THE CONSTITUTION
— AND —
AMERICAN
FOREIGN POLICY

THE CONSTITUTION
—AND—
AMERICAN
FOREIGN POLICY

Jean Edward Smith
University of Toronto

With the assistance of Sharryn Aiken and Katherine Koerner

WEST PUBLISHING COMPANY
St. Paul   New York   Los Angeles   San Francisco

COPYRIGHT © 1989 By WEST PUBLISHING COMPANY
50 W. Kellogg Boulevard
P.O. Box 64526
St. Paul, MN 55164–1003

Printed in the United States of America

Library of Congress Cataloging in
  Publication Data

Smith, Jean Edward.
    The Constitution and American Foreign Policy / Jean Edward Smith.
        p.   cm.
    Includes index.
    ISBN 0–314–42317–6
    1. United States—Foreign relations—Law and legislation—Cases.
I. Title.
KF4651.A4S65 1988
342.73'0412—dc19   88–14053
[347.302412]   CIP

CONTENTS

PREFACE

The constitutional basis of American foreign policy is generally neglected in university programs. Courses dealing with U.S. foreign policy concentrate on contemporary issues, diplomatic history, and decision making processes. Those who study constitutional law learn about America's political origins, judicial review, the separation of powers, and focus extensively on the protection of civil liberties and civil rights. But for the most part, the constitutional authority for the conduct of foreign policy—the nature of the war powers, the role of the National Security Council (NSC), and the foreign relations authority of the president—are all but ignored.

This book attempts to remedy that deficiency. It grows out of a course I have taught at the University of Toronto for the past dozen years, and seeks to provide the student with a handbook of pertinent judicial precedent defining the scope and extent of the foreign relations powers. The interested observer of America's role in world affairs, as well as practicing journalists and foreign policy professionals, also may find the book useful as a compendium of constitutional authority.

The book is organized into broad subject areas: constitutional antecedents and original intent; national supremacy and the monopoly of the federal government over foreign affairs; the act of state doctrine; the power to conclude international agreements; the doctrine of "political questions" by which the Supreme Court frequently defers to the president and Congress in foreign policy matters; the nature of the war powers; the special (almost extra-constitutional) role of the president to conduct American foreign relations; the evolution of the NSC; the intrusion of national security powers domestically, including electronic surveillance; the rights of citizenship, expatriation, and the protection of Americans abroad.

Under each subject, I have assembled the leading constitutional decisions rendered by the Supreme Court that have shaped the foreign relations power. These have been edited to retain the essence of the Court's holding and reasoning, while discarding the unnecessary verbiage and legal jargon that often make judicial decisions impenetrable. I have also provided headnotes to each case to explain the factual situation in which the dispute arose and to place it in constitutional context.

In addition to the decisions of the Supreme Court, I have also included the texts of several pieces of national security legislation that raise important constitutional questions, such as the War Powers Resolution of 1973 and the "Logan Act" of 1799 which prohibits private citizens from conducting foreign policy.

Perhaps of more general interest are the relevant excerpts reprinted from difficult-to-obtain primary sources such as the Articles of Confederation, the Debates of the Federal Convention that drafted the Constitution, the various state ratification debates, the views of Hamilton and Madison on the foreign relations power expressed in their debate over President Washington's neutrality proclamation in 1793, and above all, the *Commentaries on the Constitution* of Supreme Court Justice Joseph Story of Massachusetts. Story was not one of the Framers of the Constitution, but his *Commentaries* and written opinions provided the framework for the subsequent growth of national power and are of continuing relevance.[1]

I would like to thank my typist, Sylvia Brown, and my research assistants, Sharryn Aiken and Katherine Koerner, for their help in promptly fulfilling the numerous and demanding chores involved in preparing a manuscript for publication. I am also indebted to my students, Robert Metcs, Mary Stonehouse, Lisa Tanzi, and Toby Zanin for their helpful comments and suggestions. Susan Tubb and Mélina Brown-Hall of the editorial and production staff of West Publishing Co. were helpful beyond measure. The final responsibility for what to include and what to exclude and for the editing, headnotes and introductory commentary is of course mine.

JEAN EDWARD SMITH
Charlottesville, Virginia

Notes

1. For example, the decision of the Supreme Court establishing absolute presidential immunity from civil suits in *Nixon v. Fitzgerald* (see page 219) relied primarily on Story's treatise.

TABLE OF CASES

The principal cases are in *italic* type. Cases cited or discussed are in roman type.

THE CONSTITUTION
AND
AMERICAN
FOREIGN POLICY

INTRODUCTION

THE AMERICAN GOVERNMENT is a government of limited and enumerated powers. At the national level authority is divided among three separate branches: legislative, executive, and judicial. An elaborate system of checks and balances prevents the growth of despotic power. A written Constitution, the Bill of Rights, and the judicial review exercised by the Supreme Court restrain government in order to protect individual liberty.

All of the above are basically true in the broad area of internal affairs. The domestic powers of the national government were carved from those of the states and were strictly enumerated by the Framers of the Constitution. But foreign relations and national security are entirely different. Unlike the domestic authority of the government, the foreign affairs powers are inherent. To some extent, they exist outside the constitutional framework. The argument frequently embraced by the Supreme Court runs as follows:

- The United States came into existence when it declared independence from Great Britain, July 4, 1776.

- As an independent nation the U.S. enjoyed full sovereign power, and under that power successfully waged the war of independence and concluded a series of international treaties, including the treaty of peace with Great Britain in 1783.

- Accordingly, the United States existed *before* the Constitution, which was framed in 1787. (The Constitution, after all, was designed to create "a more perfect Union.")

- Consequently, the power of the United States to act in foreign affairs also existed prior to the Constitution. It does not depend on any affirmative grant contained in that document, although quite obviously, the government cannot do what the Constitution specifically forbids.

1

The vast authority of the national government to act in foreign relations became the basis of the Supreme Court's decision in the *Chinese Exclusion Case* [1] in which the Court upheld Congress' unlimited power to exclude Chinese aliens from the United States. Despite the lack of specific textual authority in the Constitution, the Court rested its holding on the nature of international sovereignty. According to the Court:

> [T]he United States, in their relation to foreign countries ... are one nation, invested with the powers which belong to independent nations, the exercise of which can be invoked for the maintenance of its absolute independence and security....[2]

But it was the Supreme Court's 1936 decision in *United States v. Curtiss–Wright Export Corporation* [3] that explicitly drew the distinction between the limited domestic authority of the government and the unfettered reach of its external powers. Justice George Sutherland's opinion for the Court—which remains the leading constitutional precedent on the issue—is almost breathtaking in its sweep. According to Sutherland:

> Sovereignty is never held in suspense. When, therefore, the external sovereignty of Great Britain in respect of the colonies ceased, it immediately passed to the Union.... It results that the investment of the Federal government with the powers of external sovereignty did not depend upon the affirmative grants of the Constitution. The power to declare and wage war, to conclude peace, to make treaties, to maintain diplomatic relations with other sovereignties, if they had never been mentioned in the Constitution, would have been vested in the Federal government as necessary concomitants of nationality.[4]

In effect, the power of the American government in the field of international relations is not simply a compendium of powers enumerated in the Constitution, but is an "inherent power": one that is attributable to the national government simply because the United States is a sovereign political entity in international law. As Professor Edward S. Corwin, the late dean of American constitutional scholars, remarked after World War II, "In the field of foreign relations ... the doctrine of enumerated powers has always had a difficult row to hoe, and today may be unqualifiedly asserted to be defunct." [5]

The obvious result is that the power of the American government to act in international affairs is far greater than its power to act domestically. This is not an accidental oversight, or an unfortunate omission on the part of the Framers, but an approach traditionally recognized by all nations. The security of the state is paramount. However, the government's power in foreign affairs is noteworthy because it is uncharacteristic of the elaborate constitutional restrictions that apply to the United States government domestically.

The basic premise underlying this departure is that there can be no liberty at home, unless the state is protected from its enemies abroad. John Locke, who is regarded by many as the patron saint of limited government—and who was an important reference for the Framers—wrote at length about the primary need to protect the realm from its external foes. That power (which Locke called the "federative power") could not be curtailed or restricted, but "must be left in great part to the prudence of those who have the power committed to them, to be managed by the best of their skill for the advantage of the commonwealth."[6]

Similarly, as the debates in the Federal Convention of 1787 make clear, national security was uppermost in the minds of the Framers. This was no pastoral, bucolic republic in 1787 but a revolutionary state that imperiled the stability of Europe's dynastic order. Great Britain threatened immediate intervention against the U.S. if the terms of peace were not complied with; hostile Indians menaced western settlements; Spain was intrenched in Florida and controlled New Orleans and the mouth of the Mississippi, while the British continued to press their claims to the vast Ohio region and Canada. Rather than being protected by the Atlantic Ocean, the newly independent United States was at the vortex of the struggle for North America. And in that context, those who drafted the Constitution were determined not to impede the government in its conduct of foreign affairs.

The Constitution, therefore, did not deal at length with the foreign relations power. It trusted the president to exercise executive authority to protect the country from its enemies, qualified only by the participation of Congress in the war and treaty powers; the Senate's confirmation authority; and Congress' ultimate power over appropriations.

As a result, the constitutional evolution of the authority to conduct foreign relations differs fundamentally from the constitutional development of domestic authority. Perhaps most importantly, the Supreme Court itself has been exceedingly reluctant to intervene in matters of foreign policy. Tracing to the time of Chief Justice John Marshall, the Court has held frequently (though not invariably) that such questions are "more political than legal", and has deferred to the president and Congress.[7] As the Court noted in an important 1839 case involving sovereignty over the Falkland Islands,

> ... it is not material to inquire, nor is it the province of the Court to determine, whether the executive be right or wrong. It is enough to know, that in the exercise of his constitutional functions, he has decided the question.[8]

When President Carter abrogated America's Mutual Defense Treaty with the Republic of China (Taiwan) in 1978 on his own authority, the Supreme Court declined to review the matter.[9] And more importantly, despite the clear reference in Article I, section 8 of the Constitution to Congress' power to declare war, the Supreme Court consistently refused to hear any case challenging the constitutionality of the war in Vietnam.

The clear distinction between the broad powers of the federal government in foreign policy and its limited power at home leads to curious constitutional anomalies. The most glaring of these involve the singular authority of the president to protect national security. The leading precedents, tracing to the decisions of the Supreme Court in *Martin v. Mott*[10] concerning President Madison's use of the militia in the War of 1812, and *The Prize Cases*[11] decided during the Civil War, hold that the president alone enjoys the authority to "determine the degree of force the crisis demands" [12]—a ruling that has clothed presidential use of force from Madison and Lincoln to Kennedy and Reagan with the mantle of constitutional legitimacy.

This recognition of broad presidential discretion not only stands in sharp contrast to the limited powers of the executive in domestic affairs but also varies significantly from British practice. One must go back to the reign of Charles I in 1637 to find an English court granting such discretion to the Crown; [13] of course, Charles I subsequently was executed by Parliament.

But the parallel between the royal prerogative in Great Britain and the foreign relations power of the president is striking. Surprisingly, while royal power has eroded to such an extent that it cannot be exercised without the authority of Parliament, the constitutional power of the president has increased over the years. For example:

- The president enjoys absolute immunity from civil suit. *Nixon v. Fitzgerald* (1982).

- The president, in the interest of national security, may deny access to American courts to those with claims against foreign governments. *Dames & Moore v. Regan* (1981).

- The president may order certain American citizens to be evacuated and incarcerated in time of war. *Korematsu v. United States* (1945).

- The president may properly keep secret matters pertaining to foreign affairs. *Chicago and Southern Airlines v. Waterman* (1948); *United States v. Nixon* (1974).

While the war powers are divided between the president and Congress ("an invitation to struggle for the direction of American foreign policy," in Professor Corwin's words),[14] the legal maxim *inter arma silent leges* [in time of war the laws are silent] appears alive and well in the United States. As the Supreme Court said in *United States v. Macintosh*, "The war power, when necessity calls for its exercise, tolerates no qualifications or limitations." [15] Or as Justice Goldberg stated more recently for the Court in *Kennedy v. Mendoza–Martinez*, "While the Constitution protects against invasions of individual rights, it is not a suicide pact." [16] Thus the Supreme Court has granted exceptionally wide discretion to the president and Congress.

- The Supreme Court has declined to overturn draft registration for men and not women, rejecting the argument of gender-based discrimination. *Rostker v. Goldberg* (1981).

- On the other hand, the Court has upheld Navy promotion policies that allowed female officers more time to gain promotion than their male counterparts. *Schlesinger v. Ballard* (1974).

- The Court has declined repeatedly to exercise oversight into the training and discipline of the military forces. *Gilligan v. Morgan* (1972).

On the other hand, the Supreme Court has not hesitated to curtail the executive's national security authority in purely domestic matters during peacetime. The Court overturned President Truman's seizure of the country's steel mills during the Korean War; [17] declined to enjoin the *New York*

Times and *Washington Post* from publishing excerpts from the Pentagon papers;[18] and insisted that the government must first obtain a warrant before engaging in domestic electronic surveillance even when national security is at stake.[19]

The treaty power illustrates the exceptional range of national authority. The foreign affairs of the United States are a national monopoly, and the states cannot meddle or intervene.[20] Thus the Court has regularly overturned state legislation prohibiting foreign citizens from owning land in that state when the U.S. had a treaty to the contrary with the country from which the foreigners came.[21]

Article VI of the Constitution (the Supremacy Clause) makes the Constitution, and all laws passed pursuant thereto, and all treaties made by the United States, "the supreme Law of the Land." Note again the much broader phraseology of the treaty power. For an act of Congress to become the supreme law of the land, it must be passed pursuant to (or in accordance with) the Constitution. This severely restricts Congress' legislative authority. But *all* treaties made by the United States, regardless of their content,[22] automatically become supreme law as soon as they are ratified.

Accordingly, it is sometimes possible for the federal government to accomplish tasks within the United States under the treaty power that it would be prevented from doing otherwise. For example, in the important case of *Missouri v. Holland,*[23] the Supreme Court upheld federal legislation prohibiting the hunting of wild fowl migrating between the United States and Canada, despite the lack of specific constitutional authority for Congress to take such action. The legislation was passed pursuant to a treaty with Great Britain, and the Court justified the legislation in that context.

A more far reaching example of the treaty power's scope and of the president's personal authority involves the frequent use of "executive agreements" between the United States and foreign countries. These are international agreements that are binding in every respect, but have never been submitted to the Senate for its advice and consent. They are made simply by the president. They have been upheld consistently by the Supreme Court as "a modest implied power of the President."[24] And like treaties, executive agreements are also the supreme law of the land.[25]

THE CURTISS–WRIGHT CASE

No Supreme Court decision articulates the foreign relations power with greater clarity than *United States v. Curtiss–Wright Export Corporation.*[26] The issue in *Curtiss–Wright* arose out of an attempt by the United States government to bring about a cease-fire between Bolivia and Paraguay in their war over the Chaco River. In 1934, Congress delegated broad powers to President Roosevelt to prevent the sale of arms to the belligerents, and FDR proclaimed an arms embargo immediately thereafter. The Curtiss–Wright Corporation was accused of having conspired to violate the embargo.

One of the enduring curiosities about the Supreme Court's decision in the *Curtiss–Wright* case is that it not only upheld the president's power in foreign relations, but it was delivered by the very same Supreme Court that was simultaneously invalidating much of the New Deal's domestic economic program. Also, the decision was written by Justice George Sutherland of Utah, who in many respects was the intellectual leader of the conservative Justices on the Court. Appointed to the Supreme Court by President Harding in 1922, Sutherland was the author of some of the most conservative economic decisions of an exceedingly conservative Supreme Court.[27] But Sutherland was also an ardent American nationalist. He had served prominently on the Senate Foreign Relations Committee and in 1918, while president of the American Bar Association, had delivered a series of lectures at Columbia University that supported vigorous presidential leadership in foreign affairs.[28] Chief Justice Hughes selected Sutherland to write the decision for the Court in *Curtiss–Wright,* and Sutherland produced a ringing reaffirmation of broad presidential authority.

The expansiveness of Sutherland's opinion surprised many, especially since he had just authored the Court's decision in *Carter v. Carter Coal Co.*[29] overturning the Guffy Coal Act as an unconstitutional delegation of congressional authority to the president. Why grant enormous powers to the president abroad, while restricting his authority so severely at home? The answer may lie in Sutherland's own conservatism. As the *Curtiss–Wright* decision made clear, the Supreme Court was intently concerned not to embarrass the United States government in its conduct of foreign relations. The Court recognized that the system of checks and balances so effective domestically would hamstring the government abroad. By holding that foreign relations were inherently different from domestic activity, the Court made it possible for the president to act decisively. It may also be that Justice Sutherland was determined to insure that the president would be able to intervene quickly should it be necessary to protect American interests abroad.

It is worth noting that while Sutherland's domestic economic decisions (which tilted strongly against government involvement in the economy) have all been overturned or distinguished, his foreign policy decisions— *Curtiss–Wright, Belmont,* and *Macintosh* —continue to provide the basic parameters for national and presidential authority in foreign relations.

United States v. Curtiss–Wright Export Corp.

299 U.S. 304 (1936)

This fundamental statement of presidential power in foreign affairs arose out of U.S. efforts to reduce the fighting between Bolivia and Paraguay in the headlands of the Chaco River. In May 1934, Congress passed a Joint Resolution granting to the president the power to prohibit the sales of munitions to the two countries. Curtiss–Wright was charged with conspiring to sell fifteen machine guns to Bolivia in violation of the president's proclamation and demurred to the indictment, contending that Congress' delegation of power to the president was invalid. The U.S. District Court sustained the demurrer, and the United States appealed.

Justice **Sutherland** delivered the opinion of the Court: . . . .

Whether, if the Joint Resolution had related solely to internal affairs it would be open to the challenge that it constituted an unlawful delegation of legislative power to the Executive, we find it unnecessary to determine. The whole aim of the resolution is to affect a situation entirely external to the United States, and falling within the category of foreign affairs. The determination which we are called to make, therefore, is whether the Joint Resolution, as applied to that situation, is vulnerable to attack under the rule that forbids a delegation of the law-making power. In other words, assuming (but not deciding) that the challenged delegation, if it were confined to internal affairs, would be invalid, may it nevertheless be sustained on the ground that its exclusive aim is to afford a remedy for a hurtful condition within foreign territory?

It will contribute to the elucidation of the question if we first consider the differences between the powers of the federal government in respect of foreign or external affairs and those in respect of domestic or internal affairs. That there are differences between them, and that these differences are fundamental, may not be doubted.

The two classes of powers are different, both in respect of their origin and their nature. The broad statement that the federal government can exercise no powers except those specifically enumerated in the Constitution, and such implied powers as are necessary and proper to carry into effect the enumerated powers, is categorically true only in respect of our internal affairs. In that field, the primary purpose of the Constitution was to carve from the general mass of legislative powers *then possessed by the states* such portions as it was thought desirable to vest in the federal government, leaving those not included in the enumeration still in the states. *Carter v. Carter Coal Co.*, 298 U.S. 238, 294. That this doctrine applies only to powers which the states had, is self-evident. And since the states severally never possessed international powers, such powers could not have been carved from the mass of state powers but obviously were transmitted to the United States from some other source. During the colonial period, those powers were possessed exclusively by and were entirely under the control of the Crown. By the Declaration of Independence, "the Representatives of the United States of America" declared the United [not the several] Colonies to be free and independent states, and as such to have "full Power to levy War, conclude Peace, contract Alliances, establish Commerce and to do all other Acts and Things which Independent States may of right do."

As a result of the separation from Great Britain by the colonies acting as a unit, the powers of external sovereignty passed from the Crown not to the colonies severally, but to the colonies in their collective and corporate capacity as the United States of America. Even before the Declaration, the colonies were a unit in foreign affairs, acting through a common agency— namely the Continental Congress, composed of delegates from the thirteen colonies. That agency exercised the powers of war and peace, raised an army, created a navy, and finally adopted the Declaration of Independence. Rulers come and go; governments end and forms of government change; but sovereignty survives. A political society cannot endure without a supreme will somewhere. Sovereignty is never held in suspense. When, therefore, the external sovereignty of Great Britain in respect of the colonies ceased, it immediately passed to the Union. That fact was given practical application almost at once. The treaty of peace, made on September 23, 1783, was concluded between his Britanic Majesty and the "United States of America."

The Union existed before the Constitution, which was ordained and established among other things to form "a more perfect Union." Prior to that event, it is clear that the Union, declared by the Articles of Confederation to be "perpetual," was the sole possessor of external sovereignty and in the Union it remained without change save in so far as the Constitution in express terms qualified its exercise. The Framers' Convention was called and exerted its powers upon the irrefutable postulate that though the states were several their people in respect of foreign affairs were one. . . .

It results that the investment of the federal government with the powers of external sovereignty did not depend upon the affirmative grants of the Constitution. The powers to declare and wage war, to conclude peace, to make treaties, to maintain diplomatic relations with other sovereignties, if they had never been mentioned in the Constitution, would have vested in the federal government as necessary concomitants of nationality. . . . As a member of the family of nations, the right and power of the United States in that field are equal to the right and power of the other members of the international family. Otherwise, the United States is not completely sovereign. The power to acquire territory by discovery and occupation, the power to expel undesirable aliens, the power to make such international agreements as do not constitute treaties in the constitutional sense, none of which is expressly affirmed by the Constitution, nevertheless exist as inherently inseparable from the conception of nationality. . . .

Not only . . . is the federal power over external affairs in origin and essential character different from that over internal affairs, but participation in the exercise of the power is significantly limited. In this vast external realm, with its important, complicated, delicate and manifold problems, the President alone has the power to speak or listen as a representative of the nation. He *makes* treaties with the advice and consent of the Senate; but he alone negotiates. Into the field of negotiation the Senate cannot intrude; and Congress itself is powerless to invade it. As Marshall said in his great argument of March 7, 1800, in the House of Representatives, "The President is the sole organ of the nation in its external relations, and its sole representative with foreign nations." . . .

It is important to bear in mind that we are here dealing not alone with an authority vested in the President by an exertion of legislative power, but with such an authority plus the very delicate, plenary and exclusive power of the President as the sole organ of the federal government in the field of international relations—a power which does not require as a basis for its exercise an act of Congress, but which, of course, like every other governmental power, must be exercised in subordination to the applicable provisions of the Constitution. It is quite apparent that if, in the maintenance of our international relations, embarrassment—perhaps serious embarrassment—is to be avoided and success for our aims achieved, congressional legislation which is to be made effective through negotiation and inquiry within the international field must often accord to the President a degree of discretion and freedom from statutory restriction which would not be admissible were domestic affairs alone involved. Moreover, he, not Congress, has the better opportunity of knowing the conditions which prevail in foreign countries, and especially is this true in time of war. He has his confidential sources of information. He has his agents in the form of diplomatic, consular and other officials. Secrecy in respect of information gathered by them may be highly necessary, and the premature disclosure of it productive of harmful results. Indeed, so clearly is this true that the first President refused to accede to a request to lay before the House of Representatives the instructions, correspondence and documents relating to the negotiation of the Jay Treaty—a refusal the wisdom of which was recognized by the House itself and has never since been doubted. . . .

When the President is to be authorized by legislation to act in respect of a matter intended to affect a situation in foreign territory, the legislator properly bears in mind the important consideration that the form of the President's action—or, indeed, whether he shall act at all—may well depend, among other things, upon the nature of the confidential information which he has or may thereafter receive, or upon the effect which his action may have upon our foreign relations. This consideration, in connection with what we have already said on the subject, discloses the unwisdom of requiring Congress in this field of governmental power to lay down narrowly defined standards by which the President is to be governed. As this court said in *Mackenzie v. Hare,* 239 U.S. 299, 311, "As a government, the United States is invested with all the attributes of sovereignty. As it has the character of nationality it has the powers of nationality, especially those which concern its relations and intercourse with other countries. *We should hesitate long before limiting or embarrassing such powers.*"

In the light of the foregoing observations, it is evident that this court should not be in haste to apply a general rule which will have the effect of condemning legislation like that under review as constituting an unlawful delegation of legislative power. The principles which justify such legislation find overwhelming support in the unbroken legislative practice which has prevailed almost from the inception of the national government to the present day. . . .

[At this point in the Opinion, Justice Sutherland undertook an extended examination of legislative precedent supporting a broad delegation of authority to the President in foreign affairs.]

Practically every volume of the United States Statutes contains one or more acts or joint resolutions of Congress authorizing action by the President in respect of subjects affecting foreign relations, which either leave the exercise of the power to his unrestricted judgment, or provide a standard far more general than that which has always been considered requisite with regard to domestic affairs. . . .

While this court may not, and should not, hesitate to declare acts of Congress, however many times repeated, to be unconstitutional if beyond all rational doubt it finds them to be so, an impressive array of legislation such as we have just set forth, enacted by nearly every Congress from the beginning of our national existence to the present day, must be given unusual weight in the process of reaching a correct determination of the problem. A legislative practice such as we have here, evidenced not by only occasional instances, but marked by the movement of a steady stream for a century and a half of time, goes a long way in the direction of proving the presence of unassailable ground for the constitutionality of the practice, to be found in the origin and history of the power involved, or in its nature, or in both combined . . .

It is enough to summarize by saying that, both upon principle and in accordance with precedent, we conclude there is sufficient warrant for the broad discretion vested in the President to determine whether the enforcement of the statute will have a beneficial effect upon the reestablishment of peace in the affected countries; whether he shall make proclamation to bring the resolution into operation; whether and when the resolution shall cease to operate and to make proclamation accordingly; and to prescribe limitations and exceptions to which the enforcement of the resolution shall be subject. . . .

The judgment of the court below must be reversed and the cause remanded for further proceedings in accordance with the foregoing opinion.

It is so ordered.

*Justice **McReynolds** dissented.*

Suggested Reading

The best constitutional treatise dealing with the broad flow of foreign relations remains LOUIS HENKIN'S FOREIGN AFFAIRS AND THE CONSTITUTION published by W.W. Norton in 1975. Before that, EDWARD S. CORWIN, THE PRESIDENT'S CONTROL OF FOREIGN RELATIONS (1917) and QUINCY WRIGHT, THE CONTROL OF AMERICAN FOREIGN RELATIONS (1922), provide classic insights, as does CORWIN'S exceptional text, THE CONSTITUTION AND WHAT IT MEANS TODAY, now in its 14th edition.

Earlier general treatments, frequently cited as a source of constitutional understanding, are W.W. WILLOUGHBY, PRINCIPLES OF CONSTITUTIONAL LAW OF THE UNITED STATES (2 ed. 1929); THOMAS M. COOLEY, A TREATISE ON CONSTITUTIONAL LIMITATIONS WHICH REST UPON THE LEGISLATIVE POWER OF THE STATES OF THE AMERICAN UNION (1868); and, of course, JOSEPH STORY'S COMMENTARIES ON THE CONSTITUTION (1834). For more recent observations, BERNARD SCHWARTZ, A COMMENTARY ON THE CONSTITUTION OF THE UNITED STATES (1963–68) and the ENCYCLOPEDIA OF THE AMERICAN CONSTITUTION (1987), edited by KENNETH L. KARST and DENNIS J. MAHONEY are extremely useful.

On the decision in *Curtiss–Wright,* see Charles A. Lofgren, *United States v. Curtiss–Wright Export Corporation: An Historical Reassessment,* 83 YALE LAW JOURNAL 1 (1973); Levitan, *The Foreign Relations Power: An Analysis of Mr. Justice Sutherland's Theory,* 55 YALE LAW JOURNAL 467 (1946); Patterson, *In re The United States v. The Curtiss–Wright Corpora-*

tion (pts. 1–2) 22 TEXAS LAW REVIEW 286, 445 (1944). For Justice Sutherland, see Alpheus T. Mason, *The Conservative World of Justice Sutherland,* 33 AMERICAN POLITICAL SCIENCE REVIEW (1938); J. PASCHAL, MR. JUSTICE SUTHERLAND: A MAN AGAINST THE STATE (1951), as well as the essay on Sutherland in FRIEDMAN and F. ISRAEL, THE JUSTICES OF THE SUPREME COURT OF THE UNITED STATES, vol. 3 (1969).

Notes

1. 130 U.S. 581 (1889).
2. *Id.,* at 604.
3. 299 U.S. 304 (1936).
4. *Id.,* at 316–318.
5. EDWARD S. CORWIN, ed., THE CONSTITUTION OF THE UNITED STATES OF AMERICA: ANALYSIS AND INTERPRETATION 82d Congress, 1st Session (Washington: Government Printing Office, 1952), p. 510.
6. JOHN LOCKE, SECOND TREATISE ON CIVIL GOVERNMENT section 147.
7. *Foster v. Neilson,* 2 Peters (27 U.S.) 253, 308 (1829).
8. *Williams v. Suffolk Insurance Co.,* 13 Peters (38 U.S.) 415, 419 (1839).
9. *Goldwater v. Carter,* 444 U.S. 996 (1979). The reasons for the Court's decision varied.
10. 12 Wheat. (25 U.S.) 19 (1827).
11. 2 Black (67 U.S.) 635 (1862).
12. *Id.,* at 682.
13. *Ship Money Case [Hampden's Case]* (1637), 3 St.Tr. 825.
14. EDWARD S. CORWIN, THE PRESIDENT: OFFICE AND POWERS, 1787–1957 (New York: New York University Press, 1957), p. 171.
15. 283 U.S. 605, 622 (1931).
16. 372 U.S. 144, 148 (1963).
17. *Youngstown Sheet & Tube v. Sawyer,* 343 U.S. 579 (1952).
18. *New York Times v. United States,* 403 U.S. 713 (1971).
19. *United States v. United States District Court,* 407 U.S. 297 (1972).
20. *Zschernig v. Miller,* 389 U.S. 429 (1968).
21. *Hauenstein v. Lynham,* 100 U.S. 483 (1879).
22. Although no treaty could violate an express provision of the Constitution. *Head Money Cases,* 112 U.S. 580 (1884); *Reid v. Covert,* 354 U.S. 1 (1957).
23. 252 U.S. 416 (1920).
24. *United States v. Pink,* 315 U.S. 203, 229 (1942).
25. *Weinberger v. Rossi,* 456 U.S. 25 (1982); *United States v. Belmont,* 301 U.S. 324 (1937).
26. 299 U.S. 304 (1936).
27. *Adkins v. Children's Hospital,* 261 U.S. 525 (1923); *Tyson & Brothers United Theatre Ticket Offices v. Banton,* 273 U.S. 418 (1927); *Ribnik v. McBride,* 277 U.S. 350 (1928).
28. GEORGE SUTHERLAND, CONSTITUTIONAL POWER AND WORLD AFFAIRS (New York: Columbia University Press, 1919). Many of Sutherland's phrases recur in the *Curtiss–Wright* decision.
29. 298 U.S. 238 (1936).

1

CONSTITUTIONAL ANTECEDENTS AND ORIGINAL INTENT

THE LEADERS OF revolutionary America drew their ideas from a variety of sources. In addition to the common law experience of Great Britain—the Magna Carta, the Bill of Rights, the Act of Settlement of 1701, and the *Institutes* (1628) of Sir Edward Coke—the Framers relied heavily on a host of seventeenth and eighteenth century philosophers who attacked the divine right of kings in favor of natural law, limited government, and popular sovereignty.

John Milton (1608–1674), the great Puritan poet, was also a political theorist of some consequence, and his *Areopagitica* (1644) is a classic defense of free speech in protest against the oppressive policies of Charles I. In later essays Milton championed the doctrines of limited government and the right of revolution against a tyrannous monarch.

James Harrington (1611–1677) and Algernon Sidney (1622–1683), who were Milton's contemporaries in the struggle against royal absolutism, were highly regarded by the American colonists as well. Harrington's idealistic treatise, the *Commonwealth of Oceana* (1656), advocated the equitable distribution of land, free elections, and the separation of powers. Sidney's *Discourse Concerning Government* (1698) stressed the concept of limited republican government and resistance to tyranny. Both were cited frequently in the revolutionary debate.

Perhaps equally important to the realists who made the revolution were the great scholars of international law: Hugo Grotius (1583–1645), Samuel Pufendorf (1632–1694), and Emmerich Vattel (1714–1767). Grotius' monumental work, *de jure belli ac pacis* (1625) justified the natural law–compact theory of the state, while Pufendorf's *de jure naturae et gentium* (1672), a powerful defense of the secular state, formed the basis of pastor John Wise's influential *Vindication of the Government of New England Churches* (1717). Vattel's *Law of Nations*, published in London in 1758, emphasized the importance of a

13

written constitution that was binding on Parliament. Vattel was one of the first to differentiate between the fundamental constitution, which he considered supreme, and mere legislative enactments.

But it was John Locke (1632–1704), the brilliant theorist and abstract philosopher, who set the intellectual tone of the revolution. Locke's *Second Treatise on Government* spoke convincingly of inalienable natural rights which government, even popular government, could not violate. Paramount among those rights were life, liberty and property. Jefferson's phraseology in the Declaration of Independence was modeled closely on Locke's *Second Treatise,* and the doctrine of inalienable rights subsequently emerged in the due process clauses of the Fifth and Fourteenth Amendments as one of the guiding principles of American constitutional law.

Locke's work combined four fundamental political ideas: the doctrine of natural law and inalienable rights, the compact theory of the state, the doctrine of popular sovereignty, and the right of revolution. Locke associated his doctrine of natural rights with the concept of limited legislative power. He drew a sharp distinction between executive and legislative functions, thereby contributing to the doctrine of separation of powers. Locke also wrote at length about a third function of government which he described as the "federative power." This power to protect the commonwealth from external danger would today be termed "national security." While Locke advocated the strict division of legislative and executive power to protect individual liberty from oppressive government, he recognized that there could be no liberty at home unless the state was first protected from potential enemies abroad.

Locke placed full responsibility for the "federative power" in the executive. In contrast to the domestic authority of the executive, which was severely restricted, the federative power was essentially extraconstitutional and depended upon the skill and judgment of those to whom it was entrusted. [The salient chapter of Locke's *Second Treatise* is reprinted on pages 21–22.]

ARTICLES OF CONFEDERATION

When the American colonies, acting in their collective capacity as the United States, declared independence from Great Britain on July 4, 1776, it immediately became necessary to organize for the war. The resulting Articles of Confederation, drafted by John Dickinson of Pennsylvania, were submitted to the Continental Congress, July 12, 1776. The Articles provided for a league of sovereign states rather than a strong central government and were designed primarily to facilitate a unified approach to foreign policy and national defense. Congress was given the traditional powers of the Crown to make war and peace, to send and receive ambassadors, to enter into treaties and alliances, and to conduct Indian affairs. Each state was explicitly prohibited from conducting foreign policy, engaging in war without the consent of Congress, or maintaining armed forces other than a militia.

The Articles placed full responsibility for the conduct of American foreign relations in the Congress (no executive power was provided for in the Articles), while full responsibility for domestic affairs remained with the states. Each state specifically retained "its sovereignty, freedom and independence, and every Power, Jurisdiction and right, which is not *expressly* delegated to the United States...." (emphasis added.) There was no national judiciary, and Congress lacked the power to legislate internally, including the vital powers to tax and regulate commerce.

In a very real sense, the Articles of Confederation perpetuated the distinction between foreign relations and internal affairs. Under Great Britain, the foreign relations of the colonies were the prerogative of the Crown, while domestic matters were handled more or less by each colony. The difference in 1776 was that the states, organized in the Continental Congress, would determine foreign policy collectively. Thus the Articles represented a viable compromise between those who sought a strong national government and those who wanted none at all.

The Articles of Confederation were not intended to establish a central government. But they did establish the rudiments of a common United States citizenship. Moreover, the Articles did not affect each citizen directly, but like all confederal structures dealt with the states as the basic building blocks of the Union. Finally, the lack of an executive power or a judiciary concentrated national authority in the hands of the Continental Congress. Each state had one vote, and nine states were necessary for agreement.

One should not judge a structure by tasks it was not intended to accomplish. After independence was achieved, it is clear that the Articles failed to provide the necessary framework to allow the nation to be governed effectively. But that had never been its purpose. The Articles of Confederation were intended to provide for a unitary foreign policy and to wage the War of Independence. Above all, the Articles should be seen as establishing the initial constitutional framework of the American Union. Insofar as foreign relations were concerned, the United States spoke as one. To the world the thirteen states were united; internally the states were increasingly autonomous.

THE FEDERAL CONVENTION OF 1787

By 1787 it was apparent that the Articles of Confederation were inadequate. Trade and commerce among the states were increasingly beset by local, autarkic restrictions; radicalism in some states was running at flood tide, and property rights had become grievously endangered. After much prodding by those who sought a stronger central government the Continental Congress issued a call for a special convention for the express purpose of revising the Articles of Confederation. In addition to the domestic difficulties the United States confronted, Great Britain was threatening to intervene militarily unless the U.S. complied with the terms of the peace treaty—which required compensation for confiscated Tory property. The Continental Congress had been unable to induce the States to honor the commitments it had made to Britain in 1783. As a result, France and Holland hesitated to negotiate their own treaties with the United States.

Thus, the Framers who met in Philadelphia were not only concerned to establish a central government whose writ would run internally, but also to enable the United States to speak more effectively in foreign affairs. In that sense their task was, indeed, to form "a more perfect Union."

But the basic task involved establishing a national government capable of acting domestically. In terms of foreign policy, the Confederation already enjoyed complete authority. But international authority required domestic impact. Thus Article VI, section 2 of the Constitution (the Supremacy Clause) was deliberately framed to make U.S. treaties—including those negotiated previously—"the supreme Law of the Land ... anything in the Constitution or Laws of any State to the Contrary notwithstanding." The result was to make the 1783 peace treaty with Great Britain enforceable as domestic law in the United States and to remove the doubts of other foreign countries as to the enforceability of U.S. treaty commitments. The United States thus became the only major country in which international agreements were immediately effective as domestic law without subsequent implementing legislation.

Insofar as the actual conduct of foreign relations is concerned, the Constitution did little more than specify how the respective powers of international sovereignty were to be apportioned. The national government already had the authority to act in foreign affairs. (Hence, unlike the elaborate enumeration of specific domestic powers taken from the States and entrusted to the national government, the Framers operated on the assumption that the authority for the United States to act abroad already resided there.)

What little debate the Framers had concerning foreign affairs involved the allocation of specific tasks. Congress was given the authority to "declare" war, although the president was made commander in chief of the army and navy. The original draft of the Constitution reported by the Committee on Detail empowered Congress to "make" war. But as Madison and Elbridge Gerry of Massachusetts made clear in debate, the word "make" was amended to "declare" to enable the president "to repel sudden attacks". The Framers deliberately specified the wording to allow the President to respond immediately to hostile attack but to make the initiation of offensive war a collective enterprise.

The treaty power was divided between the president and the Senate. James Wilson of Pennsylvania sought to add the House of Representatives to the treaty process arguing that if treaties were to have the force of law, the House should be involved. But he was rebuffed by Roger Sherman of Connecticut who argued that because of its unwieldy size, the House could not be relied upon to maintain the secrecy required. It is noteworthy that much went unstated or undisputed at the Convention debates. For purposes of foreign affairs the Union already existed, and the Constitution was simply tidying up the loose ends that had caused embarrassment.

It is equally clear, as the subsequent ratification debates in the various States attested, that the powers entrusted to the president bore a strong resemblance to the authority of the Crown in foreign affairs. As Gouverneur

Morris of Pennsylvania expressed it, the president was "the general Guardian of the National interests."

THE FEDERALIST PAPERS

Twentieth century Americans are inclined to overlook how bitterly contested was the ratification of the Constitution. Shortly after the Convention adjourned, a reluctant Continental Congress submitted the Constitution to the States for approval. The Constitution itself had provided for ratification by individual state conventions as a means of bypassing possible opposition in the Congress. With the exception of Rhode Island, the various state legislatures issued calls for the election of delegates.

In the fight over ratification, the supporters of the new Constitution became known as Federalists, while their opponents were dubbed Antifederalists. Although local issues often intervened, it was generally true that Federalist sentiment was concentrated along the American coastal plain from Georgia to New England, while residents of the piedmont and hill country opposed the Constitution. The division between tidewater and backcountry reflected economic and class differences. A major purpose of the Constitution was to create a strong national government that could establish a sound currency and promote deflationary credit policies. The merchants, large planters, and men of wealth living in coastal cities or on large plantations, and who often held bonds of the Confederation, strongly favored a new government which would protect commerce and restrain radicalism. But the small farmers and frontiersmen of the great upland plain, a significant portion of the United States population at that time, were opposed to programs of "sound money" and deflationary credit policies.

The ten month struggle for ratification produced an outpouring of political literature. The most important was *The Federalist*—a collection of eighty-five newspaper essays written by Hamilton, Madison, and John Jay between October 1787 and July 1788 that examined the proposed Constitution point by point.

The Federalist remains one of the great popular tracts on the American constitutional system, and it is surprising the extent to which its authors accurately anticipated how the new structure would work. Madison, Hamilton and Jay were scarcely disinterested bystanders. All three were vigorous partisans of the Constitution. They sought to convince public opinion and at the same time fashion a doctrine of national supremacy. The influence of *The Federalist* on subsequent generations has been enormous.

Federalist essays 24, 25, and 26, written by Hamilton, make clear the concern of the Framers to protect the United States from impending foreign aggression. "If we mean to be a commercial people," said Hamilton, "we must endeavor as soon as possible to have a navy." He insisted that inadequate military preparations against England and Spain "would be to desert all the usual maxims of prudence and policy." He argued strongly that a militia alone was insufficient to protect American interests and that a modest standing army was essential. This turned out to be one of the most contested issues in the entire ratification struggle, and both Hamilton and Madison, in *Federalist* No. 41, devoted considerable effort to the question of control of the military.

Hamilton's famous essay on presidential power (No. 69) represents a somewhat understated version of his views on the subject. His comments on the role of the president as commander in chief in *Federalist* No. 74 and on the treaty power in *Federalist* No. 75 appear more typical of the Founders' concerns.

DEBATES OF THE STATE CONVENTIONS

The debates of the various state conventions reflect the acrimony which the new Constitution engendered, and final adoption was not achieved until June 1788. Seven states ratified the Constitution by majorities of two-thirds or better, but in four others ratification was secured with great difficulty, and two states initially rejected it. Delaware and New Jersey, the first to ratify, gave their assent in December 1787; Georgia and Connecticut followed in January; and Maryland ratified in April 1788. Of these states only Georgia had a significant backcountry, and there the fear of the Creek Indians influenced ratification; it was hoped that a national military force would keep the Creeks under control. In Pennsylvania and South Carolina, the principal fight had been in the legislatures. Once the conventions were called, the Federalists won handily. But in Massachusetts, Virginia, New York and New Hampshire, ratification was secured only by the narrowest of margins and after hard fought struggles. Only piedmont-dominated North Carolina and Rhode Island refused to ratify and did not join the new Union until the federal government was already functioning.

The issue of maintaining standing armies in peacetime particularly aroused strong criticism—and even stronger support. James Bowdoin of Massachusetts noted the impending danger from foreign powers:

> ... their emissaries are watching our conduct ... and if we should ... reject the federal constitution proposed to us, and continue much longer our present weak, unenergetic federal government, their policy will probably induce them to plan a division or partition of the states among themselves, and unite their forces to affect it.

In New York, Alexander Hamilton led the Federalist forces, and as he told the state convention on June 27, 1788, "The great leading objects of the Federal government ... are to maintain domestic peace, and provide for the common defense." In Connecticut, Oliver Ellsworth, in his speech opening the debate, affirmed the necessity of an improved national defense. "United, we are strong," said Ellsworth, "divided, we are weak." James Wilson spoke in a similar vein in Pennsylvania; and in Maryland, the Federalists spurned proposals that would have prohibited standing armies in peacetime or prevented the state militia from being marched beyond the limits of an adjoining state without the militia's consent.

But it was in Virginia where the issue was debated most extensively. The Virginia debates, commencing June 2, 1788, pitted Madison, Governor Randolph, and John Marshall, (Federalists) against the redoubtable Antifederalists Patrick Henry and Richard Henry Lee. Lee's *Letters from the Federal Farmer,* which was published in December 1787, was the most effective Antifederalist work to appear and quickly won a large audience in Virginia. At the state convention, Henry unleashed the full force of his impressive oratorical ability in attacking the new Constitutional scheme. The criticisms Henry expressed, particularly of unresponsive executive power, have been echoed frequently over the years.

JEFFERSON—JAY CORRESPONDENCE

The early days of the Washington administration established many Constitutional precedents. One of the most important is the rule that the Supreme Court will not render advisory opinions on Constitutional matters—even if the President (or Congress) requests one. The tradition arose out of America's impending involvement in the ongoing war between England and France following the French Revolution. President Washington sought guidance from the Court as to the meaning of U.S. treaty commitments to the belligerents and the rights of commerce under international law. Accordingly on July 18, 1793, Secretary of State Thomas Jefferson wrote to the Supreme Court seeking its advice. Chief Justice Jay called the Court into special session to consider Washington's request but on August 8 replied to the President, respectfully pointing out that the separation of powers prevented the Supreme Court from acceding to his request. As judges "of a court of last resort," wrote Jay, "there are strong arguments against the propriety of our extrajudicially deciding the questions alluded to. . . ."

"PACIFICUS"—"HELVIDIUS" DEBATE

The division of authority between the president and Congress over the control of American foreign policy pitted Hamilton ("Pacificus") against Madison ("Helvidius") in a spirited exchange following Washington's 1793 proclamation of U.S. neutrality [1] in the war between England and France. The proclamation was actually drafted by John Jay and was immediately attacked by those in the U.S. who supported France. Hamilton undertook to defend Washington's action in a series of eight articles, of which only the first dealt with Constitutional issues, published in *The Gazette of the United States* (Philadelphia) under the pseudonym "Pacificus." Hamilton's argument was twofold. First, the conduct of foreign relations is an executive function. Indeed, Thomas Jefferson as secretary of state had insisted that "the transaction of business with foreign nations is executive altogether," when he refused to accept the credentials of Citizen Gênet, envoy to the United States of the First French Republic.[2] Hamilton also argued that Article II of the Constitution represented a substantive grant of authority to the president, "subject only to the *exceptions* and *qualifications* which are expressed in the instrument." [3]

Madison replied in the letters of "Helvidius," which ran in the *Gazette* from August 14 to September 18. Basically Madison argued that Congress was the principal organ of the national government and possessed full authority over foreign affairs, except for those *specifically* granted to the president. In Madison's 1793 view (which differed significantly from his opinion expressed in the Virginia ratification convention six years earlier), the control of foreign relations lay with the Congress under the Articles of Confederation, and the Constitution did not change their control. Madison placed great emphasis on Congress power to declare war and pointed out the confusion that was likely to ensue from concurrent discretionary powers in the hands of different departments. He concluded that in foreign affairs, as elsewhere, the president was only the executive agent of Congress, and that Congress power should control inconsistent presidential action.

Although Congress won the battle over neutrality proclamations (neutrality has been determined by Congress since Washington's day), Hamilton's broad interpretation of presidential authority over foreign relations generally has prevailed. But as Professor Bishop notes, "a good case can be made out for the proposition that the present imprecise situation is, in fact, reasonably satisfactory. Neither the executive nor the Congress is very sure of its rights, and both usually evince a tactful disposition not to push the assertion of their rights to abusive extremes. Of such is the system of checks and balances." [4]

STORY'S COMMENTARIES ON THE CONSTITUTION

U.S. Supreme Court Justice Joseph Story, appointed to the bench by President Madison in 1811, is generally regarded as the leading constitutional authority on the early Federal period. His extensive knowledge of admiralty and international law was a distinct asset to the Court, and though nominally a Jeffersonian Republican, he soon became Chief Justice Marshall's most able and vigorous collaborator. As Albert Beveridge observed in his book *Life of John Marshall,* "When special learning, or the examination of technicalities and the nice distinctions of the law were required, Marshall did not shine. The preparation of opinions in such cases he usually left to Story." [5] Together, Marshall and Story made the Supreme Court a nationalist (Federalist) bastion standing firmly against the forces of decentralization and agrarian radicalism. Story's *Commentaries on the Constitution of the United States,* issued in three volumes in 1833, is one of the great treatises on the American constitutional system. Indeed, Dean Roscoe Pound of the Harvard Law School credited Story's treatises with preserving the common law in America. [6]

Extracts from Story's work are included because of the impact his writings have had on the growth of American constitutional law. Story was not only an ardent nationalist but a keen observer of international politics. "[T]he surest means of avoiding war is to be prepared for it in peace," he wrote, explaining the necessity for standing armies. And he wrote extensively to justify the concentration of military authority in the president:

> ... the direction of war most particularly demands those qualities, which distinguish the exercise of power by a single hand. Unity of plan, promptitude, activity, and decision, are indispensable to success; and these can scarcely exist, except when a single magistrate is entrusted exclusively with the power.

Justice Story's explanation of the Constitution is often cited as a definitive, contemporaneous source of the Framers' intent. His writings belie the claim that national security was of little concern for the nascent Republic.

SECOND TREATISE OF CIVIL GOVERNMENT
OF THE LEGISLATIVE, EXECUTIVE, AND FEDERATIVE POWER
OF THE COMMONWEALTH

John Locke
(2nd edition, 1694)

143. THE LEGISLATIVE power is that which has a right to direct how the force of the commonwealth shall be employed for preserving the community and the members of it. But because those laws which are constantly to be executed, and whose force is always to continue, may be made in a little time, therefore there is no need that the legislative should be always in being, not having always business to do. And because it may be too great a temptation to human frailty, apt to grasp at power, for the same persons who have the power of making laws to have also in their hands the power to execute them, whereby they may exempt themselves from obedience to the laws they make, and suit the law, both in its making and execution, to their own private advantage, and thereby come to have a distinct interest from the rest of the community contrary to the end of society and government; therefore, in well ordered commonwealths, where the good of the whole is so considered as it ought, the legislative power is put into the hands of diverse persons who, duly assembled, have by themselves, or jointly with others, a power to make laws; which when they have done, being separated again, they are themselves subject to the laws they have made, which is a new and near tie upon them to take care that they make them for the public good.

144. But because the laws that are at once and in a short time made have a constant and lasting force and need a perpetual execution or an attendance thereunto; therefore, it is necessary there should be a power always in being which should see to the execution of the laws that are made and remain in force. And thus the legislative and executive power come often to be separated.

145. There is another power in every commonwealth which one may call natural, because it is that which answers to the power every man naturally had before he entered into society; for though in a commonwealth the members of it are distinct persons still in reference to one another, and as such are governed by the laws of the society, yet, in reference to the rest of mankind, they make one body which is, as every member of it before was, still in the state of nature with the rest of mankind. Hence it is that the controversies that happen between any man of the society with those that are out of it are managed by the public, and an injury done to a member of their body engages the whole in the reparation of it. So that, under this consideration, the whole community is one body in the state of nature in respect of all other states or persons out of its community.

146. This, therefore, contains the power of war and peace, leagues and alliances, and all the transactions with all persons and communities without the commonwealth, and may be called "federative," if anyone pleases. So the thing be understood, I am indifferent as to the name.

147. These two powers, executive and federative, though they be really distinct in themselves, yet one comprehending the execution of the municipal laws of the society and interest of the public without with all those that it may receive benefit or damage from, yet they are always almost united. And though this federative power in the well or ill management of it be of great moment to the commonwealth, yet it is much less capable to be directed by antecedent, standing, positive laws than the executive, and so must necessarily be left to the prudence and wisdom of those whose hands it is in to be managed for the public good; for the laws that concern subjects one amongst another, being to direct their actions may well enough precede them. But what is to be done in reference to foreigners, depending much upon their actions and the variation of designs and interests, must be left in great part to the prudence of those who have this power committed to them, to be managed by the best of their skill for the advantage of the commonwealth.

148. Though, as I said, the executive and federative power of every community be really distinct in themselves, yet they are hardly to be separated and placed at the same time in the hands of distinct persons; for both of them requiring the force of the commonwealth in distinct and not subordinate hands, or that the executive and federative power should be placed in persons that might act separately, whereby the force of the public would be under different commands, which would be apt some time or other to cause disorder and ruin.

ARTICLES OF CONFEDERATION

Reported to Congress—July 12, 1776
Submitted to States—November 17, 1777
Adopted—March 1, 1781
[Extract]

TO ALL TO WHOM these Presents shall come, we the undersigned Delegates of the States affixed to our Names send greeting. Whereas the Delegates of the United States of America in Congress assembled did on the fifteenth day of November in the Year of our Lord One Thousand Seven Hundred and Seventy-seven, and in the Second Year of the Independence of America agree to certain articles of Confederation and perpetual Union between the States of New Hampshire, Massachusetts Bay, Rhode Island and Providence Plantations, Connecticut, New York, New Jersey, Pennsylvania, Delaware, Maryland, Virginia, North Carolina, South Carolina and Georgia in the Words following, viz. . . .

Article I. The Stile of this confederacy shall be "The United States of America."

Article II. Each state retains its sovereignty, freedom and independence, and every Power, Jurisdiction and right, which is not by this confederation expressly delegated to the United States, in Congress assembled.

*   *   *

Article VI. No state without the Consent of the United States in congress assembled, shall send any embassy to, or receive any embassy from, or enter into any conference, agreement, alliance or treaty with any king, prince or state; . . . .

No two or more states shall enter into any treaty, confederation or alliance whatever between them, without the consent of the United States in congress assembled, specifying accurately the purposes for which the same is to be entered into, and how long it shall continue.

No state shall lay any imposts or duties, which may interfere with any stipulations in treaties, entered into by the United States in congress assembled, with any king, prince or state, in pursuance of any treaties already proposed by congress, to the courts of France and Spain.

No vessels of war shall be kept up in time of peace by any state, except such number only, as shall be deemed necessary by the United States in congress assembled, for the defense of such state, or its trade; nor shall any body of forces be kept up by any state, in time of peace, except such number only, as in the judgment of the United States, in congress assembled, shall be deemed requisite to garrison the forts necessary for the defense of such state; but every state shall always keep up a well regulated and disciplined militia, sufficiently armed and accoutred, and shall provide and constantly have ready for use, in public stores, a due number of field pieces and tents, and a proper quantity of arms, ammunition and camp equipage.

No state shall engage in any war without the consent of the United States in congress assembled, unless such state be actually invaded by enemies, or shall have received certain advice of a resolution being formed by some nation of Indians to invade such state, and the danger is so imminent as not to admit of a delay, till the United States in congress assembled can be consulted: nor shall any state grant commissions to any ships or vessels of war, nor letters of marque or reprisal, except it be after a declaration of war by the united states in congress assembled, and then only against the kingdom or state and the subjects thereof, against which war has been so declared, and under such regulations as shall be established by the united states in congress assembled, unless such state be infested by pirates, in which case vessels of war may be fitted out for that occasion, and kept so long as the danger shall continue, or until the united states in congress assembled shall determine otherwise.

*   *   *

Article IX. The United States in congress assembled, shall have the sole and exclusive right and power of determining on peace and war, except in the cases mentioned in the sixth article—of sending and receiving ambassadors—entering into treaties and alliances, provided that no treaty of commerce shall be made whereby the legislative power of the respective states shall be restrained from imposing such imposts and duties on foreigners, as their own people are subjected to, or from prohibiting the exportation or importation of any species of goods or commodities whatsoever—of establishing rules for deciding in all cases, what captures on land or water shall be legal, and in what manner prizes taken by land or naval forces in the service of the united states shall be divided or appropriated—of granting letters of marque and reprisal in times of peace—appointing courts for the trial of piracies and felonies committed on the high seas and establishing courts for receiving and determining finally appeals in all cases of captures, provided that no member of congress shall be appointed a judge of any of the said courts. . . .

The United States in congress assembled shall never engage in a war, nor grant letters of marque and reprisal in time of peace, nor enter into any treaties or alliances, nor coin money, nor regulate the value thereof, nor ascertain the sums and expenses necessary for the defense and welfare of the united states, or any of them, nor emit bills, nor borrow money on the credit of the united states, nor appropriate money, nor agree upon the number of vessels of war, to be built or purchased, or the number of land or sea forces to be raised, nor appoint a commander in chief of the army or navy, unless nine states assent to the same: nor shall a question on any other point, except for adjourning from day to day be determined, unless by the votes of a majority of the united states in congress assembled. . . .

*   *   *

Article XI. Canada acceding to this confederation, and joining in the measures of the United States, shall be admitted into, and entitled to all the advantages of this union: but no other colony shall be admitted into the same, unless such admission be agreed to by nine states.

*   *   *

Article XIII. Every state shall abide by the determinations of the united states in congress assembled, on all questions which by this confederation are submitted to them. And the Articles of this confederation shall be inviolably observed by every state, and the union shall be perpetual; nor shall any alteration at any time hereafter be made in any of them; unless such alteration be agreed to in a congress of the United States, and be afterwards confirmed by the legislatures of every state. . . .

——— RECORDS OF THE FEDERAL CONVENTION OF 1787 ———
AS REPORTED BY JAMES MADISON

Friday, August 17 [1787] In Convention

[Verbatim rendition]

* * *

CONGRESS' POWER TO DECLARE WAR:

. . . . Mr. **Madison** and Mr. [Elbridge] **Gerry** [of Massachusetts] moved to insert *"declare,"* striking out *"make"* war; leaving to the Executive the power to repel sudden attacks.

Mr. [Roger] **Sharman** [Sherman of Connecticut] thought it stood very well. The Executive shd. be able to repel and not to commence war. "Make" better than "declare"; the latter narrowing the power too much.

Mr. **Gerry** never expected to hear in a republic a motion to empower the Executive alone to declare war.

Mr. [Oliver] **Elsworth** [of Connecticut]. There is a material difference between the cases of making *war* and making *peace.* It shd. be more easy to get out of war, than into it. War also is a simple and overt declaration. Peace attended with intricate & secret negotiations.

Mr. [George] **Mason** [of Virginia] was agst. giving the power of war to the Executive, because not safely to be trusted with it; or to the Senate, because not so constructed as to be entitled to it. He was for clogging rather than facilitating war; but for facilitating peace. He preferred *"declare"* to *"make"*.

On the motion to insert *declare* —in place of *make,* it was agreed to.

Mr. [Charles C.] **Pinckney**'s [of South Carolina] motion to strike out whole clause, disagd. to without call of States.

Mr. [Pierce] **Butler** [of South Carolina] moved to give the Legislature power of peace, as they were to have that of war.

Mr. **Gerry** 2ds. him. 8 Senators may possibly exercise the power if vested in that body, and 14 if all should be present; and may consequently give up part of the U. States. The Senate are more liable to be corrupted by an Enemy than the whole Legislature.

Adjourned.

* * *

Friday, Septr 7, 1787. In Convention

* * *

THE TREATY POWER:

The [Article II,] Section 4.—to wit, "The President by & with the advice and consent of the Senate shall have power to make Treaties &c"

Mr. [James] **Wilson** [of Pennsylvania] moved to add, after the word "Senate" the words, "and House of Representatives." As treaties he said are to have the operation of laws, they ought to have the sanction of laws also.

The circumstance of secrecy in the business of treaties formed the only objection; but this he thought, so far as it was inconsistent with obtaining the Legislative sanction, was outweighted by the necessity of the latter.

Mr. **Sherman** thought the only question that could be made was whether the power could be safely trusted to the Senate. He thought it could; and that the necessity of secrecy in the case of treaties forbade a reference of them to the whole Legislature.

"He shall nominate &c Appoint Ambassadors &c."

Mr. **Wilson** objected to the mode of appointing, as blending a branch of the Legislature with the Executive. Good laws are of no effect without a good Executive; and there can be no good Executive without a responsible appointment of officers to execute. Responsibility is in a manner destroyed by such an agency of the Senate. He would prefer the council proposed by Col. Mason, provided its advice should not be made obligatory on the President.

Mr. **Pinckney** was against joining the Senate in these appointments, except in the instance of Ambassadors whom he thought ought not to be appointed by the President.

Mr. Govr. **Morris** [of Pennsylvania] said that as the President was to nominate, there would be responsibility, and as the Senate was to concur, there would be security. As Congress now make appointments there is no responsibility.

Mr. **Gerry**. The idea of responsibility in the nomination to offices is chimerical. The President can not know all characters, and can therefore always plead ignorance.

Mr. [Rufus] **King** [of Massachusetts]. As the idea of a Council proposed by Col. Mason has been supported by Mr. Wilson, he would remark that most of the inconveniences charged on the Senate are incident to a Council of Advice. He differed from those who thought the Senate would sit constantly. He did not suppose it was meant that all the minute officers were to be appointed by the Senate, or any other original source, but by the higher officers of the departments to which they belong. He was of opinion also that the people would be alarmed at an unnecessary creation of new Corps which must increase the expense as well as influence of the Government.

On the question on these words in the clause viz—"He shall nominate & by & with the advice and consent of the Senate, shall appoint ambassadors, and other public ministers (and Consuls) Judges of the Supreme Court." Agreed to the insertion of "and consuls" having first taken place.

Section 4. "The President by and with the advice and consent of the Senate shall have power to make Treaties"—"*But no treaty shall be made without the consent of two-thirds of the members present*"—this last being before the House.

Mr. **Wilson** thought it objectionable to require the concurrence of ⅔ which puts it in the power of a minority to control the will of a majority.

Mr. **King** concurred in the objection; remarking that as the Executive was here joined in the business, there was a check which did not exist in Congress where the concurrence of ⅔ was required.

Mr. **Madison** moved to insert after the word "treaty" the words "except treaties of peace" allowing these to be made with less difficulty than other treaties. It was agreed to.

Mr. **Madison** then moved to authorize a concurrence of two-thirds of the Senate to make treaties of peace, without the concurrence of the President.—The President he said would necessarily derive so much power and importance from a state of war that he might be tempted, if authorized, to impede a treaty of peace. Mr. **Butler** 2ned. the motion.

Mr. [Nathaniel] **Gorham** [of Massachusetts] thought the precaution unnecessary as the means of carrying on the war would not be in the hands of the President, but of the Legislature.

Mr. Govr. **Morris** thought the power of the President in this case harmless; and that no peace ought to be made without the concurrence of the President, who was the general Guardian of the National interests.

Mr. **Butler** was strenuous for the motion, as a necessary security against ambitious & corrupt Presidents. He mentioned the late perfidious policy of the Statholder in Holland; and the artifices of the Duke of Marlbro' to prolong the war of which he had the management.

Mr. **Gerry** was of opinion that in treaties of peace a greater rather than less proportion of votes was necessary, than in other treaties. In Treaties of peace the dearest interests will be at stake, as the fisheries, territory &c. In treaties of peace also there is more danger to the extremities of the Continent, of being sacrificed, than on any other occasions.

Mr. [Hugh] **Williamson** [of North Carolina] thought that Treaties of peace should be guarded at least by requiring the same concurrence as in other Treaties.

*   *   *

Saturday, September 8th in Convention

The last Report of Committee of Eleven was resumed.

Mr. **King** moved to strike out the "exception of Treaties of peace" from the general clause requiring two thirds of the Senate for making Treaties.

Mr. **Wilson** wished the requisition of two thirds to be struck out altogether if the majority cannot be trusted, it was a proof, as observed by Mr. Ghorum, that we were not fit for one Society.

A reconsideration of the whole clause was agreed to.

Mr. Govr. **Morris** was agst. striking out the "exception of Treaties of peace". If two-thirds of the Senate should be required for peace, the Legislature will be unwilling, to make war for that reason, on account of the Fisheries or the Mississippi, the two great objects of the Union. Besides, if a majority of the Senate be for peace, and are not allowed to make it, they will be apt to effect their purpose in the more disagreeable mode, of negativing the supplies for the war.

Mr. **Williamson** remarked that Treaties are to be made in the branch of the Govt. where there may be a majority of the States without a majority of the people. Eight men may be a majority of a quorum, & should not have the power to decide the conditions of peace. There would be no danger, that the exposed States, as S. Carolina or Georgia, would urge an improper war for the Western Territory.

Mr. **Wilson**. If two-thirds are necessary to make peace, the minority may perpetuate war, against the sense of the majority.

Mr. **Gerry** enlarged on the danger of putting the essential rights of the Union in the hands of so small a number as a majority of the Senate, representing, perhaps, not one-fifth of the people. The Senate will be corrupted by foreign influence.

Mr. **Sherman** was agst. leaving the rights established by the Treaty of peace, to the Senate, & moved to annex a "proviso that no such rights shd. be ceded without the sanction of the Legislature.

Mr. Govr. **Morris** seconded the ideas of Mr. Sherman.

Mr. **Madison** observed that it had been too easy in the present Congress to make Treaties altho' nine States were required for the purpose.

Mr. **Wilson** & Mr. [Jonathan] **Dayton** [of New Jersey] move to strike out the clause requiring two thirds of the Senate for making Treaties....

Mr. [John] **Rutl[e]dge** [of South Carolina] & Mr. **Gerry** move that "no Treaty be made without the consent of ⅔ of all the members of the Senate"—according to the example in the present Congs.

Mr. **Ghorum** [Gorham]. There is a difference in the case, as the President's consent will also be necessary in the new Govt.

Mr. **Sharman** [Sherman] movd. that no Treaty be made without a Majority of the whole number of the Senate. Mr. **Gerry** seconded him.

Mr. **Williamson.** This will be less security than ⅔ as now required.

Mr. **Sherman.** It will be less embarrassing.

On the question, it passed in the negative.

--------------- *THE FEDERALIST* NO. 24 (HAMILTON) ---------------

CONCERNING STANDING ARMIES

(For the *Independent Journal*)

.... A stranger to our politics, who was to read our newspapers at the present juncture, without having previously inspected the plan reported by the convention, would be naturally led to one of two conclusions: either that it contained a positive injunction, that standing armies should be kept up in time of peace; or that it vested in the EXECUTIVE the whole power of levying troops, without subjecting his discretion to the control of the legislature.

If he came afterwards to peruse the plan itself, he would be surprised to discover, that neither the one nor the other was the case; that the whole power of raising armies was lodged in the *Legislature,* not in the *Executive;* that this legislature was to be a popular body, consisting of the representatives of the people periodically elected; and that instead of the provision he had supposed in favor of standing armies, there was to be found ... an important qualification even of the legislative discretion, in that clause which forbids the appropriation of money for the support of an army for any longer period than two years. . . .

Though a wide ocean separates the United States from Europe, yet there are various considerations that warn us against an excess of confidence or security. On one side of us, and stretching far into our rear, are growing settlements subject to the dominion of Britain. On the other side, and extending to meet the British settlements, are colonies and establishments subject to the dominion of Spain. This situation and the vicinity of the West Indian Islands, belonging to these two powers, create between them, in respect to their American possessions and in relation to us, a common interest. The savage tribes on our Western frontier ought to be regarded as our natural enemies, their natural allies, because they have most to fear from us, and most to hope from them. . . . Britain and Spain are among the principal maritime powers of Europe. A future concert of views between these nations ought not to be regarded as improbable. The increasing remoteness of consanguinity is every day diminishing the force of the family compact between France and Spain. And politicians have ever with great reason considered the ties of blood as feeble and precarious links of political connection. These circumstances combined, admonish us not to be too sanguine in considering ourselves as entirely out of the reach of danger. . . .

In proportion to our increase in strength, it is probably, nay, it may be said certain, that Britain and Spain would augment their military establishments in our neighborhood. If we should not be willing to be exposed, in a naked and defenceless condition, to their insults and encroachments, we should find it expedient to increase our frontier garrisons in some ratio to the force by which our Western settlements might be annoyed. There are, and will be, particular posts, the possession of which will include the command of large districts of territory, and facilitate future invasions of the remainder. It may be added that some of those posts will be keys to the trade with the Indian nations. Can any man think it would be wise to leave such posts in a situation to be at any instant seized by one or the other of two neighboring and formidable powers? To act this part would be to desert all the usual maxims of prudence and policy. . . .

────────── *THE FEDERALIST* NO. 26 (HAMILTON) ──────────

LEGISLATIVE AUTHORITY AND DEFENCE

(For the *Independent Journal*)

. . . . It may not be amiss in this place concisely to remark the origin and progress of the idea, which aims at the exclusion of military establishments in time of peace. Though in speculative minds it may arise from a contemplation of the nature and tendency of such institutions, fortified by the events that have happened in other ages and countries, yet as a national sentiment, it must be traced to those habits of thinking which we derive from the nation from whom the inhabitants of these states have in general sprung. . . .

In [England], when the pulse of liberty was at its highest pitch, no security against the danger of standing armies was thought requisite, beyond a prohibition of their being raised or kept up by the mere authority of the executive magistrate. The patriots, who effected that memorable revolution, were too temperate, too well-informed, to think of any restraint on the legislative discretion. They were aware that a certain number of troops for guards and garrisons were indispensable; that no precise bounds could be set to the national exigencies; that a power equal to every possible contingency must exist somewhere in the government: and that when they referred the exercise of that power to the judgment of the legislature, they had arrived at the ultimate point of precaution which was reconcilable with the safety of the community.

From the same source, the people of America may be said to have derived an hereditary impression of danger to liberty, from standing armies in time of peace. The circumstances of a revolution quickened the public sensibility on every point connected with the security of popular rights, and in some instances raised the warmth of our zeal beyond the degree which consisted with the due temperature of the body politic.... The principles which had taught us to be jealous of the power of an hereditary monarch were by an injudicious excess extended to the representatives of the people in their popular assemblies....

PUBLIUS

——————— *The Federalist* No. 28 (Hamilton) ———————

THE MILITARY IN TIME OF PEACE

(For the *Independent Journal*)

To the People of the State of New York:

THAT there may happen cases in which the national government may be necessitated to resort to force, cannot be denied. Our own experience has corroborated the lessons taught by the examples of other nations; that emergencies of this sort will sometimes arise in all societies, however constituted; that seditions and insurrections are, unhappily, maladies as inseparable from the body politic as tumors and eruptions from the natural body; that the idea of governing at all times by the simple force of law (which we have been told is the only admissible principle of republican government), has no place but in the reveries of those political doctors whose sagacity disdains the admonitions of experimental instruction.

Should such emergencies at any time happen under the national government, there could be no remedy but force. The means to be employed must be proportioned to the extent of the mischief. If it should be a slight commotion in a small part of a State, the militia of the residue would be inadequate to its suppression; and the natural presumption is that they would be ready to do their duty. An insurrection, whatever may be its immediate cause, eventually endangers all government. Regard to the public peace, if not to the rights of the Union, would engage the citizens to whom the contagion had not communicated itself to oppose the insurgents; and if the general government should be found in practice conducive to the prosperity and felicity of the people, it were irrational to believe that they would be disinclined to its support. . . .

We should recollect that the extent of the military force must, at all events, be regulated by the resources of the country. For a long time to come, it will not be possible to maintain a large army; and as the means of doing this increase, the population and natural strength of the community will proportionably increase. When will the time arrive that the federal government can raise and maintain an army capable of erecting a despotism over the great body of the people of an immense empire, who are in a situation, through the medium of their State governments, to take measures for their own defence, with all the celerity, regularity, and system of independent nations? The apprehension may be considered as a disease, for which there can be found no cure in the resources of argument and reasoning.

PUBLIUS

──────────── *THE FEDERALIST* NO. 41 (MADISON) ────────────

POWERS VESTED IN THE GOVERNMENT

(For the *Independent Journal*)

. . . . Security against foreign danger is one of the primitive objects of civil society. It is an avowed and essential object of the American Union. The powers requisite for attaining it must be effectually confided to the federal councils.

Is the power of declaring war necessary? No man will answer this question in the negative. It would be superfluous, therefore, to enter into a proof of the affirmative. The existing Confederation establishes this power in the most ample form.

Is the power of raising armies and equipping fleets necessary? This is involved in the foregoing power. It is involved in the power of self-defence.

But was it necessary to give an INDEFINITE POWER of raising TROOPS, as well as providing fleets; and of maintaining both in PEACE, as well as in war?

. . . . The answer indeed seems to be so obvious and conclusive as scarcely to justify such a discussion. . . . With what color of propriety could the force necessary for defence be limited by those who cannot limit the force of offence? If a federal Constitution could chain the ambition or set bounds to the exertions of all other nations, then indeed might it prudently chain the discretion of its own government, and set bounds to the exertions for its own safety.

How could a readiness for war in time of peace be safely prohibited, unless we could prohibit, in like manner, the preparations and establishments of every hostile nation? The means of security can only be regulated

by the means and the danger of attack. They will, in fact, be ever determined by these rules, and by no others. It is in vain to oppose constitutional
barriers to the impulse of self-preservation. It is worse than in vain; because
it plants in the Constitution itself necessary usurpations of power, every
precedent of which is a germ of unnecessary and multiplied repetitions. If
one nation maintains constantly a disciplined army, ready for the service of
ambition or revenge, it obliges the most pacific nations who may be within
the reach of its enterprises to take corresponding precautions. . . .

A bad cause seldom fails to betray itself. Of this truth, the management
of the opposition to the federal government is an unvaried exemplification.
But among all the blunders which have been committed, none is more
striking than the attempt to enlist on that side the prudent jealously entertained by the people, of standing armies. The attempt has awakened fully
the public attention to that important subject; and has led to investigations
which must terminate in a thorough and universal conviction, not only that
the Constitution has provided the most effectual guards against danger from
that quarter, but that nothing short of a Constitution fully adequate to the
national defence and the preservation of the Union, can save America from
as many standing armies as it may be split into States or Confederacies, and
from such a progressive augmentation, of these establishments in each, as
will render them as burdensome to the properties and ominous to the liberties of the people, as any establishment that can become necessary, under a
united and efficient government, must be tolerable to the former and safe to
the latter.

The palpable necessity of the power to provide and maintain a navy has
protected that part of the Constitution against a spirit of censure, which has
spared few other parts. It must, indeed, be numbered among the greatest
blessings of America, that as her Union will be the only source of her
maritime strength, so this will be a principal source of her security against
danger from abroad. In this respect our situation bears another likeness to
the insular advantage of Great Britain. The batteries most capable of repelling foreign enterprises on our safety, are happily such as can never be
turned by a perfidious government against our liberties.

The inhabitants of the Atlantic frontier are all of them deeply interested
in this provision for naval protection, and if they have hitherto been suffered to sleep quietly in their beds; if their property has remained safe
against the predatory spirit of licentious adventurers; if their maritime towns
have not yet been compelled to ransom themselves from the terrors of a
conflagration, by yielding to the exactions of daring and sudden invaders,
these instances of good fortune are not to be ascribed to the capacity of the
existing government for the protection of those from whom it claims allegiance, but to causes that are fugitive and fallacious. . . . The great empori-
um of its commerce, the great reservoir of its wealth, lies every moment at
the mercy of events, and may almost be regarded as a hostage for ignomini-
ous compliances with the dictates of a foreign enemy, or even with the
rapacious demands of pirates and barbarians. . . .

PUBLIUS

─────────── *THE FEDERALIST* NO. 69 (HAMILTON) ───────────

PRESIDENTIAL POWERS

(For the *New York Packet*, March 14, 1788)

. . . . The President is to be the "commander in chief of the army and navy of the United States, and of the militia of the several States, when called into the actual service of the United States." He is to have power to grant reprieves and pardons for offences against the United States, *except in cases of impeachment;* to recommend to the consideration of Congress such measures as he shall judge necessary and expedient; to convene, on extraordinary occasions, both houses of the legislature, or either of them, and, in case of disagreement between them *with respect to the time of adjournment,* to adjourn them to such time as he shall think proper; to take care that the laws be faithfully executed; and to commission all officers of the United States." In most of these particulars, the power of the President will resemble equally that of the king of Great Britain and of the governor of New York. The most material points of difference are these: *First.* The President will have only the occasional command of such part of the militia of the nation as by legislative provision may be called into the actual service of the Union. The king of Great Britain and the governor of New York have at all times the entire command of all the militia within their several jurisdictions. In this article, therefore, the power of the President would be inferior to that of either the monarch or the governor. *Secondly.* The President is to be commander in chief of the army and navy of the United States. In this respect his authority would be nominally the same with that of the king of Great Britain, but in substance much inferior to it. It would amount to nothing more than the supreme command and direction of the military and naval forces, as first General and admiral of the Confederacy; while that of the British king extends to the *declaring* of war and to the *raising* and *regulating* of fleets and armies,—all which, by the Constitution under consideration, would appertain to the legislature. The governor of New York, on the other hand, is by the constitution of the State vested only with the command of its militia and navy. But the constitutions of several of the States expressly declare their governors to be commanders in chief, as well of the army as navy; and it may well be a question, whether those of New Hampshire and Massachusetts, in particular, do not, in this instance, confer larger powers upon their respective governors, than could be claimed by a President of the United States. . . .

The President is to have power, with the advice and consent of the Senate, to make treaties, provided two-thirds of the senators present concur. The king of Great Britain is the sole and absolute representative of the nation in all foreign transactions. He can of his own accord make treaties of peace, commerce, alliance, and of every other description. It has been insinuated, that his authority in this respect is not conclusive, and that his conventions with foreign powers are subject to the revision, and stand in need of the ratification, of Parliament. But I believe this doctrine was never heard of, until it was broached upon the present occasion. Every jurist of that king-dom, and every other man acquainted with its Constitution, knows, as an established fact, that the prerogative of making treaties exists in the crown in its utmost plenitude; and that the compacts entered into by the royal authority have the most complete legal validity and perfection, independent of any other sanction. The Parliament, it is true, is sometimes seen employ-ing itself in altering the existing laws to conform them to the stipulations in a new treaty; and this may have possibly given birth to the imagination, and its cooperation was necessary to the obligatory efficacy of the treaty. But this parliamentary interposition proceeds from a different cause: from the necessity of adjusting a most artificial and intricate system of revenue and commercial laws, to the changes made in them by the operation of the treaty; and of adapting new provisions and precautions to the new state of things, to keep the machine from running into disorder. In this respect, therefore, there is no comparison between the intended power of the Presi-dent and the actual power of the British sovereign. The one can perform alone what the other can do only with the concurrence of a branch of the legislature. It must be admitted, that, in this instance, the power of the federal Executive would exceed that of any State Executive. But this arises naturally from the sovereign power which relates to treaties. If the Confed-eracy were to be dissolved, it would become a question whether the Execu-tives of the several States were not solely invested with that delicate and important prerogative.

The President is also to be authorized to receive ambassadors and other public ministers. This, though it has been a rich theme of declamation, is more a matter of dignity than of authority. It is a circumstance which will be without consequence in the administration of the government; and it was far more convenient that it should be arranged in this manner, than that there should be a necessity of convening the legislature, or one of its branches, upon every arrival of a foreign minister, though it were merely to take the place of a departed predecessor....

PUBLIUS

────────────── *The Federalist* No. 75 (Hamilton) ──────────────

THE TREATY POWER

(For the *Independent Journal*)

To the People of the State of New York:

The President is to have power, "by and with the advice and consent of the Senate, to make treaties, provided two-thirds of the senators present concur."

Though this provision has been assailed, on different grounds, with no small degree of vehemence, I scruple not to declare my first persuasion, that it is one of the best digested and most unexceptionable parts of the plan. One ground of objection is the trite topic of the intermixture of powers; some contending that the President ought alone to possess the power of making treaties; others, that it ought to have been exclusively deposited in the Senate. Another source of objection is derived from the small number of persons by whom a treaty may be made. Of those who espouse this objection, a part are of opinion that the House of Representatives ought to have been associated in the business, while another part seem to think that nothing more was necessary than to have substituted two-thirds of *all* the members of the Senate, to two-thirds of the members *present*. . . .

With regard to the intermixture of powers, I shall rely upon the explanations already given in other places, of the true sense of the rule upon which that objection is founded; and shall take it for granted, as an inference from them, that the union of the Executive with the Senate, in the article of treaties, is no infringement of that rule. I venture to add, that the particular nature of the power of making treaties indicates a peculiar propriety in that union. Though several writers on the subject of government place that power in the class of executive authorities, yet this is evidently an arbitrary disposition; for if we attend carefully to its operation, it will be found to partake more of the legislative than of the executive character, though it does not seem strictly to fall within the definition of either of them. The essence of the legislative authority is to enact laws, or, in other words, to prescribe rules for the regulation of the society; while the execution of the laws, and the employment of the common strength, either for this purpose or for the common defence, seem to comprise all the functions of the executive magistrate. The power of making treaties is, plainly, neither the one nor the other. It relates neither to the executive of the subsisting laws, nor to the enaction of new ones; and still less to an exertion of the common strength. Its objects are CONTRACTS with foreign nations, which have the force of law, but derive it from the obligations of good faith. They are not rules prescribed by the sovereign to the subject, but agreements between sovereign and sovereign. The power in question seems therefore to form a distinct department, and to belong, properly, neither to the legislative nor to the executive. The qualities elsewhere detailed as indispensable in the management of foreign negotiations, point out the Executive as the most fit agent in those transactions; while the vast importance of the trust, and the operation of treaties as laws, plead strongly for the participation of the whole or a portion of the legislative body in the office of making them.

However proper or safe it may be in governments where the executive magistrate is an hereditary monarch, to commit to him the entire power of making treaties, it would be utterly unsafe and improper to intrust that power to an elective magistrate of four years' duration. It has been remarked, upon another occasion, and the remark is unquestionably just, that an hereditary monarch, though often the oppressor of his people, has personally too much stake in the government to be in any material danger of being corrupted by foreign powers. But a man raised from the station of a private citizen to the rank of chief magistrate, possessed of a moderate or slender fortune, and looking forward to a period not very remote when he may probably be obliged to return to the station from which he was taken might sometimes be under temptations to sacrifice his duty to his interest, which it would require superlative virtue to withstand. An avaricious man might be tempted to betray the interests of the state to the acquisition of wealth. An ambitious man might make his own aggrandizement, by the aid of a foreign power, the price of his treachery to his constituents. The history of human conduct does not warrant that exalted opinion of human virtue which would make it wise in a nation to commit interests of so delicate and momentous a kind, as those which concern its intercourse with the rest of the world, to the sole disposal of a magistrate created and circumstanced as would be a President of the United States.

To have intrusted the power of making treaties to the Senate alone, would have been to relinquish the benefits of the constitutional agency of the President in the conduct of foreign negotiations. It is true that the Senate would, in that case, have the option of employing him in this capacity, but they would also have the option of letting it alone, and pique or cabal might induce the latter rather than the former. Besides this, the ministerial servant of the Senate could not be expected to enjoy the confidence and respect of foreign powers in the same degree with the constitutional representatives of the nation, and, of course, would not be able to act with an equal degree of weight or efficacy. While the Union would, from this cause, lose a considerable advantage in the management of its external concerns, the people would lose the additional security which would result from the cooperation of the Executive. Though it would be imprudent to confide in him solely so important a trust, yet it cannot be doubted that his participation would materially add to the safety of the society. It must indeed be clear to a demonstration that the joint possession of the power in question, by the President and Senate, would afford a greater prospect of security, than the separate possession of it by either of them. And whoever has maturely weighed the circumstances which must concur in the appointment of a President, will be satisfied that the office will always bid fair to be filled by men of such character as to render their concurrence in the formation of treaties peculiarly desirable, as well on the score of wisdom, as on that of integrity. . . .

─────── DEBATES IN THE SEVERAL STATE CONVENTIONS ───────
ON THE ADOPTION OF
THE FEDERAL CONSTITUTION

MASSACHUSETTS:

In Convention, Boston, Tuesday, January 22, 1788 (Article I, section 8)

[Extract]
The War Powers of Congress

Mr. [Christopher] Gore.
. . . . Let us strip the subject of every thing that is Foreign . . . and we shall soon see that it is not only safe, but indispensably necessary to our peace and dignity, to vest Congress with the powers described in this section. . . .

To pay the debts, and provide for the common defence . . .; to declare war, &c.; to raise and support armies; to provide and maintain a navy; —these are authorities and duties incident to every government. No one has, or, I presume, will deny, that whatever government may be established over America, ought to perform such duties. . . . Is America to wait until she is attacked, before she attempts a preparation at defence? This would certainly be unwise; it would be courting our enemies to make war upon us. The operations of war are sudden. . . . But, it is said, we do not fear war; we have no enemies. Let the gentlemen consider the situation of our country; they will find we are circumscribed by enemies from Maine to Georgia. I trust, therefore, that . . . it will be found indispensably requisite to peace, dignity, and happiness, that the proposed government should be vested with all the powers granted by the section under debate.

Hon. Mr. [William] Phillips (of Boston). . . . Mention is made that Congress ought to be restricted of all power to keep an army except in time of war. I apprehend that great mischief would ensue from such a restriction. Let us take means to prevent war, by granting to Congress the power of raising an army. If a declaration of war is made against this country, and the enemy's army is coming against us, before Congress could collect the means to withstand this enemy, they would penetrate into the bounds of our country, and everything dear to us would be gone in a moment. . . .

CONNECTICUT:

In Convention, Hartford, January 4, 1788

[Extract]

Speech of **Oliver Ellsworth** on Opening the Debates:

Mr. President, ... A union is necessary for the purposes of national defense. United, we are strong; divided, we are weak. It is easy for hostile nations to sweep off a number of separate states, one after another. Witness the states in the neighborhood of ancient Rome. . . .

NEW YORK:

In Convention, Poughkeepsie, June 17, 1788

[Extract]

The **Hon. Mr. [Alexander] Hamilton** [June 24]:

. . . . There are two objects in forming systems of government—*safety* for the people, and *energy* in the administration. When the objects are united, the certain tendency of the system will be to the public welfare. . . . Good constitutions are formed upon a comparison of the liberty of the individual with the strength of government: if the tone of either be too high, the other will be weakened too much. It is the happiest possible mode of conciliating these objects, to institute one branch peculiarly endowed with sensibility, another with knowledge and firmness. Through the operation and mutual control of these bodies, the government will reach, in its operations, the perfect balance between liberty and power.

[June 27, 1788]: .... The great leading objects of the federal government ... are to maintain domestic peace, and provide for the common defence. In these are comprehended the regulation of commerce,—that is, the whole system of foreign intercourse,—the support of armies and navies, and of the civil administration. It is useless to go into detail. Everyone knows that the objects of the general government are numerous, extensive and important. Everyone must acknowledge the necessity of giving powers, in all respects, and in every degree, equal to these objects....

PENNSYLVANIA:

Philadelphia, December 11, 1787

[Extract]

Mr. [James] Wilson:
.... There is no doubt, sir, but, under this Constitution, treaties will become the supreme law of the land; nor is there any doubt but the Senate and President possess the power of making them. But though the treaties are to have the force of laws, they are in some important respects very different from other acts of legislation. In making laws, our own consent alone is necessary. In forming treaties, the concurrence of another power becomes necessary. Treaties, sir, are truly contracts, or compacts, between the different states, nations, or princes, who find it convenient or necessary to enter into them. Some gentlemen are of opinion that the power of making treaties should have been placed in the legislature at large; there are, however, reasons that operate with great force on the other side. Treaties are frequently (especially in time of war) of such a nature, that it would be extremely improper to publish them, or even commit the secret of their negotiation to any great number of persons. For my part, I am not an advocate for secrecy in transactions relating to the public; not generally even in forming treaties, because I think that the history of the diplomatic corps will evince, even in that great department of politics, the truth of an old adage, that "honesty is the best policy," and this is the conduct of the most able negotiators; yet sometimes secrecy may be necessary, and therefore it becomes an argument against committing the knowledge of these transactions to too many persons. But in their nature treaties originate differently from laws. They are made in equal parties, and each side has half of the bargain to make; they will be made between us and powers at the distance of three thousand miles. A long series of negotiation will frequently precede them; and can it be the opinion of these gentlemen that the legislature should be in session during this whole time? It well deserves to be remarked, that, though the House of Representatives possess no active part in making treaties, yet their legislative authority will be found to have strong restraining influences upon both President and Senate. In England, if the king and his ministers find themselves, during their negotiation, to be embarrassed because an existing law is not repealed, or a new law is not enacted, they give notice to the legislature of their situation, and inform them that it will be necessary, before the treaty can operate, that some law be repealed, or some be made. And will not the same thing take place here? Shall less prudence, less caution, less

moderation, take place among those who negotiate treaties for the United States, than among those who negotiate them for the other nations of the earth? And let it be attended to, that, even in the making of treaties, the states are immediately represented, and the people mediately represented; two of the constituent parts of government must concur in making them. Neither the President nor the Senate, solely, can complete a treaty; they are checks upon each other, and are so balanced as to produce security to the people.

MARYLAND:

Convened at Annapolis, April 21, 1788

[Extract]

The following amendments were laid before the committee, and negatived by a majority.

1. That the militia . . . shall not be marched beyond the limits of an adjoining state, without consent of their legislature or executive.

* * *

4. That no standing army shall be kept in time of peace, unless with the consent of two-thirds of the numbers present of each branch of Congress.

5. That the President shall not command the army in person, without the consent of Congress.

6. That no treaty shall be effectual or repeal or abrogate the constitution or bills of rights of the states, or any part of them.

* * *

VIRGINIA:

In Convention, Richmond, commencing June 2, 1788

[Extract]
The Treaty Power

Mr. [Patrick] Henry:

Mr. Chairman, gentlemen say that the King of Great Britain has the same right of making treaties that our President has here. I will have no objection to this, if you make your President a king. . . . Treaties are binding, not withstanding our laws and constitutions. . . . We may be told that we shall find ample refuge in the law of nations. When you yourselves have your necks so low that the President may dispose of your rights as he pleases, the law of nations cannot be applied to relieve you. Sure I am, if treaties are made infringing our liberties, it will be too late to say that our constitutional rights are violated. . . .

You prostrate your rights to the President and Senate. This power is therefore dangerous and destructive.

Gov. Randolph. . . . The honorable gentleman says that, if you place treaties on the same footing here as they are in England, he will consent to the power, because the king is restrained in making treaties. Will not the President and Senate be restrained? Being creatures of that Constitution, can they destroy it? Can any particular body, instituted for a particular purpose, destroy the existence of the society for whose benefit it is created? It is said there is no limitation of treaties. I defy the wisdom of that gentleman to show how they ought to be limited. When the Constitution marks out the powers to be exercised by particular departments, I say no innovation can take place. . . .

Mr. George Mason. Mr. Chairman, it is true that this is one of the greatest acts of sovereignty, and therefore ought to be most strongly guarded. The cession of such a power, without such checks and guards, cannot be justified: yet I acknowledge such a power must rest somewhere. It is so in all governments. If, in the course of an unsuccessful war, we should be compelled to give up part of our territories, or undergo subjugation if the general government could not make a treaty to give up such a part for the preservation of the residue, the government itself, and consequently the rights of the people, must fall. Such a power must, therefore, rest somewhere. For my own part, I never heard it denied that such a power must be vested in the government. Our complaint is, that it is not sufficiently guarded, and that it requires much more solemnity and caution than are delineated in that system. It is more guarded in England. . . .

Though the king can make treaties, yet he cannot make a treaty contrary to the constitution of his country. Where did their constitution originate? It is founded on a number of maxims, which, by long time, are rendered sacred and inviolable. Where are there such maxims in the American Constitution? In that country, which we formerly called our mother country, they have had, for many centuries, certain fundamental maxims, which have secured their persons and properties, and prevented a dismemberment of their country. The common law, sir, has prevented the power of the crown from destroying the immunities of the people. . . .

Mr. Henry: . . . . We are so used to speak of enormity of powers, that we are familiarized with it. To me this power appears still destructive; for they can make any treaty. If Congress forbears to exercise it, you may thank them; but they may exercise it if they please, and as they please. They have a right, from the paramount power given them, to do so. Will the gentlemen say that this power is paramount to the state laws only? Is it not paramount to the Constitution and every thing? Can any thing be paramount to what is paramount? Will not the laws of Congress be binding on Congress, as well as on any particular state? Will they not be bound by their own acts? The worthy gentleman must see the impropriety of his assertion. To render this safe, I conceive we must adopt my honorable friend's amendment. The component part of this supreme power are the President, senators, and House of Representatives. The latter is the most material part. They ought to interpose in the formation of treaties. When their consent is necessary, there will be a certainty of attending to the public interests.

Mr. Madison. Mr. Chairman, I am persuaded that, when this power comes to be thoroughly and candidly viewed, it will be found right and proper. As to its extent, perhaps it will be satisfactory to the committee that the power is, precisely, in the new Constitution as it is in the Confederation. In the existing confederacy, Congress are authorized indefinitely to make treaties. Many of the states have recognized the treaties of Congress to be the supreme law of the land. Acts have passed, within a year, declaring this to be the case. . . . Does it follow, because this power is given to Congress, that it is absolute and unlimited? I do not conceive that power is given to the President and Senate to dismember the empire, or to alienate any great, essential right. I do not think the whole legislative authority have this power. The exercise of the power must be consistent with the object of the delegation.

One objection against the amendment proposed is this, that, by implication, it would give power to the legislative authority to dismember the empire—a power that ought not to be given, but by the necessity that would force assent from every man. I think it rests on the safest foundation as it is. The object of treaties is the regulation of intercourse with foreign nations, and is external. I do not think it possible to enumerate all the cases in which such external regulations would be necessary. Would it be right to define all the cases in which Congress could exercise this authority. The definition might, and probably would, be defective. They might be restrained, by such a definition, from exercising the authority where it would be essential to the interest and safety of the community. It is most safe, therefore, to leave it to be exercised as contingencies may arise.

It is to be presumed that, in transactions with foreign countries, those who regulate them will feel the whole force of national attachment to their country. The contrast being between their own nation and a foreign nation, is it not presumable they will, as far as possible, advance the interest of their own country? . . . . Here the supremacy of a treaty is contrasted with the supremacy of the laws of the states. It cannot be otherwise supreme. If it does not supersede their existing laws, as far as they contravene its operation, it cannot be of any effect. To counteract it by the supremacy of the state laws, would bring on the Union the just charge of national perfidy, and involve us in war.

The War Powers of Congress

Mr. George Mason.

Mr. Chairman, unless there be some restrictions on the power of calling forth the militia, to execute the laws of the Union, suppress insurrections, and repel invasions, we may very easily see that it will produce dreadful oppressions. It is extremely unsafe, without some alterations. It would be to use the militia to a very bad purpose, if any disturbance happened in New Hampshire, to call them from Georgia. This would harass the people so much that they would agree to abolish the use of the militia, and establish a standing army. I conceive the general government ought to have power over the militia, but it ought to have some bounds.... I wish such an amendment as this—that the militia of any state should not be marched beyond the limits of the adjoining state; and if it be necessary to draw them from one end of the continent to the other, I wish such a check, as the consent of the state legislature, to be provided....

.... But when once a standing army is established in any country, the people lose their liberty. When, against a regular and disciplined army, yeomanry are the only defence,—yeomanry, unskillful and unarmed,—what chance is there for preserving freedom?.... The general government ought, at the same time, to have some such power. But we need not give them power to abolish our militia.... I wish that, in case the general government should neglect to arm and discipline the militia, there should be an express declaration that the state governments might arm and discipline them. With this single exception, I would agree to this part, as I am conscious the government ought to have the power....

Mr. Madison. Mr. Chairman, I most cordially agree, with the honorable member last up, that a standing army is one of the greatest mischiefs that can possibly happen.... The most effectual way to guard against a standing army, is to render it unnecessary. The most effectual way to render it unnecessary, is to give the general government full power to call forth the militia, and exert the whole natural strength of the Union, when necessary. Thus you will furnish the people with sure and certain protection, without recurring to this evil; and the certainty of this protection from the whole will be a strong inducement to individual exertion....

Mr. Henry.... The honorable member [Madison] who has risen to explain several parts of the system was pleased to say, that the best way of avoiding the danger of a standing army, was, to have the militia in such a way as to render it unnecessary; and that, as the new government would have power over the militia, we should have no standing army—it being unnecessary. This argument destroys itself. It demands a power, and denies the probability of its exercise. There are suspicions of power on one hand, and absolute and unlimited confidence on the other. I hope to be one of those who have a large share of suspicion. I leave it to this house, if there be not too small a portion on the other side, by giving up too much to that government. You can easily see which is the worst of two extremes. Too much suspicion may be corrected. If you give too little power today, you may give more tomorrow. But the reverse of the proposition will not hold. If you give too much power today, you cannot retake it tomorrow; for tomorrow will never come for that purpose. If you have the fate of other nations, you will never see it. It is easier to supply deficiencies of power than to take back excess of power. This no man can deny....

The argument of my honorable friend was, that rulers might tyrannize. The answer he received was, that they will not. In saying that they would not, he admitted they might. In this great, this essential part of the Constitution, if you are safe, it is not from the Constitution, but from the virtues of the men in government. If gentlemen are willing to trust themselves and posterity to so slender and improbable a chance, they have greater strength of nerves than I have....

I am convinced there is no safety in the paper on the table as it stands now.... Your President will not have the same motives of self-love to impel him to favor your interests. His political character is but transient, and he will promote, as much as possible, his own private interests. He will conclude, the constant observation has been that he will abuse his power, and that is expected. The king of England has a more permanent interest. His stock, his family, is to continue in possession of the same emolument. The more flourishing his nation, the more formidable and powerful is he. The sword and purse are not united, in that government, in the same hands, as in this system. Does not infinite security result from a separation?

But it is said that our Congress are more responsible than the British Parliament. It appears to me that there is no real, but there may be some specious responsibility. If Congress, in the execution of their unbounded powers, shall have done wrong, how will you come at them to punish them, if they are at the distance of five hundred miles? At such a great distance, they will evade responsibility altogether. If you have given up your militia, and Congress shall refuse to arm them, you have lost everything. Your existence will be precarious, because you depend on others, whose interests are not affected by your infelicity....

Mr. George Nicholas. Mr. Chairman, the great object of government, in every country, is security and public defence. I suppose, therefore, that what we ought to attend to here, is, what is the best mode of enabling the general government to protect us. One of three ways must be pursued for this purpose. We must either empower them to employ, and rely altogether on, a standing army; or depend altogether on militia; or else we must enable them to use the one or the other of these two ways, as may be found most expedient. The least reflection will satisfy us that the Convention has adopted the only proper method. If a standing army were alone to be employed, such an army must be kept up in time of peace as would be sufficient in war. The dangers of such an army are so striking that every man would oppose the adoption of this government, had it been proposed by it as the only mode of defence. Would it be safe to depend on militia alone, without the agency of regular forces, even in time of war? Were we to be invaded by a powerful, disciplined army, should we be safe with militia? Could men unacquainted with the hardships, and unskilled in the discipline of war,— men only inured to the peaceable occupations of domestic life—encounter with success the most skillful veterans, inured to the fatigues and toils of campaigns? Although some people are pleased with the theory of reliance on militia, as the sole defence of a nation, yet I think it will be found, in practice, to be by no means adequate. Its inadequacy is proved by the experience of other nations. But were it fully adequate, it would be unequal. If war be supported by militia, it is by personal service. The poor man does as much as the rich. Is this just? What is the consequence when war is carried on by regular troops? They are paid by taxes raised from the people, according to their property; and then the rich man pays an adequate share.

But, if you confine yourselves to militia alone, the poor man is oppressed. The rich man exempts himself by furnishing a substitute. And, although it be oppressive to the poor, is it not advantageous to the rich? For what he gives would pay regular troops. It is therefore neither safe nor just to depend entirely on militia. As these two ways are ineligible, let us consider the third method. Does this Constitution put this on a proper footing? It enables Congress to raise an army when necessary, or to call forth the militia when necessary. What will be the consequence of their having these two powers? Till there be a necessity for an army to be raised, militia will do. And when an army will be raised, the militia will still be employed, which will render a less numerous army sufficient. By these means, there will be a sufficient defence for the country, without having a standing army altogether, or oppressing the people. . . .

Mr. Madison. Mr. Chairman, the honorable gentleman has laid much stress on the maxim, that the purse and sword ought not to be put in the same hands, with a view of pointing out the impropriety of vesting this power in the general government. But it is totally inapplicable to this question. What is the meaning of this maxim? Does it mean that the sword and purse ought not to be trusted in the hands of the same government? This cannot be the meaning; for there never was, and I can say there never will be, an efficient government, in which both are not vested. The only rational meaning is, that the sword and purse are not to be given to the same member. . . . The purse is in the hands of the representatives of the people. They have the appropriation of all moneys. They have the direction and regulation of land and naval forces. They are to provide for calling forth the militia; and the President is to have the command, and, in conjunction with the Senate, to appoint the officers. The means ought to be commensurate to the end. The end is general protection. This cannot be effected without a general power to use the strength of the Union.

Mr. [John] Marshall replied that, as the government was drawn from the people, the feelings and interests of the people would be attended to, and that we should be safe in granting them power to regulate the militia. When the government is drawn from the people, continued Mr. Marshall, and depending on the people for its continuance, oppressive measures will not be attempted, as they will certainly draw on their authors the resentment of those on whom they depend. On this government, thus depending on ourselves for its existence, I will rest my safety, notwithstanding the danger depicted by the honorable gentleman. I cannot help being surprised that the worthy member thought this power so dangerous. What government is able to protect you in time of war? Will any state depend on its own exertions? The consequence of such dependence, and withholding this power from Congress, will be, that state will fall after state, and be a sacrifice to the want of power in the general government. *United we are strong, divided we fall.* Will you prevent the general government from drawing the militia of one state to another, when the consequence would be, that every state must depend on itself? The enemy, possessing the water, can quickly go from one state to another. No state will spare to another its militia, which it conceives necessary for itself. It requires a superintending power, in order to call forth the resources of all to protect all. If this be not done, each state will fall a sacrifice. This system merits the highest applause in this respect. The honorable gentleman said that a general regulation may be made to inflict punishments. Does he imagine that a militia law is to be ingrafted on the scheme of government, so as to render it incapable of being changed? The idea of the worthy member supposes that men renounce their own interests. This would produce general inconveniences throughout the Union, and would be equally opposed by all the states. But the worthy member fears, that in one part of the Union they will be regulated and disciplined, and in another neglected. This danger is enhanced by leaving this power to each state; for some states may attend to their militia, and others may neglect them. If Congress neglect our militia we can arm them ourselves. Cannot Virginia import arms? Cannot she put them into the hands of her militia-men?

He then concluded by observing, that the power of governing the militia was not vested in the states by implication, because, being possessed of it antecedent to the adoption of the government, and not being divested of it by any grant or restriction in the Constitution, they must necessarily be as fully possessed of it as ever they had been. And it could not be said that the states derived any powers from that system, but retained them, though not acknowledged in any part of it.

*   *   *

Mr. George Mason, animadverting on the magnitude of the powers of the President, was alarmed at the additional power of commanding the army in person. He admitted the propriety of his being commander in chief, so far as to give orders and have a general superintendency, but he thought it would be dangerous to let him command in person, without any restraint, as he might make a bad use of it. He was, then, clearly of opinion that the consent of a majority of both houses of Congress should be required before he could take the command in person. If at any time it should be necessary that he should take the personal command, either on account of his superior abilities or other cause, then Congress would agree to it; and all dangers would be obviated by requiring their consent. He called to gentlemen's recollection the extent of what the late commander in chief might have done, from his great abilities, and the strong attachment of both officers and soldiers towards him, if, instead of being disinterested, he had been an ambitious man. So disinterested and amiable a character as General Washington might never command again. The possibility of danger ought to be guarded against. . . .

Mr. Lee reminded his honorable friend that it did not follow, of necessity, that the President should command in person; that he was to command as a civil officer, and might only take the command when he was a man of military talents, and the public safety required it. He thought the power of pardoning, as delineated in the Constitution, could be nowhere so well placed as in the President. It was so in the government of New York, and had been found safe and convenient.

Mr. Mason replied, that he did not mean that the President was of necessity to command, but he might if he pleased; and if he was an ambitious man, he might make a dangerous use of it.

Mr. George Nicholas hoped the committee would not advert to this; that the army and navy were to be raised by Congress, and not by the President. It was on the same footing with our state government; for the governor, with the council, was to imbody the militia, but, when actually imbodied, they were under the sole command of the governor. The instance adduced was not similar. General Washington was not a President. As to possible danger, any commander might attempt to pervert what was intended for the common defence of the community to its destruction. The President, at the end of four years, was to relinquish all his offices. But if any other person was to have the command, the time would not be limited.

Mr. Mason answered, and said it did not resemble the state Constitution, because the governor did not possess such extensive powers as the President, and had no influence over the navy. The liberty of the people had been destroyed by those who were military commanders only. The danger here was greater by the junction of great civil powers to the command of the army and fleet. Although Congress are to raise the army, said he, no security arises from that; for, in time of war, they must and ought to raise an army, which will be numerous, or otherwise, according to the nature of the war, and then the President is to command without any control.

NORTH CAROLINA:

In Convention, begun at Hillsborough, July 28, 1788

Commander in Chief

Mr. [James] Iredell. Mr. Chairman,

. . . . In almost every country, the executive has the command of the military forces. From the nature of the thing, the command of armies ought to be delegated to one person only. The secrecy, despatch, and decision, which are necessary in military operations, can only be expected from one person. The President, therefore, is to command the military forces of the United States, and this power I think a proper one; at the same time it will be found to be sufficiently guarded. A very material difference may be observed between this power, and the authority of the king of Great Britain under similar circumstances. The king of Great Britain is not only the commander in chief of the land and naval forces, but has power, in time of war, to raise fleets and armies. He has also authority to declare war. The President has not the power of declaring war by his own authority, nor that of raising fleets and armies. These powers are vested in other hands. The power of declaring war is expressly given to Congress, that is, to the two branches of the legislature—the Senate, composed of representatives of the state legislatures, the House of Representatives, deputed by the people at large. They have also expressly delegated to them the powers of raising and supporting armies, and of providing and maintaining a navy.

With regard to the militia, it must be observed, that though he has the command of them when called into the actual service of the United States, yet he has not the power of calling them out. The power of calling them out is vested in Congress, for the purpose of calling them out is vested in Congress, for the purpose of executing the laws of the Union. When the militia are called out for any purpose, some person must command them; and who so proper as that person who has the best evidence of his possessing the general confidence of the people? I trust, therefore, that the power of commanding the militia, when called forth into the actual service of the United States, will not be objected to. . . .

Mr. Porter. Mr. Chairman, there is a power vested in the Senate and President to make treaties, which shall be the supreme law of the land. Which among us can call them to account? I always thought that there could be no proper exercise of power without the suffrage of the people; yet the House of Representatives had no power to intermeddle with treaties. The President and seven senators, as nearly as I can remember, can make a treaty which will be of great advantage to the Northern States, and equal injury to the Southern States. Yet, in the preamble of the Constitution, they say *all the people* have done it. I should be glad to know what power there is of calling the President and Senate to account.

Mr. Spaight answered that, under the Confederation, two-thirds of the states might make treaties; that, if the senators from all the states attended when a treaty was about to be made, two-thirds of the states would have a voice in its formation. He added, that he would be glad to ask the gentleman what mode there was of calling the present Congress to account. . . .

SOUTH CAROLINA:

In Convention, commencing May 12, 1788

Maj. Pierce Butler (one of the delegates of the Federal Convention) was one of a committee that drew up this clause, and would endeavor to recollect those reasons by which they were guided. It was at first proposed to vest the sole power of making peace or war in the Senate; but this was objected to as inimical to the genius of a republic, by destroying the necessary balance they were anxious to preserve. Some gentlemen were inclined to give this power to the President; but it was objected to, as throwing into his hands the influence of a monarch, having an opportunity of involving his country in a war whenever he wished to promote her destruction.

The House of Representatives was then named; but an insurmountable objection was made to this proposition—which was, that negotiations always required the greatest secrecy, which could not be expected in a large body. The honorable gentleman then gave a clear, concise opinion on the propriety of the proposed Constitution.

Gen. Charles Cotesworth Pinckney (one of the delegates of the Federal Convention). . . . [The treaty power] appeared to be of so much magnitude, that a committee consisting of one member from each state was appointed to consider and report upon it. His honorable friend (Major Butler) was on the committee for this state. Some members were for vesting the power for making treaties in the legislature; but the secrecy and despatch which are so frequently necessary in negotiations evinced the impropriety of vesting it there. The same reason showed the impropriety of placing it solely in the

House of Representatives. A few members were desirous that the President alone might possess this power, and contended that it might safely be lodged with him, as he was to be responsible for his conduct, and therefore would not dare to make a treaty repugnant to the interest of his country; and from his situation he was more interested in making a good treaty than any other man in the United States. This doctrine General Pinckney said he could not acquiesce in. Kings, he admitted, were in general more interested in the welfare of their country than any other individual in it, because the prosperity of the country tended to increase the lustre of the crown, and a king never could receive a sufficient compensation for the sale of his kingdoms; for he could not enjoy in any other country so advantageous a situation as he permanently possessed in his own. . . . But the situation of a President would be very different from that of a king: he might withdraw himself from the United States, so that the states could receive no advantage from his responsibility; his office is not to be permanent, but temporary; and he might receive a bribe which would enable him to live in greater splendor in another country than his own; and when out of office, he was no more interested in the prosperity of his country than any other patriotic citizen: and in framing a treaty, he might perhaps show an improper partiality for the state to which he particularly belonged. The different propositions made on this subject, the general observed, occasioned much debate. At last it was agreed to give the President a power of proposing treaties, as he was the ostensible head of the Union, and to vest the Senate (where each state had an equal voice) with the power of agreeing or disagreeing to the terms proposed. This, in some measure, took away their responsibility, but not totally. . . . On the whole, a large majority of the Convention thought this power would be more safely lodged where they had finally vested it, than anywhere else. It was a power that must necessarily be lodged somewhere: political caution and republican jealousy rendered it improper for us to vest it in the President alone; the nature of negotiation, and the frequent recess of the House of Representatives, rendered that body an improper depository of this prerogative. The President and Senate joined were, therefore, after much deliberation, deemed the most eligible corps in whom we could with safety vest the diplomatic authority of the Union.

─────────── JEFFERSON—JAY CORRESPONDENCE, 1793 ───────────

NO ADVISORY OPINIONS

Letter from Thomas Jefferson, Secretary of State, to Chief Justice Jay and Associate Justices: [7]

Philadelphia, July 18, 1793.

Gentlemen:

The war which has taken place among the powers of Europe produces frequent transactions without our ports and limits, on which questions arise of considerable difficulty, and of greater importance to the peace of the United States. These questions depend for their solution on the construction of our treaties, on the laws of nature and nations, and on the laws of the land, and are often presented under circumstances *which do not give a cognizance of them to the tribunals of the country.* Yet their decision is so little analogous to the ordinary functions of the executive, as to occasion much embarrassment and difficulty to them. The President therefore would be much relieved if he found himself free to refer questions of this description to the opinions of the judges of the Supreme Court of the United States, whose knowledge of the subject would secure us against errors dangerous to the peace of the United States, and their authority insure the respect of all parties. He has therefore asked the attendance of such of the judges as could be collected in time for the occasion, to know, in the first place, their opinion, whether the public may, with propriety, be availed of their *advice on these questions?* And if they may, to present, for their advice, the abstract questions which have already occurred, or may soon occur, from which they will themselves strike out such as any circumstances might, in their opinion, forbid them to pronounce on. I have the honour to be with sentiments of the most perfect respect, gentlemen,

Your most obedient and humble servant,

Thos. Jefferson.

Letter from Chief Justice Jay and the Associate Justices to President Washington, August 8, 1793:

Sir:

We have considered the previous question stated in a letter written by your direction to us by the Secretary of State on the 18th of last month, [concerning] the lines of separation drawn by the Constitution between the three departments of the government. These being in certain respects checks upon each other, and our being judges of a court in the last resort, are considerations which afford strong arguments against the propriety of our extrajudicially deciding the questions alluded to, especially as the power given by the Constitution to the President, of calling on the heads of departments for opinions, seems to have been *purposely* as well as expressly united to the *executive* departments.

We exceedingly regret every event that may cause embarrassment to your administration, but we derive consolation from the reflection that your judgment will discern what is right, and that your usual prudence, decision, and firmness will surmount every obstacle to the preservation of the rights, peace, and dignity of the United States.

———— PACIFICUS [HAMILTON]—HELVIDIUS [MADISON] ————
DEBATES ON THE NATURE OF THE FOREIGN RELATIONS POWER 1793

Alexander Hamilton, in *The Gazette of the United States*, Philadelphia, June 29, 1793. [Italics in original.]

* * *

The objections [to President Washington's Proclamation of Neutrality] fall under four heads:

1. That the proclamation was without authority.

2. That it was contrary to our treaties with France.

3. That it was contrary to the gratitude which is due from this to that country, for the succors afforded to us in our own revolution.

4. That it was out of time and unnecessary.

In order to judge of the solidity of the first of these objections, it is necessary to examine what is the nature and design of a proclamation of neutrality. . . .

It will not be disputed, that the management of the affairs of this country with foreign nations is confided to the government of the United States.

It can as little be disputed, that a proclamation of neutrality, when a nation is at liberty to decline or avoid a war in which other nations are engaged, and means to do so, is a *usual* and a *proper* measure. *Its main object is to prevent the nation's being responsible for acts done by its citizens, without the privity or connivance of the government, in contravention of the principles of neutrality;* an object of the greatest moment to a country whose true interest lies in the preservation of peace.

The inquiry then is, what department of our government is the proper one to make a declaration of neutrality, when the engagements of the nation permit, and its interests require that it should be done?

A correct mind will discern at once, that it can belong neither to the legislature nor judicial department, and of course must belong to the executive.

The legislative department is not the *organ* of intercourse between the United States and foreign nations. It is charged neither with *making* nor *interpreting* treaties. It is therefore not naturally that member of the government, which is to pronounce the existing condition of the nation, with regard to foreign powers, or to admonish the citizens of their obligations and duties in consequence; still less is it charged with enforcing the observance of those obligations and duties.

It is equally obvious, that the act in question is foreign to the judiciary department. The province of that department is to decide litigations in particular cases. It is indeed charged with the interpretation of treaties, but it exercises this function only where contending parties bring before it a specific controversy. It has no concern with pronouncing upon the external political relations of treaties between government and government. This position is too plain to need being insisted upon.

It must then of necessity belong to the executive department to exercise the function in question, when a proper case for it occurs.

It appears to be connected with that department in various capacities— As the *organ* of intercourse between the nation and foreign nations; as the *interpreter* of the national treaties, in those cases in which the judiciary is not competent, that is, between government and government; as the *power* which is charged with the execution of the laws, of which treaties form a part; as that which is charged with the command and disposition of the public force. . . .

The second article of the Constitution of the United States, section first, establishes this general proposition, that "the EXECUTIVE POWER shall be vested in a President of the United States of America."

The same article, in a succeeding section, proceeds to delineate particular cases of executive power. It declares, among other things, that the president shall be commander in chief of the army and navy of the United States, and of the militia of the several states, when called into the actual service of the United States; that he shall have power, by and with the advice and consent of the senate, to make treaties; that it shall be his duty to receive ambassadors and other public ministers, *and to take care that the laws be faithfully executed.*

It would not consist with the rules of sound construction, to consider this enumeration of particular authorities as derogating from the more comprehensive grant in the general clause, further than as it may be coupled with express restrictions or limitations; as in regard to the cooperation of the senate in the appointment of officers, and the making of treaties; which are plainly qualifications of the general executive powers of appointing officers and making treaties. The difficulty of a complete enumeration of all the cases of executive authority, would naturally dictate the use of general terms, and would render it improbable that a specification of certain particulars was designed as a substitute for those terms, when antecedently used. The different mode of expression employed in the constitution, in regard to the two powers, the legislative and the executive, serves to confirm this inference. In the article which gives the legislative powers of the government, the expressions are, "All legislative powers herein granted shall be vested in a congress of the United States." In that which grants the executive power, the expressions are, "*The executive power* shall be vested in a President of the United States."

The enumeration ought therefore to be considered, as intended merely to specify the principal articles implied in the definition of executive power; leaving the rest to flow from the general grant of that power, interpreted in conformity with other parts of the Constitution, and with the principles of free government.

The general doctrine of our Constitution then is, that the *executive power* of the nation is vested in the President; subject only to the *exceptions* and *qualifications,* which are expressed in the instrument.

Two of these have been already noticed; the participation of the senate in the appointment of officers, and in the making of treaties. A third remains to be mentioned; the right of the legislature "to declare war, and grant letters of marque and reprisal." . . .

If on the one hand, the legislature have a right to declare war, it is on the other, the duty of the executive to preserve peace, till the declaration is made; and in fulfilling this duty, it must necessarily possess a right of judging what is the nature of the obligations which the treaties of the country impose on the government; and when it has concluded that there is nothing in them inconsistent with neutrality, it becomes both its province and its duty to enforce the laws incident to that state of the nation. The executive is charged with the execution of all laws, the law of nations, as well as the municipal law, by which the former are recognized and adopted. It is consequently bound, by executing faithfully the laws of neutrality, when the country is in a neutral position, to avoid giving cause of war to foreign powers. . . .

The right of the executive to receive ambassadors and other public ministers, may serve to illustrate the relative duties of the executive and legislative departments. This right includes that of judging, in the case of a revolution of government in a foreign country, whether the new rulers are competent organs of the national will, and ought to be recognized, or not; which, where a treaty antecedently exists between the United States and such nation, involves the power of continuing or suspending its operation. For until the new government is *acknowledged,* the treaties between the nations, so far at least as regards *public* rights, are of course suspended.

This power of determining virtually upon the operation of national treaties, as a consequence of the power to receive public ministers, is an important instance of the right of the executive, to decide upon the obligations of the country with regard to foreign nations. To apply it to the case of France, if there had been a treaty of alliance, *offensive* and defensive between the United States and that country, the unqualified acknowledgement of the new government would have put the United States in a condition to become an associate in the war with France, and would have laid the legislature under an obligation, if required, and there was otherwise no valid excuse, of exercising its power of declaring war.

This serves as an example of the right of the executive, in certain cases, to determine the condition of the nation, though it may, in its consequences, affect the exercise of the power of the legislature to declare war. Nevertheless, the executive cannot thereby control the exercise of that power. The legislature is still free to perform its duties, according to its own sense of them; though the executive, in the exercise of its constitutional powers, may establish an antecedent state of things, which ought to weigh in the legislative decision.

The division of the executive power in the Constitution, creates a *concurrent* authority in the cases to which it relates.

Hence, in the instance stated, treaties can only be made by the president and senate jointly; but their activity may be continued or suspended by the President alone. . . .

It deserves to be remarked, that as the participation of the senate in the making of treaties, and the power of the legislature to declare war, are exceptions out of the general "executive power" vested in the President, they are to be construed strictly, and ought to be extended no further than is essential to their execution.

While, therefore, the legislature can alone declare war, can alone actually transfer the nation from a state of peace to a state of hostility, it belongs to the "executive power" to do whatever else the law of nations, cooperating with the treaties of the country, enjoin in the intercourse of the United States with foreign powers.

In this distribution of authority, the wisdom of our Constitution is manifested. It is the province and duty of the executive to preserve to the nation the blessings of peace. The legislature alone can interrupt them by placing the nation in a state of war.

But though it has been thought advisable to vindicate the authority of the executive on this broad and comprehensive ground, it was not absolutely necessary to do so. That clause of the Constitution which makes it his duty to "take care that the laws be faithfully executed," might alone have been relied upon, and this simple process of argument pursued.

The President is the Constitutional EXECUTOR of the laws. Our treaties, and the laws of nations, form a part of the law of the land. He, who is to execute the laws, must first judge for himself of their meaning.... In reference to the present war in Europe, it was necessary for the President to judge for himself, whether there was anything in our treaties, incompatible with an adherence to neutrality. Having decided that there was not, he had a right, and if in his opinion the interest of the nation required it, it was his duty as executor of the laws, to proclaim the neutrality of the nation, to exhort all persons to observe it, and to warn them of the penalties which would attend its nonobservance.

The proclamation has been represented as enacting some new law. This is a view of it entirely erroneous. It only proclaims a *fact*, with regard to the *existing* state of the nation; informs the citizens of what the laws previously established require of them in that state, and notifies them that these laws will be put in execution against the infractors of them.

PACIFICUS

James Madison, in *The Gazette of the United States*, Philadelphia,
August 24–September 18, 1793.
[Italics in original.]

NO. I

Several pieces with the signature of *Pacificus* were lately published, which have been read with singular pleasure and applause, by the foreigners and degenerate citizens among us, who hate our republican government, and the French revolution; whilst the publication seems to have been too little regarded, or too much despised by the steady friends of both....

The substance of the first piece, sifted from its inconsistencies and its vague expressions, may be thrown into the following propositions:

That the powers of declaring war and making treaties are, in their nature, executive powers:

That being particularly vested by the constitution in other departments, they are to be considered as exceptions out of the general grant to the executive department:

That being, as exceptions, to be construed strictly, the powers not strictly within them, remain with the executive:

That the executive consequently, as the organ of intercourse with foreign nations, is authorized to expound all articles of treaties, those involving questions of war and peace, as well as others—to judge of the obligations of the United States to make war or not, under any *casus foederis* or eventual operation of the contract, relating to war; and to pronounce the state of things resulting from the obligations of the United States, as understood by the executive:

That in particular the executive had authority to judge, whether in the case of the mutual guaranty between the United States and France, the former were bound by it to engage in the war:

That the executive has, in pursuance of that authority, decided that the United States are not bound—and,

That its proclamation of the 22nd of April last, is to be taken as the effect and expression of that decision. . . .

If there be any countenance to these positions, it must be found . . . in the constitution of the United States. . . .

Let us examine:

In the general distribution of powers, we find that of declaring war expressly vested in the congress, where every other legislative power is declared to be vested; and without any other qualifications than what is common to every other legislative act. The constitutional idea of this power would seem then clearly to be, that it is of a legislative and not an executive nature.

This conclusion becomes irresistible, when it is recollected, that the constitution cannot be supposed to have placed either any power legislative in its nature, entirely among executive powers, or any power executive in its nature, entirely among legislative powers, without charging the constitution, with that kind of intermixture and consolidation of different powers, which would violate a fundamental principle in the organization of free governments. If it were not unnecessary to enlarge on this topic here, it could be shown, that the constitution was originally vindicated, and has been constantly expounded, with a disavowal of any such intermixture.

The power of treaties is vested jointly in the president and in the senate, which is a branch of the legislature. From this arrangement merely, there can be no inference that would necessarily exclude the power from the executive class: since the senate is joined with the president in another power, that of appointing to offices, which, as far as relate to executive offices at least, is considered as of an executive nature. Yet on the other hand, there are sufficient indications that the power of treaties is regarded by the constitution as materially different from mere executive power, and as having more affinity to the legislative than to the executive character.

. . . That treaties, when formed according to the constitutional mode, are confessedly to have force and operation of *laws,* and are to be a rule for the courts in controversies between man and man, as much as any *other laws.*

They are even emphatically declared by the constitution to be "the supreme law of the land."

So far the argument from the constitution is precisely in opposition to the doctrine. As little will be gained in its favour from a comparison of the two powers, with those particularly vested in the president alone.

As there are but few, it will be most satisfactory to review them one by one.

"The president shall be commander in chief of the army and navy of the United States, and of the militia when called into the actual service of the United States."

There can be no relation worth examining between this power and the general power of making treaties. And instead of being analogous to the power of declaring war, it affords a striking illustration of the incompatibility of the two powers in the same hands. Those who are to *conduct a war* cannot in the nature of things, be proper or safe judges, whether a *war ought* to be *commenced, continued,* or *concluded.* They are barred from the latter functions by a great principle in free government, analogous to that which separates the sword from the purse, or the power of executing from the power of enacting laws....

Thus it appears that by whatever standard we try this doctrine, it must be condemned as no less vicious in theory than it would be dangerous in practice. It is countenanced neither by the writers on law; nor by the nature of the powers themselves; nor by any general arrangements, or particular expressions, or plausible analogies, to be found in the constitution.

Whence then can the writer have borrowed it?

There is but one answer to this question.

The power of making treaties and the power of declaring war, are *royal prerogatives* in the *British government,* and are accordingly treated as *executive prerogatives* by British *commentators*....

NO. 2

Leaving however to the leisure of the reader deductions which the author, having omitted, might not choose to own, I proceed to the examination of one, with which that liberty cannot be taken.

"However true it may be, (says he,) that the right of the legislature to declare war *includes the right of judging,* whether the legislature be under obligations to make war or not, it will not follow that the executive is *in any case* excluded from a *similar right* of judging in the execution of its own functions." ...

A concurrent authority in two independent departments, to perform the same function with respect to the same thing, would be as awkward in practice, as it is unnatural in theory.

If the legislature and executive have both a right to judge of the obligations to make war or not, it must sometimes happen, though not at present, that they will judge differently. The executive may proceed to consider the question today; may determine that the United States are not bound to take part in a war, and, *in the execution of its functions,* proclaim that declaration to all the world. Tomorrow the legislature may follow in the consideration of the same subject; may determine that the obligations impose war on the United States, and, *in the execution of its functions,* enter into a *constitutional declaration,* expressly contradicting the *constitutional proclamation.*

In what light does this present the constitution to the people who established it? In what light would it present to the world a nation, thus speaking, through two different organs, equally constitutional and authentic, two opposite languages, on the same subject, and under the same existing circumstances?

But it is not with the legislative rights alone that this doctrine interferes. The rights of the judiciary may be equally invaded. For it is clear that if a right declared by the constitution to be legislative, leaves, notwithstanding, a similar right in the executive, whenever a case for exercising it occurs, *in the course of its functions;* a right declared to be judiciary and vested in that department may, on the same principle, be assumed and exercised by the executive *in the course of its functions;* and it is evident that occasions and pretexts for the latter interference may be as frequent as for the former. So again the judiciary department may find equal occasions in the execution of *its* functions, for usurping the authorities of the executive; and the legislature for stepping into the jurisdiction of both. And thus all the powers of government, of which a partition is so carefully made among the several branches, would be thrown into absolute hotchpot and exposed to a general scramble. . . .

NO. 3

In order to give color to a right in the executive to exercise the legislative power of judging, whether there be a cause of war in a public stipulation—two other arguments are subjoined by the writer to that last examined.

The first is simply this: "It is the right and duty of the executive to judge of and interpret those articles of our treaties which give to France particular privileges, *in order to the enforcement of those privileges* "; from which it is stated, as a necessary consequence, that the executive has certain other rights, among which is the right in question.

This argument is answered by a very obvious distinction. The first right is essential to the execution of the treaty, *as a law in operation,* and interferes with no right in question, is not essential to the execution of the treaty, or any other law: on the contrary, the article to which the right is applied cannot, as has been shown, from the very nature of it, be *in operation* as a law, without a previous declaration of the legislature; and all the laws to be *enforced* by the executive remain, in the meantime, precisely the same, whatever be the disposition or judgment of the executive. This second right would also interfere with a right acknowledged to be in the legislative department.

If nothing else could suggest this distinction to the writer, he ought to have been reminded of it by his own words, "in order to the enforcement of those privileges"—Was it in order to *the enforcement* of the article of guaranty, that the right is ascribed to the executive?

The other of the two arguments reduces itself into the following form: the executive has the right to receive public ministers; this right includes the right of deciding, in the case of a revolution, whether the new government, sending the minister, ought to be recognized, or not; and this, again, the right to give or refuse operation to preexisting treaties.

The power of the legislature to declare war, and judge of the causes for declaring it, is one of the most express and explicit parts of the constitution. To endeavour to abridge or *affect* it by strained inferences, and by hypothetical or singular occurrences, naturally warns the reader of some lurking fallacy.

The words of the constitution are, "He (the president) shall receive ambassadors, other public ministers, and consuls." I shall not undertake to examine, what would be the precise extent and effect of this function in various cases which fancy may suggest, or which time may produce. It will be more proper to observe, in general, and every candid reader will second the observation, that little, if anything, more was intended by the clause, than to provide for a particular mode of communication, *almost* grown into a right among modern nations; by pointing out the department of the government, most proper for the ceremony of admitting public ministers, of examining their credentials, and of authenticating their title to the privileges annexed to their character by the law of nations. This being the apparent design of the constitution, it would be highly improper to magnify the function into an important prerogative, even where no rights of other departments could be affected by it. . . .

But how does it follow from the function to receive ambassadors and other public ministers, that so consequential a prerogative may be exercised by the executive? When a foreign minister presents himself, two questions immediately arise: Are his credentials from the existing and acting government of his country? Are they properly authenticated? These questions belong of necessity to the executive; but they involve no cognizance of the question, whether those exercising the government have the right along with the possession. This belongs to the nation, and to the nation alone, on whom the government operates. The questions before the executive are merely questions of fact; and the executive would have precisely the same right, or rather be under the same necessity of deciding them, if its function was simply to receive *without any discretion to reject* public ministers. It is evident, therefore, that if the executive has a right to reject a public minister, it must be founded on some other consideration than a change in the government, or the newness of the government; and consequently a right to refuse to acknowledge a new government cannot be implied by the right to refuse a public minister. . . .

That the authority of the executive does not extend to a question, whether an *existing* government ought to be recognized or not, will still more clearly appear from an examination of the next inference of the writer, to wit: that the executive has a right to give or refuse activity and operation to preexisting treaties. . . .

As a change of government then makes no change in the obligations or rights of the party to a treaty, it is clear that the executive can have no more right to suspend or prevent the operation of a treaty, on account of the change, than to suspend or prevent the operation, where no such change has happened. Nor can it have any more right to suspend the operation of a treaty in force as a law, than to suspend the operation of any other law. . . .

Yet allowing it to be, as contended, that a suspension of treaties might happen from a *consequential* operation of a right to receive public ministers, which is an *express right* vested by the constitution; it could be no proof, that the same or a *similar* effect could be produced by the *direct* operation of a *constructive power.*

Hence the embarrassments and gross contradictions of the writer in defining, and applying his ultimate inference from the operation of the executive power with regard to public ministers.

At first it exhibits an "important instance of the right of the executive to decide the obligation of the nation with regard to foreign nations."

Rising from that, it confers on the executive, a right "to put the United States in a condition to become an associate in war."

And at its full height, it authorizes the executive "to lay the legislature under *an obligation* of declaring war."

From this towering prerogative, it suddenly brings down the executive to the right of *"consequentially affecting* the proper or improper exercise of the power of the legislature to declare war."

And then, by a caprice as unexpected as it is sudden, it espouses the cause of the legislature; rescues it from the executive right "to lay it under an *obligation* of declaring war"; and asserts it to be "free to perform its *own* duties according to its *own* sense of them," without any other control than what it is liable to, in every other legislative act.

The point at which it finally seems to rest, is, that "the executive, in the exercise of its *constitutional powers,* may establish an antecedent state of things, which ought to *weigh* in the *legislative decisions* "; a prerogative which will import a great deal, or nothing, according to the handle by which you take it; and which at the same time, you can take by no handle that does not clash with some inference preceding. . . .

If the meaning be as is implied by the force of the terms "constitutional powers," that the antecedent state of things produced by the executive, ought to have a *constitutional weight* with the legislature; or, in plainer words, imposes a *constitutional obligation;* the writer will not only have to combat the arguments by which such a prerogative has been disproved; but to reconcile it with his last concession, that "the legislature is *free* to perform its duties according to its *own* sense of them." He must show that the legislature is, at the same time *constitutionally free* to pursue its *own judgment,* and *constitutionally bound* by the *judgment of the executive.*

HELVIDIUS

COMMENTARIES ON THE CONSTITUTION
OF THE UNITED STATES

by Joseph Story
1833

THE WAR POWERS

[Book III, Chapter XXI]

Section 1165. The only practical question upon this subject would seem to be, to what department of the national government it would be most wise and safe to confide this high prerogative, emphatically called the last resort of sovereigns, *ultima ratio regum.* In Great Britain it is the exclusive prerogative of the crown; and in other counties, it is usually, if not universally, confided to the executive department. It might by the constitution have been confided to the executive, or to the senate, or to both conjointly.

Section 1166. In the plan offered by an eminent statesman in the convention, it was proposed, that the senate should have the sole power of declaring war. The reasons, which may be urged in favour of such an arrangement, are, that the senate would be composed of representatives of the states, of great weight, sagacity, and experience, and that being a small and select body, promptitude of action, as well as wisdom, and firmness, would, as they ought, accompany the possession of the power. Large bodies necessarily move slowly; and where the cooperation of different bodies is required, the retardation of any measure must be proportionally increased. In the ordinary course of legislation this may be no inconvenience. But in the exercise of such a prerogative, as declaring war, despatch, secrecy, and vigour are often indispensable, and always useful towards success. On the other hand it may be urged in reply, that the power of declaring war is not only the highest sovereign prerogative; but that it is in its own nature and effects so critical and calamitous, that it requires the utmost deliberation, and successive review of all the councils of the nation. War, in its best estate, never fails to impose upon the people the most burthensome taxes, and personal sufferings. It is always injurious, and sometimes subversive of the great commercial, manufacturing, and agricultural interests. Nay, it always involves the prosperity, and not unfrequently the existence, of a nation. It is sometimes fatal to public liberty itself, by introducing a spirit of military glory, which is ready to follow, wherever a successful commander will lead; and in a republic, whose institutions are essentially founded on the basis of peace, there is infinite danger, that war will find it both imbecile in defense, and eager for contest. Indeed, the history of republics has but too fatally proved, that they are too ambitious of military fame and conquest, and too easily devoted to the views of demagogues, who flatter their pride, and betray their interests. It should therefore be difficult in a republic to declare war; but not to make peace. The representatives of the people are to lay the taxes to support a war, and therefore have a right to be consulted, as to its propriety and necessity. The executive is to carry it on, and therefore should be consulted, as to its time, and the ways and means of making it effective. The cooperation of all the branches of the legislative power ought, upon principle, to be required in this the highest act of legislation, as it is in all others. Indeed, there might be a propriety even in enforcing still greater restrictions, as by requiring a concurrence of two-thirds of both houses.

* * *

Section 1172. The power to declare war is exclusive in congress; and (as will be hereafter seen) the states are prohibited from engaging in it, unless in cases of actual invasion or imminent danger thereof. It includes the exercise of all the ordinary rights of belligerents; and congress may therefore pass suitable laws to enforce them. They may authorize the seizure and condemnation of the property of the enemy within, or without the territory of the United States; and the confiscation of debts due to the enemy. But, until laws have been passed upon these subjects, no private citizens can enforce any such rights; and the judiciary is incapable of giving them any legitimate operation.

*　　*　　*

Section 1178. .... [T]he power [to raise and support armies] must be unlimited. It is impossible to foresee, or define the extent and variety of national exigencies, and the correspondent extent of national means necessary to satisfy them. The power must be co-extensive with all possible combinations of circumstances, and under the direction of the councils entrusted with the common defense. To deny this would be to deny the means, and yet require the end. These must, therefore, be unlimited in every matter essential to its efficacy, that is, in the formation, direction, and support of the national forces.... Indeed, in regard to times of war, it seems utterly preposterous to impose any limitations upon the power; since it is obvious, that emergencies may arise, which would require the most various, and independent exercises of it. The country would otherwise be in danger of losing both its liberty and its sovereignty, from its dread of investing the public councils with the power of defending it. It would be more willing to submit to foreign conquest, than to domestic rule.

Section 1179. But in times of peace the power may be at least equally important, though not so often required to be put in full exercise. The United States are surrounded by the colonies and dependencies of potent foreign governments, whose maritime power may furnish them with the means of annoyance, and mischief, and invasion. To guard ourselves against evils of this sort, it is indispensable for us to have proper forts and garrisons, stationed at the weak points, to overawe or check incursions. Besides; it will be equally important to protect our frontiers against the Indians, and keep them in a state of due submission and control. The garrisons can be furnished only by occasional detachments of militia, or by regular troops in the pay of the government. The first would be impracticable, or extremely inconvenient, if not positively pernicious. The militia would not, in times of profound peace, submit to be dragged from their occupations and families to perform such a disagreeable duty. And if they would, the increased expenses of a frequent rotation in the service; the loss of time and labour; and the breaking up of the ordinary employments of life; would make it an extremely ineligible scheme of military power. The true and proper recourse should, therefore, be to a permanent, but small standing army for such purposes. And it would only be, when our neighbours should greatly increase their military force, that prudence and a due regard to our own safety would require any augmentation of our own....

Section 1180. It is important also to consider, that the surest means of avoiding war is to be prepared for it in peace. If a prohibition should be imposed upon the United States against raising armies in time of peace, it would present the extraordinary spectacle to the world of a nation incapacitated by a constitution of its own choice from preparing for defence before an actual invasion. As formal denunciations of war are in modern times often neglected, and are never necessary, the presence of an enemy within our territories would be required, before the government would be warranted to begin levies of men for the protection of the state. The blow must be received, before any attempts could be made to ward it off, or to return it. Such a course of conduct would at all times invite aggression and insult; and enable a formidable rival or secret enemy to seize upon the country, as a defenseless prey; or to drain its resources and ruinous. It would be in vain to look to the militia for an adequate defense under such circumstances. This reliance came very near losing us our independence, and was the occasion of the useless expenditure of many millions. The history of other countries, and our past experience, admonish us, that a regular force, well-disciplined and well-supplied, is the cheapest, and the only effectual means of resisting the inroads of a well-disciplined foreign army. In short, under such circumstances the constitution must be either violated (as it in fact was by the states under the confederation) or our liberties must be placed in extreme jeopardy. Too much precaution often leads to as many difficulties as too much confidence. How could a readiness for war in time of peace be safely prohibited, unless we could in like manner prohibit the preparations and establishments of every hostile nation? The means of security can be only regulated by the means and the danger of attack. They will, in fact, ever be determined by these rules, and no other. It will be in vain to oppose constitutional barriers to the impulse of self-preservation.

* * *

THE COMMANDER IN CHIEF

[Book III, Chapter XXXVII]

Section 1485. The command and application of the public force, to execute the laws, to maintain peace, and to resist foreign invasion, are powers so obviously of an executive nature, and require the exercise of qualities so peculiarly adapted to this department, that a well-organized government can scarcely exist, when they are taken away from it. Of all the cases and concerns of government, the direction of war most peculiarly demands those qualities, which distinguish the exercise of power by a single hand. Unity of plan, promptitude, activity, and decision, are indispensable to success; and these can scarcely exist, except when a single magistrate is entrusted exclusively with the power. Even the coupling of the authority of an executive council with him, in the exercise of such powers, enfeebles the system, divides the responsibility, and not unfrequently defeats every energetic measure. Timidity, indecision, obstinacy, and pride of opinion, must mingle in all such councils, and infuse a torpor and sluggishness, destructive of all military operations. Indeed, there would seem to be little reason to enforce the propriety of giving this power to the executive department, (whatever may be its actual organization,) since it is in exact coincidence with the provisions of our state constitutions; and therefore seems to be universally deemed safe, if not vital to the system.

Section 1486. Yet the clause did not wholly escape animadversion in the state conventions. The propriety of admitting the president to be commander in chief, so far as to give orders, and have a general superintendency, was admitted. But it was urged, that it would be dangerous to let him command in person without any restraint, as he might make a bad use of it. The consent of both houses of congress ought, therefore, to be required, before he should take the actual command. The answer then given was, that though the president might, there was no necessity that he should take the command in person; and there was no probability that he would do so except in extraordinary emergencies and when he was possessed of superior military talents. But if his assuming the actual command depended upon the assent of congress, what was to be done, when an invasion, or insurrection took place during the recess of congress? Besides; the very power of restraint might be so employed, as to cripple the executive department, when filled by a man of extraordinary military genius. The power of the president, too, might well be deemed safe; since he could not, of himself, declare war, raise armies, or call forth the militia, or appropriate money for the purpose; for these powers all belonged to congress. . . .

THE TREATY POWER

[Book III, Chapter XXXVII]

Section 1500. The . . . power, "to make treaties," was not in the original draft of the constitution; but was afterwards reported by a committee; and after some ineffectual attempts to amend, it was adopted, in substance, as it now stands, except, that in the report the advice and consent of two-thirds of the senators was not required to a treaty of peace. This exception was struck out by a vote of eight states against three. The principal struggle was to require two-thirds of the whole number of members of the senate, instead of two-thirds of those present.

Section 1501. Under the confederation congress possessed the sole and exclusive power of "entering into treaties and alliances, provided, that no treaty of commerce shall be made, whereby the legislative power of the respective states shall be restrained from imposing such imposts and duties on foreigners, as their own people were subjected to; or from prohibiting the exportation or importation of any species of goods or commodities whatsoever." But no treaty or alliance could be entered into, unless by the assent of nine of the states. These limitations upon the power were found very inconvenient in practice; and indeed, in conjunction with other defects, contributed to the prostration, and utter imbecility of the confederation.

Section 1502. The power "to make treaties" is by the constitution general; and of course it embraces all sorts of treaties, for peace or war; for commerce or territory; for alliance or succours; for indemnity for injuries or payment of debts; for the recognition and enforcement of principles of public law; and for any other purposes, which the policy or interests of independent sovereigns may dictate in their intercourse with each other. But though the power is thus general and unrestricted, it is not to be so construed, as to destroy the fundamental laws of the state. A power given by the constitution cannot be construed to authorize a destruction of other powers given in the same instrument. It must be construed, therefore, in subordination to it; and cannot supersede, or interfere with any other of its fundamental provisions. Each is equally obligatory, and of paramount authority within its scope; and no one embraces a right to annihilate any other. A treaty to change the organization of the government, or annihilate its sovereignty, to overturn its republican form, or to deprive it of its constitutional powers, would be void; because it would destroy, what it was designed merely to fulfill, the will of the people. Whether there are any other restrictions, necessarily growing out of the structure of the government, will remain to be considered, whenever the exigency shall arise.

Section 1503. The power of making treaties is indispensable to the due exercise of national sovereignty, and very important, especially as it relates to war, peace, and commerce. That it should belong to the national government would seem to be irresistibly established by every argument deduced from experience, from public policy, and a close survey of the objects of government. It is difficult to circumscribe the power within any definite limits, applicable to all times and exigencies, without impairing its efficacy, or defeating its purposes. The constitution has, therefore, made it general and unqualified. This very circumstance, however, renders it highly important, that it should be delegated in such a mode, and with such precautions, as will afford the highest security, and it will be exercised by men the best qualified for the purpose, and in the manner most conducive to the public good. With such views, the question was naturally presented in the convention, to what body shall it be delegated? It might be delegated to congress generally, as it was under the confederation, exclusive of the president, or in conjunction with him. It might be delegated to either branch of the legislature, exclusive of the President, or in conjunction with him. Or it might be exclusively delegated to the president.

Section 1504. In the formation of treaties, secrecy and immediate despatch are generally requisite, and sometimes absolutely indispensable. Intelligence may often be obtained, and measures matured in secrecy, which could never be done, unless in the faith and confidence of profound secrecy. No man at all acquainted with diplomacy, but must have felt, that the success of negotiations as often depends upon their being unknown by the public, as upon their justice or their policy. Men will assume responsibility in private, and communicate information, and express opinions, which they would feel the greatest repugnance publicly to avow; and measures may be defeated by the intrigues and management of foreign powers, if they suspect them to be in progress, and understand their precise nature and extent. In this view the executive department is a far better depositary of the power, than congress would be. The delays incident to a large assembly; the differences of opinion; the time consumed in debate; and the utter impossibility of secrecy, all combine to render them unfitted for the purposes of diplomacy. And our own experience during the confederation abundantly demonstrated all the evils, which the theory would lead us to expect. Besides; there are tides in national affairs, as well as in the affairs of private life. To discern and profit by them is the part of true political wisdom; and the loss of a week, or even of a day, may sometimes change the whole aspect of affairs, and render negotiations wholly nugatory, or indecisive.... The executive, having a constant eye upon foreign affairs, can promptly meet, and even anticipate such emergencies, and avail himself of all the advantages accruing from them; while a large assembly would be coldly deliberating on the changes of success, and the policy of opening negotiations. It is manifest, then, that congress would not be a suitable depositary of the power.

Section 1505. The same difficulties would occur from confiding it exclusively to either branch of congress. Each is too numerous for prompt and immediate action, and secrecy. The matters in negotiations, which usually require these qualities in the highest degree, are the preparatory and auxiliary measures; and which are to be seized upon, as it were, in an instant. The president could easily arrange them. But the house, or the senate, if in session, could not act, until after great delays; and in the recess could not act at all. To have entrusted the power to either would have been to relinquish the benefits of the constitutional agency of the president in the conduct of foreign negotiations. It is true, that the branch so entrusted might have the option to employ the president in that capacity; but they would also have the option of refraining from it; and it cannot be disguised, that pique, or cabal, or personal or political hostility, might induce them to keep their pursuits at a distance from his inspection and participation. Nor could it be expected, that the president, as a mere ministerial agent of such branch, would enjoy the confidence and respect of foreign powers to the same extent, as he would, as the constitutional representative of the nation itself; and his interposition would of course have less efficacy and weight.

*   *   *

THE DIPLOMATIC POWER

[Book III, Chapter XXXVII]

Section 1560. The power to receive ambassadors and ministers is always an important, and sometimes a very delicate function; since it constitutes the only accredited medium, through which negotiations and friendly relations are ordinarily carried on with foreign powers. A government may in its discretion lawfully refuse to receive an ambassador, or other minister, without its affording any just cause of war. But it would generally be deemed an unfriendly act, and might provoke hostilities, unless accompanied by conciliatory explanations.... But a much more delicate occasion is, when a civil war breaks out in a nation, and two nations are formed, or two parties in the same nation, each claiming the sovereignty of the whole, and the contest remains as yet undecided, *flagrante bello*. In such a case a neutral nation may very properly withhold its recognition of the supremacy of either party, or of the existence of two independent nations; and on that account refuse to receive an ambassador from either. It is obvious, that in such cases the simple acknowledgment of the minister of either party, or nation, might be deemed taking part against the other; and thus as affording a strong countenance, or opposition, to rebellion and civil dismemberment. On this account, nations, placed in such a predicament, have not hesitated sometimes to declare war against neutrals, as interposing in the war; and have made them the victims of their vengeance, when they have been anxious to assume a neutral position. The exercise of this prerogative of acknowledging new nations, or ministers, is, therefore, under such circumstances, an executive function of great delicacy, which requires the utmost caution and deliberation. If the executive receives an ambassador, or other minister, as the representative of a new nation, or of a party in a civil war in an old nation, it is an acknowledgment of the sovereign authority *de facto* of such new nation, or party. If such recognition is made, it is conclusive upon the nation, unless indeed it can be reversed by an act of congress repudiating it. If, on the other hand, such recognition has been refused by the executive, it is said, that congress may, notwithstanding, solemnly acknowledge the sovereignty of the nation, or party. These, however, are propositions, which have hitherto remained, as abstract statements, under the constitution; and, therefore, can be propounded, not as absolutely true, but as still open to discussion, if they should ever arise in the course of our foreign diplomacy. The constitution has expressly invested the executive with power to receive ambassadors, and other ministers. It has not expressly invested congress with the power, either to repudiate, or acknowledge them. At all events, in the case of a revolution, or dismemberment of a nation, the judiciary cannot take notice of any new government, or sovereignty, until it has been duly recognized by some other department of the government, to whom the power is constitutionally confided.

Section 1561. That a power, so extensive in its reach over our foreign relations, could not be properly conferred on any other than the executive department will admit of little doubt. That it should be exclusively confided to that department, without any participation of the senate in the functions, (that body being conjointly entrusted with the treaty-making power,) is not so obvious. Probably the circumstance, that in all foreign governments the power was exclusively confided to the executive department, and the utter impracticability of keeping the senate constantly in session, and the suddenness of the emergencies, which might require the action of the government, conduced to the establishment of the authority in its present form. It is not, indeed, a power likely to be abused; though it is pregnant with consequences, often involving the question of peace and war. And, in our own short experience, the revolutions in France and the revolutions in South America have already placed us in situations, to feel its critical character, and the necessity of having, at the head of the government, an executive of sober judgment, enlightened views, and firm and exalted patriotism.

Section 1562. As incidents to the power to receive ambassadors and foreign ministers, the president is understood to possess the power to refuse them, and to dismiss those who, having been received, become obnoxious to censure, or unfit to be allowed the privilege, by their improper conduct, or by political events. While, however, they are permitted to remain, as public functionaries, they are entitled to all the immunities and rights, which the law of nations has provided at once for their dignity, their independence, and their inviolability.

Suggested Reading

For discussions of John Locke's views on the foreign relations power, see RICHARD COX, LOCKE ON WAR AND PEACE (1960), as well as the more general works by JOHN CLOUGH, JOHN LOCKE'S POLITICAL PHILOSOPHY (1950), and WILLMORE KENDALL, JOHN LOCKE AND THE DOCTRINE OF MAJORITY–RULE (1941).

Sympathetic interpretations of the Articles of Confederation are provided by MERRILL JENSEN in THE ARTICLES OF CONFEDERATION: AN INTERPRETATION OF THE SO-CIAL–CONSTITUTIONAL HISTORY OF THE AMERICAN REVOLUTION, 1774–1781 (1940); THE NEW NATION: A HISTORY OF THE UNITED STATES DURING THE CONFEDERATION 1781–1789 (1950). ANDREW C. MCLAUGHLIN'S THE CONFEDERATION AND THE CONSTITUTION, 1781–1789 (1905) is the classic nationalist critique. Equally useful, and of more recent vintage, is FORREST MCDONALD'S E PLURIBUS UNUM: THE FORMATION OF THE AMERICAN REPUBLIC 1776–1790 (1965).

On the Federal Convention itself, MAX FERRAND, ed., THE RECORDS OF THE FEDER-AL CONVENTION OF 1787, 4 vols. is the standard documentary source. Edward S. Corwin's article *The Progress of Constitutional Theory between the Declaration of Independence and the Meeting of the Philadelphia Convention.* AMERICAN HISTORICAL REVIEW 30 (1925) provides authoritative insight, while CHARLES WARREN'S THE MAKING OF THE CONSTITUTION (1929) is the classic account. Also useful are FREDERICK W. MARKS III, INDEPENDENCE ON TRIAL: FOREIGN AFFAIRS AND THE MAKING OF THE CONSTITUTION (1973); Bernard Donahoe and Marshall Smelser, *The Congressional Power to Raise Armies: The Constitutional and Ratifying Conventions of 1787–1788,* REVIEW OF POLITICS 33 (1971); and Charles Lofgren, *War–Making Under the Constitution: The Original Understanding,* 81 YALE LAW JOURNAL 672 (1972). For a more general treatment, see Jefferson Powell, *The Original Understanding of the Original Intent,* 98 HARVARD LAW REVIEW 885 (1985).

For an analysis of *The Federalist,* see Alpheus T. Mason, *The Federalist—A Split Personality,* AMERICAN HISTORICAL REVIEW 58 (1952); Martin Diamond, *Democracy and the Federalist: A Reconsideration of the Framers Intent,* AMERICAN POLITICAL SCIENCE REVIEW 53 (1959); and for the other side, HERBERT J. STORING, ed., THE COMPLETE ANTI–FEDERAL-IST, 7 vols. (1982).

The basic documentation on the State ratifying conventions is JONATHAN ELLIOT, ed., THE DEBATES IN THE SEVERAL STATE CONVENTIONS ON THE ADOPTION OF THE FEDERAL CONSTITUTION, 5 vols. (1936). The "Pacificus"—"Helvidius" Debate between Hamilton and Jefferson forms a major part of CORWIN'S THE PRESIDENT'S CONTROL OF FOREIGN RELATIONS (1917). The renewal of the debate by Senators Tillman of South Carolina and Spooner of Wisconsin during the administration of Theodore Roosevelt is included in Professor Corwin's work.

A sympathetic treatment of STORY'S COMMENTARIES is contained in Jefferson Powell's *Judge Story's Commentaries on the Constitution: A Belated Review,* 94 YALE LAW JOURNAL 1285 (1985). Two useful biographies of Judge Story are JAMES MCCLELLAN, JOSEPH STORY AND THE AMERICAN CONSTITUTION: A STUDY IN POLITICAL AND LEGAL THOUGHT (1971), and GERALD T. DUNNE, JUSTICE JOSEPH STORY AND THE RISE OF THE SUPREME COURT (1970). Also see HENRY STEELE COMMAGER'S "JOSEPH STORY" in THE CASPAR G. BACON LECTURES ON THE CONSTITUTION OF THE UNITED STATES (1953).

NOTES

1. For text, see MacDonald, Documentary Source Book of American History 243 (1908).

2. 5 Thomas Jefferson, Writings 161–162 (Ford ed. 1892). Gênet's credentials had been addressed to Congress, whereupon Jefferson had informed Gênet that "the President was the only channel of communications between the United States and foreign nations, and that it was from him alone that foreign nations or their agents are to learn what is or has been the will of the nation." 4 J. Moore, International Law Digest 680–681 (1906).

3. Hamilton was merely interpreting the executive power clause in light of the views of Blackstone, Locke and Montesquieu as to the location of power to conduct foreign relations. See Edward S. Corwin, The President: Office and Powers 416–418 (1957).

4. Bishop, *The Executive's Right of Privacy: An Unresolved Constitutional Question,* 66 Yale L.J. 477, 491 (1957).

5. 4 A. Beveridge, The Life of John Marshall 119 (1919).

6. Pound, *The Place of Judge Story in the Making of American Law,* 48 Am.L.Rev. 676.

7. Source: 3 H. Johnson, *Correspondence and Public Papers of John Jay,* 486–89 (1891). Judge Story, in his Commentaries on the Constitution of the United States, notes that "[T]he president possesses the right to require the written advice and opinions of his cabinet ministers, upon all questions connected with their respective departments. But, he does not possess a like authority, in regard to the judicial department. That branch of the government can be called upon only to decide controversies, brought before them in a legal form; and therefore are bound to abstain from any extra-judicial opinions upon points of law, even though solemnly requested by the Executive." Also see *Hayburn's Case,* 2 Dall. (2 U.S.) 409, 441 (1792); *Marbury v. Madison,* 1 Cranch (5 U.S.) 137, 171 (1803).

2

FOREIGN AFFAIRS, NATIONAL
SUPREMACY, AND THE
ACT OF STATE DOCTRINE

THE FEDERAL GOVERNMENT enjoys a monopoly on foreign relations. The individual states cannot intrude. In the words of Justice Bradley in the *Legal Tender Cases*,[1] "The United States is not only a government, but it is a national government, and the only government in this country that has the character of nationality. It is invested with power over all the foreign relations of the country, war, peace, and negotiations and intercourse with other nations; all of which are forbidden to the State governments."

Or as Justice Field said on behalf of the Supreme Court in *Chae Chan Ping v. United States* (The *Chinese Exclusion* Case):[2]

> For local interests the several States of the Union exist, but for international purposes, embracing our relations with foreign nations, we are but one people, one nation, one power.

The control of foreign relations by the national government traces to the Declaration of Independence and the Articles of Confederation. In *Curtiss–Wright*, Justice Sutherland based the Court's decision on the collective action of the United States in declaring its independence from Great Britain. As a result, sovereignty passed from the Crown to the United States as a whole—and not to the states individually.

The Articles of Confederation also made it clear that the states had no role in foreign affairs. Under Article VI the states were explicitly denied the power to send and receive ambassadors, enter into agreements with foreign countries, or engage in war without the consent of Congress. Article IX reaffirmed "the sole and exclusive right and power" of Congress to determine war and peace, to send and receive ambassadors, and to conclude treaties and alliances. Even the Constitution of the Confederate States of America—a veritable monument to states' rights—provided for the exclusive jurisdiction of the Confederate government over foreign relations.

The United States Constitution continued the distinction laid down in the Articles of Confederation and expressly prohibited the states from engaging in foreign relations. According to Article I, section 10:

> No State shall enter into any Treaty, Alliance or Confederation....
>
> No State shall, without the Consent of Congress, keep Troops, or Ships of War in time of Peace, enter into any Agreement or Compact with a foreign Power, or engage in War, unless actually invaded, or in such imminent Danger as will not admit of delay.

The decisions of the Supreme Court are equally clear. The Marshall Court, in particular, was under no illusions as to the national monopoly over foreign affairs. As Justice William Johnson observed in *Gibbons v. Ogden*,[3] "The States are unknown to Foreign nations." Chief Justice Taney spoke to the same effect in *Holmes v. Jennison:* "One of the main objects of the constitution [was] to make us, as far as regarded our foreign relations, one people, one nation; and to cut off all communications between foreign governments, and the several state authorities."

Mr. Justice Gray expressed the same view on behalf of the Court in *Fong Yue Ting v. United States* :[4]

> The United States are a sovereign and independent nation, and are vested by the Constitution with the entire control of international relations, and with all the powers of government necessary to maintain that control and make it effective. The only government of this country, which other governments recognize or treat with, is the government of the Union....

The modern Supreme Court has been no less emphatic. In *United States v. Belmont,* Justice Sutherland noted that ".... in respect of our foreign relations generally, state lines disappear. As to such purpose the State ... does not exist."

Accordingly, it is now a well settled rule that state legislation cannot stand when encroaching on the authority of the federal government in foreign affairs. Not only does the Supremacy Clause of Article VI make treaties the supreme law of the land, but as Justice Douglas stated in *Zschernig v. Miller,* "even in the absence of a treaty, a State's policy may disturb foreign relations."

THE NATURE OF THE UNION

In many respects, the Constitution left the nature of the federal union ambiguous. Advocates of national power could point to the Preamble ("We the people of the United States ...") and the various grants of authority contained in Article I to argue that the Union was created by the people of the United States; that it was ratified by those same people in special conventions, and that the Constitution stood supreme over the states as a result. On the other hand, advocates of states' rights could argue that the concluding words of the Constitution ("Done in Convention by the Unanimous Consent of the individual States"), the express reservations of the Tenth Amendment, plus the fact that the state legislatures had convened the ratifying conventions, made it clear that the Union was the creature of the states. The definitive answer to this dispute was provided less by logical analysis and syllogism than by the ultimate victory of the Union forces in the Civil War.

The early Supreme Court subscribed to the doctrine of national supremacy. In *Chisholm v. Georgia,* the Court rejected the claims of states' rights advocates that a state could not be sued in federal court. "As to the purposes of the union," said Justice Wilson, "the State of Georgia is not a sovereign state. . . ." Wilson reasoned that Georgia had been created by the people of Georgia. In coming together to form the Union, those same people could take powers they had previously given to Georgia and vest them in the United States. Chief Justice John Jay, anticipating the doctrine announced by Sutherland in *Curtiss–Wright,* observed that with the Declaration of Independence sovereignty passed "From the crown of Great Britain . . . not to the people [of the separate states], but to the whole people of the United States."

The Supreme Court's decision in *Chisholm* provoked widespread criticism, and the Eleventh Amendment to the Constitution was passed shortly thereafter denying the federal judiciary jurisdiction over the states in private litigation. But the rationale of the Court's decision in *Chisholm* laid the groundwork for the more sweeping claims of national power made soon afterward by the Marshall Court.

TREATY VERSUS STATE LAW

The first case involving a conflict between a treaty and a state law was *Ware v. Hylton* in 1796. The case was typical of many during the post-Revolutionary period. It pitted a Virginia statute of 1777, which sequestered the debts owed by Virginians to British creditors, against the treaty of peace which expressly provided that such debts should be paid. Virginia and several other states had steadfastly refused to honor that provision of the treaty, and under the Articles of Confederation the federal government could not force the states to comply. In fact, the British government considered reopening hostilities in 1787 after the states failed to uphold the peace treaty. To avoid the possibility of British intervention, Article VI of the new federal Constitution made all treaties the supreme law of the land, including the peace treaty with Great Britain, retroactively.

Armed with the Supremacy Clause, the Supreme Court held in *Ware v. Hylton* that the Treaty of Paris nullified the earlier Virginia law, revived the debts owed to British creditors, and gave a right of recovery, state law to the contrary notwithstanding. This sweeping interpretation of the Supremacy Clause again subjected the Supreme Court to considerable attack, but in subsequent cases the Court has invariably ruled that inconsistent state legislation must fall in the face of treaty commitments. Thus in *Hopkirk v. Bell*[5] the Court held that the Virginia statute of limitations did not bar collection of pre–Revolutionary debts under the peace treaty.

The leading case of *Martin v. Hunter's Lessee,* which established the ultimate authority of the Supreme Court over state judicial systems, also involved the treaty of peace with Great Britain and the Jay Treaty of 1794.
Paradoxically, it was the claims of British loyalists and their descendents
(Martin was the nephew of Lord Fairfax) that helped consolidate national
power in the United States. Justice Story's opinion for the Court is a *tour-de-
force* on behalf of federal supremacy and restates the Federalist claim that the
Union was superior to state authority. In Story's words, "The constitution of
the United States was ordained and established, not by the states in their
sovereign capacities, but emphatically, as the preamble of the constitution
declares, by 'the people of the United States'." Accordingly, said Story,
"There can be no doubt that it was competent to the people to invest the
general government with all the powers which they might deem proper and
necessary ... and to give them a paramount and supreme authority."

In *McCulloch v. Maryland,*[6] another landmark case of the Federalist era,
Chief Justice Marshall expanded this latitudinarian concept of national
power, asserting that "the sword and the purse, all the external relations,
and no inconsiderable portion of the industry of the nation, are intrusted to
its [national] government." Nine years later in *American Insurance Co. v. Canter,*
Marshall introduced what Story in his *Commentaries* called the concept of
"resulting powers" of the federal government: powers which flowed not
merely from a combination of the enumerated powers contained in Article I,
but "from the aggregate powers of the national government" itself. The
Canter case involved the authority of the United States to acquire territory
from a foreign country without the consent of the states. Such acquisitions,
of course, could potentially upset the balance of the Union. Because there
was no explicit constitutional authority to justify such acquisitions, Marshall said that "the Constitution confers absolutely on the government of
the Union, the powers of making war, and of making treaties; consequently,
that government possesses the power of acquiring territory, either by conquest or by treaty." And from the power to acquire territory, Marshall noted
that the right to govern it was an "inevitable consequence."

Chief Justice Taney, who succeeded Marshall in 1836 and who was
generally more sympathetic to states' rights, nevertheless adhered to the
nationalist position the earlier Supreme Courts had adopted concerning foreign relations. In the case of *Holmes v. Jennison* in 1840, Taney rejected the
authority of the Governor of Vermont to extradite a fugitive to Canada in
the absence of a treaty on the subject. Taney's opinion made it clear that
every aspect of foreign relations was a national prerogative. In his words,
"The states, by their adoption of the existing Constitution, have become
divested of all their national attributes, except as relate purely to their
internal concerns."

After the Civil War in the case of *Texas v. White*, the Supreme Court was
given another opportunity to pronounce on the nature of the Union. The
case involved the status of Texas during the war and the authority of the
president to establish a provisional government for Texas immediately afterwards. The Court held that throughout the Civil War Texas remained a
State of the Union, and that the ordinance of seccession was "absolutely

null." "The Constitution," said Chief Justice Chase, "looks to an indestructible Union, composed of indestructible states."

> If this were otherwise, the State must have become foreign, and her citizens foreigners. The war must have ceased to be a war for the suppression of the rebellion, and must have become a war for conquest and subjugation.

The Court upheld the president's authority to establish a temporary government in Texas after the war based on his authority as commander in chief, although Justice Grier, joined by Justices Swayne and Miller, dissented vigorously.

STATES' RIGHTS AND THE TREATY POWER

The leading case dealing with the conflict between states' rights and the treaty power is *Missouri v. Holland,* involving the use of a treaty to accomplish legislative goals within the United States itself. From the adoption of the Constitution onward, states' rights advocates had strongly contested the authority of the treaty power to infringe on rights guaranteed to the states. The broad language of the Supremacy Clause doomed such protestations, although in *Frederickson v. Louisiana* [7] the Supreme Court, with civil war looming, appeared sympathetic to state concerns. But when the issue arose once more in 1923, the Court, speaking through Justice Holmes, upheld in sweeping terms the virtually unlimited scope of the federal government's treaty power.

The issue in *Missouri v. Holland* involved a treaty between the United States and Great Britain providing for the protection of migrating birds making seasonal flights between Canada and the United States. Pursuant to the treaty, Congress had enacted legislation authorizing the Department of Agriculture to draw up regulations to govern the hunting of such birds. The State of Missouri challenged both the law and the treaty as an invasion of the power of the state to protect game within its borders. But Holmes (whose nationalist sympathies were as great as Story's or Sutherland's), curtly dismissed Missouri's claim. "Acts of Congress," he said, "are the supreme law of the land only when made in pursuance of the Constitution, while treaties are declared so when made under the authority of the United States." The distinction that Holmes drew between statutes and treaties suggests that the power of the national government in foreign affairs is far more encompassing than it is domestically. In Holmes' words:

> It is obvious that there may be matters of the sharpest exigency for national well being that an act of Congress could not deal with but that a treaty followed by such an act could, and it is not lightly to be assumed that, in matters requiring national action, 'a power which must belong to and reside in every civilized government' is not to be found.

Since the power to enact legislation necessary to execute a treaty was expressly granted to Congress, the validity of such legislation does not depend upon whether its subject matter is included within the legislative powers of Congress. Instead it depends upon whether the treaty that is being enforced is within the treaty-making power of the United States.

Holmes' admonition that treaties cannot contravene the express words of the Constitution provided little solace to those who sought to preserve states' rights. In fact, it was the smoldering resentment against the Court's decision in *Missouri v. Holland* that helped fuel the drive to curb the treaty power with the Bricker Amendment after World War II (see Chapter III).

Fourteen years after *Missouri v. Holland,* the Supreme Court held that executive agreements (agreements with foreign countries that have not been submitted to the Senate for its advise and consent) enjoyed the same status as treaties insofar as state legislation was concerned. The case was *United States v. Belmont,* and the question involved an agreement between the United States and the Soviet Union that accompanied the establishment of diplomatic relations between the two countries in 1933. "We do not pause to inquire," wrote Justice Sutherland, "whether in fact there was any policy of the State of New York to be infringed, since we are of the opinion that no state policy can prevail against the international compact here involved."

According to the Court, the president's act in recognizing the Soviet government, and the accompanying executive agreements, were justified by the president's authority "as the sole organ" of the United States in foreign affairs. The agreements did not require Senate approval, and as binding international commitments, they fell within the ambit of the Supremacy Clause of Article VI.

The decision in *Belmont* came just one year after the Supreme Court (also speaking through Sutherland) had sustained the broad foreign relations authority of the president in *United States v. Curtiss–Wright.* The two decisions greatly facilitated the president's subsequent conduct of World War II. As some scholars have observed, the *Belmont* and *Curtiss–Wright* decisions decisively altered the balance of national power in the United States concerning foreign affairs.[8]

Two subsequent cases, *Clark v. Allen* decided in 1947 and *Zschernig v. Miller* handed down 21 years later, illustrate the continuing need to differentiate between the legitimate authority of a state to regulate matters within its borders and the possible impact of such regulation on foreign affairs. In *Clark,* the Supreme Court upheld a California statute that allowed an alien to inherit property in the state only if the alien's country permitted Americans to inherit in that nation. In the view of Justice Douglas, the California law had only an "incidental or indirect effect" on foreign relations and therefore, in the absence of treaty commitments to the contrary, did not invade "the forbidden domain of negotiating with a foreign country."[9]

But in *Zschernig* the Court overturned an Oregon statute that denied an inheritance to a resident of East Germany who could not satisfy a state probate court that East Germany allowed Americans to inherit there or that his inheritance would not be confiscated by his government. In the opinion of the Supreme Court, again written by Justice Douglas, the Oregon statute radiated "some of the attitudes of the 'cold war', where the search is for the 'democratic quotient' of a foreign regime as opposed to the Marxist theory." Such efforts by the State of Oregon, said Douglas, represented "an intrusion by the State into the field of foreign affairs which the Constitution entrusts to the President and the Congress."

ACT OF STATE DOCTRINE

The Act of State doctrine in international affairs, as defined by Chief Justice Fuller in *Underhill v. Hernandez* (1897), means that "Every sovereign State is bound to respect the independence of every other sovereign State, and the courts of one country will not sit in judgment on the acts of the government of another done within its own territory." The *Underhill* case involved a suit for damages against a revolutionary movement in Venezuela that was subsequently recognized by the United States as the official government. The Supreme Court dismissed the suit, holding that:

> Where a civil war prevails ... generally speaking foreign nations do not assume to judge the merits of the quarrel. If the party seeking to dislodge the existing government succeeds, and the independence of the government it has set up is recognized, then the acts of such government from the commencement of its existence are regarded as those of an independent nation. If the political revolt fails of success, still if actual war has been waged, acts of legitimate warfare cannot be made the bases of individual liability.

For the most part the United States has subscribed to the Act of State doctrine, although the post-World War II emergence of numerous Communist governments bent on nationalizing private investment without prompt, adequate and effective compensation has modified the application of the doctrine substantially. In *Banco Nacional de Cuba v. Sabbatino,* a case that involved Castro's expropriation of American sugar interests in Cuba, the Supreme Court confronted the question of whether the doctrine applied to acts of foreign governments that violated international law. After concluding that the Act of State doctrine was not required by the Constitution, the Court, speaking through Justice Harlan, said:

> The act of state doctrine does, however, have "constitutional" underpinnings. It arises out of the basic relationships between branches of government in a system of separation of powers.... The doctrine as formulated in past decisions expresses a strong sense of the Judicial Branch that its engagement in the task of passing on the validity of foreign acts of state may hinder rather than further this country's pursuit of goals ... in the international sphere.

Despite the fact that Castro's seizure of American sugar interests may have violated international law, the Court felt compelled to apply the Act of State doctrine and uphold it. This unleashed a torrent of criticism, culminating in Congress' passage of the so-called "Hickenlooper Amendment" to the 1964 Foreign Assistance Act. The Amendment directed the courts not to apply the Act of State doctrine to expropriations for which adequate compensation had not been provided, unless the president specifically requests the courts to do so based on "the foreign policy interests of the United

States." In two subsequent cases, *First National City Bank v. Banco National de Cuba* (1972), and *Alfred Dunhill v. Cuba* (1976), the Supreme Court divided 5–4 in declining to apply the Act of State doctrine to expropriation actions taken by Cuba. In the *City Bank* case, the State Department expressly announced that the Act of State doctrine should not bar City Bank's claims, and while the court of appeals disregarded the statement, Justice Rehnquist, speaking for the Supreme Court's majority, gave it great weight. In *Dunhill,* the Supreme Court's five-man majority appeared to attach special significance to Cuba's involvement in the commercial cigar trade and doubted the applicability of the Act of State doctrine to commercial activities undertaken by a government.

CHISHOLM V. GEORGIA

2 Dallas (2 U.S.) 419 (1793)

During the Revolutionary War, the state of Georgia purchased supplies valued at $169,613.33 from Robert Farquhar, a merchant in Charleston, South Carolina. Farquhar never received payment, and his claim was still unsatisfied when he was killed in a shipping accident. Alexander Chisholm, another Charleston merchant, became executor of Farquhar's estate and pressed the claim against the state of Georgia in U.S. Circuit Court. Georgia maintained that as a sovereign state it could not be sued in Federal court, and the court upheld Georgia's objections.

In 1792, Chisholm resumed litigation in the U.S. Supreme Court. The State of Georgia refused to respond, and after several unsuccessful attempts by the Court to compel Georgia to appear, the Justices delivered their seriatim opinions February 19, 1793.

In a sense, Georgia lost the case by default. But the hostile outcry was immediate and effective. The Eleventh Amendment forbidding federal jurisdiction in suits brought by citizens of one state against another state was proposed and ratified within two years.

Wilson, Justice:

. . . . This is a case of uncommon magnitude. One of the parties to it is a state; certainly respectable, claiming to be sovereign. The question to be determined is whether this state, so respectable, and whose claim soars so high, is amenable to the jurisdiction of the supreme court of the United States? This question may, perhaps, be ultimately resolved into one, no less radical than this—"do the people of the United States form a nation?" . . .

As a judge of this court, I know, and can decide upon the knowledge, that the citizens of Georgia, when they acted upon the large scale of the union, as part of the "People of the United States," did not surrender the supreme or sovereign power to that state; but, as to the purposes of the union, retained it to themselves. As to the purposes of the union, therefore, Georgia is not a sovereign state. . . . A state I cheerfully admit, is the noblest work of man: But man himself, free and honest, is, I speak as to this world, the noblest work of God. . . .

With the strictest propriety, therefore, classical and political, our national scene opens with the most magnificent object which the nation could present. "The people of the United States" are the first personages introduced. Who were those people? They were the citizens of thirteen states, each of which had a separate constitution and government, and all of which were connected together by articles of confederation. To the purposes of public strength and felicity that confederacy was totally inadequate. A requisition on the several states terminated its legislative authority; executive or judicial authority it had none. In order, therefore, to form a more perfect union, to establish justice, to insure domestic tranquility, to provide for common defense, and to secure the blessing of liberty, those people, among whom were the people of Georgia, ordained and established the present constitution. By that constitution, legislative power is vested, executive power is vested, judicial power is vested.

The question now opens fairly to our view, could the people of those states, among whom were those of Georgia, bind those states, and Georgia, among the others, by the legislative, executive, and judicial power so vested? If the principles on which I have founded myself are just and true, this question must, unavoidably, receive an affirmative answer. If those States were the work of those people, those people, and that I may apply the case closely, the people of Georgia, in particular, could alter, as they pleased, their former work; to any given degree, they could diminish as well as enlarge it. Any or all of the former State powers they could extinguish or transfer. The inference which necessarily results is, that the constitution ordained and established by those people, and still closely to apply the case, in particular, by the people of Georgia, could vest jurisdiction or judicial power over those states, and over the state of Georgia in particular. . . .

Whoever considers, in a combined and comprehensive view, the general texture of the constitution, will be satisfied that the people of the United States intended to form themselves into a nation for national purposes. They instituted, for such purposes, a national government complete in all its parts, with powers legislative, executive and judiciary; and in all those powers extending over the whole nation. Is it congruous that, with regard to such purposes, any man or body of men, any person, natural or artificial, should be permitted to claim successfully an entire exemption from the jurisdiction of the national government? Would not such claims, crowned with success, be repugnant to our very existence as a nation? When so many trains of deduction, coming from different quarters, converge and unite at last in the same point, we may safely conclude, as the legitimate result of this constitution, that the State of Georgia is amenable to the jurisdiction of this court. . . .

Jay, Chief Justice: The question we are now to decide has been accurately stated, viz.: Is a state suable by individual citizens of another state?
. . .

The revolution, or rather the Declaration of Independence, found the people already united for general purposes, and at the same time, providing for their more domestic concerns, by state conventions, and other temporary arrangements. From the crown of Great Britain, the sovereignty of their country passed to the people of it.... Afterwards, in the hurry of the war, and in the warmth of mutual confidence, they made a confederation of the States, the basis of a general Government. Experience disappointed the expectations they had formed from it; and then the people, in their collective and national capacity, established the present Constitution. It is remarkable that in establishing it, the people exercised their own rights, and their own proper sovereignty, and conscious of the plenitude of it, they declared with becoming dignity, "We the people of the United States," do ordain and establish this Constitution. Here we see the people acting as sovereigns of the whole country; and in the language of sovereignty, establishing a Constitution by which it was their will, that the State Governments should be bound, and to which the State Constitutions should be made to conform. Every State Constitution is a compact made by and between the citizens of a state to govern themselves in a certain manner; and the Constitution of the United States is likewise a compact made by the people of the United States to govern themselves as to general objects, in a certain manner....

Iredell, Justice, dissented....

WARE V. HYLTON

3 Dallas (3 U.S.) 199 (1796)

During the Revolutionary War, the Virginia legislature passed a series of laws that provided for the confiscation of the property of British loyalists, and nullified debts of Virginia citizens that were owed to British creditors. These laws conflicted with the subsequent peace treaty with Great Britain (Treaty of Paris, 1783), which expressly provided for the recovery by British creditors of the value in sterling of debts that had been contracted by American citizens before the Treaty. Ware, on behalf of British creditors, brought suit in the United States Circuit Court for recovery of debts owed by Hylton, a citizen of Virginia. The circuit court upheld the Virginia statute, and ruled in favor of the defendant. The case went to the Supreme Court on a writ of error.

Justice **Chase:**

.... The question then may be stated thus: Whether the 4th article of the said treaty *nullifies* the law of Virginia, passed on the 20th of *October,* 1777; destroys the payment made under it; and revives the debt, and gives a right of recovery thereof, against the *original debtor?*

.... It seems to me that treaties made by Congress, according to the [Articles of] Confederation, were superior to the laws of the states; because the Confederation made them obligatory on all the states. They were so declared by Congress on the 13th of April, 1787; were so admitted by the legislatures and executives of most of the states; and were so decided by the judiciary of the general government, and by the judiciaries of some of the state governments.

If *doubts* could exist *before* the establishment of the present national government, they must be *entirely* removed by the 6th article of the Constitution, which provides "That all treaties *made,* or which shall be made, under the authority of the *United States,* shall be the *Supreme law of the land;* and the

Judges in every State shall be bound thereby, any thing in the *Constitution,* or *laws,* of any State to the contrary notwithstanding." There can be no limitation on the power of the *people* of the *United States.* By their authority the State Constitutions were made, and by their authority the Constitution of the *United States* was established; and they had the power to change or abolish the State Constitutions, or to make them yield to the general government, and to treaties made by their authority. A treaty cannot be the *supreme law of the land, that is of all the United States,* if any act of a *State Legislature* can stand in its way. If the Constitution of a State (which is the *fundamental* law of the State, and paramount to its Legislature) must give way to a treaty, and fall before it; can it be questioned, whether the *less power, an act of the State Legislature, must not be prostrate? It is the declared will of the people of the United States* that every treaty made, by the authority of the *United States,* shall be superior to the *Constitution and laws* of *any individual State;* and their will alone is to decide.... If a law of a State, contrary to a treaty, is not void, but *voidable only* by a repeal, or nullification by a State Legislature, this certain consequence follows, that the will of a *small part of the United States* may control or defeat the will of the *whole. The people of America* have been pleased to declare, that all treaties made *before* the establishment of the National *Constitution,* or *laws* of any of the States, contrary to a treaty, shall be disregarded.

Four things are apparent on a view of this 6th article of the National Constitution. 1st. That it is *Retrospective,* and is to be considered in the *same* light as if the Constitution had been established before the making of the treaty of 1783. 2nd. That the Constitution, or laws, of any of the States so far as either of them shall be found contrary to that treaty are by force of the said article, prostrated before the treaty. 3d. That consequently the treaty of 1783 has superior power to the *Legislature* of any State, because no Legislature of any State has any kind of power over the Constitution, which was its *creator.* 4th. That it is the declared duty of the State Judges to determine any Constitution, or laws of any State, contrary to that treaty (or any other) made under the authority of the *United States null and void.* National or Federal Judges are bound by duty and oath to the same conduct....

Our Federal Constitution establishes the power of a treaty over the constitution and laws of any of the States; and I have shewn that the words of the 4th article were intended, and are sufficient to *nullify* the *law of Virginia,* and the payment under it. It was contended that *Virginia* is interested in this question, and ought to compensate the Defendants in error, if obliged to pay the Plaintiff under the treaty. If *Virginia* had a *right* to receive the money, which I hope I have clearly established, by what law is she obliged to return it? The treaty only speaks of the *original debtor,* and says nothing about a recovery from any of the States.

It was said that the defendant ought to be *fully indemnified,* if the *treaty* compels him to pay his debt over again; as his rights have been sacrificed for the *benefit of the public....*

Although *Virginia* is not bound to make compensation to the debtors, yet it evident [sic] that they ought to be indemnified, and it is not to be supposed, that those whose duty it may be to make the compensation, will permit the *rights* of our citizens to be sacrificed to a *public object*, without the fullest indemnity.

On the best investigation I have been able to give the 4th article of the treaty.... I am satisfied, that the words, in their natural import, and common use, give a recovery to the *British* creditor from his original *debtor* of the debt contracted *before* the treaty, notwithstanding the payment thereof into the public treasuries, or loan offices, under the authority of any State law; and, therefore, I am of the opinion, that the judgment of the Circuit Court ought to be reversed....

————————— MARTIN V. HUNTER'S LESSEE —————————

1 Wheaton (14 U.S.) 304 (1816)

This is another important case pertaining to the supremacy of U.S. treaties over state law, and the ultimate authority of the Supreme Court to enforce the treaty provisions. It involves competing ownership claims to vast timber and tobacco lands originally owned by Lord Fairfax in the Northern neck of Virginia.

Lord Fairfax owned the lands under royal charters originally granted by Charles II and James II. When he died in England in 1781, he devised the land to his nephew, Denny Martin. But the state of Virginia maintained that he had confiscated the Fairfax estate in 1777, along with all other real property in Virginia belonging to British loyalists, and that in any event an alien could not inherit land in Virginia.

The state of Virginia sold a portion of the estate to David Hunter in 1789, and in 1791 Hunter began the first of many court actions to eject Martin and take possession. Martin maintained that the Treaty of Peace with Great Britain (1783), and the Jay Treaty of 1794, protected the Fairfax lands against seizure by the state of Virginia.

In 1810, the Virginia Court of Appeals, the highest court in the state, upheld Hunter's claim, and in 1813 the U.S. Supreme Court reversed, siding with Martin (Fairfax's Devisee v. Hunter's Lessee, 7 Cranch 603 (1813).) In a direct challenge to the ultimate jurisdiction of the Supreme Court, the Virginia Court of Appeals rejected the decision on the grounds that "... the appellate power of the Supreme Court of the United States does not extend to this court, under a sound construction of the Constitution of the United States...."

Justice **Story** delivered the opinion of the Court:

.... The constitution of the United States was ordained and established, not by the states in their sovereign capacities, but emphatically, as the preamble of the constitution declares, by "the people of the United States." There can be no doubt that it was competent to the people to invest the general government with all the powers which they might deem proper and necessary; to extend or restrain these powers according to their own good pleasure, and to give them a paramount and supreme authority. As little doubt can there be, that the people had a right to prohibit to the states the exercise of any powers which were, in their judgment, incompatible with the objects of the general compact; to make the powers of the state governments, in given cases, subordinate to those of the nation, or to reserve to themselves those sovereign authorities which they might not choose to delegate to either. The constitution was not, therefore, necessarily carved out of existing state sovereignties, nor a surrender of powers already existing in state institutions, for the powers of the states depend upon their own constitutions; and the people of every state had the right to modify and restrain them, according to their own views of policy or principle....

[I]t is plain that the framers of the constitution did contemplate that cases within the judicial cognizance of the United States not only might but would arise in the state courts, in the exercise of their ordinary jurisdiction. With this view the sixth article declares, that "this constitution, and the laws of the United States which shall be made in pursuance thereof, and all treaties made, or which shall be made, under the authority of the United States, shall be the supreme law of the land, and the judges in every state shall be bound thereby, any thing in the constitution or laws of any state to the contrary notwithstanding." It is obvious that this obligation is imperative upon the state judges in their official, and not merely in their private, capacities. From the very nature of their judicial duties they would be called upon to pronounce the law applicable to the case in judgment. They were not to decide merely according to the laws or constitution of the state, but according to the constitution, laws and treaties of the United States—"the supreme law of the land." ...

It must, therefore, be conceded that the constitution not only contemplated, but meant to provide for cases within the scope of the judicial power of the United States, which might yet depend before state tribunals. It was foreseen that in the exercise of their ordinary jurisdiction, state courts would incidentally take cognizance of cases arising under the constitution, the laws, and treaties of the United States. Yet to all these cases the judicial power, by the very terms of the constitution, is to extend.... It would seem to follow that the appellate power of the United States must, in such cases, extend to state tribunals; and if in such cases, there is no reason why it should not equally attach upon all others within the purview of the constitution.

It has been argued that such an appellate jurisdiction over state courts is inconsistent with the genius of our governments, and the spirit of the constitution. That the latter was never designed to act upon state sovereignties, but only upon the people, and that if the power exists, it will materially impair the sovereignty of the states, and the independence of their courts. We cannot yield to the force of this reasoning, it assumes principles which we cannot admit, and draws conclusions to which we do not yield our assent.

It is a mistake that the constitution was not designed to operate upon states, in their corporate capacities. It is crowded with provisions which restrain or annul the sovereignty of the states in some of the highest branches of their prerogatives. The tenth section of the first article contains a long list of disabilities and prohibitions imposed upon the states. Surely, when such essential portions of state sovereignty are taken away, or prohibited to be exercised, it cannot be correctly asserted that the constitution does not act upon the states. The language of the constitution is also imperative upon the states as to the performance of many duties.... When, therefore, the states are stripped of some of the highest attributes of sovereignty, and the same are given to the United States; when the legislatures of the states are, in some respects, under the control of congress, and in every case are, under the constitution, bound by the paramount authority of the United States; it is certainly difficult to support the argument that the appellate power over the decisions of state courts is contrary to the genius of our institutions. The courts of the United States can, without question, revise the proceedings of the executive and legislative authorities of the states, and if they are found to be contrary to the constitution, may declare them to be of no legal validity. Surely the exercise of the same right over judicial tribunals is not a higher or more dangerous act of sovereign power. . . .

A motive of another kind, perfectly compatible with the most sincere respect for state tribunals, might induce the grant of appellate power over their decisions. That motive is the importance, and even necessity of *uniformity* of decisions throughout the whole United States, upon all subjects within the purview of the constitution. Judges of equal learning and integrity, in different states, might differently interpret a statute, or a treaty of the United States, or even the constitution itself: the constitution has presumed that state attachments, state prejudices, state jealousies and state interests might sometimes obstruct or retard the regular administration of justice. If there were no revising authority to control these jarring and discordant judgments, and harmonize them into uniformity, the laws, the treaties, and the constitution of the United States would be different in different states, and might, perhaps, never have precisely the same construction, obligation, or efficacy, in any two states. The public mischiefs that would attend such a state of things would be truly deplorable; and it cannot be believed that they could have escaped the enlightened convention which formed the constitution. What, indeed, might then have been only prophecy, has now become fact; and the appellate jurisdiction must continue to be the only adequate remedy for such evils. . . .

On the whole, the courts are of opinion, that the appellate power of the United States does extend to cases pending in the state courts; and that the 25th section of the judiciary act, which authorizes the exercise of this jurisdiction in the specified cases, by a writ of error, is supported by the letter and spirit of the constitution. We find no clause in that instrument which limits this power; and we dare not interpose a limitation where the people have not been disposed to create one. . . .

It is the opinion of the whole court, that the judgement of the court of appeals of Virginia
. . . be reversed. . . .

AMERICAN INSURANCE CO.
v. CANTER

1 Peters (26 U.S.) 511 (1828)

In many areas the authority of the national government in relation to the States was left unresolved by the Constitution. One of the critical questions unanswered was whether the government of the United States, on its own authority, and without approval of the States, could acquire territory by treaty with a foreign power, and thus alter the original structure of the Union. The Marshall Court, as usual, provided firm support for national authority.

In 1819, the United States concluded a treaty with Spain by which the territory of Florida was ceded to the U.S. Three years later, Congress passed legislation "for the establishment of a territorial government in Florida." That Act included authority for the Florida territorial legislature to establish such inferior courts as it deemed necessary. The issue in Canter *turned on the legality of the original acquisition of Florida; the authority of Congress to legislate for the territory, and whether the Florida territorial legislature was competent to establish the inferior courts authorized under the Act.*

The case arose out of proceedings in salvage following the wreck of the ship Point a Petre *off the coast of Florida. The ship was bound from New Orleans to France with a load of cotton when it foundered. The cargo was saved, taken to Key West, and purchased by Canter at public auction held pursuant to a decree of a Florida territorial court to satisfy salvage claims. American Insurance Co., the insurers of the cargo, brought suit in U.S. District Court to recover the cotton, and were awarded partial restitution. The U.S. Circuit Court reversed, and upheld the original sale. The insurance company appealed.*

Chief Justice **Marshall** delivered the opinion of the Court:

. . . . The course which the argument has taken, will require, that, in deciding this question, the Court should take into view the relation in which Florida stands to the United States.

The Constitution confers absolutely on the government of the Union, the powers of making war, and of making treaties; consequently, that government possesses the power of acquiring territory, either by conquest or by treaty.

The usage of the world is, if a nation be not entirely subdued, to consider the holding of conquered territory as a mere military occupation, until its fate shall be determined at the treaty of peace. If it be ceded by the treaty, the acquisition is confirmed, and the ceded territory becomes a part of the nation to which it is annexed; either on the terms stipulated in the treaty of cession, or on such as its new master shall impose. On such transfer of territory, it has never been held, that the relations of the inhabitants with each other undergo any change. Their relations with their former sovereign are dissolved, and new relations are created between them, and the government which has acquired their territory. The same Act which transfers their country, transfers the allegiance of those who remain in it; and the law, which may be denominated political, is necessarily changed, although that which regulates the intercourse, and general conduct of individuals, remains in force, until altered by the newly created power of the state.

On the 2d of February 1819, Spain ceded Florida to the United States. The 6th article of the treaty of cession, contains the following provision—"The inhabitants of the territories, which his Catholic majesty cedes to the United States by this treaty, shall be incorporated in the Union of the United States, as soon as may be consistent with the principles of the federal Constitution; and admitted to the enjoyment of the privileges, rights, and immunities of the citizens of the United States."

This treaty is the law of the land, and admits the inhabitants of Florida to the enjoyment of the privileges, rights, and immunities, of the citizens of the United States.... They do not, however, participate in political power; they do not share in the government, till Florida shall become a state. In the mean time, Florida continues to be a territory of the United States; governed by virtue of that clause in the Constitution, which empowers Congress "to make all needful rules and regulations, respecting the territory, or other property belonging to the United States."

Perhaps the power of governing a territory belonging to the United States, which has not, by becoming a state, acquired the means of self-government, may result necessarily from the facts, that it is not within the jurisdiction of any particular state, and is within the power and jurisdiction of the United States. The right to govern, may be the inevitable consequence of the right to acquire territory. Whichever may be the source, whence the power is derived, the possession of it is unquestioned. In execution of it, Congress, in 1822, passed "an Act for the establishment of a territorial government in Florida;" and, on the 3d of March 1823, passed another Act to amend the Act of 1822. Under this Act, the territorial legislature enacted the law now under consideration.

We think, then, that the Act of the territorial legislature, erecting the Court by whose decree the cargo of the *Point a Petre* was sold, is not "inconsistent with the laws and Constitution of the United States," and is valid. Consequently, the sale made in pursuance of it changed the property, and the decree of the Circuit Court, awarding restitution of the property to the claimant [Canter], ought to be affirmed with costs.

―――――――――――― HOLMES V. JENNISON ――――――――――――

14 Peters (39 U.S.) 540 (1840)

In 1839, George Holmes, a resident of Canada, was indicted for murder there and fled to Vermont. Although there was no extradition treaty between the United States and Great Britain (then responsible for Canada's foreign relations), the Governor of Vermont signed a warrant for Holmes' arrest and extradition to Canada. Holmes' appeal was dismissed by the Supreme Court because the justices were evenly divided as to whether Governor Jennison's decision to extradite constituted an agreement with a foreign government prohibited by Article I, section 10, of the Constitution. After the Supreme Court disposed of the case, a writ of habeas corpus was issued by the Vermont Supreme Court and Holmes was discharged.

Chief Justice **Taney** (joined by Justices **Story, McLean,** and **Wayne**): . . .

This case presents a question of great importance, upon which eminent jurists have differed in opinion. Can a state, since the adoption of the constitution of the United States, deliver up an individual found within its territory, to a foreign government, to be there tried for offences alleged to have been committed against it? This involves an inquiry into the relative powers of the federal and state governments, upon a subject which is sometimes one of great delicacy....

The power which has thus been exercised by the state of Vermont, is a part of the foreign intercourse of this country; and has undoubtedly been conferred on the federal government. Whether it be exclusive or not, is another question, of which we shall hereafter speak. But we presume, that no one will dispute the possession of this power by the general government. It is clearly included in the treaty-making power, and the corresponding power of appointing and receiving ambassadors and other public ministers. The power to make treaties is given by the constitution, in general terms, without any description of the objects intended to be embraced by it; and consequently, it was designed to include all those subjects, which, in the ordinary intercourse of nations, had usually been made subjects of negotiation and treaty; and which are consistent with the nature of our institutions, and the distribution of powers between the general and state governments. And without attempting to define the exact limits of this treaty-making power, or to enumerate the subjects intended to be included in it; it may safely be assumed, that the recognition and enforcement of the principles of public law, being one of the ordinary subjects of treaties, were necessarily included in the power conferred on the general government....

And the use of all of these terms, "treaty," "agreement," "compact," show that it was the intention of the framers of the constitution to use the broadest and most comprehensive terms; and that they anxiously desired to cut off all connection or communication between a state and a foreign power; and we shall fail to execute that evident intention, unless we give to the word "agreement" its most extended signification; and so apply it as to prohibit every agreement, written or verbal, formal or informal, positive or implied, by the mutual understanding of the parties....

The framers of the constitution manifestly believed, that any intercourse between a state and a foreign nation was dangerous to the Union; that it would open a door of which foreign powers would avail themselves, to obtain influence in separate states. Provisions were, therefore, introduced, to cut off all negotiations and intercourse between the state authorities and foreign nations. If they could make no agreement, either in writing or by parol, formal or informal, there would be no occasion for negotiation or intercourse between the state authorities and a foreign government. Hence, prohibitions were introduced, which were supposed to be sufficient to cut off all communication between them....

The first clause of the tenth section of the first article of the constitution, among other limitations of state power, declares, that "no state shall enter into any treaty, alliance or confederation;" the second clause of the same section, among other things, declares, that no state, without the consent of congress, shall "enter into any agreement or compact with another state, or with a foreign power." ...

In expounding the constitution of the United States, every word must have its due force, and appropriate meaning; for it is evident from the whole instrument, that no word was unnecessarily used, or needlessly added. The many discussions which have taken place upon the construction of the constitution, have proved the correctness of this proposition; and shown the high talent, the caution, and the foresight of the illustrious men who framed it. Every word appears to have been weighed with the utmost deliberation, and its force and effect to have been fully understood. No word in the instrument, therefore, can be rejected as superfluous or unmeaning; and this principle of construction applies with peculiar force to the two clauses of the tenth section of the first article, of which we are now speaking, because the whole of this short section is directed to the same subject; that is to say, it is employed altogether in enumerating the rights surrendered by the states; and this is done with so much clearness and brevity, that we cannot for a moment believe, that a single superfluous word was used, or words which meant merely the same thing. When, therefore, the second clause declares, that no state shall enter into "any agreement or compact" with a foreign power, without the assent of congress, the words "agreement" and "compact," cannot be construed as synonymous with one another; and still less can either of them be held to mean the same thing with the word "treaty" in the preceding clause, into which the states are positively and unconditionally forbidden to enter; and which even the consent of congress could not authorize.

.... But the question does not rest upon the prohibition to enter into a treaty. In the very next clause of the constitution, the states are forbidden to enter into any "agreement" or "compact" with a foreign nation; and as these words could not have been idly or superfluously used by the framers of the constitution, they cannot be construed to mean the same thing with the word treaty. They evidently mean something more, and were designed to make the prohibition more comprehensive....

.... Every part of [the Constitution] shows that our whole foreign intercourse was intended to be committed to the hands of the general government; and nothing shows it more strongly than the treaty-making power, and the power of appointing and receiving ambassadors; both of which are immediately connected with the question before us, and undoubtedly belong exclusively to the federal government. It was one of the main objects of the constitution to make us, so far as regarded our foreign relations, one people, and one nation; and to cut off all communications between foreign governments, and the several state authorities. The power now claimed for the states, is utterly incompatible with this evident intention; and would expose us to one of those dangers, against which the framers of the constitution have so anxiously endeavored to guard....

Upon the whole, therefore, my three brothers, before mentioned, and myself, after the most careful and deliberate examination, are of opinion, that the power to surrender fugitives, who, having committed offences in a foreign country, have fled to this for shelter, belongs, under the constitution of the United States, exclusively to the federal government; and that the authority exercised in this instance by the governor of Vermont, is repugnant to the constitution of the United States.

─────────── TEXAS V. WHITE ───────────

7 Wallace (74 U.S.) 700 (1868)

This case deals with the nature of the Union and inquires as to the status of Texas during the Civil War. Was Texas still a state of the Union in spite of its ordinance of secession, and was it still a state of the Union after its attempt to leave had failed and it was being governed by military authorities under the "Reconstruction Acts"? Though President Lincoln acted to terminate the secession based on his belief that the states of the Confederacy had no right to leave the Union, the Supreme Court had taken no stand on the issue.

Texas v. White *provided that opportunity. It involved an attempt by the post-Civil War government of Texas to recover certain United States bonds that the Confederate government of Texas had sold during the war. The issue was whether a state could unilaterally secede from the Union.*

Chief Justice **Chase** delivered the opinion of the Court:

The first inquiries to which our attention was directed by counsel, arose upon the allegations . . . that the State, having severed her relations with a majority of the States of the Union, and having by her ordinance of secession attempted to throw off her allegiance to the Constitutional government of the United States, has so far changed her status as to be disabled from prosecuting suits in the National courts. . . .

It is needless to discuss, at length, the question whether the right of a State to withdraw from the Union for any cause, regarded by herself as sufficient, is consistent with the Constitution of the United States.

The Union of the States never was a purely artificial and arbitrary relation. It began among the Colonies, and grew out of common origin, mutual sympathies, kindred principles, similar interests, and geographical relations. It was confirmed and strengthened by the necessities of war, and received definite form, and character, and sanction from the Articles of Confederation. By these the Union was solemnly declared to "be perpetual." And when these articles were found to be inadequate to the exigencies of the country, the Constitution was ordained "to form a more perfect Union." It is difficult to convey the idea of indissoluble unity more clearly than by these words. What can be indissoluble if a perpetual Union, made more perfect, is not?

But the perpetuity and indissolubility of the Union, by no means implies the loss of distinct and individual existence, or of the right of self-government by the States. Under the Articles of Confederation each State retained its sovereignty, freedom, and independence, and every power, jurisdiction, and right not expressly delegated to the United States. Under the Constitution, though the powers of the States were much restricted, still, all powers not delegated to the United States, nor prohibited to the States, are reserved to the States respectively, or to the people. . . . Not only, therefore, can there be no loss of separate and independent autonomy to the States, through their union under the Constitution, but it may be not unreasonably said that the preservation of the States, and the maintenance of their governments, are as much within the design and care of the Constitution as the preservation of the Union and the maintenance of the National government. The Constitution, in all its provisions, looks to an indestructible Union, composed of indestructible States.

When, therefore, Texas became one of the United States, she entered into an indissoluble relation. All the obligations of perpetual union, and all the guaranties of republican government in the Union, attached at once to the State. The act which consummated her admission into the Union was something more than a compact; it was the incorporation of a new member into the political body. And it was final. The union between Texas and the other States was as complete, as perpetual, and as indissoluble as the union between the original States. There was no place for reconsideration, or revocation, except through revolution, or through consent of the States.

Considered therefore as transactions under the Constitution, the ordinance of secession, adopted by the convention and ratified by a majority of the citizens of Texas, and all the acts of her legislature intended to give effect to that ordinance, were absolutely null. They were utterly without operation in law. The obligations of the State, as a member of the Union, and of every citizen of the State, as a citizen of the United States, remained perfect and unimpaired. It certainly follows that the State did not cease to be a State, nor her citizens to be citizens of the Union. If this were otherwise, the State must have become foreign, and her citizens foreigners. The war must have ceased to be a war for the suppression of rebellion, and must have become a war for conquest and subjugation.

Our conclusion therefore is, that Texas continued to be a State, and a State of the Union, notwithstanding the transactions to which we have referred. And this conclusion, in our judgment, is not in conflict with any act or declaration of any department of the National government, but entirely in accordance with the whole series of such acts and declarations since the first outbreak of the rebellion.

No one has been bold enough to contend that, while Texas was controlled by a government hostile to the United States, and in affiliation with a hostile confederation, waging war upon the United States, senators chosen by her legislature, or representatives elected by her citizens, were entitled to seats in Congress; or that any suit, instituted in her name, could be entertained in this court. All admit that, during this condition of civil war, the rights of the State as a member, and of her people as citizens of the Union, were suspended. The government and the citizens of the State, refusing to recognize their constitutional obligations, assumed the character of enemies, and incurred the consequences of rebellion.

. . . . Almost immediately after the cessation of organized hostilities, and while the war yet smouldered in Texas, the President of the United States issued his proclamation appointing a provisional governor for the State, and providing for the assembling of a convention, with a view to the reestablishment of a republican government, under an amended constitution, and to the restoration of the State to her proper constitutional relations. A convention was accordingly assembled, the constitution amended, elections held, and a State government, acknowledging its obligations to the Union, established.

Whether the action then taken was, in all respects, warranted by the Constitution, it is not now necessary to determine. The power exercised by the President was supposed, doubtless, to be derived from his constitutional functions, as commander in chief; and, so long as the war continued, it cannot be denied that he might institute temporary government within insurgent districts, occupied by the National forces, or take measures, in any State, for the restoration of State government faithful to the Union, employing, however, in such efforts, only such means and agents as were authorized by constitutional laws.

But, the power to carry into effect the clause of guarantee is primarily a legislative power, and resides in Congress. . . .

On the whole case, therefore, our conclusion is that the State of Texas is entitled to the relief sought by her bill, and a decree must be made accordingly.

Justice **Grier**, *dissenting*. . . .

Justice **Swayne** *and Justice* **Miller**, *dissenting in part, and* **concurring** *in part.*

MISSOURI V. HOLLAND

252 U.S. 416 (1920)

In 1913 Congress enacted legislation to regulate the hunting of migratory birds. The law was subsequently declared invalid in the district courts as beyond the scope of congressional authority. To protect the migrating birds from extinction, the president negotiated the Migratory Bird Treaty of 1916 with Great Britain (acting on behalf of Canada). Pursuant to the treaty, Congress in 1918 enacted the Migratory Bird Treaty Act which restricted the hunting of the birds during their spring and autumn migrations. The state of Missouri sought to prevent enforcement of the Act by federal game warden Holland, claiming that the measures constituted an infringement of the rights reserved to the states under the Tenth Amendment.

Justice **Holmes** delivered the opinion of the Court:

. . . . Acts of Congress are the supreme law of the land only when made in pursuance of the Constitution, while treaties are declared to be so when made under the authority of the United States. It is open to question whether the authority of the United States means more than the formal acts prescribed to make the convention. We do not mean to imply that there are no qualifications to the treaty-making power; but they must be ascertained in a different way. It is obvious that there may be matters of the sharpest exigency for the national well being that an act of Congress could not deal with but that a treaty followed by such an act could, and it is not lightly to be assumed that, in matters requiring national action, "a power which must belong to and somewhere reside in every civilized government" is not to be found. . . . The treaty in question does not contravene any prohibitory words to be found in the Constitution. The only question is whether it is forbidden by some invisible radiation from the general terms of the Tenth Amendment. We must consider what this country has become in deciding what that Amendment has reserved.

The State as we have intimated founds its claim of exclusive authority upon an assertion of title to migratory birds, an assertion that is embodied in statute. No doubt it is true that as between a State and its inhabitants the State may regulate the killing and sale of such birds, but it does not follow that its authority is exclusive of paramount powers. To put the claim of the State upon title is to lean upon a slender reed. Wild birds are not in the possession of anyone; and possession is the beginning of ownership. The whole foundation of the State's rights is the presence within their jurisdiction of birds that yesterday had not arrived, tomorrow may be in another State and in a week a thousand miles away. If we are to be accurate we cannot put the case of the State upon higher ground than that the treaty deals with creatures that for the moment are within the state borders, that it must be carried out by officers of the United States within the same territory, and that but for the treaty the State would be free to regulate this subject itself.

As most of the laws of the United States are carried out within the States and as many of them deal with matters which in the silence of such laws the State might regulate, such general grounds are not enough to support Missouri's claim. Valid treaties of course "are as binding within the territorial limits of the States as they are elsewhere throughout the dominion of the United States." No doubt the great body of private relations usually fall within the control of the State, but a treaty may override its power.

. . . Here a national interest of very nearly the first magnitude is involved. It can be protected only by national action in concert with that of another power. The subject-matter is only transitorily within the State and has no permanent habitat therein. But for the treaty and the statute there soon might be no birds for any powers to deal with. We see nothing in the Constitution that compels the Government to sit by while a food supply is cut off and the protectors of our forests and our crops are destroyed. It is not sufficient to rely upon the States. The reliance is vain, and were it otherwise, the question is whether the United States is forbidden to act. We are of opinion that the treaty and statute must be upheld.

Decree affirmed.

Justice **Van Devanter** *and Justice* **Pitney** *dissent*.

──────────── UNITED STATES V. BELMONT ────────────

301 U.S. 324 (1937)

The United States and the Soviet Union exchanged diplomatic recognition in 1933. In an effort to settle claims between the two countries, the Soviet Union assigned to the United States all claims due the Soviet Union arising out of its earlier nationalization decrees. The United States would act as agent for the Soviet government in collecting those claims for Russian property located in the United States. In return, the funds collected would be used to offset American claims against the Soviet government for American property in Russia that had been nationalized. Pursuant to that agreement, the United States brought suit to recover funds deposited by the Petrograd Metal Works with the New York bank of August Belmont prior to 1918. The U.S. Court of Appeals rejected the U.S. claim, holding that the deposits in question were not within Soviet territory, and that the nationalization decree, if enforced, would amount to an act of confiscation.

Justice **Sutherland** delivered the opinion of the Court:

. . . . We are of opinion that no state policy can prevail against the international compact here involved.

This court has held that every sovereign state must recognize the independence of every other sovereign state; and that the courts of one will not sit in judgment upon the acts of the government of another, done within its own territory. . . .

We take judicial notice of the fact that coincident with the assignment set forth in the complaint, the President recognized the Soviet Government, and normal diplomatic relations were established between that government and the Government of the United States, followed by an exchange of ambassadors. The effect of this was to validate, so far as this country is concerned, all acts of the Soviet Government here involved from the commencement of its existence. The recognition, establishment of diplomatic relations, the assignment, and agreements with respect thereto, were all parts of one transaction, resulting in an international compact between the two governments. That the negotiations, acceptance of the assignment and agreements and understandings in respect thereof were within the competence of the President may not be doubted. Governmental power over internal affairs is distributed between the national government and the several states. Governmental power over external affairs is not distributed, but is vested exclusively in the national government. And in respect of what was done here, the Executive had authority to speak as the sole organ of that government. The assignment and the agreements in connection therewith did not, as in the case of treaties, as that term is used in the treaty making clause of the Constitution (Art. II, ss. 2), require the advice and consent of the Senate.

A treaty signifies "a compact made between two or more independent nations with a view to the public welfare." But an international compact, as this was, is not always a treaty which requires the participation of the Senate. There are many such compacts, of which a protocol, a *modus vivendi,* a postal convention, and agreements like that now under consideration are illustrations.

Plainly, the external powers of the United States are to be exercised without regard to state laws or policies. The supremacy of a treaty in this respect has been recognized from the beginning. And while this rule in respect of treaties is established by the express language of cl. 2, Art. VI, of the Constitution, the same rule would result in the case of all international compacts and agreements from the very fact that complete power over international affairs is in the national government and is not and cannot be subject to any curtailment or interference on the part of the several states. In respect of all international negotiations and compacts, and in respect of our foreign relations generally, state lines disappear. As to such purposes the State of New York does not exist. Within the field of its powers, whatever the United States rightfully undertakes, it necessarily has warrant to consummate. And when judicial authority is invoked in aid of such consummation, state constitutions, state laws, and state policies are irrelevant to the inquiry and decision. It is inconceivable that any of them can be interposed as an obstacle to the effective operation of a federal constitutional power.

Second. The public policy of the United States relied upon as a bar to the action is that declared by the Constitution, namely, that private property shall not be taken without just compensation. But the answer is that our Constitution, laws and policies have no extraterritorial operation, unless in respect of our own citizens. What another country has done in the way of taking over property of its nationals, and especially of its corporations, is not a matter for judicial consideration here. Such nationals must look to their own government for any redress to which they may be entitled. So far as the record shows, only the rights of the Russian corporation have been affected by what has been done; and it will be time enough to consider the rights of our nationals when, if ever, by proper judicial proceeding, it shall be made to appear that they are so affected as to entitle them to judicial relief. The substantive right to the moneys, as now disclosed, became vested in the Soviet Government as the successor to the corporation; and this right that government has passed to the United States. It does not appear that respondents have any interest in the matter beyond that of a custodian. Thus far no question under the Fifth Amendment is involved.

Judgement reversed.

ZSCHERNIG V. MILLER

389 U.S. 429 (1968)

Zschernig, a resident of East Germany, was the sole heir to the personal estate of an American citizen living in Oregon who died without a will in 1962. Zschernig was denied the inheritance by the courts of Oregon under the terms of a state statute that provided a three-tiered test when a nonresident alien sought to inherit. The statute required that:

(1) there is a reciprocal right of a United States citizen to take property on the same terms as the citizen of a foreign nation,

(2) American citizens have the right to receive payment here of funds from estates in the foreign country,

(3) foreign heirs have the right to receive the proceeds of Oregon estates without confiscation.

Justice **Douglas** delivered the opinion of the Court:

The Oregon Supreme Court held that the appellants could take the Oregon realty involved in the present case by reason of Article IV of the 1923 Treaty of Friendship, Commerce and Consular Rights with Germany but that by reason of the same Article, as construed in *Clark v. Allen* they could not take the personalty. We noted probable jurisdiction.

We do not accept the invitation to reexamine our ruling in *Clark v. Allen.* For we conclude that the history and operation of this Oregon statute make clear that [it] is an intrusion by the State into the field of foreign affairs which the Constitution entrusts to the President and the Congress.

As already noted one of the conditions of inheritance under the Oregon statute requires "proof that such foreign heirs, distributees, devisees or legatees may receive the benefit, use or control of money or property from estates of persons dying in this state without confiscation, in whole or in part, by the governments of such foreign countries," the burden being on the nonresident alien to establish that fact.... State courts, of course, must frequently read, construe, and apply laws of foreign nations. It has never been seriously suggested that state courts are precluded from performing that function, albeit there is a remote possibility that any holding may disturb a foreign nation—whether the matter involves commercial cases, tort cases, or some other type of controversy. At the time *Clark v. Allen* was decided, the case seemed to involve no more than a routine reading of foreign laws. It now appears that in this reciprocity area under inheritance statutes, the probate courts of various States have launched inquiries into the type of governments that obtain in particular foreign nations—whether aliens under their law have enforceable rights, whether the so-called "rights" are merely dispensations turning upon the whim or caprice of government officials, whether the representation of consuls, ambassadors, and other representatives of foreign nations is credible or made in good faith, whether there is in the actual administration in the particular foreign system of law any element of confiscation. . . .

As we read the decisions that followed in the wake of *Clark v. Allen,* we find that they radiate some of the attitudes of the "cold war," where the search is for the "democracy quotient" of a foreign regime as opposed to the Marxist theory. The Oregon statute introduces the concept of "confiscation," which is of course opposed to the Just Compensation Clause of the Fifth Amendment. And this has led into minute inquiries concerning the actual administration of foreign law, into the credibility of foreign diplomatic statements, and into speculation whether the fact that some received delivery of funds should "not preclude wonderment as to how many may have been denied 'the right to receive'. . . ."

That kind of state involvement in foreign affairs and international relations—matters which the Constitution entrusts solely to the Federal Government—is not sanctioned by *Clark v. Allen.* . . .

As one reads the Oregon decisions, it seems that foreign policy attitudes, the freezing or thawing of the "cold war," and the like are the real desiderata. Yet they of course are matters for the Federal Government, not for local probate courts. . . .

The statute as construed seems to make unavoidable judicial criticism of nations established on a more authoritarian basis than our own.

It seems inescapable that the type of probate law that Oregon enforces affects international relations in a persistent and subtle way. The practice of state courts in withholding remittances to legatees residing in Communist countries or in preventing them from assigning them is notorious. The several States, of course, have traditionally regulated the descent and distribution of estates. But those regulations must give way if they impair the effective exercise of the Nation's foreign policy. Where those laws conflict with a treaty, they must bow to the superior federal policy. Yet, even in absence of a treaty, a State's policy may disturb foreign relations. As we stated in *Hines v. Davidowitz,* "Experience has shown that international controversies of the gravest moment, sometimes even leading to war, may arise from real or imagined wrongs to another's subjects inflicted, or permitted, by a government." Certainly a State could not deny admission to a traveler from East Germany nor bar its citizens from going there. If there are to be such restraints, they must be provided by the Federal Government. The present Oregon law is not as gross an intrusion in the federal domain as those others might be. Yet, as we have said, it has a direct impact upon foreign relations and may well adversely affect the power of the central government to deal with those problems.

The Oregon law does, indeed, illustrate the dangers which are involved if each State, speaking through its probate courts, is permitted to establish its own foreign policy.

Reversed.

Justice **Stewart,** joined by Justice **Brennan,** concurring:

In my view, each of the three provisions of the Oregon law suffers from the same fatal infirmity. All three launch the State upon a prohibited voyage into a domain of exclusively federal competence. Any realistic attempt to apply any of the three criteria would necessarily involve the Oregon courts in an evaluation, either expressed or implied, of the administration of foreign law, the credibility of foreign diplomatic statements, and the policies of foreign governments. Of course state courts must routinely construe foreign law in the resolution of controversies properly before them, but here the courts of Oregon are thrust into these inquiries only because the Oregon Legislature has framed its inheritance laws to the prejudice of nations whose policies it disapproves and thus has trespassed upon an area where the Constitution contemplates that only the National Government shall operate. "For local interests the several States of the Union exist, but for national purposes, embracing our relations with foreign nations, we are but one people, one nation, one power." *Chinese Exclusion Case.* "Our system of government is such that the interest of the cities, counties and states, no less than the interest of the people of the whole nation, imperatively requires that federal power in the field affecting foreign relations be left entirely free from local interference."

The Solicitor General, as *amicus curiae,* says that the Government does not "contend that the application of the Oregon escheat statute in the circumstances of this case unduly interferes with the United States' conduct of foreign relations." But that is not the point. We deal here with the basic allocation of power between the States and the Nation. Resolution of so fundamental a constitutional issue cannot vary from day to day with the shifting winds at the State Department. Today, we are told, Oregon's statute does not conflict with the national interest. Tomorrow it may. But, however that may be, the fact remains that the conduct of our foreign affairs is entrusted under the Constitution to the National Government, not to the probate courts of the several States....

——————————— UNDERHILL V. HERNANDEZ ———————————

168 U.S. 250 (1897)

In 1892 Venezuela was beset by revolution. General Hernandez, commander of the revolutionary army, defeated the government forces and occupied the capital city of Bolivar.

Underhill was a U.S. citizen living in Bolivar, who previously had constructed the city's waterworks. He applied for a passport to leave the city—which General Hernandez denied. The passport was later issued, but Underhill filed suit for damages alleging assaults and affronts by Hernandez's soldiers. (The revolutionary government under which Hernandez fought was subsequently recognized by the United States.)

Chief Justice **Fuller** delivered the opinion of the Court:

Every sovereign State is bound to respect the independence of every other sovereign State, and the courts of one country will not sit in judgment on the acts of the government of another done within its own territory....

Nor can the principle be confined to lawful or recognized governments, or to cases where redress can manifestly be had through public channels. The immunity of individuals from suits brought in foreign tribunals for acts done within their own States, in the exercise of governmental authority, whether as civil officers or as military commanders, must necessarily extend to the agents of governments ruling by paramount force as matter of fact. Where a civil war prevails, that is, where the people of a country are divided into two hostile parties.... generally speaking foreign nations do not assume to judge of the merits of the quarrel. If the party seeking to dislodge the existing government succeeds, and the independence of the government it has set up is recognized, then the acts of such government from the commencement of its existence are regarded as those of an independent nation. If the political revolt fails of success, still if actual war has been waged, acts of legitimate warfare cannot be made the basis of individual liability.

Revolutions or insurrections may inconvenience other nations, but by accommodation to the facts the application of settled rules is readily reached. And where the fact of the existence of war is in issue in the instance of complaint of acts committed within foreign territory, it is not an absolute prerequisite that that fact should be made out by an acknowledgment of belligerency, as other official recognition of its existence may be sufficient proof thereof.

In this case, the archives of the State Department show that civil war was flagrant in Venezuela from the spring of 1892; that the revolution was successful; and that the revolutionary government was recognized by the United States as the government of the country, it being, to use the language of the Secretary of State in a communication to our minister to Venezuela, "accepted by the people, in the possession of the power of the nation and fully established." ...

It is idle to argue that the proceedings of those who thus triumphed should be treated as the acts of banditti or mere mobs.

We entertain no doubt upon the evidence that Hernandez was carrying on military operations in support of the revolutionary party.... The acts complained of were the acts of a military commander representing the authority of the revolutionary party as a government, which afterwards succeeded and was recognized by the United States. We think the Circuit Court of Appeals was justified in concluding "that the acts of the defendant were the acts of the government of Venezuela, and as such are not properly the subject of adjudication in the courts of another government." . . .

We agree with the Circuit Court of Appeals, that "the evidence upon the trial indicated that the purpose of the defendant in his treatment of the plaintiff was to coerce the plaintiff to operate his waterworks and his repair works for the benefit of the community and the revolutionary forces," and that "it was not sufficient to have warranted a finding by the jury that the defendant was actuated by malice or any personal or private motive;" and we concur in its disposition of the rulings below. The decree of the Circuit Court is

Affirmed.

BANCO NACIONAL DE CUBA V. SABBATINO

376 U.S. 398 (1964)

In early 1960, an American commodity broker contracted with a Cuban corporation (largely owned by U.S. residents) to buy Cuban sugar. In July, 1960, pursuant to Congressional legislation, President Eisenhower reduced the American import quota for Cuban sugar. The Cuban Council of Ministers retaliated by authorizing nationalization of property or enterprises in which American nationals had an interest.

On the day the contracted sugar was loaded for shipment, President Castro, acting pursuant to his government's authorization, ordered the expropriation of certain companies, including the company which owned the sugar. The American brokers thereupon entered into a new and identical contract with the Cuban government for the sugar. When the sugar was sold, the American brokers declined to turn over the proceeds to Cuba, but gave them instead to Sabbatino, the temporary receiver of the corporation that originally owned the sugar.

Banco Nacional brought suit in U.S. District Court to recover the sale proceeds, and the court ruled that since the expropriation violated international law, the Cuban government did not have title to the sugar.

Justice **Harlan** delivered the opinion of the Court:

. . . . It is first contended that this petitioner, an instrumentality of the Cuban Government, should be denied access to American courts because Cuba is an unfriendly power and does not permit nationals of this country to obtain relief in its courts. . . .

Under principles of comity governing this country's relations with other nations, sovereign states are allowed to sue in the courts of the United States. This Court has called "comity" in the legal sense "neither a matter of absolute obligation, on the one hand, nor of mere courtesy and good will, upon the other." Although comity is often associated with the existence of friendly relations between states, prior to some recent lower court cases which have questioned the right of instrumentalities of the Cuban Government to sue in our courts, the privilege of suit has been denied only to governments at war with the United States, or to those not recognized by this country. . . .

It is perhaps true that nonrecognition of a government in certain circumstances may reflect no greater unfriendliness than the severance of diplomatic relations with a recognized government, but the refusal to recognize has a unique legal aspect. It signifies this country's unwillingness to acknowledge that the government in question speaks as the sovereign authority for the territory it purports to control. Political recognition is exclusively a function of the Executive. The possible incongruity of judicial "recognition," by permitting suit, of a government not recognized by the Executive is completely absent when merely diplomatic relations are broken. . . .

. . . . The courts, whose powers to further the national interest in foreign affairs are necessarily circumscribed as compared with those of the political branches, can best serve the rule of law by not excluding otherwise proper suitors because of deficiencies in their legal systems.

We hold that this petitioner is not barred from access to the federal courts. . . .

The classic American statement of the act of state doctrine, which appears to have taken root in England as early as 1674, and began to emerge in the jurisprudence of this country in the late eighteenth and early nineteenth centuries, is found in *Underhill v. Hernandez*, where Chief Justice Fuller said for a unanimous Court:

> "Every sovereign State is bound to respect the independence of every other sovereign State, and the courts of one country will not sit in judgment on the acts of the government of another done within its own territory. Redress of grievances by reason of such acts must be obtained through the means open to be availed of by sovereign powers as between themselves." . . .

We do not believe that this doctrine is compelled either by the inherent nature of sovereign authority . . . or by some principle of international law. If a transaction takes place in one jurisdiction and the forum is in another, the forum does not by dismissing an action or by applying its own law purport to divest the first jurisdiction of its territorial sovereignty; it merely declines to adjudicate or makes applicable its own law to parties or property before it. . . .

Despite the broad statement in *Oetjen* that "The conduct of the foreign relations of our Government is committed by the Constitution to the Executive and Legislative . . . Departments," it cannot of course be thought that "every case or controversy which touches foreign relations lies beyond judicial cognizance." *Baker v. Carr.* The text of the Constitution does not require the act of state doctrine; it does not irrevocably remove from the judiciary the capacity to review the validity of foreign acts of state.

The act of state doctrine does, however, have "constitutional" underpinnings. It arises out of the basic relationships between branches of government in a system of separation of powers. It concerns the competency of dissimilar institutions to make and implement particular kinds of decisions in the area of international relations. The doctrine as formulated in past decisions expresses the strong sense of the Judicial Branch that its engagement in the task of passing on the validity of foreign acts of state may hinder rather than further this country's pursuit of goals both for itself and for the community of nations as a whole in the international sphere. . . . Whatever considerations are thought to predominate, it is plain that the problems involved are uniquely federal in nature. If federal authority, in this instance this Court, orders the field of judicial competence in this area for the federal courts, and the state courts are left free to formulate their own rules, the purposes behind the doctrine could be as effectively undermined as if there had been no federal pronouncement on the subject. . . .

If the act of state doctrine is a principle of decision binding on federal and state courts alike but compelled by neither international law nor the Constitution, its continuing vitality depends on its capacity to reflect the proper distribution of functions between the judicial and political branches of the Government on matters bearing upon foreign affairs. It should be apparent that the greater the degree of codification or consensus concerning a particular area of international law, the more appropriate it is for the judiciary to render decisions regarding it, since the courts can then focus on the application of an agreed principle to circumstances of fact rather than on the sensitive task of establishing a principle not inconsistent with the national interest or with international justice. It is also evident that some aspects of international law touch much more sharply on national nerves than do others; the less important the implications of an issue are for our foreign relations, the weaker the justification for exclusivity in the political branches. The balance of relevant considerations may also be shifted if the government which perpetuated the challenged act of state is no longer in existence . . . for the political interest of this country may, as a result, be measurably altered. Therefore, rather than laying down or reaffirming an inflexible and all-encompassing rule in this case, we decide only that the Judicial Branch will not examine the validity of a taking of property within its own territory by a foreign sovereign government, extant and recognized by this country at the time of suit, in the absence of a treaty or other unambiguous agreement regarding controlling legal principles, even if the complaint alleges that the taking violates customary international law.

There are few if any issues in international law today on which opinion seems to be so divided as the limitations on a state's power to expropriate the property of aliens. There is, of course, authority, in international judicial and arbitral decisions, in the expressions of national governments, and among commentators for the view that a taking is improper under international law if it is not for a public purpose, is discriminatory, or is without provision for prompt, adequate, and effective compensation. However, Communist countries, although they have in fact provided a degree of compensation after diplomatic efforts, commonly recognize no obligation on the part of the taking country. Certain representatives of the newly independent and underdeveloped countries have questioned whether rules of state responsibility toward aliens can bind nations that have not consented to them and it is argued that the traditionally articulated standards governing expropriation of property reflect "imperialist" interests and are inappropriate to the circumstances of emergent states.

The disagreement as to relevant international law standards reflects an even more basic divergence between the national interests of capital importing and capital exporting nations and between the social ideologies of those countries that favor state control of a considerable portion of the means of production and those that adhere to a free enterprise system. It is difficult to imagine the courts of this country embarking on adjudication in an area which touches more sensitively the practical and ideological goals of the various members of the community of nations.

. . . . While each of the leading cases in this Court may be argued to be distinguishable on its facts from this one . . . the plain implication of all these opinions, is that the act of state doctrine is applicable even if international law has been violated. . . .

The possible adverse consequences of a conclusion to the contrary of that implicit in these cases is highlighted by contrasting the practices of the political branch with the limitations of the judicial process in matters of this kind. Following an expropriation of any significance, the Executive engages in diplomacy aimed to assure that United States citizens who are harmed are compensated fairly. Representing all claimants of this country, it will often be able, either by bilateral or multilateral talks, by submission to the United Nations, or by the employment of economic and political sanctions, to achieve some degree of general redress. Judicial determinations of invalidity of title can, on the other hand, have only an occasional impact, since they depend on the fortuitous circumstance of the property in question being brought into this country. Such decisions would, if the acts involved were declared invalid, often be likely to give offense to the expropriating country; since the concept of territorial sovereignty is so deep seated, any state may resent the refusal of the courts of another sovereign to accord validity to acts within its territorial borders. Piecemeal dispositions of this sort involving the probability of affront to another state could seriously interfere with negotiations being carried on by the Executive Branch and might prevent or render less favorable the terms of an agreement that could otherwise be reached. Relations with third countries which have engaged in similar expropriations would not be immune from effect.

The dangers of such adjudication are present regardless of whether the State Department has, as it did in this case, asserted that the relevant act violated international law. If the Executive Branch has undertaken negotiations with an expropriating country, but has refrained from claims of violation of the law of nations, a determination to that effect by a court might be regarded as a serious insult, while a finding of compliance with international law, would greatly strengthen the bargaining hand of the other state with consequent detriment to American interests.

Even if the State Department has proclaimed the impropriety of the expropriation, the stamp of approval of its view by a judicial tribunal, however impartial, might increase any affront and the judicial decision might occur at a time, almost always well after the taking, when such an impact would be contrary to our national interest. Considerably more serious and far-reaching consequences would flow from a judicial finding that international law standards had been met if that determination flew in the face of a State Department proclamation to the contrary. When articulating principles of international law in its relations with other states, the Executive Branch speaks not only as an interpreter of generally accepted and traditional rules, as would the courts, but also as an advocate of standards it believes desirable for the community of nations and protective of national concerns. In short, whatever way the matter is cut, the possibility of conflict between the Judicial and Executive Branches could hardly be avoided....

... [W]e find respondents' countervailing arguments quite unpersuasive. Their basic contention is that United States courts could make a significant contribution to the growth of international law, a contribution whose importance, it is said, would be magnified by the relative paucity of decisional law by international bodies. But given the fluidity of present world conditions, the effectiveness of such a patchwork approach toward the formulation of an acceptable body of law concerning state responsibility for expropriations is, to say the least, highly conjectural. Moreover, it rests upon the sanguine presupposition that the decisions of the courts of the world's major capital exporting country and principal exponent of the free enterprise system would be accepted as disinterested expressions of sound legal principle by those adhering to widely different ideologies.... Respondents claim that the economic pressure resulting from the proposed exception to the act of state doctrine will materially add to the protection of United States investors. We are not convinced, even assuming the relevance of this contention. Expropriations take place for a variety of reasons, political and ideological as well as economic. When one considers the variety of means possessed by this country to make secure foreign investment, the persuasive or coercive effect of judicial invalidation of acts of expropriation dwindles in comparison. The newly independent states are in need of continuing foreign investment; the creation of a climate unfavorable to such investment by wholesale confiscations may well work to their long-run economic disadvantage. Foreign aid given to many of these countries provides a powerful lever in the hands of the political branches to ensure fair treatment of United States nationals. Ultimately the sanctions of economic embargo and the freezing of assets in this country may be employed. Any country willing to brave any or all of these consequences is unlikely to be deterred by sporadic judicial decisions directly affecting only property brought to our shores. If the political branches are unwilling to exercise their ample powers to effect compensation, this reflects a judgment of the national interest which the judiciary would be ill-advised to undermine indirectly....

However offensive to the public policy of this country and its constituent States an expropriation of this kind may be, we conclude that both the national interest and progress toward the goal of establishing the rule of law among nations are best served by maintaining intact the act of state doctrine in this realm of its application....

The judgment of the Court of Appeals is reversed and the case is remanded to the District Court for proceedings consistent with this opinion.

It is so ordered.

*Justice **White**, dissenting.*

—————————————— HICKENLOOPER AMENDMENT ——————————————

Pub.L. 88–633; 78 Stat. 1009, 1013 (1964)
22 United States Code 2370(e)(2)

Notwithstanding any other provision of law, no court in the United States shall decline on the ground of the federal act of state doctrine to make a determination on the merits giving effect to the principles of international law in a case in which a claim of title or other right to property is asserted by any party including a foreign state (or a party claiming through such state) based upon (or traced through) a confiscation or other taking after January 1, 1959, by an act of that state in violation of the principles of international law, including the principles of compensation and the other standards set out in this subsection: *Provided,* That this subparagraph shall not be applicable (1) in any case in which an act of a foreign state is not contrary to international law or with respect to a claim of title or other right to property acquired pursuant to an irrevocable letter of credit of not more than 180 days duration issued in good faith prior to the time of the confiscation or other taking, or (2) in any case with respect to which the President determines that application of the act of state doctrine is required in that particular case by the foreign policy interests of the United States and a suggestion to this effect is filed on his behalf in that case with the court.

—————————————— FIRST NATIONAL CITY BANK ——————————————
v. BANCO NACIONAL DE CUBA

406 U.S. 759 (1972)

In 1960, the Castro government nationalized City Bank's eleven branches in Cuba. City Bank responded by selling the collateral securing a $10 million loan it had made to Cuba. The sale of the collateral netted an excess of $1.8 million above the principal and interest due on the loan. Banco Nacional, the financial arm of the Cuban government, sued to recover the excess. City Bank defended its action as a set-off, and filed a counter-claim for losses sustained through the Cuban nationalization of its property. The lower federal courts held that the Sabbatino ruling applied, and ruled in favor of Banco Nacional.

While the matter was pending before the Supreme Court, the legal adviser of the Department of State advised the Court that the foreign policy interests of the United States did not require application of the Act of State doctrine, and that the doctrine should not be applied to defeat City Bank's counterclaim. The "Hickenlooper Amendment" (passed by Congress to overrule the Sabbatino decision) provided that the courts may not apply the act of state doctrine unless instructed to do so by the executive.

Justice **Rehnquist** delivered the opinion of the Court:

. . . . The act of state doctrine represents an exception to the general rule that a court of the United States, where appropriate jurisdictional standards are met, will decide cases before it by choosing the rules appropriate for decision from among various sources of law including international law. The doctrine precludes any review whatever of the acts of the government of one sovereign State done within its own territory by the courts of another sovereign

State. It is clear, however, from both history and the opinions of this Court that the doctrine is not an inflexible one. . . .

[T]his Court has recognized the primacy of the Executive in the conduct of foreign relations quite as emphatically as it has recognized the act of state doctrine. The Court in *Sabbatino* throughout its opinion emphasized the lead role of the Executive in foreign policy, particularly in seeking redress for American nationals who had been the victims of foreign expropriation, and concluded that any exception to the act of state doctrine based on a mere silence or neutrality on the part of the Executive might well lead to a conflict between the Executive and Judicial Branches. Here, however, the Executive Branch has expressly stated that an inflexible application of the act of state doctrine by this Court would not serve the interests of American foreign policy.

The act of state doctrine is grounded on judicial concern that application of customary principles of law to judge the acts of a foreign sovereign might frustrate the conduct of foreign relations by the political branches of the government. We conclude that where the Executive Branch, charged as it is with primary responsibility for the conduct of foreign affairs, expressly represents to the Court that application of the act of state doctrine would not advance the interests of American foreign policy, that doctrine should not be applied by the courts. . . .

Our holding is in no sense an abdication of the judicial function to the Executive Branch. The judicial power of the United States extends to this case, and the jurisdictional standards established by Congress for adjudication by the federal courts have been met by the parties. The only reason for not deciding the case by use of otherwise applicable legal principles would be the fear that legal interpretation by the judiciary of the act of a foreign sovereign within its own territory might frustrate the conduct of this country's foreign relations. But the branch of the government responsible for the conduct of these foreign relations has advised us that such a consequence need not be feared in this case. The judiciary is therefore free to decide the case without the limitations that would otherwise be imposed upon it by the judicially created act of state doctrine. . . .

The act of state doctrine, as reflected in the cases culminating in *Sabbatino,* is a judicially accepted limitation on the normal adjudicative processes of the courts, springing from the thoroughly sound principle that on occasion individual litigants may have to forgo decision on the merits of their claims because the involvement of the courts in such a decision might frustrate the conduct of the Nation's foreign policy. It would be wholly illogical to insist that such a rule, fashioned because of fear that adjudication would interfere with the conduct of foreign relations, be applied in the face of an assurance from that branch of the Federal Government that conducts foreign relations that such a result would not obtain. Our holding confines the courts to adjudication of the case before them, and leaves to the Executive Branch the conduct of foreign relations. In so doing, it is both faithful to the principle of separation of powers and consistent with earlier cases applying the act of state doctrine where we lacked the sort of representation from the Executive Branch that we have in this case.

We therefore reverse the judgment of the Court of Appeals, and remand the case to it for consideration of respondent's alternative bases of attack on the judgment of the District Court.

Reversed and remanded.

*Justice **Douglas** and Justice **Powell** filed separate **concurring** opinions.*

*Justice **Brennan**, joined by Justice **Stewart**, Justice **Marshall**, and Justice **Blackmun**, dissenting.*

———————————— ALFRED DUNHILL V. CUBA ————————————

425 U.S. 682 (1976)

In 1960, the Cuban government confiscated and took control of the Cuban cigar industry. This complicated litigation involved offsetting counterclaims between Dunhill and the Cuban government for excess monies paid by Dunhill for cigars shipped before the nationalization decree. The Cuban government denied any obligation to repay this money, based on the "act of state" doctrine, and their position had been sustained by the court of appeals.

Justice **White** delivered the opinion of the Court:

. . . . The major underpinning of the act of state doctrine is the policy of foreclosing court adjudications involving the legality of acts of foreign states on their own soil that might embarrass the Executive Branch of our Government in the conduct of our foreign relations. But based on the presently expressed views of those who conduct our relations with foreign countries, we are in no sense compelled to recognize as an act of state the purely commercial conduct of foreign governments in order to avoid embarrassing conflicts with the Executive Branch. On the contrary, for the reasons to which we now turn, we fear that embarrassment and conflict would more likely ensue if we were to require that the repudiation of a foreign government's debts arising from its operation of a purely commercial business be recognized as an act of state and immunized from question in our courts.

Although it had other views in years gone by, in 1952, the United States abandoned the absolute theory of sovereign immunity and embraced the restrictive view under which immunity in our courts should be granted only with respect to causes of action arising out of a foreign state's public or governmental actions and not with respect to those arising out of its commercial or proprietary actions. . . . Repudiation of a commercial debt cannot, consistent with this restrictive approach to sovereign immunity, be treated as an act of state; for if it were, foreign governments, by merely repudiating the debt before or after its adjudication, would enjoy an immunity which our Government would not extend them under prevailing sovereign immunity principles in this country. . . .

Participation by foreign sovereigns in the international commercial market has increased substantially in recent years. The potential injury to private businessmen—and ultimately to international trade itself—from a system in which some of the participants in the international market are not subject to the rule of law has therefore increased correspondingly. . . . In their commercial capacities, foreign governments do not exercise powers peculiar to sovereigns. Instead, they exercise only those powers that can also be exercised by private citizens. Subjecting them in connection with such acts to the same rules of law that apply to private citizens is unlikely to touch very sharply on "national nerves.". . . There may be little codification or consensus as to the rules of international law concerning exercises of *governmental* powers, including military powers and expropriations, within a sovereign state's borders affecting the property or persons of aliens. However, more discernible rules of international law have emerged with regard to the commercial dealings of private parties in the international market. The restrictive approach to sovereign immunity suggests that these established rules should be applied to the commercial transactions of sovereign states. . . .

. . . . Nothing in our national policy calls on us to recognize as an act of state a repudiation by Cuba of an obligation adjudicated in our courts and arising out of the operation of a commercial business by one of its instrumentalities. For all the reasons which led the Executive Branch to adopt the restrictive theory of sovereign immunity, we hold that the mere assertion of sovereignty as a defense to a claim arising out of purely commercial acts by a foreign sovereign is no more effective if given the label "Act of State" than if it is given the label "sovereign immunity." In describing the act of state doctrine in the past we have said that it "precludes the courts of this country from inquiring into the validity of the *public* acts a recognized foreign sovereign power committed within its own territory." We decline to extend the act of state doctrine to acts committed by foreign sovereigns in the course of their purely commercial operations. Because the act relied on by respondents in this case was an act arising out of the conduct by Cuba's agents in the operation of cigar businesses for profit, the act was not an act of state.

Reversed.

Chief Justice **Burger,** *and Justices* **Powell** *and* **Rehnquist,** *concurred. Justice Stevens concurred separately.*

Justice **Marshall** *with whom Justice* **Brennan,** *Justice* **Stewart,** *and Justice* **Blackmun,** *join,* **dissenting:**
     The act of state doctrine commits the courts of the country not to sit in judgment on the acts of a foreign government performed within its own territory. Under any realistic view of the facts of this case, the interventors' retention of and refusal to return funds paid to them by Dunhill constitute an act of state, and no affirmative recovery by Dunhill can rest on the invalidity of that conduct.

Suggested Reading

The best general review of the early Supreme Court is still CHARLES WARREN'S, THE SUPREME COURT IN UNITED STATES HISTORY (1937). Also see, HOMER CAREY HOCKETT, THE CONSTITUTIONAL HISTORY OF THE UNITED STATES, 1776–1826 (1939), and W.W.

WILLOUGHBY, THE SUPREME COURT OF THE UNITED STATES, ITS HISTORY AND INFLUENCE IN OUR CONSTITUTIONAL SYSTEM (1890).

For the special significance of *Chisholm v. Georgia,* see Doyle Mathis, Chisholm v. Georgia: *Background and Settlement,* 54 JOURNAL OF AMERICAN HISTORY 19 (1967). Also see Van Tyne, *Sovereignty in the American Revolution: An Historical Study,* 12 AMERICAN HISTORICAL REVIEW 529 (1907), and Edward S. Corwin, *National Power and State Interposition,* 3 SELECTED ESSAYS IN CONSTITUTIONAL LAW 1181 (1938).

Among the numerous works on Federalism, see especially John C. Ranney, *The Basis of American Federalism,* 3 WILLIAM AND MARY QUARTERLY (3rd series) 1 (1946); Moore, *Federalism and Foreign Relations,* (1965) DUKE LAW JOURNAL 248; Koenig, *Federal and State Cooperation Under the Constitution,* 36 MICHIGAN LAW REVIEW 752 (1938).

ALBERT J. BEVERIDGE'S, THE LIFE OF JOHN MARSHALL, 4 vols. (1916–19) remains the best source on the Marshall period, complemented by CORWIN'S JOHN MARSHALL AND THE CONSTITUTION (1919). CARL SWISHER'S ROGER B. TANEY (1935), and CHARLES SMITH, ROGER B. TANEY: JACKSONIAN JURIST (1936) provide useful insights into another great Chief Justice.

For an analysis of *Texas v. White,* see JOHN BURGESS, THE CIVIL WAR AND THE CONSTITUTION, 2 vols. (1901), as well as J.G. RANDALL'S CONSTITUTIONAL PROBLEMS UNDER LINCOLN (rev.ed.1951).

For alternative views of executive agreements see Mathews, *The Constitutional Power of the President to Conclude Executive Agreements,* 64 YALE LAW REVIEW 345 (1955); Frankfurter and Landis, *The Compact Clause of the Constitution—A Study in Interstate Adjustments,* 34 YALE LAW JOURNAL 685 (1925); Naujoks, *Compacts and Agreements Between States and Between States and Foreign Countries,* 36 MARQUETTE LAW REVIEW 219 (1952); Weinfield, *What Did the Framers Mean by 'Agreements or Compacts'?,* 3 UNIVERSITY OF CHICAGO LAW REVIEW 453 (1936); and *The Capacity of States of the Union to Conclude International Agreements,* 61 AMERICAN JOURNAL OF INTERNATIONAL LAW 1021 (1967). On the role of cities and other local jurisdictions in foreign policy, see Michael H. Shuman, *Dateline Main Street: Local Foreign Policies,* FOREIGN POLICY (Winter 1985) 154–171.

The Act of State doctrine is discussed in Henkin, *The Foreign Affairs Power and the Federal Courts,* Sabbatino, 64 COLUMBIA LAW REVIEW 805 (1964); Henkin, *Act of State Today: Recollections in Tranquility,* 6 COLUMBIA JOURNAL OF TRANSNATIONAL LAW 175 (1967), and RICHARD FALK, THE AFTERMATH OF SABBATINO (1965).

Notes

1. 12 Wall. (79 U.S.) 457, 555 (1870).
2. 130 U.S. 581, 606 (1889).
3. 9 Wheat. (22 U.S.) 1, 228 (1824).
4. 149 U.S. 698 (1893).
5. 3 Cranch (7 U.S.) 454 (1806).
6. 4 Wheat. (17 U.S.) 316 (1819).
7. 23 How. (64 U.S.) 445, 448 (1859).
8. See Levitan, *The Foreign Relations Power: An Analysis of Mr. Justice Sutherland's Theory,* 55 YALE L.J. 467 (1946).
9. Greenough v. Tax Assessors of Newport, 331 U.S. 486 (1947).

3

TREATIES AND
EXECUTIVE AGREEMENTS

ARTICLE II OF the Constitution provides that the president "shall have Power, by and with the Advice and Consent of the Senate, to make Treaties, provided two-thirds of the Senators present concur." Article VI, section 2 (the Supremacy Clause) provides that "all Treaties made, or which shall be made, under the Authority of the United States, shall be the supreme Law of the Land, and the Judges in every State shall be bound thereby, any Thing in the Constitution or Laws of any State to the Contrary notwithstanding." These two Constitutional provisions describe how treaties shall be made, and what their effect shall be domestically.

PRESIDENT AND SENATE

At the Constitutional Convention, the Committee of Detail's original plan provided that "the Senate of the United States shall have power to make treaties, and to appoint Ambassadors, and Judges of the Supreme Court." Not until the last ten days of the Convention was the president given primary responsibility for these functions. But the close relation between executive and legislative power in the various states at that time suggests that the final version of Article II assumed the president and Senate would be closely associated throughout the entire treaty process.[1] As Senator Rufus King of New York (who had been a member of the Constitutional Convention) told the Senate in 1818:

> In these concerns the Senate are the Constitutional and only responsible counsellors of the President. And in this capacity the Senate may, and ought to, look into and watch over every branch of the foreign affairs of the nation....[2]

But since the time of George Washington, the negotiation of treaties has been taken over exclusively by the president.[3] As Justice Sutherland observed in *United States v. Curtiss–Wright,* the president "alone negotiates. Into the field of negotiation the Senate cannot intrude; and Congress itself is powerless to invade it." Moreover, despite Senator King's views, the Senate must content itself with such information as the president chooses to furnish. In effect, the Senate has four options when a treaty is presented:

1. It may consent unconditionally to the treaty as it has been proposed.

2. It may reject the treaty.

3. It may request amendments to the treaty. These require the consent of the other party or parties before the treaty becomes effective.

4. It may attach reservations which affect the substance of the proposed treaty. These are binding only on the United States, but the other signatures may reject the treaty because of U.S. reservations.

The formal ratification of a treaty is a presidential act and has the effect of binding the United States to its terms. But ratification cannot be undertaken by the president unless Senate has given the required two-thirds consent. Conversely, a president is not bound to ratify a treaty that the Senate has agreed to and may simply abandon it.[4]

The domestic effect of treaties in the United States is unique. Unlike other countries, American treaties have immediate internal impact. They require no separate implementing legislation. Chief Justice Marshall explained the distinction in *Foster v. Neilson* in 1829:

> A treaty is . . . a contract between two nations, not a legislative act. It does not generally effect, of itself, the object to be accomplished; especially so far as its operation is infraterritorial. . . . *In the United States, a different principle is established.* Our constitution declares a treaty to be the law of the land. It is, consequently, to be regarded in courts of justice as equivalent to an act of the legislature. . . . (Emphasis added.)

This difference traces to the difficulty the United States experienced with Great Britain after the Revoluntionary War because various states did not comply with the peace treaty terms. The first case to arise under the Supremacy Clause was *Ware v. Hylton* in 1796. The treaty of peace with Great Britain, which provided for the restitution of Loyalist assets, contradicted Virginian sequestration statutes of the Revolutionary period. The Supreme Court vigorously upheld the supremacy of American treaties over state laws to the contrary—a ruling so emphatic that it continues to be the leading case on the issue.

Later, in *Hauenstein v. Lynham* the Supreme Court upheld the right of a Swiss national to inherit property under the terms of an 1850 treaty between the United States and Switzerland despite another Virginia law to the contrary. Said Justice Swayne, "It must always be borne in mind that the Constitution, laws and treaties of the United States are as much a part of the laws of every State as its own local laws and Constitution. This is a fundamental principle in our system of complex national polity." Thus while states may enact legislation placing property restrictions on foreign nationals, those restrictions must yield in the face of treaties to the contrary.

In the early case of *United States v. Schooner Peggy,* the Supreme Court, again speaking through Chief Justice Marshall, held that treaties created self-executing domestic commitments which the courts were obliged to enforce. The treaty in question, a friendship treaty with France seeking to end tensions of the 1790s, was held by the Court to be "the law of the land, and as such affects the rights of the parties litigating in court . . . and is as much to be regarded by the court as an act of congress."

AUTHORITY OF CONGRESS

If a treaty, once ratified, is the supreme law of the land, is it binding on the U.S. government? Is Congress obliged to comply with its provisions? Specifically, is Congress required to appropriate money to carry a treaty into effect? The issue arose in 1796 concerning the Jay Treaty with Great Britain where certain provisions required Congressional appropriations. But the Constitution gives Congress exclusive authority over appropriations, and it was quickly agreed by all concerned that no money could be spent without Congress' approval. Did the Supremacy Clause require Congress to act? Hamilton, Chief Justice Oliver Ellsworth, and several members of Washington's cabinet argued that the House of Representatives had no choice; the treaty, duly ratified with the advice and consent of the Senate, had become "the supreme law of the land," and the legislative branch was bound by it. But James Madison, a member of the House at that time, rejected the thesis. Instead Madison proposed a series of resolutions that would establish the independence of Congress to decide the question. According to Madison, "It is the clear constitutional right and duty of the House of Representatives . . . to deliberate on the expediency or inexpediency of carrying such Treaty into effect, and to determine and act thereon, as, in their judgment, may be most conducive to the public good." [5] The result was a compromise. The House of Representatives attached Madison's resolutions to the appropriations Washington had requested. The House then passed the appropriations and the president signed the measure. (Later in *DeLima v. Bidwell,* [6] a case involving the 1899 peace treaty between the United States and Spain, the Court stated "We express no opinion as to whether Congress is bound to appropriate the money [stipulated in the treaty].")

Reaction to the Jay Treaty established the precedent that Congress is not bound to implement a treaty, and the House of Representatives, especially, is under no constitutional obligation to appropriate the funds that a treaty may require. For all practical purposes, this involves the House of Representatives in the treaty process whenever funds are required. President Carter discovered this in 1978 when the House initially declined to appropriate the funds required to implement the Panama Canal Treaty ratified the year before. A massive lobbying effort by the administration was required to convince the House to go along with the U.S. treaty commitment.

CONGRESSIONAL REPEAL OF TREATIES

An analogous problem relates to the possible conflict between a federal law and a treaty. Since both are defined by Article VI as the supreme law of the land, which prevails when the two conflict? Neither has any intrinsic superiority over the other. Since both represent legitimate expressions of the sovereign purpose, the most recent will control. The legal maxim, *leges posteriores priores contrarias abrogant,* developed to govern the possible conflict of laws, is applicable in every respect.

Justice Curtis considered the issue in *Taylor v. Morton* in 1855, and Curtis' conclusion has been frequently invoked by the Court in the years since. According to Curtis, "There is nothing in the mere fact that a treaty is a law, which would prevent Congress from repealing it."

> To refuse to execute a treaty ... is a matter of the utmost gravity and delicacy; but the power to do so is prerogative, of which no nation can be deprived, without deeply affecting its independence. That the people of the United States have deprived their government of this power ... I do not believe. That it must reside somewhere ... I am convinced. I feel no doubt that it belongs to Congress.

Speaking for the Court in the *Head Money Cases,* Justice Miller noted that "A treaty is primarily a compact between independent nations. It depends for the enforcement of its provisions on the interest and the honor of the governments which are parties to it." Accordingly, since situations might arise where it is no longer in the interests of the United States to observe a treaty (the question in the *Head Money Cases* involved alleged Congressional violation of treaty commitments), the Court sustained the power of Congress to modify or even abrogate a treaty. In the words of Justice Miller:

> A treaty is made by the President and the Senate. Statutes are made by the President, the Senate and House of Representatives. The addition of the latter body to the other two in making a law certainly does not render it less entitled to respect.... If there be any difference in this regard, it would seem to be in favor of an act in which all three of the bodies participate.

The obvious proof, said Miller, involved a declaration of war by Congress, which "when made, usually suspends or destroys existing treaties between the nations then at war."

In 1888 the Court applied the same reasoning in *Whitney v. Robertson* involving a conflict between an 1867 treaty with the Dominican Republic and subsequent tariff legislation. As Justice Field said for the Court, when a treaty and a law "relate to the same subject, the courts will always endeavor to construe them so as to give effect to both, ... but if the two are inconsistent, the one last in date will control the other...." Field went on to say that if the country involved was dissatisfied with Congress' action, the country could take its complaint to the president, but "the courts can afford no redress." Of course, should Congress repeal a treaty, the United States might be in violation of its international responsibilities and could be acting contrary to international law. The 1987 action by Congress to close the PLO

(Palestine Liberation Organization) observer office at the United Nations may be one such example.

TREATIES AND PRIOR ACTS OF CONGRESS

There are numerous cases in which the courts have recognized statutes superseding prior treaty commitments. Instances where treaties were held to overturn prior legislative enactment are less common. In the early case of the *Schooner Peggy* certain statutory provisions dealing with the trial of prize cases were held to have been modified by a subsequent treaty with France. In another case from the Marshall period, *Foster v. Neilson,* (see Chapter 4), Chief Justice Marshall noted by way of *dicta* that an 1818 treaty with Spain would have repealed acts of Congress repugnant to it. But these examples appear to be exceptions. They are disparaged by Professor Willoughby as follows:

> ... [T]here have been few (the writer is not certain that there have been any) instances in which a treaty inconsistent with a prior act of Congress has been given full force and effect ... without the consent of Congress. There may indeed have been cases in which, by treaty, certain action has been taken without reference to existing Federal laws, ... but such treaty action has not operated to repeal or annul existing Federal law on the subject.[7]

The exception noted by Willoughby is *Cook v. United States* in which a sharply divided Court, speaking through Justice Brandeis, held that the Tariff Acts of 1922 and 1930 relating to the seizure of liquor had been modified by a 1924 treaty with Great Britain. The facts of the case are unique and the issue of Prohibition so peculiar that *Cook* must be regarded as a judicial anomaly.

THE LIMITS OF TREATY–MAKING

The question of the extent of a treaty power—what a treaty can regulate or accomplish—was deliberately left open by the Framers. Given the largely extra-constitutional nature of the foreign relations power, the general view seems to be that whatever the United States and a foreign government deem to be an appropriate subject for a treaty is by definition an appropriate subject. In fact the Supreme Court has never declared any treaty, or any provision thereof, to be unconstitutional. The sole qualification is that the United States cannot do anything by treaty that the Constitution explicitly forbids. Outside of this requirement, there appears to be no limit.

The rule was enunciated most clearly by Justice Field, speaking for the Court in *Geofroy v. Riggs* in 1890. Said Field:

> The treaty power, as expressed in the Constitution, is in terms unlimited except by those restraints which are found in that instrument against the action of the government or of its departments, and those arising from the nature of the government itself and of that of the States. It would not be

contended that it extends so far as to authorize what the Constitution forbids, or a change in the character of the government or in that of one of the States, or the cession of any portion of the territory of the latter without its consent. . . . But with these exceptions, it is not perceived that there is any limit to the questions which can be adjusted touching any matter which is properly the subject of negotiation with a foreign country.

A second general principle enunciated in *Geofroy v. Riggs* is that treaties shall be liberally construed so as to carry out the intention of the parties to secure equality and reciprocity between them. This was reaffirmed by the Court in *Tucker v. Alexandroff* in 1902. "Treaties are solemn engagements," said Justice Brown, and "should be interpreted in that broad and liberal spirit which is calculated to make for the existence of a perpetual state of amity, so far as it can be done without the sacrifice of individual rights or those principles of personal liberty which lie at the foundation of our jurisprudence . . ."

Fifty–five years later in *Reid v. Covert* the Supreme Court reaffirmed that the treaty power was limited only by the express prohibitions contained in the Constitution. As Justice Black noted, "The prohibitions of the Constitution were designed to apply to all branches of the National Government and they cannot be nullified by the Executive or by the Executive and the Senate combined." The *Covert* case is sometimes cited as being contrary to the broad interpretation granted by the Court to the treaty power. While the language of Justice Black sometimes appears to be very restrictive, a careful reading of the case suggests that the Court merely affirmed that the express terms of the Constitution necessarily place limits on the treaty power—a holding in no way contrary to *Geofroy v. Riggs* or *Missouri v. Holland*.

EXECUTIVE AGREEMENTS

Treaties are not the only method by which the United States can enter into agreements with other nations. The Constitution recognizes a distinction between treaties and "agreements" or "compacts" but does not indicate how they differ. In *Holmes v. Jennison* (see Chapter 2), Chief Justice Taney sought to distinguish among the various terms, relying principally on the work of Vattel. In *United States v. Belmont* (see Chapter 2), Justice Sutherland noted the difference as well. Judge Story defined such executive agreements as "the private rights of sovereignty." [8] More recently, Professor Myles McDougal of Yale and his predecessor Professor Edwin Borchard debated the distinction in the *Yale Law Journal*.[9] The issue, as McDougal suggests, is that today the only real distinction between a treaty and an executive agreement is that the former requires the consent of two-thirds of the Senate while the latter can be concluded by the president alone.

From the days of the first Congress, the United States has entered into executive agreements with other countries concerning such matters as postal rates, trademark and copyright, and reciprocal trade arrangements. Executive agreements are of constitutional significance when they become a critical factor in American foreign policy, and these instances—such as the Yalta and Potsdam agreements in World War II, or the Berlin Accords of 1971—have become much more frequent as the United States has assumed a more active role in world affairs.

In an early instance of executive treaty-making, President Monroe brought about the limitation of armaments on the Great Lakes with the Rush–Bagehot Agreement of 1817. Similarly, between 1882 and 1896, various American presidents concluded agreements with Mexico according each country the right to pursue marauding Indians across the border. The use of such agreements for major foreign policy purposes increasingly became manifest during the administration of President McKinley. The armistice agreement with Spain concluded by the president in August 1898 determined the shape of the subsequent peace treaty, just as the executive-written armistice of November 11, 1918 determined the conditions of peace with Germany. It was also President McKinley who dispatched troops to China to suppress the Boxer Rebellion and who signed, without reference to the Senate, the Boxer Indemnity Protocol for the United States.

The "Open Door" policy in China, the 1908 Root–Takahira agreement between the United States and Japan to uphold the status quo in the Pacific, the "Gentlemen's Agreement" to curb Japanese immigration to the United States, and the Lansing–Ishii Agreement in 1917 by which the United States recognized Japan's special interests in China were all consummated without reference to the Senate. So, too, was the Hull–Lothian Agreement of 1940 under which the U.S. provided Great Britain with fifty recommissioned destroyers (in apparent violation of the Neutrality Acts) in return for ninety-nine year leases to certain naval bases in the western Atlantic.

DOMESTIC EFFECTS OF EXECUTIVE AGREEMENTS

It was under President Franklin Roosevelt that the executive agreement reached its fullest development. Roosevelt's first important utilization of the procedure involved an exchange of notes with the Soviet Union on November 16, 1933, by which the two countries established diplomatic recognition. Known as the Hull–Litvinov Agreement, or the Litvinov Assignment, these arrangements gave rise to two leading cases, *United States v. Belmont* in 1937, and *United States v. Pink* in 1942. The effect of these cases has elevated executive agreements to the same constitutional status as treaties.

Speaking through Justice Sutherland in the *Belmont* case, the Court held that President Roosevelt's act in recognizing the Soviet Union, and the accompanying agreements, constituted a binding international compact which the president, "as the sole organ of international relations for the United States," was authorized to conclude without consulting the Senate. According to the Court state laws contrary to the agreements were of no effect because executive agreements, like treaties, were the supreme law of the land. In *United States v. Pink,* the same reasoning was applied with even greater emphasis. According to Justice Douglas the agreements with the Soviet Union were "a modest implied power of the President who is the 'sole organ of the Federal Government in the field of international relations'."

More recently, in *Weinberger v. Rossi,* the Court, speaking through Justice Rehnquist (as he then was), held that the word "treaty" in the Supremacy Clause of the Constitution extended to executive agreements unless Congress explicitly provided otherwise.

THE BRICKER AMENDMENT

Hostile reaction to the decisions in *Missouri v. Holland, Belmont,* and *Pink,* as well as the extensive use of executive agreements during World War II, prompted a series of efforts to amend the Constitution. In 1954 these efforts culminated in the Bricker Amendment named for its original sponsor, Senator John Bricker of Ohio. The Bricker Amendment would have nullified *Missouri v. Holland* by ending the distinction between laws and treaties as domestic legislation. To be effective as domestic law treaties would have to be made pursuant to powers granted to the national government in the Constitution. The Amendment also took aim at the power of the president to conclude executive agreements and gave Congress power to annul them. The Bricker Amendment (actually, the "George Substitute") came within one vote of the required two-thirds of the Senate on February 26, 1954.

HAUENSTEIN V. LYNHAM

100 U.S. 483 (1879)

A treaty between the United States and Switzerland ratified in 1850 provided that citizens of each country could inherit land in the other despite state legislation prohibiting aliens from doing so. In 1861, Solomon Hauenstein died in Richmond, Virginia, without having made a will. His next of kin was a Swiss citizen. Pursuant to Virginia law, which prohibited aliens from inheriting real property, Hauenstein's estate was sold and the proceeds reverted to the State. Hauenstein's Swiss heirs brought suit to recover under terms of the treaty.

Justice **Swayne** delivered the opinion of the Court:

. . . . That the laws of the State, irrespective of the treaty, would put the fund into her coffers, is no objection to the right or the remedy claimed by the plaintiffs in error.

The efficacy of the treaty is declared and guaranteed by the Constitution of the United States. That instrument took effect on the fourth day of March, 1789. In 1796, but a few years later, this court said: "If doubts could exist before the adoption of the present national government, they must be entirely removed by the sixth article of the Constitution, which provides that 'all treaties made or which shall be made under the authority of the United States, shall be the *supreme law of the land,* and the judges in every State shall be bound thereby, any thing in the Constitution or laws of any State to the contrary notwithstanding.' There can be no limitation on the power of the people of the United States. By their authority the State Constitutions were made, and by their authority the Constitution of the United States was established; and they had the power to change or abolish the State Constitutions or to make them yield to the general government and to treaties made by their authority. A treaty cannot be the *supreme law of the land,* that is, of all the United States, if any act of a State legislature can stand in its way. If the Constitution of a State (which is the fundamental law of the State and paramount to its legislature) must give way to a treaty and fall before it, can it be questioned whether the less power, an act of the State legislature, must not be prostrate? It is the declared will of the people of the United States that every treaty made by the authority of the United States shall be superior to the Constitution and laws of any individual State, and their will alone is to decide. If a law of a State contrary to a treaty is not void, but voidable only, by a repeal or nullification by a State legislature, this certain consequence follows,—that the will of a small part of the United States may control or defeat the will of the whole." ...

It must always be borne in mind that the Constitution, laws, and treaties of the United States are as much a part of the law of every State as its own local laws and Constitution. This is a fundamental principle in our system of complex national polity.... We have no doubt that this treaty is within the treaty-making power conferred by the Constitution. And it is our duty to give it full effect....

The judgment of the Court of Appeals of Virginia ... will be reversed....

So ordered.

UNITED STATES V. SCHOONER PEGGY

1 Cranch (5 U.S.) 103 (1801)

In 1800, the American ship Trumbull *was commissioned by President Adams to apprehend and capture any vessels sailing under authority of the French Republic. Acting on these instructions, the commander of the* Trumbull *captured the French schooner* Peggy *off shore from Port au Prince, and brought her into port, where she was condemned as a lawful prize. The following year, while appeal to the Supreme Court was pending, the United States and France concluded a treaty of friendship that provided for the mutual restoration of captured property "not yet* definitely *condemned."*

Chief Justice **Marshall** delivered the opinion of the Court:

In this case the court is of opinion that the schooner *Peggy* is within the provisions of the treaty entered into with France and ought to be restored. This vessel is not considered as being definitely condemned....

The Constitution of the United States declares a treaty to be the supreme law of the land. Of consequence its obligation on the courts of the United States must be admitted.... But yet where a treaty is the law of the land, and as such affects the rights of parties litigating in court, that treaty as much binds those rights and is as much to be regarded by the court as an act of congress; and although restoration may be an executive, when viewed as a substantive, act independent of, and unconnected with, other circumstances, yet to condemn a vessel, the restoration of which is directed by a law of the land, would be a direct infraction of that law, and of consequence, improper.

It is in general true that the province of an appellate court is only to enquire whether a judgment when rendered was erroneous or not. But if subsequent to the judgment and before the decision of the appellate court, a law intervenes and positively changes the rule which governs, the law must be obeyed, or its obligation denied. If the law be constitutional, and of that no doubt in the present case has been expressed, I know of no court which can contest its obligation. It is true that in mere private cases between individuals, a court will and ought to struggle hard against a construction which will, by a retrospective operation, affect the rights of parties, but in great national concerns where individual rights, acquired by war, are sacrificed for national purposes, the contract, making the sacrifice, ought always to receive a construction conforming to its manifest import; and if the nation has given up the vested rights of its citizens, it is not for the court, but for the government, to consider whether it be a case proper for compensation. In such a case the court must decide according to existing laws, and if it be necessary to set aside a judgment, rightful when rendered, but which cannot be affirmed but in violation of law, the judgment must be set aside.

───────────── TAYLOR ET AL. V. MORTON ─────────────

23 Fed.Cas. 784 (No. 13,799)
(U.S. Circuit Court, Massachusetts, 1855)
Affirmed, 2 Black (67 U.S.) 481 (1862)

The 1832 commercial treaty between the United States and Russia stipulated that products imported into the U.S. from Russia would not be subjected to a higher rate of duty than like products imported from other countries. The U.S. Tariff Act of 1842 imposed a duty of $40 per ton on all hemp imported, except that from India, on which a duty of $25 was levied.

In 1846, Charles Taylor imported a quantity of hemp from Russia, and was required to pay duty of $40 per ton. Taylor claimed that the treaty with Russia should be controlling and brought suit against the collector of customs to recover the difference.

Justice **Curtis** (sitting as Circuit Judge):

.... By the eighth section of the first article of the Constitution, power is conferred on congress to regulate commerce with foreign nations, and to lay duties, and to make all laws necessary and proper for carrying those powers into execution. That the act now in question is within the legislative power of congress, unless that power is controlled by the treaty, is not doubted. It must be admitted, also, that in general, power to legislate on a particular subject, includes power to modify and repeal existing laws on that subject, and either substitute new laws in their place, or leave the subject without regulation, in those particulars to which the repealed laws applied. There is therefore nothing in the mere fact that a treaty is a law, which would prevent congress from repealing it. Unless it is for some reason distinguishable from other laws, the rule which it gives may be displaced by the legislative power, at its pleasure.

The first and most obvious distinction between a treaty and an act of congress is, that the former is made by the president and ratified by two-thirds of the senators present; the latter by majorities of both houses of congress and the president, or by the houses only, by constitutional majorities, if the president refuses his assent. Ordinarily, it is certainly true, that the powers of enacting and repealing laws reside in the same persons. But there is no reason, in the nature of things, why it may not be otherwise. . . . I think it is impossible to maintain that, under our constitution, the president and senate exclusively, possess the power to modify or repeal a law found in a treaty. If this were so, inasmuch as they can change or abrogate one treaty, only by making another inconsistent with the first, the government of the United States could not act at all, to that effect, without the consent of some foreign government; for no new treaty, affecting, in any manner, one already in existence, can be made without the concurrence of two parties, one of whom must be a foreign sovereign. That the constitution was designed to place our country in this helpless condition, is a supposition wholly inadmissable. It is not only inconsistent with the necessities of a nation, but negatived by the express words of the Constitution. That gives to congress, in so many words, power to declare war, an act which, *ipso jure,* repeals all provisions of all existing treaties with the hostile nation, inconsistent with a state of war. To refuse to execute a treaty, for reasons which approve themselves to the conscientious judgment of the nation, is a matter of the utmost gravity and delicacy; but the power to do so, is prerogative, of which no nation can be deprived, without deeply affecting its independence. That the people of the United States have deprived their government of this power in any case, I do not believe. That it must reside somewhere, and be applicable to all cases, I am convinced. I feel no doubt that it belongs to congress. That, inasmuch as treaties must continue to operate as part of our municipal law, and be obeyed by the people, applied by the judiciary and executed by the president, while they continue unrepealed, and inasmuch as the power of repealing these municipal laws must reside somewhere, and no body other than congress possesses it, then legislative power is applicable to such laws whenever they relate to subjects, which the constitution has placed under that legislative power. . . .

Is it a judicial question, whether a treaty with a foreign sovereign has been violated by him; whether the consideration of a particular stipulation in a treaty, has been voluntarily withdrawn by one party, so that it is no longer obligatory on the other; whether the views and acts of a foreign sovereign, manifested through his representative have given just occasion to the political departments of our government to withhold the execution of a promise contained in a treaty, or to act in direct contravention of such promise? I apprehend not. These powers have not been confided by the people to the judiciary, which has no suitable means to exercise them; but to the executive and the legislative departments of our government. They belong to diplomacy and legislation, and not to the administration of existing laws. And it necessarily follows, that if they are denied to congress and the executive, in the exercise of their legislative power, they can be found nowhere, in our system of government. On the other hand, if it be admitted that congress has these powers, it is wholly immaterial to inquire whether they have, by the act in question, departed from the treaty or not; or if they have, whether such departure were accidental or designed, and if the latter, whether the reasons therefore were good or bad. If by the act in question they have not departed from the treaty, the plaintiff has no case. If they have, their act is the municipal law of the country, and any complaint, either by the citizen, or the foreigner, must be made to those, who alone are empowered by the Constitution, to judge of its grounds, and act as may be suitable and just. . . .

For these reasons, I am of opinion that, inasmuch as the duty paid in this case was duly assessed and levied pursuant to the act of congress, there is no further or other question to be tried, and the plaintiffs cannot recover. I desire to add, what perhaps is not necessary, that the various suppositions of violation or departure from treaties by foreign sovereigns, or by our country, which are put by way of argument in the course of this opinion, have no reference whatever to the treaty now in question, or to any actual case; that I have not formed, or intended to intimate, any opinion, upon the question whether the duty levied upon hemp, the product of Russia, is, or is not higher, than a just interpretation and application of the treaty with the sovereign of that country would allow; as, in my judgment, it belongs to the political department of the government of the United States to determine this question.

—————————————— HEAD MONEY CASES ——————————————

112 U.S. 580 (1884)

In 1882 Congress enacted legislation requiring ship owners to pay a duty of fifty cents for every passenger entering the United States who was not an American citizen. The Act provided that the money collected would be paid into the Treasury for the establishment of an immigrant fund to be used to defray the expenses of regulating immigration and for the care of immigrants in distress. In 1884, partners in a New York shipping firm brought action contesting the requirement, arguing that Congress lacked constitutional authority to impose such a levy, and that the Act violated American treaty obligations.

The Circuit Court for the Southern District of New York dismissed the complaint, and the petitioners appealed to the Supreme Court on a Writ of Error.

Justice **Miller** delivered the opinion of the Court:

. . . . The precise question involved here, namely, a supposed conflict between an act of Congress imposing a customs duty, and a treaty with Russia on that subject, in force when the act was passed, came before the Circuit Court for the District of Massachusetts in 1855. It received the consideration of that eminent jurist, Mr. Justice Curtis of this court, who in a very learned opinion exhausted the sources of argument on the subject, holding that if there were such conflict the act of Congress must prevail in a judicial forum. And Mr. Justice Field, in a very recent case in the Ninth Circuit has delivered an opinion sustaining the same doctrine in reference to a statute regulating the immigration of Chinamen into this country....

It is very difficult to understand how any different doctrine can be sustained.

A treaty is primarily a compact between independent nations. It depends for the enforcement of its provisions on the interest and the honor of the governments which are parties to it. If these fail, its infraction becomes the subject of international negotiations and reclamations, so far as the injured party chooses to seek redress, which may in the end be enforced by actual war. It is obvious that with all this the judicial courts have nothing to do and can give no redress. But a treaty may also contain provisions which confer certain rights upon the citizens or subjects of one of the nations residing in the territorial limits of the other, which partake of the nature of municipal law, and which are capable of enforcement as between private parties in the courts of the country. An illustration of this character is found in treaties, which regulate the mutual rights of citizens and subjects of the contracting nations in regard to rights of property by descent or inheritance, when the individuals concerned are aliens. The Constitution of the United States places such provisions as these in the same category as other laws of Congress by its declaration that "this Constitution and the laws made in pursuance thereof, and all treaties made or which shall be made under authority of the United States, shall be the supreme law of the land." A treaty, then, is a law of the land as an act of Congress is, whenever its provisions prescribe a rule by which the rights of the private citizen or subject may be determined. And when such rights are of a nature to be enforced in a court of justice, that court resorts to the treaty for a rule of decision for the case before it as it would to a statute.

But even in this aspect of the case there is nothing in this law which makes it irrepealable or unchangeable. The Constitution gives it no superiority over an act of Congress in this respect, which may be repealed or modified by an act of a later date. Nor is there anything in its essential character, or in the branches of the government by which the treaty is made, which gives it this superior sanctity.

A treaty is made by the President and the Senate. Statutes are made by the President, the Senate and the House of Representatives. The addition of the latter body to the other two in making a law certainly does not render it less entitled to respect in the matter of its repeal or modification than a treaty made by the other two. If there be any difference in this regard, it would seem to be in favor of an act in which all three of the bodies participate. And such is, in fact, the case in a declaration of war, which must be made by Congress, and which, when made, usually suspends or destroys existing treaties between the nations thus at war.

In short, we are of opinion that, so far as a treaty made by the United States with any foreign nation can become the subject of judicial cognizance in the courts of this country, it is subject to such acts as Congress may pass for its enforcement, modification, or repeal. . . .

The judgment of the Circuit Court in all the cases is

Affirmed.

WHITNEY V. ROBERTSON

124 U.S. 190 (1888)

In 1867, the United States ratified a treaty with the Dominican Republic whereby the two countries agreed not to enact discriminatory legislation against one another's products in favor of similar articles imported from other countries. Eight years later, the U.S. ratified a treaty with Hawaii that provided for duty-free trade between the two countries.

In 1882, Whitney, a New York merchant, imported a large quantity of molasses from the Dominican Republic that was similar to sugars imported duty-free from Hawaii. Whitney paid the duty levied on the molasses, but brought suit to recover the money based on the 1867 treaty provisions. The Circuit Court rendered judgment for Robertson, the tax collector, and Whitney appealed on a Writ of Error.

Justice **Field** delivered the opinion of the Court:

. . . . The act of Congress under which the duties were collected authorized their exaction. It is of general application, making no exception in favor of goods of any country. It was passed after the treaty with the Dominican Republic, and, if there be any conflict between the stipulations of the treaty and the requirements of the law, the latter must control. A treaty is primarily a contract between two or more independent nations, and is so regarded by writers on public law. For the infraction of its provisions a remedy must be sought by the injured party through reclamations upon the other. When the stipulations are not self-executing they can only be enforced pursuant to legislation to carry them into effect, and such legislation is as much subject to modification and repeal by Congress as legislation upon any other subject. If the treaty contains stipulations which are self-executing, that is, require no legislation to make them operative, to that extent they have the force and effect of a legislative enactment. Congress may modify such provisions, so far as they bind the United States, or supersede them altogether. By the Constitution a treaty is placed on the same footing, and made of like obligation, with an act of legislation. Both are declared by that instrument to be the supreme law of the land, and no superior efficacy is given to either over the other. When the two relate to the same subject, the courts will always endeavor to construe them so as to give effect to both, if that can be done without violating the language of either; but if the two are inconsistent, the one last in date will control the other, provided always the stipulation of the treaty on the subject is self-executing. If the country with which the treaty is made is dissatisfied with the action of the legislative department, it may present its complaint to the executive head of the government, and take such other measures as it may deem essential for the protection of its interests. The courts can afford no redress. Whether the complaining nation has just cause of complaint, or our country was justified in its legislation, are not matters for judicial cognizance. In *Taylor v. Morton,* this subject was very elaborately considered at the circuit by Mr. Justice Curtis, of this court, and he held that whether a treaty with a foreign sovereign had been violated by him; whether the consideration of a particular stipulation of the treaty had been voluntarily withdrawn by one party so that it was no longer obligatory on the other; whether the views and acts of a foreign sovereign had given just occasion to the legislative department of our government to withhold the execution of a promise contained in a treaty, or to act in direct contravention of such promise, were not judicial questions; that the power to determine these matters had not been confided to the judiciary, which has no suitable means to exercise it, but to the executive and legislative departments of our government; and that they belong to diplomacy and legislation, and not to the administration of the laws. And he justly observed, as a necessary consequence of these views, that if the power to determine these matters is vested in Congress, it is wholly immaterial to inquire whether by the act assailed it has departed from the treaty or not, or whether such departure was by accident or design, and, if the latter, whether the reasons were good or bad.

In these views we fully concur. It follows, therefore, that when a law is clear in its provisions, its validity cannot be assailed before the courts for want of conformity to stipulations of a previous treaty not already executed. Considerations of that character belong to another department of the government. The duty of the courts is to construe and give effect to the latest expression of the sovereign will.

Judgment affirmed.

Cook v. United States

288 U.S. 102 (1933)

After adoption of the Eighteenth Amendment [Prohibition], the United States concluded a treaty with Great Britain in 1924 authorizing the search and seizure of British vessels suspected of carrying liquor that were located within one hour's sailing distance of the United States. The treaty modified earlier statutes which authorized a four-league [12 mile] limit for such searches and seizures. Cook was the owner of a British-flag vessel, ostensibly bound for Nassau, that was seized by the Coast Guard in international waters 11½ miles off the Massachusetts coast carrying a large supply of unmanifested intoxicating liquor. Based on the Treaty provision, Cook contested the seizure, and was upheld by the district court. The circuit court of appeals reversed, and the Supreme Court granted certiorari.

Justice **Brandeis** delivered the opinion of the Court:

The main question for decision is whether . . . the Tariff Act . . . is modified . . . by the Treaty between the country and Great Britain proclaimed May 22, 1924.

. . . . The Treaty, being later in date than the Act of 1922, superseded, so far as inconsistent with the terms of the Act, the authority which had been conferred by [the Act] upon officers of the Coast Guard to board, search and seize beyond our territorial waters. For in a strict sense the Treaty was self-executing, in that no legislation was necessary to authorize executive action pursuant to its provisions....

The Treaty was not abrogated by reenacting [section] 581 in the Tariff Act of 1930 in the identical terms of the Act of 1922. A treaty will not be deemed to have been abrogated or modified by a later statute unless such purpose on the part of Congress has been clearly expressed. Here, the contrary appears. The committee reports and the debates upon the Act of 1930, like the reenacted section itself, make no reference to the Treaty of 1924. Any doubt as to the construction of the section should be deemed resolved by the consistent departmental practice existing before its reenactment....

Searches and seizures in the enforcement of the laws prohibiting alcoholic liquors are governed, since the 1930 Act, as they were before, by the provisions of the Treaty. [The Tariff Act], with its scope narrowed by the Treaty, remained in force after its reenactment in the Act of 1930. The section continued to apply to the boarding, search and seizure of all vessels of all countries with which we had no relevant treaties. It continued also, in the enforcement of our customs laws not related to the prohibition of alcoholic liquors, to govern the boarding of vessels of those countries with which we had entered into treaties like that with Great Britain....

*The decree of the Circuit Court of Appeals is **Reversed**.*

*Justice **Sutherland** and Justice **Butler**, dissenting.*

GEOFROY V. RIGGS

133 U.S. 258 (1890)

Two separate conventions between the United States and France, concluded in 1800 and 1853, respectively, provided reciprocal rights for French and American citizens to acquire and inherit property in both countries. In 1888, Lawson Riggs, a wealthy American landowner, died in Washington, D.C. without having made a will. The inheritance was contested by Riggs' brother and sisters, who were American citizens, and his nephews, who were citizens of France. The nephew's suit was dismissed by the Supreme Court of the District of Columbia, and they appealed.

Justice **Field** delivered the opinion of the Court:

.... The question presented for solution ... is whether the complainants, being citizens and residents of France, inherit an interest in the real estate in the District of Columbia of which their uncle, a citizen of the United States and a resident of the District, died seized. In more general terms the question is: can citizens of France take land in the District of Columbia by descent from citizens of the United States?....

On the 30th of September, 1800, a convention of peace, commerce and navigation was concluded between France and the United States, the 7th article of which provided that "the citizens and inhabitants of the United

States shall be at liberty to dispose by testament, donation or otherwise, of their goods, movable and immovable, holden in the territory of the French Republic in Europe, and the citizens of the French Republic shall have the same liberty with regard to goods movable and immovable, holden in the territory of the United States, in favor of such persons as they shall think proper. The citizens and inhabitants of either of the two countries, who shall be heirs of goods, movable or immovable, in the other, shall be able to succeed *ab intestato*, without being obliged to obtain letters of naturalization, and without having the effect of this provision contested or impeded under any pretext whatever."

This article, by its terms, suspended, during the existence of the treaty, the provisions of the common law of Maryland and of the statutes of that State of 1780 and of 1791, so far as they prevented citizens of France from taking by inheritance from citizens of the United States, property, real or personal, situated therein.

That the treaty power of the United States extends to all proper subjects of negotiation between our government and the governments of other nations, is clear. It is also clear that the protection which should be afforded to the citizens of one country owning property in another, and the manner in which that property may be transferred, devised or inherited, are fitting subjects for such negotiation and of regulation by mutual stipulations between the two countries. As commercial intercourse increases between different countries the residence of citizens of one country within the territory of the other naturally follows, and the removal of their disability from alienage to hold, transfer and inherit property in such cases tends to promote amicable relations. Such removal has been within the present century the frequent subject of treaty arrangement. The treaty power, as expressed in the Constitution, is in terms unlimited except by those restraints which are found in that instrument against the action of the government or of its departments, and those arising from the nature of the government itself and of that of the States. It would not be contended that it extends so far as to authorize what the Constitution forbids, or a change in the character of the government or in that of one of the States, or a cession of any portion of the territory of the latter, without its consent. But with these exceptions, it is not perceived that there is any limit to the questions which can be adjusted touching any matter which is properly the subject of negotiation with a foreign country....

Reversed.

TUCKER V. ALEXANDROFF

183 U.S. 424 (1902)

Alexandroff, a recruit in the Russian navy, was ordered to Philadelphia along with other Russian sailors to become part of the crew of a Russian ship still under construction. Alexandroff deserted, went to New York, renounced his Russian citizenship, and declared his intention to become a U.S. citizen. Pursuant to a warrant sworn out by the Russian consul

(Tucker), he was arrested by U.S. authorities and imprisoned pending orders from the captain of the Russian vessel. Alexandroff petitioned for a writ of habeas corpus *which was granted by the U.S. District Court and approved by the Circuit Court for the Third Circuit. The Supreme Court granted* certiorari.

Justice **Brown** delivered the opinion of the Court:

. . . . The vice-consul, who prosecutes this appeal on behalf of the Russian government, relies chiefly upon Art. IX of the treaty of December, 1832, which reads as follows: "The said Consuls, Vice–Consuls and Commercial Agents are authorized to require the assistance of the local authorities, for the search, arrest, detention and imprisonment of the deserters from the ships of war and merchant vessels of their country. For this purpose they shall apply to the competent tribunals, judges and officers, and shall in writing demand said deserters, proving by the exhibition of the registers of the vessels, the rolls of the crews, or by other official documents, that such individuals formed part of the crews; and, this reclamation being thus substantiated, the surrender shall not be refused." . . .

We are cited to no case holding that courts have the power, in the absence of treaty stipulations, to order the arrest and return of seamen deserting from foreign ships; and it would appear there was no such power in this country, inasmuch as [the statutes] under which the commissioner is bound to proceed, limits his jurisdiction to applications by a consul or vice-consul of a foreign government *"having a treaty with the United States"* for that purpose. . . .

The only case in our reports even indirectly considering such a case as one of international comity is that of the *Exchange*. . . . This court, through Mr. Chief Justice Marshall, held that . . . "perfect equality and absolute independence of sovereigns, and this common interest impelling them to mutual intercourse, and an interchange of good offices with each other, have given rise to a class of cases in which every sovereign is understood to waive the exercise of a part of that complete exclusive territorial jurisdiction, which has been stated to be the attribute of every nation." He divided these cases into three classes:

1. The exemption of the person of the sovereign from arrest or detention in a foreign country.

2. The immunity which all civilized nations allow to foreign ministers.

3. Where the sovereign allows the troops of a foreign prince to pass through his dominions.

. . . . But whatever view might be taken of the question of delivering over foreign seamen in the absence of a treaty, we are of opinion that the treaty with Russia, having contained a convention upon this subject, that convention must alone be looked to in determining the rights of the Russian authorities to the reclamation of the relator. Where the signatory powers have themselves fixed the terms upon which deserting seamen shall be surrendered, we have no right to enlarge those powers upon the principles of comity so as to embrace cases not contemplated by the treaty. Upon general principles applicable to the construction of written instruments, the enumeration of certain powers with respect to a particular subject matter is a negation of all other analogous powers with respect to the same subject matter. . . .

As treaties are solemn engagements entered into between independent nations for the common advancement of their interests and the interests of civilization, and as their main object is not only to avoid war and secure a lasting and perpetual peace, but to promote a friendly feeling between the people of the two countries, they should be interpreted in that broad and liberal spirit which is calculated to make for the existence of a perpetual amity, so far as it can be done without the sacrifice of individual rights or those principles of personal liberty which lie at the foundation of our jurisprudence. . . .

We are of opinion that this case is within the treaty, and the judgments of both courts below are therefore reversed, and the case remanded to the District Court for the Eastern District of Pennsylvania for further proceedings consistent with this opinion.

Justice **Gray**, *joined by Chief Justice* **Fuller** *and Justices* **Harlan** *and* **White**, *dissenting.*

--------------- REID V. COVERT ---------------

354 U.S. 1 (1957)

Mrs. Clarice Covert was accused of killing her husband, a sergeant in the United States Air Force, at an airbase in England. Mrs. Covert, who was not a member of the armed services, was residing with her husband on the base at the time. Under an executive agreement between the United States and Great Britain, American military courts were given exclusive jurisdiction over offenses committed by American servicemen and their dependents. Mrs. Covert was tried by court-martial, convicted, and sentenced to life imprisonment. She appealed, claiming that the denial of trial by jury violated her rights under the Fifth and Sixth Amendments.

Justice **Black** delivered the opinion of the Court:

At the beginning we reject the idea that when the United States acts against citizens abroad it can do so free of the Bill of Rights. The United States is entirely a creature of the Constitution. Its power and authority have no other source. It can only act in accordance with all the limitations imposed by the Constitution. When the Government reaches out to punish a citizen who is abroad, the shield which the Bill of Rights and other parts of the Constitution provide to protect his life and liberty should not be stripped away just because he happens to be in another land.

. . . . Even though a court-martial does not give an accused trial by jury and other Bill of Rights protections, the Government contends that Art. 2(11) of the U[niform] C[ode] [of] M[ilitary] J[ustice], insofar as it provides for the military trial of dependents accompanying the armed forces in Great Britain and Japan, can be sustained as legislation which is necessary and proper to carry out the United States' obligations under the international agreements made with those countries. The obvious and decisive answer to this, of course, is that no agreement with a foreign nation can confer power on the Congress, or on any other branch of Government, which is free from the restraints of the Constitution.

Article VI, the Supremacy Clause of the Constitution, declares:

> "This Constitution, and the Laws of the United States which shall be made in Pursuance thereof; and all Treaties made, or which shall be made, under the Authority of the United States, shall be the supreme Law of the Land; . . . ."

There is nothing in this language which intimates that treaties and laws enacted pursuant to them do not have to comply with the provisions of the Constitution. Nor is there anything in the debates which accompanied the drafting and ratification of the Constitution which even suggests such a result. These debates as well as the history that surrounds the adoption of the treaty provision in Article VI make it clear that the reason treaties were not limited to those made in "pursuance" of the Constitution was so that agreements made by the United States under the Articles of Confederation, including the important peace treaties which concluded the Revolutionary War, would remain in effect. It would be manifestly contrary to the objectives of those who created the Constitution, as well as those who were responsible for the Bill of Rights—let alone alien to our entire constitutional history and tradition—to construe Article VI as permitting the United States to exercise power under an international agreement without observing constitutional prohibitions. In effect, such construction would permit amendment of that document in a manner not sanctioned by Article V. The prohibitions of the Constitution were designed to apply to all branches of the National Government and they cannot be nullified by the Executive or by the Executive and the Senate combined. . . .

This Court has also repeatedly taken the position that an Act of Congress, which must comply with the Constitution, is on a full parity with a treaty, and that when a statute which is subsequent in time is inconsistent with a treaty, the statute to the extent of conflict renders the treaty null. It would be completely anomalous to say that a treaty need not comply with the Constitution when such an agreement can be overridden by a statute that must conform to that instrument.

There is nothing in *Missouri v. Holland* which is contrary to the position taken here. There the Court carefully noted that the treaty involved was not inconsistent with any specific provision of the Constitution. The Court was concerned with the Tenth Amendment which reserves to the States or the people all power not delegated to the National Government. To the extent that the United States can validly make treaties, the people and the States have delegated their power to the National Government and the Tenth Amendment is no barrier.

In summary, we conclude that the Constitution in its entirety applied to the trial of . . . Mrs. Covert. Since [her] court-martial did not meet the requirements of Art. III, ss. 2 or the Fifth and Sixth Amendments we are compelled to determine if there is anything *within* the Constitution which authorizes the military trial of dependents accompanying the armed forces overseas....

Ours is a government of divided authority on the assumption that in division there is not only strength but freedom from tyranny. And under our Constitution courts of law alone are given power to try civilians for their offenses against the United States. The philosophy expressed by Lord Coke, speaking long ago from a wealth of experience, is still timely:

> "God send me never to live under the Law of Conveniency or Discretion. Shall the Soldier and Justice Sit on one Bench, the Trumpet will not let the Cryer speak in *Westminster–Hall*."

In ... *Reid v. Covert,* the judgment of the District Court directing that Mrs. Covert be released from custody is

Affirmed.

UNITED STATES V. PINK

315 U.S. 203 (1942)

The First Russian Insurance Company, organized under Czarist Russia, established a New York branch in 1907. In 1919, the Soviet government nationalized the country's insurance business and all property, wherever situated, of Russian insurance companies, including the First Russian Insurance Company. Despite the nationalization order, the First Russian Insurance Company continued to do business in New York until 1925, when the State Superintendent of Insurance (Pink), took possession of its assets to satisfy claims of American policyholders and creditors.

In 1933, the United States recognized the Soviet Union, and incident to that recognition accepted an assignment (known as the Litvinov Assignment) of Soviet claims arising out of the nationalization decree of 1919. In 1934, the United States brought action pursuant to that assignment, seeking to recover the assets of the First Russian Insurance Company remaining with Pink. Pink denied the U.S. claim, contending that the Soviet nationalization decrees had no extraterritorial effect, and were contrary to the public policy of the United States and the state of New York. The claim of the United States was dismissed by the New York Supreme Court, the New York Court of Appeals affirmed, and the U.S. appealed.

Justice **Douglas** delivered the opinion of the Court:

.... The contest here is between the United States and creditors of the Russian corporation who, we assume, are not citizens of this country and whose claims did not arise out of transactions with the New York branch. The United States is seeking to protect not only claims which it holds but also claims of its nationals.... The existence of such claims and their non-payment had for years been one of the barriers to recognition of the Soviet regime by the Executive Department. The purpose of the discussions leading to the policy of recognition was to resolve "all questions outstanding" between the two nations. Settlement of all American claims against Russia was one method of removing some of the prior objections to recognition based on the Soviet policy of nationalization. The Litvinov Assignment was not only part and parcel of the new policy of recognition, it was also the method adopted by the Executive Department for alleviating in this country the rigors of nationalization. Congress tacitly recognized that policy. Acting in anticipation of the realization of funds under the Litvinov Assignment, it authorized the appointment of a Commissioner to determine the claims of American nationals against the Soviet Government....

The powers of the President in the conduct of foreign relations included the power, without consent of the Senate, to determine the public policy of the United States with respect to the Russian nationalization decrees. "What government is to be regarded here as representative of a foreign sovereign state is a political rather than a judicial question, and is to be determined by the political department of the government." That authority is not limited to a determination of the government to be recognized. It includes the power to determine the policy which is to govern the question of recognition. Objections to the underlying policy as well as objections to recognition are to be addressed to the political department and not to the courts....

.... Power to remove such obstacles to full recognition as settlement of claims of our nationals certainly is a modest implied power of the President who is the "sole organ of the federal government in the field of international relations." Effectiveness in handling the delicate problems of foreign relations requires no less. Unless such a power exists, the power of recognition might be thwarted or seriously diluted. No such obstacle can be placed in the way of rehabilitation of relations between this country and another nation, unless the historic conception of the powers and responsibilities of the President in the conduct of foreign affairs is to be drastically revised. It was the judgment of the political department that full recognition of the Soviet Government required the settlement of all outstanding problems including the claims of our nationals. Recognition and the Litvinov Assignment were interdependent. We would usurp the executive function if we held that that decision was not final and conclusive in the courts....

It is, of course, true that even treaties with foreign nations will be carefully construed so as not to derogate from the authority and jurisdiction of the States of this nation unless clearly necessary to effectuate the national policy.... But state law must yield when it is inconsistent with, or impairs the policy or provisions of, a treaty or of an international compact or agreement. Then, the power of a State to refuse enforcement of rights based on foreign law which runs counter to the public policy of the forum must give way before the superior Federal policy evidenced by a treaty or international compact or agreement....

The action of New York in this case amounts in substance to a rejection of a part of the policy underlying recognition by this nation of Soviet Russia. Such power is not accorded a State in our constitutional system. To permit it would be to sanction a dangerous invasion of Federal authority. For it would "imperil the amicable relations between governments and vex the peace of nations." It would tend to disturb that equilibrium in our foreign relations which the political departments of our national government had diligently endeavored to establish.

.... No state can rewrite our foreign policy to conform to its own domestic policies. Power over external affairs is not shared by the States; it is vested in the national government exclusively. It need not be so exercised as to conform to state laws or state policies, whether they be expressed in constitutions, statutes, or judicial decrees. And the policies of the States become wholly irrelevant to judicial inquiry when the United States, acting within its constitutional sphere, seeks enforcement of its foreign policy in the courts.

We hold that the right to the funds or property in question became vested in the Soviet Government as the successor to the First Russian Insurance Co.; that this right has passed to the United States under the Litvinov Assignment; and that the United States is entitled to the property as against the corporation and the foreign creditors.

The judgment is reversed and the cause is remanded to the Supreme Court of New York for proceedings not inconsistent with this opinion.

Reversed.

Chief Justice **Stone, dissenting.**

WEINBERGER V. ROSSI

456 U.S. 25 (1982)

In 1968, the President concluded an Executive Agreement with the Philippines providing for the preferential employment of Filipino citizens at U.S. military bases in the Philippines. Two years later Congress enacted legislation prohibiting employment discrimination against U.S. citizens on military bases overseas unless permitted by "treaty." In 1978, Rossi and others, all United States citizens residing in the Philippines, were notified that their jobs at the U.S. Navy base at Subic Bay were being converted into local national positions in accord with the 1968 agreement, and that they would be discharged from their employment with the Navy. Rossi, et al., thereupon filed suit alleging that preferential treatment for Filipinos violated U.S. statutes. The U.S. District Court ruled in favor of the government, the court of appeals reversed, and the secretary of defense petitioned for certiorari.

Justice **Rehnquist** delivered the opinion of the Court:

.... The question in this case is whether "treaty" includes executive agreements concluded by the President with the host country, or whether the term is limited to those international agreements entered into by the President with the advice and consent of the Senate....

Simply because the question presented is entirely one of statutory construction does not mean that the question necessarily admits of an easy answer. Chief Justice Marshall long ago observed that "[w]here the mind labors to discover the design of the legislature, it seizes everything from which aid can be derived...." More recently, the Court has stated:

> "Generalities about statutory construction help us little. They are not rules of law but merely axioms of experience. They do not solve the special difficulties in constructing a particular statute. The variables render every problem of statutory construction unique." ....

The word "treaty" has more than one meaning. Under principles of international law, the word ordinarily refers to an international agreement concluded between sovereigns, regardless of the manner in which the agreement is brought into force. Under the United States Constitution, of course, the word "treaty" has a far more restrictive meaning. Article II, section 2, cl. 2, of that instrument provides that the President "shall have Power, by and with the Advice and Consent of the Senate, to make Treaties, provided two-thirds of the Senators present concur."

Congress has not been consistent in distinguishing between Art. II treaties and other forms of international agreements. . . .

The fact that Congress has imparted no precise meaning to the word "treaty" as that term is used in its various legislative Acts was recognized by this Court in *B. Altman & Co. v. United States,* 224 U.S. 583 (1912). There this Court construed "treaty" in section 5 of the Circuit Court of Appeals Act of 1891 to include international agreements concluded by the President under congressional authorization. The Court held that the word "treaty" in the jurisdictional statute extended to such an agreement, saying: "If not technically a treaty requiring ratification, nevertheless it was a compact authorized by the Congress of the United States, negotiated and proclaimed under the authority of its President. We think such a compact is a treaty under the Circuit Court of Appeals Act. . . ."

It has been a maxim of statutory construction since the decision in *Murray v. The Charming Betsy* (1804), that "an act of congress ought never to be construed to violate the law of nations, if any other possible construction remains. . . ." In *McCulloch v. Sociedad Nacional de Marineros de Honduras* (1963), this principle was applied to avoid construing the National Labor Relations Act in a manner contrary to State Department regulations, for such a construction would have been contrary to a "well-established rule of international law." While these considerations apply with less force to a statute which by its terms is designed to affect conditions on United States enclaves outside of the territorial limits of this country than they do to the construction of statutes couched in general language which are sought to be applied in an extraterritorial way, they are nonetheless not without force in either case.

At the time [the statute] was enacted, there were in force 12 agreements in addition to the [one with the Philippines] providing for preferential hiring of local nationals on United States military bases overseas. Since the time of the enactment of [the statute], four more such agreements have been concluded, and none of these were submitted to the Senate for its advice and consent. We think that some affirmative expression of congressional intent to abrogate the United States' international obligations is required in order to construe the word "treaty" in as meaning only Art. II treaties. . . .

While the question is not free from doubt, we conclude that the "treaty" exception contained in [the statute] extends to executive agreements as well as to Art. II treaties. The judgment of the Court of Appeals is reversed, and the case is remanded for proceedings consistent with this opinion.

It is so ordered.

———————— THE BRICKER AMENDMENT OF 1954 ————————

S.J.Res. 1
83rd Congress, 2d Session

Section 1. A provision of a treaty which conflicts with this Constitution shall not be of any force or effect.

Section 2. A treaty shall become effective as internal law in the United States only through legislation *which would be valid in the absence of treaty.*

Section 3. Congress shall have power to regulate all executive and other agreements with any foreign power or international organization. All such agreements shall be subject to the limitations imposed on treaties by this article.

Section 4. The Congress shall have power to enforce this article by appropriate legislation.

Section 5. This article shall be inoperative unless it shall have been ratified as an amendment to the Constitution by the legislatures of three-fourths of the several States within seven years from the date of its submission. [Emphasis supplied.]

[After President Eisenhower indicated his strong objection to the Bricker Amendment, the following substitute proposal, introduced by Senator Walter F. George (D–Ga.), was defeated 60–31 by the Senate on February 26, 1954.]

GEORGE SUBSTITUTE

Sec. 1. A provision of a treaty or other international agreement which conflicts with this Constitution shall not be of any force or effect.

Sec. 2. An international agreement other than a treaty shall become effective as internal law in the United States only by an act of the Congress.

Sec. 3. On the question of advising and consenting to the ratification of a treaty the vote shall be determined by yeas and nays, and the names of the persons voting for and against shall be entered on the Journal of the Senate.

Sec. 4. This article shall be inoperative unless it shall have been ratified as an amendment to the Constitution by the legislatures of three-fourths of the several States within 7 years from the date of its submission.

Suggested Reading

The classic studies of the treaty power are C. BUTLER, THE TREATY–MAKING POWER OF THE UNITED STATES (1902); S. CRANDALL, TREATIES, THEIR MAKING AND ENFORCEMENT (2 ed. 1916); C. HAYDEN, THE SENATE AND TREATIES; W. HOLT, TREATIES DEFEATED BY THE SENATE (1933); and W. MALLOY, TREATIES, CONVENTIONS, INTERNATIONAL ACTS, PROTOCOLS AND AGREEMENTS BETWEEN THE UNITED STATES AND OTHER POWERS. On the intention of the Framers, see David Gray Adler, *Framers and Treaty Termination: A Matter of Symmetry,* 1981 ARIZONA STATE LAW JOURNAL 891.

Before 1950, American treaties and executive agreements were published in the United States Statutes-at-Large with an index at 64 Stat. B1107. From 1950 onward they have been published by the Department of State in a new series, *U.S. Treaties and Other International Agreements* which is usually abbreviated TIAS.

On specialized subjects dealing with the treaty power, see Manley O. Hudson, *The 'Injunction of Secrecy' With Respect to American Treaties,* 23 AMERICAN JOURNAL OF INTERNATIONAL LAW 329 (1929); A. Sutherland, *Restricting the Treaty Power,* 65 HARVARD LAW REVIEW 1305 (1952); Mikell, *The Extent of the Treaty–Making Power of the President and Senate of the United States,* 57 UNIVERSITY OF PENNSYLVANIA LAW REVIEW 435 (1909); Quincy Wright, *The Constitutionality of Treaties,* 13 AMERICAN JOURNAL OF INTERNATIONAL LAW 242 (1919), and Louis Henkin, *The Treaty Makers and the Law Makers: The Law of the Land and Foreign Relations,* 107 UNIVERSITY OF PENNSYLVANIA LAW REVIEW 903 (1959).

For further study of Executive Agreements, see W. MCCLURE, INTERNATIONAL EXECUTIVE AGREEMENTS: THE DEMOCRATIC PROCEDURE UNDER THE CONSTITUTION OF THE UNITED STATES (1941); Mathews, *The Constitutional Power of the President to Conclude International Agreements,* 64 YALE LAW REVIEW 345 (1955). On the conflict between President and Congress, see the two articles by G.J. Schmitt, *Separation of Powers: Introduction to the Study of Executive Agreements,* 27 AMERICAN JOURNAL OF JURISPRUDENCE 114 (1982); *Executive Agreements and Separation of Powers: A Reconsideration,* 28 AMERICAN JOURNAL OF JURISPRUDENCE 189 (1983); M.J. Glennon, *Senate Role in Treaty Ratification,* 77 AMERICAN JOURNAL OF INTERNATIONAL LAW 257 (1983); and most topically, A.D. Sofaer, *The ABM Treaty and the Strategic Defense Initiative,* 99 HARVARD LAW REVIEW 1972 (1986).

Notes

1. But compare Hamilton's view in *Federalist* 64 that the president must often seize the initiative without benefit of the Senate's advice.

2. As quoted in 3 M. FERRAND, THE RECORDS OF THE FEDERAL CONVENTION OF 1787 424 (1937).

3. For details of Washington's unsatisfactory efforts to involve the Senate in treaty negotiations, see CORWIN, THE PRESIDENT: OFFICE AND POWERS 207–217 (1957).

4. In this connection see S. CRANDALL, TREATIES, THEIR MAKING AND ENFORCEMENT sec. 53 (1916).

5. J. MADISON, WRITINGS 264 (Hunt ed. 1906).

6. 182 U.S. 1, 198 (1901).

7. 1 W. WILLOUGHBY, THE CONSTITUTIONAL LAW OF THE UNITED STATES 555 (1929).

8. 2 STORY, COMMENTARIES, section 1403 (1833).

9. See E. Borchard, *Shall the Executive Agreement Replace the Treaty,* 53 YALE LAW JOURNAL 644 (1944); M. McDougal and A. Lans, *Treaties and Congressional–Executive or Presidential Agreements: Interchangeable Instruments of National Policy,* 54 YALE LAW JOURNAL 181, 534 (1945); Borchard, *Treaties and Executive Agreements—A Reply, Id.,* at 616.

4

THE DOCTRINE OF POLITICAL QUESTIONS

FOREIGN RELATIONS ARE by definition political relations and are the responsibility of the political branches of government—the president and Congress—not the courts. Not only do foreign relations derive from the nation's sovereignty and thus lie outside the Constitutional grant of powers, but they deal with inherently political issues. As a result, the courts will rarely, if ever, intervene in fundamental matters of foreign policy. The constitutionality of the war in Vietnam, President Carter's unilateral decision to terminate America's defense treaty with Taiwan, and the conduct and discipline of the armed forces have all been ruled "political questions" and are therefore beyond the scrutiny of the courts.

The doctrine of political questions arises from the separation of powers. Under the Constitution, national authority is divided among three branches of government—legislative, executive, and judicial—each coordinate and coequal. The domestic structure of government depends on the dynamic interplay among these branches and the overlapping power they share.

But foreign relations are not subject to the same constraints as domestic relations. Foreign relations are the distinctive responsibility of the president and Congress. The doctrine of political questions, which is a judicial construct, allows the Court to step aside gracefully from matters not properly within its ken. Although the doctrine is often criticized and somewhat formless in its dimensions, it is essentially a doctrine of judicial discretion that keeps the Court from becoming embroiled in the nation's foreign policy.

The doctrine of political questions is also uniquely American, both in its origin and its exercise. Countries with parliamentary regimes usually subscribe to the theory of parliamentary supremacy. Judicial authority is constitutionally subordinate. There is no possibility for the courts to embarrass or restrain government's conduct of foreign policy. The same holds true in authoritarian or one-party regimes. But in the United States, where the Supreme Court is an equal participant in power, genuine confusion might ensue if the Court took one position on foreign policy, while the president and Congress maintained another. Thus, the doctrine of political questions allows the Court to defer to the "political branches."

The basis for the Supreme Court's authority to exercise judicial review stems from the landmark decision written by Chief Justice John Marshall in *Marbury v. Madison.*[1] Marshall hinged the Court's authority on three principles: First, the Constitution, framed by the people, was superior to ordinary statute law passed by Congress. Second, the Constitution was law and could thus be adjudicated by the courts. Third, the decision of the courts on matters of law were absolute and final. The ultimate authority of the Supreme Court in constitutional matters has evolved from these three principles.

But in *Marbury v. Madison* Marshall also recognized that not all constitutional issues were legal issues. Some were clearly *political* and thus outside the jurisdiction of the Court. "[T]he Constitution," said Marshall, invests the president "with certain important political powers, in the exercise of which he is to use his own discretion, and is accountable only to his country in his political character, and to his own conscience." Accordingly,

> Whatever opinion may be entertained of the manner in which executive discretion may be used, still there exists, and can exist, no power to control that discretion. The subjects are political. They respect the nation, not individual rights, and being entrusted to the executive, the decision of the executive is conclusive.

This is particularly true in foreign relations. For example, the early case of *United States v. Palmer* involved various insurrections against Spanish rule in Latin America. The Supreme Court, again speaking through Marshall, held that the status of the numerous revolutionary movements was a political question. In such matters the courts must be guided by the decisions of president and Congress.

The leading foreign policy case involving application of the political questions doctrine is *Foster v. Neilson,* a controversy arising out of conflicting land claims in West Florida—the region along the Gulf Coast between the Mississippi and Perdido Rivers. Chief Justice Marshall held that, regardless of the normal rules of property law, the Court was bound by the action of the president and Congress who claimed the land for the United States. According to Marshall:

> If those departments which are intrusted with the foreign intercourse of the nation, which assert and maintain its interests against foreign powers, have unequivocally asserted its right of dominion over a country of which it is in possession, and which it claims under a treaty; if the legislature has acted on the construction thus asserted, it is not in its own courts that this construction is to be denied. *A question like this respecting the boundaries of nations, is,* as has been truly said, *more a political than a legal question,* and in its discussion, the courts of every country must respect the pronounced will of the legislature.

Marshall was concerned that the conduct of U.S. foreign policy be unified and that the Supreme Court should not proceed haphazardly to intrude its judgment on matters contrary to the pronounced will of the government. The doctrine was even more clearly enunciated by the Taney Court in 1839 in the case of *Williams v. Suffolk Insurance Co.* The issue involved sovereignty over the Falkland Islands. The Argentines were in obvious possession, but the United States recognized Great Britain's claim to the islands. President Jackson had stated explicitly that the islands were not part of Argentina. In upholding the president's decision, the Supreme Court said: "Can there be any doubt, that when the executive branch of the government, which is charged with our foreign relations, shall, in its correspondence with a foreign nation, assume a fact in regard to the sovereignty of any island or country, it is conclusive on the judicial department? *And in this view, it is not material to inquire, nor is it in the province of the court to determine, whether the executive be right or wrong. It is enough to know, that in the exercise of his constitutional functions, he has decided the question. Having done this . . . it is obligatory on the people and government of the Union.*" (Emphasis added.)

Justice McLean explained that "If this were not the rule, cases might often arise, in which, on most important questions of foreign jurisdiction, there would be an irreconcilable difference between the executive and judicial departments. By one of those departments, a foreign island or country might be considered as at peace with the United States; whilst the other could consider it in a state of war. No well-regulated government has ever sanctioned a principle so unwise, and so destructive of national character."

Thus, in *Doe v. Braden* the question of Spain's 1819 ratification of a treaty with the United States was held to be a political question decided by the president, not the courts. In *Jones v. United States* in 1890, the Court reaffirmed that "Who is the sovereign, *de jure* or *de facto*, of a territory is not a judicial, but a political question," and in *Neely v. Henkel* (1901), the duration of the American military occupation of Cuba was held to be beyond judicial cognizance.

Chief Justice Fuller, speaking for the Court in *Terlinden v. Ames* the following year, stated that the executive, not the courts, should determine the obligations of a foreign country under a treaty. In the important case of *Oetjen v. Central Leather Company* involving action by General "Pancho" Villa during the Mexican revolution, the Court applied the Act of State doctrine (see Chapter 2) to acts taken by Villa during the struggle. Said the Court:

> The conduct of the foreign relations of our Government is committed by the Constitution to the Executive and Legislature—"the political"—Departments of the Government, and the propriety of what may be done in the exercise of this political power is not subject to judicial inquiry or decision.

MODERN HOLDINGS

After World War II, Justice Jackson, speaking for the Court in *Chicago and Southern Airlines v. Waterman,* upheld the broad powers of the president to act on behalf of the United States in foreign affairs. Elaborating on the necessity for judicial abstinence, Jackson stated that "The President, both as Commander in Chief and as the Nation's organ for foreign affairs, has available intelligence services whose reports are not and ought not to be published to the world. It would be intolerable that courts, without the relevant information, should review and perhaps nullify actions of the Executive taken on information properly held secret. Nor can courts sit *in camera* in order to be taken into executive confidences. But even if courts could require full disclosure, the very nature of executive decisions as to foreign policy is political, not judicial. Such decisions are wholly confided by our Constitution on the political departments of the government, Executive and Legislative. They are delicate, complex, and involve large elements of prophecy. They are and should be undertaken only by those directly responsible to the people whose welfare they advance or imperil. They are decisions of a kind for which the Judiciary has neither aptitude, facilities nor responsibility and which has long been held to belong in the domain of political power not subject to judicial intrusion or inquiry."

Similarly, in *Ludecke v. Watkins* which involves the president's authority to order the deportation of a German alien after the cessation of hostilities in 1945, Justice Frankfurter said for the Court:

> War does not cease with a cease-fire order.... The Court would be assuming the functions of the political agencies of the Government to yield to the suggestion that the unconditional surrender of Germany and the disintegration of the Nazi Reich have left Germany without a government capable of negotiating a treaty of peace. It is not for us to question a belief by the President that enemy aliens ... do not lose their potency for mischief during the period of confusion and conflict which is characteristic of a state of war even when the guns are silent.... These are matters of political judgment for which judges have neither technical competence nor official responsibility.

IMPACT OF THE VIETNAM WAR

During the early 1960s there was some indication that the Court might be prepared to reconsider application of the doctrine of political questions to foreign relations. In *Baker v. Carr* for example, the Court rejected the applicability of the doctrine to legislative apportionment, and there was language in Justice Brennan's opinion that suggested foreign affairs would come under increasing judicial scrutiny. But with the Vietnam War the Court retreated to its traditional stance. Foreign relations were a political matter. Not one case contesting the constitutionality of the war in Vietnam ever came before the Supreme Court, and the lower courts consistently dismissed such actions, citing the doctrine of political questions. Although Justice Douglas consistently dissented from the Court's refusal to grant *certiorari* to the Vietnam cases, the outcome was to reemphasize that matters of war and peace should be left to the political branches.

Likewise, in *Gilligan v. Morgan* in 1972 the Court dismissed complaints about the level of training of the Ohio National Guard following the tragic events at Kent State. As Chief Justice Burger said for the Court: "It would be difficult to think of a clearer example of the type of governmental action that was intended by the Constitution to be left to the political branches directly responsible—as the Judicial Branch is not—to the political process. Moreover, it is difficult to conceive of an area—in which the courts have less competence. The complex, subtle, and professional decisions as to the composition, training, equipping, and control of a military force are essentially professional military judgments, subject *always* to civilian control of the Legislative and Executive Branches." Similarly, in *Schlesinger v. Ballard*, the Court, speaking this time through Justice Stewart, dismissed a challenge to Navy promotion criteria that appeared to favor women over men. "The responsibility for determining how best our Armed Forces shall attend to the business [of being] ready to fight wars should the occasion arise rests with the Congress and with the President."

Finally, in the leading case of *Goldwater v. Carter* in 1979, a plurality of the Court (Justice Rehnquist, Chief Justice Burger, Justices Stewart and Stevens) rejected a constitutional challenge by Senator Goldwater and others to President Carter's termination without Senate approval of the U.S. mutual defense treaty with the Republic of China (Taiwan). Said Justice Rehnquist, "In light of the absence of any constitutional provision governing the termination of a treaty, . . . the instant case in my view must surely be controlled by political standards."

The *Goldwater* decision has been cited with regularity by lower courts dismissing other appeals against executive action in foreign relations. It suggests that the views of the Framers and earlier Supreme Courts—that the foreign affairs power is largely beyond judicial review—continue to prevail.

UNITED STATES V. PALMER

3 Wheaton (16 U.S.) 610 (1818)

John Palmer, along with several associates, was indicted for piracy on the high seas stemming from an assault on the Spanish merchant ship Industria Raffaelli, *July 4, 1817. Palmer took valuable cargo, including large quantities of sugar, rum, silver and gold, and generally made the crew of the* Raffaelli *fear for their lives and safety. At trial Palmer produced evidence that he was acting under authority of Latin American revolutionaries led by Simón Bolívar. The United States did not recognize Bolívar's government at the time, although it did recognize that a state of civil war existed. The judges of the circuit court were divided as to whether charges of piracy could be sustained in this context and certified the question to the Supreme Court.*

Chief Justice **Marshall** delivered the opinion of the Court:

. . . Those questions which respect the rights of a part of a foreign empire, which asserts, and is contending for its independence, and the conduct which must be observed by the courts of the Union towards the subjects of such section of an empire who may be brought before the tribunals of this country, are equally delicate and difficult. As it is understood, that the construction which has been given to the act of congress, will render a particular answer to them unnecessary, the court will only observe, that such questions are generally political rather than legal in their character. They belong more properly to those who can declare what the law shall be; who can place the nation in such a position with respect to foreign powers as to their own judgment shall appear wise; to whom are intrusted all its foreign relations; than to that tribunal whose power as well as duty is confined to the application of the rule which the legislature may prescribe for it. In such contests, a nation may engage itself with the one party or the other; may observe absolute neutrality; may recognize the new state absolutely; or may make a limited recognition of it. The proceeding in courts must depend so entirely on the course of the government, that it is difficult to give a precise answer to questions which do not refer to a particular nation. It may be said generally, that if the government remains neutral, and recognizes the existence of a civil war, its courts cannot consider as criminal, those acts of hostility which war authorizes, and which the new government may direct against its enemy. To decide otherwise, would be to determine that the war prosecuted by one of the parties was unlawful, and would be to arrange the nation to which the court belongs against that party. This would transcend the limits prescribed to the judicial department....

.... This court is further of opinion, that when a civil war rages in a foreign nation, one part of which separates itself from the old established government, and erects itself into a distinct government, the courts of the Union must view such newly-constituted government as it is viewed by the legislative and executive departments of the government of the United States. If the government of the Union remains neutral, but recognizes the existence of a civil war, the courts of the Union cannot consider as criminal, those acts of hostility, which war authorizes, and which the new government may direct against its enemy. In general, the same testimony which would be sufficient to prove that a vessel or a person is in the service of an acknowledged state, must be admitted to prove that a vessel or person is in the service of such newly erected government....

FOSTER V. NEILSON

2 Peters (27 U.S.) 253 (1829)

By the treaty of St. Ildefonso (1800), Spain ceded the Louisiana territory to France; and France, by the treaty of Paris (1803), ceded it to the United States in the "Louisiana Purchase." As part of the Purchase, the United States claimed the lands between the Iberville and Perdido rivers, then known as West Florida, and what today constitutes the Gulf Coast of Alabama, Mississippi and that portion of Louisiana lying east of the Mississippi River. Spain contended that her cession to France included only that territory west of the Mississippi and the island of New Orleans and disputed the American claim to West Florida.

Foster and Elam claimed title to a tract of land in the disputed territory under a grant made by the Spanish governor of Florida and ratified by the king of Spain in 1804. Neilson held title to the same land under acts of Congress and the State of Louisiana. Foster and Elam brought suit to recover the land, and the U.S. District Court dismissed their claim, holding that the Spanish Governor had no authority in 1804 to grant lands in the territory. The plaintiffs appealed.

Chief Justice **Marshall** delivered the opinion of the Court:

... The case presents this very intricate, and at one time very interesting question: To whom did the country between the Iberville and the Perdido rightfully belong, when the title now asserted by the plaintiffs was acquired?

This question has been repeatedly discussed with great talent and research by the government of the United States and that of Spain. The United States have perseveringly and earnestly insisted that by the treaty of St. Ildefonso, made on the 1st of October, in the year 1800, Spain ceded the disputed territory as part of Louisiana to France; and that France, by the treaty of Paris ... ceded it to the United States. Spain has with equal perseverance and earnestness maintained, that her cession to France comprehended that territory only which was at that time denominated Louisiana, consisting of the island of New Orleans, and the country she received from France west of the Mississippi.

.... In a controversy between two nations concerning boundary, it is scarcely possible that the Courts of either should refuse to abide by the measures adopted by its own government. There being no common tribunal to decide between them, each determines for itself on its own rights, and if they cannot adjust their differences peaceably, the right remains with the strongest. The judiciary is not that department of the government, to which the assertion of its interests against foreign powers is confided; and its duty commonly is to decide upon individual rights, according to those principles which the political departments of the nation have established. If the course of the nation has been a plain one, its Courts would hesitate to pronounce it erroneous.

We think, then, however individual judges might construe the treaty of Ildefonso, it is the province of the Court to conform its decisions to the will of the legislature, if that will has been clearly expressed....

The convulsed state of European Spain affected her influence over her colonies; and a degree of disorder prevailed in the Floridas, at which the United States could not look with indifference. In October 1810, the president issued his proclamation, directing the governor of the Orleans territory to take possession of the country as far east as the Perdido, and to hold it for the United States. This measure was avowedly intended as an assertion of the title of the United States....

In April 1812, Congress passed "an act to enlarge the limits of the state of Louisiana." This act describes lines which comprehend the land in controversy and declares that the country included within them shall become and form a part of the state of Louisiana.

In May of the same year, another act was passed, annexing the residue of the country west of the Perdido to the Mississippi territory.

And in February 1813, the president was authorized "to occupy and hold all that tract of country called West Florida, which lies west of the river Perdido, not now in possession of the United States...."

After these acts of sovereign power over the territory in dispute, asserting the American construction of the treaty by which the government claims it, to maintain the opposite construction in its own Courts would certainly be an anomaly in the history and practice of nations. If those departments which are intrusted with the foreign intercourse of the nation, which assert and maintain its interests against foreign powers, have unequivocally asserted its rights of dominion over a country of which it is in possession, and which it claims under a treaty; if the legislature has acted on the construction thus asserted, it is not in its own Courts that this construction is to be denied. A question like this respecting the boundaries of nations, is, as has been truly said, more a political than a legal question, and in its discussion, the Courts of every country must respect the pronounced will of the legislature....

─────────── WILLIAMS V. SUFFOLK INSURANCE CO. ───────────

13 Peters (38 U.S.) 415 (1839)

In the early nineteenth century, Great Britain and the Republic of Buenos Ayres [Buenos Aires] both claimed sovereignty over the Falkland Islands. The Buenos Ayres government took control of the islands in 1829, established a settlement, and proclaimed a ban on seal fishing in territorial waters surrounding the islands. The American government refused to recognize the claim of Buenos Ayres to the Falklands, and insisted that "the seal fishery at those islands is a trade free and lawful to the citizens of the United States, and beyond the competency of the Buenos Ayres government to regulate, prohibit or punish." Two American sealing ships, Harriet and Breakwater, defied the Buenos Ayres ban and were seized and condemned by the Argentines. The vessels had been insured by the Suffolk Insurance Co., and the owners brought suit to recover.

Justice **McLean** delivered the opinion of the Court:

Prior to the revolution in South America, it is known that the Malvinas, or Falkland Islands, were attached to the vice-royalty of La Plata, which included Buenos Ayres. And if this were an open question, we might inquire whether the jurisdiction over these islands did not belong to some other part, over which this ancient vice-royalty extended, and not to the government of Buenos Ayres: but we are saved from this inquiry by the attitude of our own government....

And can there be any doubt, that when the executive branch of the government, which is charged with our foreign relations, shall in its correspondence with a foreign nation assume a fact in regard to the sovereignty of any island or country, it is conclusive on the judicial department? And in this view it is not material to inquire, nor is it the province of the Court to determine, whether the executive be right or wrong. It is enough to know, that in the exercise of his constitutional functions, he has decided the question. Having done this under the responsibilities which belong to him, it is obligatory on the people and government of the Union.

If this were not the rule, cases might often arise in which, on the most important questions of foreign jurisdiction, there would be an irreconcilable difference between the executive and judicial departments. By one of these departments, a foreign island or country might be considered as at peace with the United States; whilst the other would consider it in a state of war. No well regulated government has ever sanctioned a principle so unwise, and so destructive of national character. . . .

If these islands are not within the jurisdiction of the Buenos Ayrean government, the power assumed and exercised by Governor Vernet was unauthorized, and the master was not bound to regard it. He was not necessarily to be diverted from the objects of his voyage, and the exercise of rights which belonged in common to the citizens of the United States by an unauthorized threat to the seizure of his vessel. . . .

It was the duty of the master to prosecute his voyage, and attain the objects of it, for the benefit of his owners: and, in doing this, he was not bound to abandon the voyage by any threat of illegal seizure. We think, therefore, that the underwriters are not discharged from liability, by the conduct of the master. . . .

[I]t is the opinion of this Court, 1st, That, inasmuch as the American government has insisted and still does insist, through its regular executive authority, that the Falkland Islands do not constitute any part of the dominions within the sovereignty of the government of Buenos Ayres, the action of the American government on this subject is binding on the said Circuit Court, as to whom the sovereignty of those islands belongs. And, secondly: That the seizure and condemnation of the *Harriet* was a loss for which the plaintiff is entitled to recover in this case.

[After seizure of the Harriet *and* Breakwater *by the Buenos Ayres authority, the U.S. sloop-of-war* Lexington *proceeded to the Falklands, laid waste the Argentine settlement, and proclaimed the islands free of all governance. Great Britain resumed official occupation in 1833.]*

--------------------- DOE V. BRADEN ---------------------

16 Howard (57 U.S.) 635 (1853)

By treaty in 1819, Spain ceded Florida to the United States. The treaty stipulated that all land grants made by the Spanish crown in Florida after January 24, 1818 were annulled and made void. Included in that category was a grant made to the Duke of Alagon. An American who had purchased land from the Duke of Alagon sought to recover title to the lands, contending that the King of Spain lacked constitutional authority within Spain to annul the grant. The U.S. District Court ruled against the recovery, and the claimant appealed to the Supreme Court on a writ of error.

Chief Justice **Taney** delivered the opinion of the Court:

. . . . It is said that the King of Spain, by the constitution under which he was then acting and administering the government, had not the power to annul [the grant to the Duke of Alagon] by treaty or otherwise; that if the power existed anywhere in the Spanish government it resided in the courts; and that it does not appear, in the ratification, that it was annulled by that body or by its authority or consent.

But these are political questions and not judicial. They belong exclusively to the political department of the government.

By the Constitution of the United States, the president has the power, by and with the advice and consent of the Senate, to make treaties provided two-thirds of the Senators present concur. And he is authorized to appoint ambassadors, other public ministers and consuls, and to receive them from foreign nations; and is thereby enabled to obtain accurate information of the political condition of the nation with which he treats; who exercises over it the powers of sovereignty, and under what limitations; and how far the party who ratifies the treaty is authorized, by its form of government, to bind the nation and persons and things within its territory and dominion, by treaty stipulations. And the Constitution declares that all treaties made under the authority of the United States shall be the supreme law of the land.

The treaty is therefore a law made by the proper authority, and the courts of justice have no right to annul or disregard any of its provisions, unless they violate the Constitution of the United States. It is their duty to interpret it and administer it according to its terms. And it would be impossible for the executive department of the government to conduct our foreign relations with any advantage to the country, and fulfil the duties which the Constitution has imposed upon it, if every court in the country was authorized to inquire and decide whether the person who ratified the treaty on behalf of a foreign nation had the power, by its constitution and laws, to make the engagements into which he entered.

In this case the King of Spain has by the treaty stipulated that the grant to the Duke of Alagon, previously made by him, had been and remained annulled, and that neither the Duke of Alagon nor any person claiming under him could avail himself of this grant. It was for the president and Senate to determine whether the king, by the constitution and laws of Spain, was authorized to make this stipulation and to ratify a treaty containing it. They have recognized his power by accepting this stipulation as a part of the compact, and ratifying the treaty which contains it. The constituted and legitimate authority of the United States, therefore, has acquired and received this land as public property. In that character it became a part of the United States, and subject to and governed by their laws. And as the treaty is by the Constitution the supreme law, and that law declared it public domain when it came to the possession of the United States, the courts of justice are bound so to regard it and treat it, and cannot sanction any title not derived from the United States....

In this view of the case it is not necessary to examine the other questions which appear in the exception or have been raised in the argument. The treaty is the supreme law, and the stipulations in it dispose of the case. The judgment of the District Court must therefore be affirmed.

——————————— JONES V. UNITED STATES ———————————

137 U.S. 202 (1890)

The Guano Islands Act of 1856 provided that when a citizen of the United States discovered a deposit of guano on an island not within the jurisdiction of any other government, the president enjoyed the discretionary power to proclaim that such island "appertained to the United States." The Act extended the criminal jurisdiction of the United States to such islands.

In 1889, Henry Jones was indicted and tried in U.S. circuit court for the murder of Thomas Foster on the island of Navassa, a Carribean island claimed by the United States under the Guano Islands Act. Jones was convicted, but appealed challenging the constitutionality of the Act, and therefore the criminal jurisdiction of the U.S. court.

Justice **Gray** delivered the opinion of the Court:

By the law of nations, recognized by all civilized States, dominion of new territory may be acquired by discovery and occupation, as well as by cession or conquest; and when citizens or subjects of one nation, in its name, and by its authority or with its assent, take and hold actual, continuous and useful possession, (although only for the purpose of carrying on a particular business, such as catching and curing fish, or working mines,) of territory unoccupied by any other government or its citizens, the nation to which they belong may exercise such jurisdiction and for such period as it sees fit over territory so acquired. This principle affords ample warrant for the legislation of Congress concerning guano islands. . . .

Who is the sovereign, *de jure* or *de facto,* of a territory is not a judicial, but a political question, the determination of which by the legislative and executive departments of any government conclusively binds the judges, as well as all other officers, citizens and subjects of that government. This principle has always been upheld by this court, and has been affirmed under a great variety of circumstances. . . .

All courts of justice are bound to take judicial notice of the territorial extent of the jurisdiction exercised by the government whose laws they administer, or of its recognition or denial of the sovereignty of a foreign power, as appearing from the public acts of the legislature and executive, although those acts are not formally put in evidence, nor in accord with the pleadings. . . .

In the case at bar, the indictment alleges that the Island of Navassa, on which the murder is charged to have been committed, was at the time under the sole and exclusive jurisdiction of the United States, and out of the jurisdiction of any particular State or district of the United States, and recognized and considered by the United States as containing a deposit of guano within the meaning and terms of the laws of the United States relating to such islands, and recognized and considered by the United States as appertaining to the United States and in the possession of the United States under those laws.

The power, conferred on the President of the United States by . . . act of Congress . . . to determine that a guano island shall be considered as appertaining to the United States, being a strictly executive power, affecting foreign relations, and the manner in which his determination shall be made known not having been prescribed by statute, there can be no doubt that it may be declared through the Department of State, whose acts in this regard are in legal contemplation the acts of the President.

For the reasons above stated, our conclusion is that the Guano Islands Act of August 18, 1856, c. 164, reenacted in Title 72 of the Revised Statutes, is constitutional and valid; that the Island of Navassa must be considered as appertaining to the United States; that the Circuit Court of the United States for the District of Maryland had jurisdiction to try this indictment; and that there is no error in the proceedings.

Judgment affirmed.

NEELY V. HENKEL

180 U.S. 109 (1901)

After the liberation of Cuba from Spain in 1898, the United States undertook a temporary military occupation of the island pending the establishment of an independent Cuban government. Subsequently, Congress enacted legislation providing for the extradition from the United States of persons accused of crimes in occupied areas. Neely was accused of feloniously embezzling a large sum of money from the Cuban Post Office, arrested in the United States, and ordered to be extradited. Neely sought a writ of habeas corpus *claiming that the military occupation of Cuba was unconstitutional. His petition was denied by the circuit court, and he appealed.*

Justice **Harlan** delivered the opinion of the Court:

. . . . III.   Another contention of the appellant is that as Congress, by the joint resolution of April 20, 1898, declared that "the people of Cuba are, and of right ought to be free and independent" and as peace has existed since, at least, the military forces of Spain evacuated Cuba on or about January 1899, the occupancy and control of that island, under the military authority of the United States is without warrant in the Constitution and an unauthorized interference with the internal affairs of a friendly power; consequently it is argued the appellant should not be extradited for trial in the courts established under the orders issued by the Military Governor of the Island. In support of this proposition it is said that the United States recognized the existence of the Republic of Cuba, and that the war with Spain was carried on jointly by the allied forces of the United States and of that Republic.

Apart from the view that it is not competent for the judiciary to make any declaration upon the question of the length of time during which Cuba may be rightfully occupied and controlled by the United States in order to effect its pacification—it being the function of the political branch of the Government to determine when the troops of the United States shall be withdrawn from Cuba—the contention that the United States recognized the existence of an established government known as the Republic of Cuba, but is now using its military or executive power to displace or overthrow it, is without merit. The declaration by Congress that the people of Cuba were and of right ought to be free and independent was not intended as a recognition of the existence of an organized government instituted by the people of that Island in hostility to the government maintained by Spain. Nothing more was intended than to express the thought that the Cubans were entitled to enjoy—to use the language of the President in his message of December 5, 1897—that "measure of self control which is the inalienable right of man, protected in their right to reap the benefit of the exhaustless treasure of their country." . . .

The judgment of the Circuit Court is, therefore,

Affirmed.

──────────────── TERLINDEN V. AMES ────────────────

184 U.S. 270 (1902)

In 1852 the United States and Prussia concluded an extradition treaty. Gerhard Terlinden, a Prussian subject, was charged with forging and counterfeiting in Prussia and fled to the United States in 1901 to seek asylum. The German Consul sought Terlinden's extradition to Prussia under the treaty, while Terlinden contended the treaty was terminated by the creation of the German Empire in 1871. Terlinden was taken into custody and petitioned the U.S. District Court for a writ of habeas corpus, *which was denied.*

Chief Justice **Fuller** delivered the opinion of the Court:

This brings us to the real question, namely, the denial of the existence of a treaty of extradition between the United States and the Kingdom of Prussia, or the German Empire. In these proceedings the application was made by the official representative of both the Empire and the Kingdom of Prussia, but was based on the extradition treaty of 1852. The contention is that, as the result of the formation of the German Empire, this treaty had been terminated by operation of law. . . .

Undoubtedly treaties may be terminated by the absorption of Powers into other Nationalities and the loss of separate existence, as in the case of Hanover and Nassau, which became by conquest incorporated into the Kingdom of Prussia in 1866. Cessation of independent existence rendered the execution of treaties impossible. But where sovereignty in that respect is not extinguished, and the power to execute remains unimpaired, outstanding treaties cannot be regarded as avoided because of impossibility of performance. . . .

We concur in the view that the question whether power remains in a foreign State to carry out its treaty obligations is in its nature political and not judicial, and that the courts ought not to interfere with the conclusions of the political department in that regard. . . .

The decisions of the Executive Department in matters of extradition, within its own sphere, and in accordance with the Constitution, are not open to judicial revision, and it results that where proceedings for extradition, regularly and constitutionally taken under the acts of Congress, are pending, they cannot be put an end to by writs of *habeas corpus.*

> *The District Court was right, and its final order is*
>
> *Affirmed.*

——————— OETJEN V. CENTRAL LEATHER CO. ———————

246 U.S. 297 (1918)

During the Mexican Civil War (1913–17), General "Pancho" Villa, commander of the Constitutionalist forces in the north, confiscated two large consignments of hides from a Mexican dealer in a town recently taken by Villa's forces. The hides were purchased from General Villa by a Texas corporation, and resold to the defendants. Plaintiffs claimed ownership of the hides on behalf of the original Mexican dealer, and brought suit to recover on the grounds that General Villa's confiscation was contrary to the Hague Convention of 1907. The Circuit Court for Hudson County, New Jersey, dismissed the suit, and the New Jersey Court of Errors and Appeals sustained the judgment.

Justice **Clarke** delivered the opinion of the Court:

A somewhat detailed description will be necessary of the political conditions in Mexico prior to and at the time of the seizure of the property in controversy by the military authorities. It appears in the record, and is a matter of general history, that on February 23, 1913, Madero, President of the Republic of Mexico, was assassinated; that immediately thereafter General Huerta declared himself Provisional President of the Republic and took the oath of office as such; that on the twenty-sixth day of March following General Carranza, who was then Governor of the State of Coahuila, inaugurated a revolution against the claimed authority of Huerta and in a "Manifesto addressed to the Mexican Nation" proclaimed the organization of a constitutional government under "The Plan of Guadalupe," and that civil war was at once entered upon between the followers and forces of the two leaders. When General Carranza assumed the leadership of what were called the Constitutionalist forces he commissioned General Villa his representative, as "Commander of the North," and assigned him to an independent command in that part of the country. Such progress was made by the Carranza forces that in the autumn of 1913 they were in military possession . . . of approximately two-thirds of the area of the entire country . . . and after a battle lasting several days the City of Torreon . . . was captured by General Villa on October 1 of that year. Immediately after the capture of Torreon, Villa proposed levying a military contribution on the inhabitants, for the support of his army. . . . Martinez, the owner from whom the plaintiff in error claims title to the property involved in this case, was a wealthy resident of Torreon and was a dealer in hides in a large way. Being an adherent of Huerta, when Torreon was captured Martinez fled the city and failed to pay the assessment imposed upon him, and it was to satisfy this assessment that, by order of General Villa, the hides in controversy were seized and on January 3, 1914, were sold in Mexico to the Finnegan–Brown Company.

They were paid for in Mexico, and were thereafter shipped into the United States.

This court will take judicial notice of the fact that, since the transactions thus detailed and since the trial of this case in the lower courts, the Government of the United States recognized the Government of Carranza as the *de facto* government of the Republic of Mexico, on October 19, 1915, and as the *de jure* government on August 31, 1917. . . .

The conduct of the foreign relations of our Government is committed by the Constitution to the Executive and Legislative—"the political"—Departments of the Government, and the propriety of what may be done in the exercise of this political power is not subject to judicial inquiry or decision. It has been specifically decided that "Who is the sovereign, *de jure* or *de facto,* of a territory is not a judicial, but is a political question, the determination of which by the legislative and executive departments of any government conclusively binds the judges, as well as all other officers, citizens and subjects of that government. This principle has always been upheld by this court, and has been affirmed under a great variety of circumstances."

It is also the result of the interpretation by this court of the principles of international law that when a government which originates in revolution or revolt is recognized by the political department of our government as the *de jure* government of the country in which it is established, such recognition is retroactive in effect and validates all the actions and conduct of the government so recognized from the commencement of its existence.

To these principles we must add that: "Every sovereign State is bound to respect the independence of every other sovereign State, and the courts of one country will not sit in judgment on the acts of the government of another done within its own territory. Redress of grievances by reason of such acts must be obtained through the means open to be availed of by sovereign powers as between themselves."

Applying these principles of law to the case at bar, we have a duly commissioned military commander of what must be accepted as the legitimate government of Mexico, in the progress of a revolution, and when conducting active independent operations, seizing and selling in Mexico, as a military contribution, the property of a citizen of Mexico, the assignor of the plaintiff in error. Plainly this was the action, in Mexico, of the legitimate Mexican government when dealing with a Mexican citizen, and, as we have seen, for the soundest reasons, and upon repeated decisions of this court such action is not subject to reexamination and modification by the courts of this country.

The principle that the conduct of one independent government cannot be successfully questioned in the courts of another . . . rests at last upon the highest consideration of international comity and expediency. To permit the validity of the acts of one sovereign State to be reexamined and perhaps condemned by the courts of another would very certainly "imperil the amicable relations between governments and vex the peace of nations". . . .

The remedy of the former owner, or of the purchaser from him, of the property in controversy, if either has any remedy, must be found in the courts of Mexico or through the diplomatic agencies of the political department of our Government. The judgments of the Court of Errors and Appeals of New Jersey must be

Affirmed.

———————— CHICAGO AND SOUTHERN AIRLINES ———————— V. WATERMAN CORP.

333 U.S. 103 (1948)

The Civil Aeronautics Act authorized judicial review of decisions of the Civil Aeronautics Board [C.A.B.] to grant or deny licenses to U.S. air carriers for overseas routes. The Act further specified that the president would exercise final approval.

The C.A.B. issued an order, with the express approval of the president, denying a license for a particular route to Waterman Steamship Corporation and awarding one to C & S Airlines, a rival applicant. Waterman filed for judicial review, C & S Airlines moved to dismiss the case on the grounds that an order opposed by the president was not reviewable, the court of appeals denied the motion to dismiss, and the Supreme Court granted certiorari.

Justice **Jackson** delivered the opinion of the Court:

. . . The court below considered, and we think quite rightly, that it could not review such provisions of the order as resulted from Presidential direction. The President, both as Commander in Chief and as the Nation's organ for foreign affairs, has available intelligence services whose reports are not and ought not to be published to the world. It would be intolerable that courts, without the relevant information, should review and perhaps nullify actions of the Executive taken on information properly held secret. Nor can courts sit *in camera* in order to be taken into executive confidences. But even if courts could require full disclosure, the very nature of executive decisions as to foreign policy is political, not judicial. Such decisions are wholly confided by our Constitution to the political departments of the government, Executive and Legislative. They are delicate, complex, and involve large elements of prophecy. They are and should be undertaken only by those directly responsible to the people whose welfare they advance or imperil. They are decisions of a kind for which the Judiciary has neither aptitude, facilities nor responsibility and which has long been held to belong in the domain of political power not subject to judicial intrusion or inquiry. . . . We therefore agree that whatever of this order emanates from the President is not susceptible of review by the Judicial Department. . . .

To revise or review an administrative decision which has only the force of a recommendation to the President would be to render an advisory opinion in its most obnoxious form—advice that the President has not asked, tendered at the demand of a private litigant, on a subject concededly within the President's exclusive, ultimate control. This Court early and wisely determined that it would not give advisory opinions even when asked by the Chief Executive. It has also been the firm and unvarying practice of Constitutional Courts to render no judgments not binding and

conclusive on the parties and none that are subject to later review or alteration by administrative action. . . .

We conclude that orders of the Board as to certificates for overseas or
foreign air transportation are not mature and are therefore not susceptible of
judicial review at any time before they are finalized by Presidental approval.
After such approval has been given, the final orders embody Presidential
discretion as to political matters beyond the competence of the courts to
adjudicate. This makes it unnecessary to examine the other questions raised.
The petition of the Waterman Steamship Corp. should be dismissed.

Judgment reversed.

Justice **Douglas**, *joined by Justices* **Black, Reed** *and* **Rutledge,** *dissented.*

─────────── LUDECKE V. WATKINS ───────────

335 U.S. 160 (1948)

*The Alien Enemy Act of 1798 empowered the president to remove enemy aliens from the
United States whenever there was a "declared war" between the U.S. and a foreign country.
On July 14, 1945, President Truman directed the removal of all enemy aliens "deemed by
the Attorney General to be dangerous." On January 18, 1946—eight months after Germany's surrender and five months after VJ–Day—the attorney general ordered the removal of
Ludecke, a German national, from the United States. Ludecke was taken into custody and
petitioned for a writ of* habeas corpus, *which was denied.*

Justice **Frankfurter** delivered the opinion of the Court:

. . . . As Congress explicitly recognized in the recent Administrative Procedure Act, some statutes "preclude judicial review." Barring questions of
interpretation and constitutionality, the Alien Enemy Act of 1798 is such a
statute. Its terms, purpose, and construction leave no doubt. The very nature
of the President's power to order the removal of all enemy aliens rejects the
notion that courts may pass judgment upon the exercise of his discretion.
This view was expressed by Mr. Justice Iredell shortly after the Act was
passed and every judge before whom the question has since come has held
that the statute barred judicial review. We would so read the Act if it came
before us without the impressive gloss of history.

The power with which Congress vested the President had to be executed by him through others. He provided for the removal of such enemy aliens
as were "deemed by the Attorney General" to be dangerous. But such a
finding, at the President's behest, was likewise not to be subjected to the
scrutiny of courts. For one thing, removal was contingent not upon a finding
that in fact an alien was "dangerous." The President was careful to call for
the removal of aliens "deemed by the Attorney General to be dangerous."
But the short answer is that the Attorney General was the President's voice
and conscience. A war power of the President not subject to judicial review
is not transmuted into a judicially reviewable action because the President
chooses to have that power exercised within narrower limits than Congress
authorized.

And so we reach the claim that while the President had summary power under the Act, it did not survive cessation of actual hostilities. This claim in effect nullifies the power to deport alien enemies, for such deportations are hardly practicable during the pendency of what is colloquially known as the shooting war. Nor does law lag behind common sense. War does not cease with a cease-fire order, and power to be exercised by the President such as that conferred by the Act of 1798 is a process which begins when war is declared but is not exhausted when the shooting stops. "The state of war" may be terminated by treaty or legislation or Presidential proclamation. Whatever the mode, its termination is a political act. Whether and when it would be open to this Court to find that a war though merely formally kept alive had in fact ended, is a question too fraught with gravity even to be adequately formulated when not compelled. . . .

The political branch of the Government has not brought the war with Germany to an end. On the contrary, it has proclaimed that "a state of war still exists." The Court would be assuming the functions of the political agencies of the Government to yield to the suggestion that the unconditional surrender of Germany and the disintegration of the Nazi Reich have left Germany without a government capable of negotiating a treaty of peace. It is not for us to question a belief by the President that enemy aliens who were justifiably deemed fit subjects for internment during active hostilities do not lose their potency for mischief during the period of confusion and conflict which is characteristic of a state of war even when the guns are silent. . . . These are matters of political judgment for which judges have neither technical competence nor official responsibility.

This brings us to the final question. Is the statute valid as we have construed it? The same considerations of reason, authority, and history, that led us to reject reading the statutory language "declared war" to mean "actual hostilities," support the validity of the statute. The war power is the war power. If the war, as we have held, has not in fact ended, so as to justify local rent control, a fortiori, it validly supports the power given to the President by the Act of 1798 in relation to alien enemies. Nor does it require protracted argument to find no defect in the Act because resort to the courts may be had only to challenge the construction and validity of the statute and to question the existence of the "declared war," as has been done in this case. The Act is almost as old as the Constitution, and it would savor of doctrinaire audacity now to find the statute offensive to some emanation of the Bill of Rights. . . .

Such great war powers may be abused, no doubt, but that is a bad reason for having judges supervise their exercise, whatever the legal formulas within which such supervision would nominally be confined. . . .

Accordingly, we hold that full responsibility for the just exercise of this great power may validly be left where the Congress has constitutionally placed it—on the President of the United States. The Founders in their wisdom made him not only the Commander in Chief but also the guiding organ in the conduct of our foreign affairs. He who was entrusted with such vast powers in relation to the outside world was also entrusted by Congress, almost throughout the whole life of the nation, with the disposition of alien enemies during a state of war. Such a page of history is worth more than a volume of rhetoric.

Judgment affirmed.

Justice **Black,** *joined by Justices* **Douglas, Murphy,** *and* **Rutledge,** *dissenting.*

──────────────────── BAKER V. CARR ────────────────────

369 U.S. 186 (1962)

Historically, the question of legislative apportionment was considered a nonjusticeable political question, resting on the guaranty clause of the Constitution [Article IV, section 4]. Baker v. Carr, *involving the malapportionment of the Tennessee General Assembly, represented the first application of the equal protection clause of the Fourteenth Amendment to the question of legislative apportionment, and provided the basis for the Supreme Court's subsequent involvement in legislative redistricting. Although the decision relates exclusively to domestic issues, Justice Brennan, in his opinion for the Court, discussed the general doctrine of political questions at length. That portion of the opinion pertaining to foreign relations, though essentially* dictum, *is reprinted.*

Justice **Brennan** delivered the opinion of the Court:

. . . . [N]onjusticiability of a political question is primarily a function of the separation of powers. Much confusion results from the capacity of the "political question" label to obscure the need for case-by-case inquiry. Deciding whether a matter has in any measure been committed by the Constitution to another branch of government, or whether the action of that branch exceeds whatever authority has been committed, is itself a delicate exercise in constitutional interpretation, and is a responsibility of this Court as ultimate interpreter of the Constitution. To demonstrate this requires no less than to analyze representative cases and to infer from them the analytical threads that make up the political question doctrine. . . .

Foreign relations: There are sweeping statements to the effect that all questions touching foreign relations are political questions. Not only does resolution of such issues frequently turn on standards that defy judicial application, or involve the exercise of a discretion demonstrably committed to the executive or legislature; but many such questions uniquely demand single-voiced statement of the Government's views. Yet it is error to suppose that every case or controversy which touches foreign relations lies beyond judicial cognizance. Our cases in this field seem invariably to show a discriminating analysis of the particular question posed, in terms of the history of its management by the political branches, of its susceptibility to judicial handling in the light of its nature and posture in the specific case, and of the possible consequences of judicial action. For example, though a court will not ordinarily inquire whether a treaty has been terminated, since on that question "governmental action . . . must be regarded as of controlling importance," if there has been no conclusive "governmental action" then a court can construe a treaty and may find it provides the answer. . . . Though a court will not undertake to construe a treaty in a manner inconsistent with a subsequent federal statute, no similar hesitancy obtains if the asserted clash is with state law. . . .

While recognition of foreign governments so strongly defies judicial treatment that without executive recognition a foreign state has been called "a republic of whose existence we know nothing," and the judiciary ordinarily follows the executive as to which nation has sovereignty over disputed territory, once sovereignty over an area is politically determined and declared, courts may examine the resulting status and decide independently whether a statute applies to that area. Similarly, recognition of belligerency abroad is an executive responsibility, but if the executive proclamations fall short of an explicit answer, a court may construe them seeking, for example, to determine whether the situation is such that statutes designed to assure American neutrality have become operative. Still again, though it is the executive that determines a person's status as representative of a foreign government, the executive's statements will be construed where necessary to determine the court's jurisdiction. Similar judicial action in the absence of a recognizedly authoritative executive declaration occurs in cases involving the immunity from seizure of vessels owned by friendly foreign governments.

Dates of duration of hostilities: Though it has been stated broadly that "the power which declared the necessity is the power to declare its cessation, and what the cessation requires," here too analysis reveals isolable reasons for the presence of political questions, underlying this Court's refusal to review the political departments' determination of when or whether a war has ended. Dominant is the need for finality in the political determination, for emergency's nature demands "A prompt and unhesitating obedience." Moreover, "the cessation of hostilities does not necessarily end the war power. . . ." But deference rests on reason, not habit. The question in a particular case may not seriously implicate considerations of finality—e.g., a public program of importance (rent control) yet not central to the emergency effort. Further, clearly definable criteria for decision may be available. In such case the political question barrier falls away: "[A] Court is not at liberty to shut its eyes to an obvious mistake, when the validity of the law depends upon the truth of what is declared. . . . [It can] inquire whether the exigency still existed upon which the continued operation of the law depended." On the other hand, even in private litigation which directly implicates no feature of separation of powers, lack of judicially discoverable standards and the drive for even-handed application may impel reference to the political departments' determination of dates of hostilities beginning and ending.

It is apparent that several formulations which vary slightly according to the settings in which the questions arise may describe a political question, although each has one or more elements which identify it as essentially a function of the separation of powers. Prominent on the surface of any case held to involve a political question is found a textually demonstrable constitutional commitment of the issue to a coordinate political department; or a lack of judicially discoverable and manageable standards for resolving it; or the impossibility of deciding without an initial policy determination of a kind clearly for nonjudicial discretion; or the impossibility of a court's undertaking independent resolution without expressing lack of the respect due coordinate branches of government; or an unusual need for unquestioning adherence to a political decision already made; or the potentiality of embarrassment from multifarious pronouncements by various departments on one question.

Unless one of these formulations is inextricable from the case at bar, there should be no dismissal for nonjusticiability on the ground of a political question's presence. The doctrine of which we treat is one of "political questions," not one of "political cases." The courts cannot reject as "no law suit" a bona fide controversy as to whether some action dominated "political" exceeds constitutional authority. The cases we have reviewed show the necessity for discriminating inquiry into the precise facts and posture of the particular case, and the impossibility of resolution by any semantic cataloguing. . . .

Justice **Frankfurter,** *dissenting:* . . . From its earliest opinions this Court has consistently recognized a class of controversies which do not lend themselves to judicial standards and judicial remedies. To classify the various instances as "political questions" is rather a form of stating this conclusion than revealing of analysis. Some of the cases so labelled have no relevance here. But from others emerge unifying considerations that are compelling.

1. The cases concerning war or foreign affairs, for example, are usually explained by the necessity of the country's speaking with one voice in such matters. While this concern alone undoubtedly accounts for many of the decisions, others do not fit the pattern. It would hardly embarrass the conduct of war were this Court to determine, in connection with private transactions between litigants, the date upon which war is to be deemed terminated. But the Court has refused to do so. . . . It does not suffice to explain such cases as *Ludecke v. Watkins* deferring to political determination the question of the duration of war for purposes of the Presidential power to deport alien enemies—that judicial intrusion would seriously impede the President's power effectively to protect the country's interests in time of war. Of course, this is true; but the precise issue presented is the duration of the time of war which demands the power. And even for the purpose of determining the extent of congressional regulatory power over the tribes and dependent communities of Indians, it is ordinarily for Congress, not the Court, to determine whether or not a particular Indian group retains the characteristics constitutionally requisite to confer the power. A controlling factor in such cases is that, decision respecting these kinds of complex matters of policy being traditionally committed not to courts but to the political agencies of government for determination by criteria of political expediency, there exists no standard ascertainable by settled judicial experience or process by reference to which a political decision affecting the question at issue between the parties can be judged. Where the question arises in the course of a litigation involving primarily the adjudication of other issues between the litigants, the Court accepts as a basis for adjudication the political departments' decision of it. But where its determination is the sole function to be served by the exercise of the judicial power, the Court will not entertain the action. . . . The dominant consideration is "the lack of satisfactory criteria for a judicial determination. . . ."

This may be, like so many questions of law, a matter of degree. Questions have arisen under the Constitution to which adjudication gives answer although the criteria for decision are less than unwavering bright lines. Often in these cases illumination was found in the federal structures established by, or the underlying presuppositions of, the Constitution. With respect to such questions, the Court has recognized that, concerning a particular power of Congress put in issue, ". . . effective restraints on its exercise must proceed from political rather than from judicial processes." It is also true that even regarding the duration of war and the status of Indian tribes, referred to above as subjects ordinarily committed exclusively to the nonjudicial branches, the Court has suggested that some limitations exist upon the range within which the decisions of those branches will be permitted to go unreviewed. But this is merely to acknowledge that particular circumstances may differ so greatly in degree as to differ thereby in kind, and that, although within a certain range of cases on a continuum, no standard of distinction can be found to tell between them, other cases will fall above or below the range. The doctrine of political questions, like any other, is not to be applied beyond the limits of its own logic, with all the quiddities and abstract disharmonies it may manifest. . . .

—————————— GILLIGAN V. MORGAN ——————————

413 U.S. 1 (1973)

In the face of widespread student demonstrations against the war in Vietnam, Governor Gilligan of Ohio ordered National Guard troops to the Kent State campus to preserve order and protect public property. The deployment of the Guard resulted in a confrontation with the students; and in the ensuing melee, the Guard opened fire, killing several students and injuring others. Several students at Kent State brought suit, claiming that use of the Guard had violated the students' rights of peace and assembly, and caused injury and death. They sought to enjoin the governor from prematurely ordering National Guard troops to duty in civil disorders, and to hold unconstitutional that portion of the Ohio statutes which provided that law enforcement personnel were "guiltless" of the consequences for the use of necessary and proper force to suppress a riot. The U.S.District Court dismissed the suit. The court of appeals affirmed the dismissal with respect to injunctive relief.

Chief Justice **Burger** delivered the opinion of the Court:

It is important to note at the outset that this is not a case in which damages are sought for injuries sustained during the tragic occurrence at Kent State. Nor is it an action seeking a restraining order against some specified and imminently threatened unlawful action. Rather, it is a broad call on judicial power to assume continuing regulatory jurisdiction over the activities of the Ohio National Guard. This far-reaching demand for relief presents important questions of justiciability. . . . This would plainly and explicitly require a judicial evaluation of a wide range of possibly dissimilar procedures and policies approved by different law enforcement agencies or other authorities.... Trained professionals, subject to the day-to-day control of the responsible civilian authorities, necessarily must make comparative judgments on the merits as to evolving methods of training, equipping, and controlling military forces with respect to their duties under the Constitution. It would be inappropriate for a district judge to undertake this responsibility in the unlikely event that he possessed requisite technical competence to do so....

In *Flast v. Cohen*, this Court noted that:

> Justiciability is itself a concept of uncertain meaning and scope. Its reach is illustrated by the various grounds upon which questions sought to be adjudicated in federal courts have been held not to be justiciable. Thus, no justiciable controversy is presented when the parties seek adjudication of only a political question, when the parties are asking for an advisory opinion, when the question sought to be adjudicated has been mooted by subsequent developments, and when there is no standing to maintain the action. Yet it remains true that '[j]usticiability is ... not a legal concept with a fixed content or susceptible of scientific verification. Its utilization is the resultant of many subtle pressures....'

In testing this case by these standards drawn specifically from *Flast*, there are serious deficiencies with respect to each. The advisory nature of the judicial declaration sought is clear from respondents' argument and, indeed, from the very language of the court's remand. Added to this is that the nature of the questions to be resolved on remand are subjects committed expressly to the political branches of government. These factors, when coupled with the uncertainties as to whether a live controversy still exists and the infirmity of the posture of respondents as to standing, render the claim and the proposed issues on remand nonjusticiable.

It would be difficult to think of a clearer example of the type of governmental action that was intended by the Constitution to be left to the political branches directly responsible—as the Judicial Branch is not—to the electoral process. Moreover, it is difficult to conceive of an area of governmental activity in which the courts have less competence. The complex, subtle, and professional decisions as to the composition, training, equipping, and control of a military force are essentially professional military judgments, subject *always* to civilian control of the Legislative and Executive Branches. The ultimate responsibility for these decisions is appropriately vested in branches of the government which are periodically subject to electoral accountability. It is this power of oversight and control of military force by elected representatives and officials which underlies our entire constitutional system; the majority opinion of the Court of Appeals failed to give appropriate weight to this separation of powers.

Voting rights cases such as *Baker v. Carr, Reynolds v. Sims,* and prisoner rights cases such as *Haines v. Kerner,* are cited by the court [of appeals] as supporting the "diminish[ing] vitality of the political question doctrine." Yet, because this doctrine has been held inapplicable to certain carefully delineated situations, it is no reason for federal courts to assume its demise.

The voting rights cases, indeed, have represented the Court's efforts to strengthen the political system by assuring a higher level of fairness and responsiveness to the political processes, not the assumption of a continuing judicial review of substantive political judgments entrusted expressly to the coordinate branches of government.

In concluding that no justiciable controversy is presented, it should be clear that we neither hold nor imply that the conduct of the National Guard is always beyond judicial review or that there may not be accountability in a judicial forum for violations of law or for specific unlawful conduct by military personnel, whether by way of damages or injunctive relief. We hold only that no such questions are presented in this case. We decline to require a United States District Court to involve itself so directly and so intimately in the task assigned that court by the Court of Appeals.

Reversed.

SCHLESINGER V. BALLARD

419 U.S. 498 (1975)

Robert Ballard was a lieutenant in the United States Navy. After nine years of service, he failed for a second time to be selected for promotion, and thus became subject to mandatory discharge. Ballard brought suit, claiming that had he been a female officer he would have been allowed thirteen years of commissioned service before a mandatory discharge for want of promotion. Ballard claimed the distinction constituted unconstitutional gender discrimination in violation of the Due Process Clause of the Fifth Amendment. A three-judge panel of the U.S. District Court for the Southern District of California ruled in favor of Ballard, and the Secretary of Defense appealed.

Justice **Stewart** delivered the opinion of the Court:

At the base of the system governing the promotion and attrition of male line officers in the Navy is a congressional designation of the authorized number of the Navy's enlisted personnel and a correlative limitation upon the number of active line officers as a percentage of that figure. Congress has also established the ratio of discrimination of line officers in the several grades above lieutenant in fixed proportions to the total number of line officers.

The Secretary of the Navy is required periodically to convene selection boards to consider and recommend for promotion male line officers in each of the separate ranks and must provide the boards so convened with the number of male line officers that may be recommended for promotion to the next higher grade. . . .

Because the Navy has a pyramidal organizational structure, fewer officers are needed at each higher rank than are needed in the rank below. In the absence of some mandatory attrition of naval officers, the result would be stagnation of promotion of younger officers and disincentive to naval service. If the officers who failed to be promoted remained in the service, the promotion of younger officers through the ranks would be retarded. Accordingly, a basic "up or out" philosophy was developed to maintain effective leadership by heightening competition for the higher ranks while providing junior officers with incentive and opportunity for promotion. It is for this reason, and not merely because of administrative or fiscal policy considerations, that [the statute] requires that lieutenants be discharged when they are "considered as having failed of selection for promotion to the grade of lieutenant commander . . . for the second time." Similar selection-out rules apply to officers in different ranks who are twice passed over for promotion. . . .

It is against this background that we must decide whether, agreeably to the Due Process Clause of the Fifth Amendment, the Congress may accord to women naval officers a 13–year tenure of commissioned service . . . before mandatory discharge for want of promotion, while requiring . . . the mandatory discharge of male lieutenants who have been twice passed over for promotion but who, like Ballard, may have had less than 13 years of commissioned service. In arguing that Congress has acted unconstitutionally, appellee relies primarily upon the Court's recent decisions in *Frontiero v. Richardson* and *Reed v. Reed*. . . .

In both *Reed* and *Frontiero* the challenged classifications based on sex were premised on overbroad generalizations that could not be tolerated under the Constitution. . . .

In contrast, the different treatment of men and women naval officers . . . reflects, not archaic and overbroad generalizations, but, instead, the demonstrable fact that male and female line officers in the Navy are *not* similarly situated with respect to opportunities for professional service. . . .

In both *Reed* and *Frontiero* the reason asserted to justify the challenged gender-based classifications was administrative convenience, and that alone. Here, on the contrary, the operation of the statutes in question results in a flow of promotions commensurate with the Navy's current needs and serves to motivate qualified commissioned officers to so conduct themselves that they may realistically look forward to higher levels of command. This Court has recognized that "it is the primary business of armies and navies to fight or be ready to fight wars should the occasion arise." The responsibility for determining how best our Armed Forces shall attend to that business rests with Congress and with the President. We cannot say that, in exercising its broad constitutional power here, Congress has violated the Due Process Clause of the Fifth Amendment.

The judgment is reversed.

─────────── GOLDWATER ET AL. ───────────
V. CARTER

444 U.S. 996 (1979)

In December 1978, President Carter announced that the United States would extend diplomatic recognition to the Peoples' Republic of China, and would simultaneously withdraw recognition from the Republic of China (Taiwan). One week later the State Department notified the Taiwan Government that the U.S. would terminate the 1955 Mutual Defense

Treaty between the United States and the Republic of China on January 1, 1980, in accordance with treaty provisions which permitted either party to terminate the agreement on one year's notice. Senator Barry Goldwater, joined by twenty members of Congress, brought suit to enjoin the president from terminating the treaty without approval by two-thirds of the Senate. The U.S. District Court ruled in favor of the plaintiffs, and the court of appeals reversed.

Certiorari *granted, judgment of the Court of Appeals vacated, and remanded to the District Court with instructions to dismiss the complaint.*

Justice **Powell** (*concurring*):

Although I agree with the result reached by the Court, I would dismiss the complaint as not ripe for judicial review.

I

This Court has recognized that an issue should not be decided if it is not ripe for judicial review. Prudential considerations persuade me that a dispute between Congress and the President is not ready for judicial review unless and until each branch has taken action asserting its constitutional authority. Differences between the President and the Congress are commonplace under our system. The differences should, and almost invariably do, turn on political rather than legal considerations. The Judicial Branch should not decide issues affecting the allocation of power between the President and Congress until the political branches reach a constitutional impasse. Otherwise, we would encourage small groups or even individual Members of Congress to seek judicial resolution of issues before the normal political process has the opportunity to resolve the conflict.

In this case, a few Members of Congress claim that the President's action in terminating the treaty with Taiwan has deprived them of their constitutional role with respect to a change in the supreme law of the land. Congress has taken no official action. In the present posture of this case, we do not know whether there ever will be an actual confrontation between the Legislative and Executive Branches. Although the Senate has considered a resolution declaring that Senate approval is necessary for the termination of any mutual defense treaty, no final vote has been taken on the resolution. . . . Moreover, it is unclear whether the resolution would have retroactive effect. It cannot be said that either the Senate or the House has rejected the President's claim. If the Congress chooses not to confront the President, it is not our task to do so. I therefore concur in the dismissal of this case.

II

Justice Rehnquist suggests, however, that the issue presented by this case is a nonjusticiable political question which can never be considered by this Court. I cannot agree. In my view, reliance upon the political-question doctrine is inconsistent with our precedents. As set forth in the seminal case of *Baker v. Carr,* the doctrine incorporates three inquiries: (i) Does the issue involve resolution of questions committed by the text of the Constitution to a coordinate branch of Government? (ii) Would resolution of the question demand that a court move beyond areas of judicial expertise? (iii) Do prudential considerations counsel against intervention? In my opinion the answer to each of these inquiries would require us to decide this case if it were ready for review. . . .

In my view, the suggestion that this case presents a political question is incompatible with this Court's willingness on previous occasions to decide whether one branch of our Government has impinged upon the power of another. Under the criteria enunciated in *Baker v. Carr,* we have the responsibility to decide whether both the Executive and Legislative Branches have constitutional roles to play in termination of a treaty. If the Congress, by appropriate formal action, had challenged the President's authority to terminate the treaty with Taiwan, the resulting uncertainty could have serious consequences for our country. In that situation, it would be the duty of this Court to resolve the issue.

Justice **Rehnquist,** with whom the **Chief Justice,** Justice **Stewart** and Justice **Stevens** join, *concurring* in the judgment: I am of the view that the basic question presented by the petitioners in this case is "political" and therefore nonjusticiable because it involves the authority of the President in the conduct of our country's foreign relations and the extent to which the Senate or the Congress is authorized to negate the action of the President. . . .

In light of the absence of any constitutional provision governing the termination of a treaty, and the fact that different termination procedures may be appropriate for different treaties, the instant case in my view also "must surely be controlled by political standards."

The present case differs in several important respects from *Youngstown Sheet & Tube Co. v. Sawyer,* cited by petitioners as authority both for reaching the merits of this dispute and for reversing the Court of Appeals. In *Youngstown,* private litigants brought a suit contesting the President's authority under his war powers to seize the Nation's steel industry, an action of profound and demonstrable domestic impact. Here, by contrast, we are asked to settle a dispute between coequal branches of our Government, each of which has resources available to protect and assert its interests, resources not available to private litigants outside the judicial forum. Moreover, as in *Curtiss–Wright,* the effect of this action, as far as we can tell, is "entirely external to the United States, and [falls] within the category of foreign affairs." Finally, as already noted, the situation presented here is closely akin to that presented in *Coleman,*[2] where the Constitution spoke only to the procedure for ratification of an amendment, not to its rejection.

Having decided that the question presented in this action is nonjusticiable, I believe that the appropriate disposition is for this Court to vacate the decision of the Court of Appeals and remand with instructions for the District Court to dismiss the complaint.

Justice **Blackmun,** with whom Justice **White** joins, *dissenting* in part:

In my view, the time factor and its importance are illusory; if the President does not have the power to terminate the treaty (a substantial issue that we should address only after briefing and oral argument), the notice of intention to terminate surely has no legal effect. It is also indefensible, without further study, to pass on the issue of justiciability or on the issues of standing or ripeness. While I therefore join in the grant of the petition for certiorari, I would set the case for oral argument and give it the plenary consideration it so obviously deserves.

Justice **Brennan,** *dissenting:*

I respectfully dissent from the order directing the District Court to dismiss this case, and would affirm the judgment of the Court of Appeals insofar as it rests upon the President's well-established authority to recognize, and withdraw recognition from, foreign governments.

In stating that this case presents a nonjustificiable "political question," Mr. Justice Rehnquist, in my view, profoundly misapprehends the political-question principle as it applies to matters of foreign relations. Properly understood, the political-question doctrine restrains courts from reviewing an exercise of foreign policy judgment by the coordinate political branch to which authority to make that judgment has been "constitutional[ly] commit[ted]." But the doctrine does not pertain when a court is faced with the *antecedent* question whether a particular branch has been constitutionally designated as the repository of political decisionmaking power. The issue of decision-making authority must be resolved as a matter of constitutional law, not political discretion; accordingly, it falls within the competence of the courts.

The constitutional question raised here is prudently answered in narrow terms. Abrogation of the defense treaty with Taiwan was a necessary incident to Executive recognition of the Peking Government, because the defense treaty was predicated upon the now-abandoned view that the Taiwan Government was the only legitimate political authority in China. Our cases firmly establish that the Constitution commits to the President alone the power to recognize, and withdraw recognition from, foreign regimes. That mandate being clear, our judicial inquiry into the treaty rupture can go no further.

Suggested Readings

The most perceptive discussion of the doctrine of political question remains that of ALEXANDER BICKEL in his text, THE LEAST DANGEROUS BRANCH (1962). More skeptical treatments include Louis Henkin, *Is There a 'Political Question' Doctrine,* 85 YALE LAW JOURNAL 597 (1976); Fritz W. Scharpf, *Judicial Review and the Political Question: A Functional Analysis,* 75 YALE LAW JOURNAL 517 (1966); Tigar, *Judicial Power, the Political Question Doctrine, and Foreign Relations,* 17 U.C.L.A. LAW REVIEW 1135 (1970); Firmage, *The War Powers and the Political Questions Doctrine,* 49 UNIVERSITY OF COLORADO LAW REVIEW 65 (1977–78), and Newberry, *Constitutional Law: Political Questions and the Conduct of Foreign Policy,* 25 HARVARD INTERNATIONAL LAW JOURNAL 433 (1984).

Earlier treatments can be found in Field, *The Doctrine of Political Questions in the Federal Courts,* 8 MINNESOTA LAW REVIEW 485 (1924); Finkelstein, *Judicial Self–Limitation,* 37 HARVARD LAW REVIEW 338 (1924); Weston, *Political Questions,* 38 HARVARD LAW

REVIEW 296 (1925); and Tollett, *Political Questions and the Law,* 42 UNIVERSITY OF DETROIT LAW JOURNAL 499 (1965).

For topical application of the doctrine, see Ann Van Wynen Thomas and A.J. Thomas, Jr. *Presidential War–Making Power: A Political Question,* 35 SOUTHWESTERN LAW JOURNAL 879 (1981); David Cole, *Challenging Covert War: The Politics of the Political Questions Doctrine,* 26 HARVARD INTERNATIONAL LAW JOURNAL 155 (1985); Howard Konar, *Termination of Treaties as a Political Question: The Role of Congress after* Goldwater v. Carter, 4 FORDHAM INTERNATIONAL LAW JOURNAL 81 (1981); Louis Henkin, *Litigating the President's Power to Terminate Treaties,* 73 AMERICAN JOURNAL OF INTERNATIONAL LAW 647 (1979); Karin Lee Lawson, *The Twilight Zone of Treaty–Termination:* Goldwater v. Carter, 20 VIRGINIA JOURNAL OF INTERNATIONAL LAW 147 (1979).

Recent general treatments include Martin H. Redish, *Judicial Review and the "Political Question,"* 79 NORTHWESTERN UNIVERSITY LAW REVIEW 1031 (1984); and Linda Champlin and Alan Schwartz, *Political Question Doctrine and Allocation of the Foreign Affairs Power,* 13 HOFSTRA LAW REVIEW 215 (1985).

Notes

1. 1 Cranch (5 U.S.) 137 (1803).
2. *Coleman v. Miller,* 307 U.S. 433 (1939).

5

INTERPRETATIONS OF EXECUTIVE POWER

THE TAUT PHRASEOLOGY of Article II of the Constitution concerning presidential power has led to a continuing struggle to define the nature of the office. However, it has been agreed since George Washington's time that the president is primarily responsible for the conduct of American foreign relations. Even such constitutional antagonists as Thomas Jefferson and John Marshall found common ground when it came to the president's power in foreign affairs. In 1790, when the first French Republic dispatched Citizen Gênet to the United States with diplomatic credentials addressed to Congress instead of the president, Jefferson (who was then secretary of state) informed Gênet that "The transaction of business with foreign nations is Executive altogether. It belongs then to the head of that department, except as to such portions of it as are specially submitted to the Senate. Exceptions are to be strictly construed." [1]

In 1800 John Marshall, addressing the House of Representatives in support of President Adams, stated that "The President is the sole organ of the nation in its external relations, and its sole representative with foreign nations. . . . [T]he demand of a foreign nation can only be made on him. He possesses the whole Executive power. He holds and directs the force of the nation." [2] Marshall's views were quoted with approval by the Supreme Court in *United States v. Curtiss–Wright*, which went on to speak of "the very delicate, plenary and exclusive power of the President as the sole organ of the federal government in the field of international relations."

The presidential monopoly over foreign relations was given explicit congressional approval with the passage of the Logan Act in 1799. In 1798 a Philadelphia Quaker named Logan travelled to Paris to negotiate with the French government in an effort to avoid war between France and the United States. Congress responded by passing "An Act to Prevent Usurpation of Executive Functions," which still survives on the statute books. During the

163

1972 presidential campaign, Pierre Salinger undertook to initiate discussions with the North Vietnamese peace negotiators in Paris on behalf of George McGovern. He was quickly called to order by the Nixon administration's invocation of the Logan Act. But in 1984 President Reagan chose to overlook the strictures of the Act when the Reverend Jesse Jackson went to Syria to secure release of a downed Navy pilot. In fact, as Professor Charles Warren once pointed out, the Logan Act has been "more honored in the breach than the observance." [3]

The cryptic Constitutional authority of the president to send and receive ambassadors provides the textual basis for the president's monopoly over foreign affairs. But the president's monopoly derives as much from an inherent authority as chief executive as from the words of the Constitution itself. Nevertheless, by the beginning of the twentieth century it is clear that the president's authority had evolved to the point where John Bassett Moore in his famous *International Law Digest* could state without fear of contradiction that "In every case . . . the question of recognition was determined solely by the Executive." [4] The potential of non-recognition as a diplomatic weapon also rests exclusively in the hands of the president. This was illustrated by President Woodrow Wilson's refusal to recognize the Heurta government in Mexico in 1913, thereby contributing to its downfall the following year. Conversely, since 1939 every successive administration has continued to recognize the existence of Estonia, Latvia, and Lithuania—with less sanguine results. More recently, when the United States under Presidents Nixon and Carter shifted recognition from the Republic of China (Taiwan) to the People's Republic of China, the Supreme Court in *Goldwater v. Carter* considered the authority of the president to be so well-settled that it scarcely warranted comment.

COMMANDER IN CHIEF

But the major source of presidents' authority in foreign relations traces to their power as commander in chief. The importance of the president's command of the armed forces was stressed at the Federal Convention in 1787 as essential to national security. It is directly analogous to the ancient power of kingship to command a country's army and navy. It is curious that the power of the American president embedded in the black-letter text of Article II of the Constitution has expanded with time while the power of monarchy, except perhaps in the princely states of the Middle East, has been eroded severely by parliamentary authority.

It may be even more intriguing that the expansion of the president's authority as commander in chief has been vigorously supported by the Supreme Court. Speaking through Justice Story in the early case of *Martin v. Mott,* the Court upheld President Madison's unlimited discretion to call out the individual state militias during the War of 1812. The sweeping language employed by Story had not been used by an English–speaking jurist since the days of Charles I, but it has since become the standard by which presidential discretion is measured. In time of crisis, said Story, the president "is necessarily constituted the judge of the existence of the exigency, and is bound to act according to his belief of the facts." Moreover, the Court held that presidents, as well as their military subordinates, were immune from civil suit challenging the validity of their orders. "Such a course would be subversive of all discipline, and expose the best disposed officers to the chances of ruinous litigation."

The purely military aspects of the commander in chief power were stressed by the Court in *Fleming v. Page,* arising out of the Mexican War. While the decision is sometimes cited as restricting presidential power, the commander in chief's authority in military terms is analogous to that of an absolute monarch of the seventeenth or eighteenth century—the sole distinction being that the president is responsible to the people and serves for a four-year term. As expressed by Chief Justice Taney, "His [the president's] duty and his power are purely military. As commander in chief, he is authorized to direct the movements of the naval and military forces placed by law at his command, and to employ them in the manner he may deem most effectual to harass and conquer and subdue the enemy." Within the military sphere, the president's power was absolute.

But it is the *Prize Cases* in 1863 that provide the basis for the modern war powers of the president. In his famous July 4, 1861, message to Congress, Lincoln laid claim to the "war power" of the Union to suppress the rebellion of the southern states. In the *Prize Cases* a sharply divided Court supported him. The immediate issue was the validity of the naval blockade Lincoln imposed on the South following the attack on Fort Sumter. The opponents of presidential power argued that a blockade could only be imposed through a validly declared "public war," and that under the Constitution only Congress could declare war. Justice Grier, speaking for the Court's majority, dismissed the argument. "If a war be made by invasion of a foreign nation, the President is not only authorized but bound to resist force by force. He does not initiate the war, but is found to accept the challenge without waiting for any special legislative authority. And whether the hostile party be a foreign invader, or State organized in rebellion, it is none the less a war, although the declaration be *unilateral."*

But it is the following two sentences of Justice Grier that have sustained presidential initiatives from McKinley to Reagan and which remain the definitive pronouncement of the Supreme Court on the use of force:

> Whether the President in fulfilling his duties, as Commander in Chief, in suppressing an insurrection, has met with such armed hostile resistance, and a civil war of such alarming proportions as will compel him to accord them the character of belligerents, is a question to be decided by *him,* and this Court must be governed by the decisions and acts of the political department of the Government to which this power was entrusted. 'He must determine the degree of force the crisis demands.' [Grier's emphasis.]

President Lincoln's wartime suspension of the privilege of *habeas corpus* was sustained initially by the Supreme Court in *Ex Parte Vallandigham.* Once the war was safely over, a sharply divided Court rejected the president's action in the leading case of *Ex Parte Milligan.* It is difficult to reconcile *Vallandigham* and *Milligan,* but the Union had been saved and victory achieved when *Milligan* was decided: *inter arma silent leges.* Nevertheless the vigorous dissent of Chief Justice Chase in *Milligan* (joined by Justices Wayne, Swayne and Miller), asserted that Congress could have authorized the president's action:

> Congress has the power not only to raise and support and govern armies but to declare war. It has, therefore, the power to provide by law for carrying on war. This power necessarily extends to all legislation essential for the prosecution of the war with vigor and success, except such as interferes with the command of the forces and the conduct of campaigns. That power and duty belongs to the President as Commander in Chief. Both these powers are derived from the Constitution, but neither is defined by that instrument. Their extent must be determined by their nature, and by the principles of our institutions.

After the Civil War, the powers of the president were tested further in *Mississippi v. Johnson,* which involved an attempt by the State of Mississippi to enjoin President Johnson from enforcing the Reconstruction Acts on the grounds that they were unconstitutional. But the Supreme Court rejected Mississippi's argument, effectively placing the president beyond the reach of judicial intervention in the exercise of his official powers. The initial argument for the president was made by Attorney General Stanbery, who said, "It is not upon any peculiar immunity that the individual has who happens to be President; upon any idea that he cannot do wrong; upon any idea that there is any particular sanctity belonging to him as an individual, . . . but it is on account of the office he holds that . . . the President is above the process of any court . . . to bring him to account as President." Stanbery maintained that the impeachment court of the Senate was the only court that could call the president to account for his official acts.

Speaking through Chief Justice Chase, the Supreme Court agreed. "The Congress is the legislative department of the government; the President is the executive department. Neither can be restrained in its action by the judicial department; though the acts of both, when performed, are, in proper cases, subject to judicial cognizance."

During World War II, the Court appears to have come close to embracing the dissenting opinion in *Milligan* in the case of *Ex Parte Quirin,* involving four captured Nazi saboteurs tried by a special military commission established by President Roosevelt. Said Chief Justice Stone, speaking for a unanimous Court, the powers of the president as Commander in Chief in time of war "are not to be set aside by the courts without clear conviction that they are in conflict with the Constitution . . ."

IMPLIED POWERS

The duty of the president to take care that the laws be faithfully executed is not "limited to the enforcement of acts of Congress or of treaties according to their express terms" but encompasses a far broader discretionary power. In the famous case of *In re Neagle* in 1890, the Supreme Court held that the president's duty also embraced "the rights, duties, and obligation growing out of the Constitution itself, our international relations, and all the protection implied by the nature of the government under the Constitution."[5] Five years later in the *Debs* case,[6] the Court unanimously upheld the right of the executive to secure an injunction against striking railway employees, although there was no statutory basis for such action.

The extraordinary growth of presidential power during the last fifty years may actually have begun with William McKinley and Theodore Roosevelt. The Spanish–American War and McKinley's deployment of troops in China during the Boxer Rebellion brought the United States onto the world scene as a major actor. Theodore Roosevelt claimed in his *Autobiography* that he not only had a right but a duty "to do anything that the needs of the Nation demanded unless such action was forbidden by the Constitution or by the laws." Woodrow Wilson, writing about the presidency in his book on *Constitutional Government,* said that "the President is at liberty, both in law and in conscience, to be as big a man as he can."

But it was the presidency of Franklin Delano Roosevelt that marked the final elevation of the office to its current status. The economic crisis of the early thirties followed by World War II provided both the opportunity and the necessity to exercise broad discretionary powers, on a virtually continuous basis.

WORLD WAR II

The most drastic example of the president's implied war powers undoubtedly relates to the 1942 "relocation" of Americans of Japanese ancestry living on the West Coast. On February 19, 1942, President Roosevelt issued an Executive Order directing the secretary of war "to prescribe military areas in such places and in such extent as he or the appropriate Military Commanders may determine, from which any or all persons may be excluded...." As a result, more than 120,000 persons of Japanese descent, two-thirds of whom were natural born United States citizens, were removed from their homes and transferred first to temporary camps and later to "relocation centers" in the desert. These measures came before the Supreme Court in *Korematsu v. United States*[7] in 1944. The anguish of the Court is apparent in the majority decision written by Justice Black. But just as during the Civil War, it is apparent that the Court did not wish to embarrass the president's conduct of the war or substitute its judgment for his in matters of military necessity. Said Black:

> We uphold the exclusion order as of the time it was made and when petitioner violated it. In doing so, we are not unmindful of the hardships imposed by it upon a large group of American citizens. But hardships are part of war, and war is an aggregation of hardships. .... Compulsory exclusion of large groups of citizens from their homes except under circumstances of direst emergency and peril, is inconsistent with our basic governmental institutions. But when under conditions of modern warfare our shores are threatened by hostile forces, the power to protect must be commensurate with the threatened danger.

Two years later with the war safely won, a sharply divided Court, again speaking through Black, overturned the executive's imposition of martial law in Hawaii following the attack on Pearl Harbor.[8]

The execution of General Yamashita for alleged war crimes presents a related example of the breadth of the president's powers in wartime. Another sharply divided Court held that the findings of properly constituted military trial commissions are not reviewable by civilian courts. But as Justices Rutledge and Murphy protested in dissent, the Court's decision meant that such military proceedings are effectively placed beyond the "rule of law." The dissent by Justice Murphy in *Yamashita* is perhaps the most moving critique of a military conviction in modern judicial history.

As the Steel Seizure Case of 1952 suggests, the president's "inherent" emergency powers can be scrutinized quite closely by the Court when the emergency is not so apparent or when Congress has entered the field contrary to the president. The Court divided 6–3 rejecting President Truman's authority to seize the nation's steel mills in *Youngstown Sheet and Tube v. Sawyer*, and the Justices in the majority wrote six separate opinions. While the case produced no clear rule regarding limits of presidential authority, it does suggest that executive power, particularly when exercised in the domestic context, must proceed cautiously when taking private property. The decision also illustrates that while presidents may not be enjoined by the Court (*Mississippi v. Johnson*), their subordinates may be the objects of injunctive relief when they threaten to act illegally.

NATIONAL SECURITY IN THE DOMESTIC CONTEXT

The Pentagon Papers case during the Vietnam War (*New York Times v. United States*), provides another example in which the Supreme Court declined to accept executive branch protestations of national security. In June 1971 the Department of Justice sought to enjoin the *New York Times* and the *Washington Post* from publishing the contents of a classified Defense Department study about U.S. decision making on Vietnam. The brief *per curiam* decision by the Court merely stated that the government had not met the burden of "showing justification for . . . such restraint." But like the Steel Seizure Case, the complexity of the issue is illustrated in that the Justices wrote nine separate opinions, six concurring and three dissenting.

Similarly, in *United States v. United States District Court* in 1972, the Supreme Court rejected the argument of Attorney General Mitchell that "the President, acting through the Attorney General, may constitutionally authorize the use of electronic surveillance without court approval in cases when he has determined that, in order to preserve national security the use of such surveillance is reasonable." Speaking for a unanimous Court, Justice Powell said: "The price of lawful public dissent must not be a dread of subjection to an unchecked surveillance power. Nor must the fear of unauthorized official eavesdropping deter vigorous citizen dissent and discussion of Government action in private conversation. For private dissent, no less than open public discourse, is essential to our free society." But in *Laird v. Tatum,* a seemingly related case involving Army surveillance of domestic political activity, a sharply divided court dismissed a class action suit challenging the Army's activities.

The landmark case of *United States v. Nixon* produced another set back for extravagant claims of presidential power as a unanimous Court rejected President Nixon's claims of absolute executive privilege—that is, the right of the executive branch to shield its communications from the courts and Congress. The Supreme Court held that neither the separation of powers nor the confidentiality of executive communications barred the federal courts from access to presidential tapes needed as evidence in a criminal case. Chief Justice Burger, who spoke for the Court, was careful to point out that the president had made no "claim of need to protect military, diplomatic, or sensitive national secrets," and implied that in these circumstances the Court's decision might have been different.

More recently, in *Dames & Moore v. Regan* in 1981, the Court appears to have retreated from the *Youngstown* holding when it upheld President Carter's extraordinary financial agreement with Iran to secure the release of the American Embassy hostages. The effect of Carter's action denied American companies with financial claims against Iran access to U.S. courts. Those claims were instead placed before a special arbitration commission. As Justice Rehnquist observed in sustaining the president's action, the Framers "did not make the judiciary the overseer of our government." As a result of the decision in *Dames & Moore,* the presidency enjoys much greater discretionary power to employ the economic resources of the United States for national security purposes. The passage of the International Emergency Economic Powers Act in 1977 provided broad congressional authorization for presidents to act when in their judgment, the situation requires it. The Executive Order issued by President Reagan severing economic relations with Libya is a recent example of the exercise of such discretionary authority.

In *Nixon v. Fitzgerald* in 1982, the Court held that presidents are absolutely immune from civil suits arising out of their official acts. This is an extention of the earlier 1827 rendering by Justice Story in *Martin v. Mott.* Speaking through Justice Powell, the Court said: "The President occupies a unique position in the constitutional scheme," and that "[b]ecause of the singular importance of the President's duties, diversion of his energies by concern with private lawsuits would raise unique risks to the effective functioning of government."

The authority of the executive to withhold sensitive intelligence information was sustained recently by a unanimous Court in *CIA v. Sims.* In the words of Chief Justice Burger, "The national interest sometimes makes it advisable, or even imperative, not to disclose information that may lead to the identity of intelligence sources. And it is the responsibility of the Director of Central Intelligence, not that of the judiciary, to weigh the variety of complex and subtle factors in determining whether disclosure of information may lead to an unacceptable risk...."

PRESIDENTIAL RESPONSIBILITY

Within the executive branch itself, final responsibility rests exclusively with the president. As Chief Justice Taft made clear in *Myers v. United States,* [9] the executive power entrusted to the president in Article II is complete and indivisible. After World War II, when the National Security Council was established,[10] President Truman insisted that the NSC was merely advisory to the president: that it did not enjoy decision-making authority.[11] The language of the Act is explicit:

> The function of the Council *shall be to advise the President* with respect to the integration of domestic, foreign and military policies relating to the national security.... [Emphasis added.]

Senator John Tower, chairman of President Reagan's Special Review Board to investigate the activities of the National Security Council, was equally explicit when he presented findings of the Board [12] at a nationally televised press conference on February 26, 1987. Said Tower:

> The President is the ultimate decision-maker in national security. No one can or should pretend otherwise. We could not long endure exercise of Executive power by committee. A strong Executive with the flexibility to conduct foreign and diplomatic affairs is an essential feature of our form of government.

The Report of the Review Board restated the president's constitutional authority. "Ours is a government of checks and balances, of shared power and responsibility. The Constitution places the President and the Congress in dynamic tension. They both cooperate and compete in making national policy.

"National security is no exception. The Constitution gives both the President and the Congress an important role. The Congress is critical in formulating national policies and in marshalling the resources to carry them out. But those resources—the nation's military personnel, its diplomats, its intelligence capability—are lodged in the Executive Branch. As Chief Executive and Commander in Chief, and with broad authority in the area of foreign affairs, it is the President who is empowered to act for the nation and protect its interests." [13]

THE LOGAN ACT

January 30, 1799

ACTS OF THE FIFTH CONGRESS OF THE UNITED STATES

Passed at the third session, which was begun and held at the City of Philadelphia, in the state of Pennsylvania, on Monday, the third day of December, 1798, and ended on the third day of March, 1799.

STATUTE III

Chapter I—An Act for the Punishment of certain Crimes therein specified.[14]

Be it enacted by the Senate and House of Representatives of the United States of America in Congress assembled, That if any person, being a citizen of the United States, whether he be actually resident, or abiding within the United States, or in any foreign country, shall, without the permission or authority of the government of the United States, directly or indirectly, commence, or carry on, any verbal or written correspondence or intercourse with any foreign government, or any officer or agent thereof, with an intent to influence the measures or conduct of any foreign government, or of any officer or agent thereof, in relation to any disputes or controversies with the United States, or defeat the measures of the government of the United States; or if any person, being a citizen of, or resident within the United States, and not duly authorized, shall counsel, advise, aid or assist in any such correspondence, with intent, as aforesaid, he or they shall be deemed guilty of a high misdemeanor, and on conviction before any court of the United States having jurisdiction thereof, shall be punished by a fine not exceeding five thousand dollars, and by imprisonment during a term not less than six months, nor exceeding three years: *Provided always,* that nothing in this act contained shall be construed to abridge the right of individual citizens of the United States to apply, by themselves, or their lawful agents, to any foreign government, or the agents thereof, for the redress of any injuries in relation to person or property which such individuals may have sustained from such government, or any of its agents, citizens or subjects.

———— MARTIN V. MOTT ————

12 Wheaton (25 U.S.) 19 (1827)

During the War of 1812, President Madison ordered portions of the New York militia into active federal service. Jacob Mott, a private in the militia, was ordered to report for duty in August 1814, but refused to do so. He was tried by court martial, convicted, and fined $96. When Mott failed to pay, the U.S. deputy marshall [Martin] seized certain goods of equivalent value belonging to Mott. Mott initiated suit in New York state court to recover the goods, claiming, among other things, that the president did not provide sufficient justification for calling forth the militia and had abused his authority as commander in chief. Mott was awarded judgment, the New York Supreme Court affirmed, and Martin appealed on a writ of error to the U.S. Supreme Court.

Justice **Story** delivered the opinion of the Court:

The Constitution declares that Congress shall have power "to provide for calling forth the militia, to execute the laws of the Union, suppress insurrections, and repel invasions:" and also "to provide for organizing, arming, and disciplining the militia, and for governing such part of them as may be employed in the service of the United States." In pursuance of this authority, the act of 1795 has provided, "that whenever the United States shall be invaded, or be in imminent danger of invasion from any foreign nation or

Indian tribe, it shall be lawful for the President of the United States to call forth such number of the militia of the State or States most convenient to the place of danger, or scene of action, as he may judge necessary to repel such invasion, and to issue his order for that purpose to such officer or officers of the militia as he shall think proper." . . . [T]he power to provide for repelling invasions includes the power to provide against the attempt and danger of invasion, as the necessary and proper means to effectuate the object. One of the best means to repel invasion is to provide the requisite force for action before the invader himself has reached the soil.

The power thus confided by Congress to the President is, doubtless, of a very high and delicate nature. A free people are naturally jealous of the exercise of military power; and the power to call the militia into actual service is certainly felt to be one of no ordinary magnitude. But it is not a power which can be executed without a correspondent responsibility. It is, in its terms, a limited power, confined to cases of actual invasion, or of imminent danger of invasion. If it be a limited power, the question arises, by whom is the exigency to be judged of and decided? Is the President the sole and exclusive judge whether the exigency has arisen, or is it to be considered as an open question, upon which every officer to whom the orders of the President are addressed, may decide for himself, and equally open to be contested by every militiaman who shall refuse to obey the orders of the President? We are all of opinion, that the authority to decide whether the exigency has arisen, belongs exclusively to the President, and that his decision is conclusive upon all other persons. We think that this construction necessarily results from the nature of the power itself, and from the manifest object contemplated by the act of Congress. The power itself is to be exercised upon sudden emergencies, upon great occasions of state, and under circumstances which may be vital to the existence of the Union. A prompt and unhesitating obedience to orders is indispensable to the complete attainment of the object. The service is a military service, and the command of a military nature; and in such cases, every delay, and every obstacle to an efficient and immediate compliance, necessarily tend to jeopardize the public interests. . . . If "the power of regulating the militia, and of commanding its services in times of insurrection and invasion, are (as it has been emphatically said they are) natural incidents to the duties of superintending the common defense, and of watching over the internal peace of the confederacy" [*The Federalist*, No. 29], these powers must be so construed as to the modes of their exercise as not to defeat the great end in view. If a superior officer has a right to contest the orders of the President upon his own doubts as to the exigency having arisen, it must be equally the right of every inferior officer and soldier; and any act done by any person in furtherance of such orders would subject him to responsibility in a civil suit, in which his defense must finally rest upon his ability to establish the facts by competent proofs. Such a course would be subversive of all discipline, and expose the best disposed officers to the chances of ruinous litigation. Besides, in many instances, the evidence upon which the President might decide that there is imminent danger of invasion, might be of a nature not constituting strict technical proof, or the disclosure of the evidence might reveal important secrets of state, which the public interest, and even safety, might imperiously demand to be kept in concealment.

.... [The President] is necessarily constituted the judge of the existence of the exigency in the first instance, and is bound to act according to his belief of the facts. If he does so act, and decides to call forth the militia, his orders for this purpose are in strict conformity with the provisions of the law; and it would seem to follow as a necessary consequence, that every act done by a subordinate officer, in obedience to such orders, is equally justifiable. The law contemplates that, under such circumstances, orders shall be given to carry the power into effect; and it cannot therefore be a correct inference that any other person has a just right to disobey them. The law does not provide for any appeal from the judgment of the President, or for any right in subordinate officers to review his decision, and in effect defeat it. Whenever a statute gives a discretionary power to any person, to be exercised by him upon his own opinion of certain facts, it is a sound rule of construction, that the statute constitutes him the sole and exclusive judge of the existence of those facts....

Reversed and Annulled.

FLEMING V. PAGE

9 Howard (50 U.S.) 603 (1850)

During the Mexican War the United States captured and occupied the port of Tampico on the Gulf of Mexico. In June 1847, the schooner Catharine *sailed from Tampico to Philadelphia, and was denied entry unless duty was paid on her cargo. The owners of the cargo [Fleming et al.] paid the duty but brought suit to recover from the collector of customs [Page], claiming that because Tampico was under U.S. occupation, it was not a foreign port under the meaning of the Tariff Act of July 30, 1846. The circuit court was divided on the issue, and certified the case to the Supreme Court for a ruling.*

Chief Justice **Taney** delivered the opinion of the Court:

The question certified by the Circuit Court turns upon the construction of the act of Congress of July 30, 1846. The duties levied upon the cargo of the schooner *Catharine* were the duties imposed by this law upon goods imported from a foreign country. And if at the time of this shipment Tampico was not a foreign port within the meaning of the act of Congress, then the duties were illegally charged, and, having been paid under protest, the plaintiffs would be entitled to recover in this action the amount exacted by the collector.

The port of Tampico, at which the goods were shipped, and the Mexican State of Tamaulipas, in which it is situated, were undoubtedly at the time of the shipment subject to the sovereignty and dominion of the United States. The Mexican authorities had been driven out, or had submitted to our army and navy; and the country was in the exclusive and firm possession of the United States, and governed by its military authorities, acting under the orders of the President. But it does not follow that it was a part of the United States, or that it ceased to be a foreign country, in the sense in which these words are used in the acts of Congress....

The genius and character of our institutions are peaceful, and the power to declare war was not conferred upon Congress for the purposes of aggression or aggrandizement, but to enable the general government to vindicate by arms, if it should become necessary, its own rights and the rights of its citizens.

A war, therefore, declared by Congress, can never be presumed to be waged for the purpose of conquest or the acquisition of territory; nor does the law declaring the war imply an authority to the President to enlarge the limits of the United States by subjugating the enemy's country. The United States, it is true, may extend its boundaries by conquest or treaty, and may demand the cession of territory as the condition of peace, in order to indemnify its citizens for the injuries they have suffered, or to reimburse the government for the expenses of the war. But this can be done only by the treaty-making power or the legislative authority, and is not a part of the power conferred upon the President by the declaration of war. His duty and his power are purely military. As commander in chief, he is authorized to direct the movements of the naval and military forces placed by law at his command, and to employ them in the manner he may deem most effectual to harass and conquer and subdue the enemy. He may invade the hostile country, and subject it to the sovereignty and authority of the United States. But his conquests do not enlarge the boundaries of this Union, nor extend the operation of our institutions and laws beyond the limits before assigned to them by the legislative power....

Every nation which acquires territory by treaty or conquest holds it according to its own institutions and laws. And the relation in which the port of Tampico stood to the United States while it was occupied by their arms did not depend upon the laws of nations, but upon our own Constitution and acts of Congress. The power of the President under which Tampico and the State of Tamaulipas were conquered and held in subjection was simply that of a military commander prosecuting a war waged against a public enemy by the authority of his government. And the country from which these goods were imported was invaded and subdued, and occupied as the territory of a foreign hostile nation, as a portion of Mexico, and was held in possession in order to distress and harass the enemy. While it was occupied by our troops, they were in an enemy's country, and not in their own; the inhabitants were still foreigners and enemies, and owed to the United States nothing more than the submission and obedience, sometimes called temporary allegiance, which is due from a conquered enemy, when he surrenders to a force which he is unable to resist. But the boundaries of the United States, as they existed when war was declared against Mexico, were not extended by the conquest; nor could they be regulated by the varying incidents of war, and be enlarged or diminished as the armies on either side advanced or retreated. They remained unchanged. And every place which was out of the limits of the United States, as previously established by the political authorities of the government, was still foreign; nor did our laws extend over it. Tampico was, therefore, a foreign port when this shipment was made....

.... Our own Constitution and form of government must be our only guide. And we are entirely satisfied that, under the Constitution and laws of the United States, Tampico was a foreign port, within the meaning of the act of 1846, when these goods were shipped, and that the cargoes were liable to the duty charged upon them. And we shall certify accordingly to the Circuit Court.

*Justice **McLean** dissented.*

———————————— THE PRIZE CASES ————————————

2 Black (67 U.S.) 635 (1862)

In the spring of 1861, the southern states, led by South Carolina, began to secede from the Union. When the Confederates fired on Fort Sumter, President Lincoln, with Congress in recess, issued a proclamation stating that the execution of federal laws was being obstructed "by combinations too powerful to be suppressed by the ordinary course of judicial proceedings." He called the militia to federal service to suppress the rebellion and on April 27, 1861, ordered a blockade of southern ports. When Congress reconvened in July, it passed legislation recognizing that a state of insurrection existed (Act of July 13, 1861) and on August 6 approved the proclamations and orders previously issued by the president.

During the interval between President Lincoln's proclamation of the blockade and action by Congress recognizing the existence of the rebellion, a number of neutral ships and cargoes moving to and from southern ports were seized by the United States Navy and condemned as prizes in the federal courts. The original owners appealed.

Justice **Grier** delivered the opinion of the Court:

.... By the Constitution, Congress alone has the power to declare a national or foreign war. It cannot declare war against a State, or any number of States, by virtue of any clause in the Constitution. The Constitution confers on the President the whole Executive power. He is bound to take care that the laws be faithfully executed. He is Commander in chief of the Army and Navy of the United States, and of the militia of the several States when called into the actual service of the United States. He has no power to initiate or declare a war either against a foreign nation or a domestic State. But by the Acts of Congress of February 28th, 1795, and 3rd of March, 1807, he is authorized to call out the militia and use the military and naval forces of the United States in case of invasion by foreign nations, and to suppress insurrection against the government of a State or of the United States.

If a war be made by invasion of a foreign nation, the President is not only authorized but bound to resist force by force. He does not initiate the war, but is bound to accept the challenge without waiting for any special legislative authority. And whether the hostile party be a foreign invader, or States organized in rebellion, it is none the less a war, although the declaration of it be "unilateral." Lord Stowell observes, "It is not the less a war on *that account,* for war may exist without a declaration on either side.... A declaration of war by one country only, is not a mere challenge to be accepted or refused at pleasure by the other."

.... This greatest of civil wars was not gradually developed by popular commotion, tumultuous assemblies, or local unorganized insurrections. However long may have been its previous conception, it nevertheless sprung forth suddenly from the parent brain, a Minerva in the full panoply of *war.* The President was bound to meet it in the shape it presented itself, without waiting for Congress to baptize it with a name; and no name given to it by him or them could change the fact.

.... Whether the President in fulfilling his duties, as Commander in chief, in suppressing an insurrection, has met such armed hostile resistance, and a civil war of such alarming proportions as will compel him to accord to them the character of belligerents, is a question to be decided *by him,* and this Court must be governed by the decisions and acts of the political department of the Government to which this power was entrusted. "He must determine what degree of force the crisis demands." The proclamation of blockade is itself official and conclusive evidence to the Court that a state of war existed which demanded and authorized a recourse to such a measure, under the circumstances peculiar to the case....

If it were necessary to the technical existence of a war, that it should have a legislative sanction, we find it in almost every act passed at the extraordinary session of the Legislature of 1861, which was wholly employed in enacting laws to enable the Government to prosecute the war with vigor and efficiency. And finally, in 1861, we find Congress *"ex majore caute-la "* and in anticipation of such astute objections, passing an act "approving, legalizing, and making valid all the acts, proclamations, and orders of the President, &c., as if they had been *issued and done under the previous express authority* and direction of the Congress of the United States."

Without admitting that such an act was necessary under the circumstances it is plain that if the President had in any manner assumed powers which it was necessary should have the authority or sanction of Congress, that on the well known principle of law, *"amnis ratihabitio retrotrahitur et mandato equiparatur,"* this ratification has operated to perfectly cure the defect.

.... The objection made to this act of ratification, that is *ex post facto,* and therefore unconstitutional and void, might possibly have some weight on the trial of an indictment in a criminal Court. But precedents from that source cannot be received as authoritative in a tribunal administering public and international law.

.... [T]herefore we are of the opinion that the President had a right, *jure belli,* to institute a blockade of ports in possession of the States in rebellion, which neutrals are bound to regard.

Justice **Nelson,** *dissenting.* By our Constitution ... Congress shall have power "to declare war, grant letters of marque and reprisal, and make rules concerning captures on land and water...."

In the case of a rebellion or resistance of a portion of the people of a country against the established government, there is no doubt, if in its progress and enlargement the government thus sought to be overthrown sees fit, it may by the competent power recognize or declare the existence of a state of civil war, which will draw after it all the consequences and rights of war between the contending parties as in the case of a public war.... But before this insurrection against the established Government can be dealt with on the footing of a civil war, within the meaning of the law of nations and the Constitution of the United States, and which will draw after it belligerent rights, it must be recognized or declared by the war-making power of the Government. No power short of this can change the legal status of the Government or the relations of its citizens from that of peace to a state of war....

Now, in one sense, no doubt this is war, ... but it is a statement simply of its existence in a material sense, and has no relevancy or weight when the question is what constitutes war in a legal sense, in the sense of the law of nations, and of the Constitution of the United States? For it must be a war in this sense to attach to it all the consequences that belong to belligerent rights. Instead, therefore, of inquiring after armies and navies, and victories lost and won, or organized rebellion against the general Government, the inquiry should be into the law of nations and into the municipal fundamental laws of the Government. For we find there that to constitute a civil war in the sense in which we are speaking, before it can exist, in contemplation of law, it must be recognized or declared by the sovereign power of the State, and which sovereign power by our Constitution is lodged in the Congress of the United States—civil war, therefore, under our system of government, can exist only by an act of Congress, which requires the assent of two of the great departments of the Government, the Executive and Legislative.

.... I am compelled to the conclusion that no civil war existed between this Government and the States in insurrection till recognized by the Act of Congress 13th of July, 1861; that the President does not possess the power under the Constitution to declare war or recognize its existence within the meaning of the law of nations, which carries with it belligerent rights, and thus change the country and all its citizens from a state of peace to a state of war; that this power belongs exclusively to the Congress of the United States, and, consequently, that the President had no power to set on foot a blockade under the law of nations, and that the capture of the vessel and cargo in this case, and in all cases before us in which the capture occurred before the 13th of July, 1861, for breach of blockade, or as enemies' property, are illegal and void, and that the decrees of condemnation should be reversed and the vessel and cargo restored.

*Chief Justice **Taney**, Justice **Catron** and Justice **Clifford**, concurred in the dissenting opinion of Justice **Nelson**.*

Ex Parte Vallandigham

1 Wallace (68 U.S.) 243 (1863)

Pursuant to military directives issued with the approval of President Lincoln, General Burnside, commander of the military department of Ohio, appointed a military commission to try all persons assisting or declaring sympathy for the rebels. On May 5, 1863, Val-landigham was arrested by military authorities and charged with "having expressed sympa-thy for those in arms against the Government of the United States, and having uttered, in a speech at a public meeting, disloyal sentiments and opinions, with the object and purpose of weakening the power of the Government. . . ." He was tried by military commission, convicted, and sentenced to confinement for the duration of the war. The sentence was approved by General Burnside, and Vallandigham moved for certiorari, *claiming that the military commission lacked jurisdiction.*

Justice **Wayne** delivered the opinion of the Court:

. . . . It is affirmed . . . that military jurisdiction is of two kinds. First, that which is conferred and defined by statute; second, that which is derived from the common law of war. "Military offences, under the statute, must be tried in the manner therein directed; but military offences, which do not come within the statute, must be tried and punished under the common law of war. . . ."

These jurisdictions are applicable, not only to war with foreign nations, but to a rebellion, when a part of a country wages war against its legitimate government, seeking to throw off all allegiance to it, to set up a government of its own.

Our first remark upon *the motion for a certiorari* is, that . . . [t]he courts of the United States derive authority to issue such a writ from the Constitution and the legislation of Congress. . . .

The appellate powers of the Supreme Court, as granted by the Consti-tution, are limited and regulated by the acts of Congress, and must be exercised subject to the exceptions and regulations made by Congress. In other words, the petition before us we think not to be within the letter or spirit of the grants of appellate jurisdiction to the Supreme Court. It is not in law or equity within the meaning of those terms as used in the 3d article of the Constitution. Nor is a military commission a court within the meaning of the 14th section of the Judiciary Act of 1789. That act is denominated to be one to establish the judicial courts of the United States, and the 14th section declares that all the "before-mentioned courts" of the United States shall have power to issue writs of *scire facias, habeas corpus,* and all other writs not specially provided for by statute, which may be necessary for the exer-cise of their respective jurisdictions, agreeably to the principles and usages of law. The words in the section, "the before-mentioned" courts, can only have reference to such courts as were established in the preceding part of the act, and excludes the idea that a court of military commission can be one of them.

Whatever may be the force of Vallandigham's protest, that he was not triable by a court of military commission, it is certain that his petition cannot be brought within the 14th section of the act; and further, that the court cannot, without disregarding its frequent decisions and interpretation of the Constitution in respect to its judicial power, originate a writ of *certiorari* to review or pronounce any opinion upon the proceedings of a military commission. It was natural, before the sections of the 3d article of the Constitution had been fully considered in connection with the legislation of Congress, giving to the courts of the United States power to issue writs of *scire facias, habeas corpus,* and all other writs not specially provided for by statute, which might be necessary for the exercise of their respective jurisdiction, that by some members of the profession it should have been thought, and some of the early judges of the Supreme Court also, that the 14th section of the act of 24th September, 1789, gave to this court a right to originate processes of *habeas corpus ad subjiciendum,* writs of *certiorari* to review the proceedings of the inferior courts as a matter of original jurisdiction, without being in any way restricted by the constitutional limitation, that in all cases affecting ambassadors, other public ministers and consuls, and those in which a State shall be a party, the Supreme Court shall have original jurisdiction. This limitation has always been considered restrictive of any other original jurisdiction. *The rule of construction of the Constitution being, that affirmative words in the Constitution, declaring in what cases the Supreme Court shall have original jurisdiction, must be construed negatively as to all other cases.* The nature and extent of the court's appellate jurisdiction and its want of it to issue writs of *habeas corpus ad subjiciendum* have been fully discussed by this court at different times....

And as to the President's action in such matters, and those acting in them under his authority, we refer to the opinions expressed by this court, in the cases of *Martin v. Mott,* and *Dynes v. Hoover.*

For the reasons given, our judgment is, that the writ of *certiorari* prayed for to revise and review the proceedings of the military commission, by which Clement L. Vallandigham was tried, sentenced, and imprisoned, must be denied, and so do we order accordingly.

Certiorari Refused.

Nelson, *J.*, Grier, *J.*, and **Field, *J.*,** *concurred in the result of this opinion.* **Miller, *J.*,** *was not present at the argument, and took no part.*

Ex Parte Milligan

4 Wallace (71 U.S.) 2 (1866)

During the Civil War, Congress passed several acts authorizing the suspension of the writ of habeas corpus. *Pursuant to this legislation, President Lincoln issued a proclamation suspending the writ in cases where members of the military held "persons in their custody either as prisoners of war, spies, or aiders and abettors of the enemy...." In 1864, Milligan, a U.S. citizen and resident of Indiana, was arrested and tried before a military commission for "affording aid and comfort to the rebels against the authority of the United States." He was convicted and sentenced to hang.*

Milligan petitioned the federal courts for a writ of habeas corpus, *contending that the military commission had no jurisdiction to try him since the civil courts of Indiana were still in operation. The judges of the circuit court divided on the issue, and the case was certified to the Supreme Court.*

Justice **Davis** delivered the opinion of the Court:

Have any of the rights guaranteed by the Constitution been violated in the case of Milligan? and if so, what are they?

Every trial involves the exercise of judicial power; and from what source did the military commission that tried him derive their authority? Certainly no part of the judicial power of the country was conferred on them; because the Constitution expressly vests it "in one supreme court and such inferior courts as the Congress may from time to time ordain and establish," and it is not pretended that the commission was a court ordained and established by Congress....

But it is said that the jurisdiction is complete under the "laws and usages of war."

It can serve no useful purpose to inquire what those laws and usages are, whence they originated, where found, and on whom they operate; they can never be applied to citizens in states which have upheld the authority of the government, and where the courts are open and their process unobstructed. This court has judicial knowledge that in Indiana the Federal authority was always unopposed, and its courts always open to hear criminal accusations and redress grievances; and no usage of war could sanction a military trial there for any offence whatever of a citizen in civil life, in nowise connected with the military service....

One of the plainest constitutional provisions was, therefore, infringed when Milligan was tried by a court not ordained and established by Congress, and not composed of judges appointed during good behavior.

Why was he not delivered to the Circuit Court of Indiana to be proceeded against according to law? No reason of necessity could be urged against it; because Congress had declared penalties against the offences charged, provided for their punishment, and directed that court to hear and determine them. And soon after this military tribunal was ended, the Circuit Court met, peacefully transacted its business, and adjourned....

The government had no right to conclude that Milligan, if guilty, would not receive in that court merited punishment; for its records disclose that it was constantly engaged in the trial of similar offences, and was never interrupted in its administration of criminal justice. If it was dangerous, in the distracted condition of affairs, to leave Milligan unrestrained of his liberty, because he "conspired against the government, afforded aid and comfort to rebels, and incited the people to insurrection," the *law* said arrest him, confine him closely, render him powerless to do further mischief; and then present his case to the grand jury of the district, with proofs of his guilt, and, if indicted, try him according to the course of the common law. If this had been done, the Constitution would have been vindicated, the law of 1863 enforced, and the securities for personal liberty preserved and defended.

Another guarantee of freedom was broken when Milligan was denied a trial by jury.... The right to trial by jury is *now* assailed; but if ideas can be expressed in words, and language has any meaning, *this right* —one of the most valuable in a free country—is preserved to every one accused of crime who is not attached to the army, or navy, or militia in actual service. The sixth amendment affirms that "in all criminal prosecutions the accused shall enjoy the right to a speedy and public trial by an impartial jury," language broad enough to embrace all persons and cases; but the fifth, recognizing the necessity of an indictment, or presentment, before any one can be held to answer for high crimes, *"excepts* cases arising in the land or naval forces, or in the militia, when in actual service, in time of war or public danger;" and the framers of the Constitution, doubtless, meant to limit the right of trial by jury, in the sixth amendment, to those persons who were subject to indictment or presentment in the fifth.

The discipline necessary to the efficiency of the army and navy, required other and swifter modes of trial than are furnished by the common law courts; and, in pursuance of the power conferred by the Constitution, Congress has declared the kinds of trial, and the manner in which they shall be conducted, for offences committed while the party is in the military or naval service. Every one connected with these branches of the public service is amenable to the jurisdiction which Congress has created for their government, and, while thus serving, surrenders his right to be tried by the civil courts. *All other persons,* citizens of states where the courts are open, if charged with crime, are guaranteed the inestimable privilege of trial by jury. This privilege is a vital principle, underlying the whole administration of criminal justice; it is not held by sufferance, and cannot be frittered away on any plea of state or political necessity. When peace prevails, and the authority of the government is undisputed, there is no difficulty of preserving the safeguards of liberty; for the ordinary modes of trial are never neglected, and no one wishes it otherwise; but if society is disturbed by civil commotion—if the passions of men are aroused and the restraints of law weakened, if not disregarded—these safeguards need, and should receive, the watchful care of those intrusted with the guardianship of the Constitution and laws. In no other way can we transmit to posterity unimpaired the blessings of liberty, consecrated by the sacrifices of the Revolution.

It is claimed that martial law covers with its broad mantle the proceedings of this military commission. The proposition is this: that in a time of war the commander of an armed force (if in his opinion the exigencies of the country demand it, and of which he is to judge), has the power, within the lines of his military district, to suspend all civil rights and their remedies, and subject citizens as well as soldiers to the rule of *his will;* and in the exercise of his lawful authority cannot be restrained, except by his superior officer or the President of the United States.

If this position is sound to the extent claimed, then when war exists, foreign or domestic, and the country is subdivided into military departments for mere convenience, the commander of one of them can, if he chooses, within his limits, on the plea of necessity, with the approval of the Executive, substitute military force for and to the exclusion of the laws, and punish all persons, as he thinks right and proper, without fixed or certain rules.

The statement of this proposition shows its importance; for, if true, republican government is a failure, and there is an end of liberty regulated by law. Martial law, established on such a basis, destroys every guarantee of the Constitution, and effectually renders the "military independent of and superior to the civil power"—the attempt to do which by the King of Great Britain was deemed by our fathers such an offence, that they assigned it to the world as one of the causes which impelled them to declare their independence. Civil liberty and this kind of martial law cannot endure together; the antagonism is irreconcilable; and, in the conflict, one or the other must perish. . . .

The necessities of the service, during the late Rebellion, required that the loyal states should be placed within the limits of certain military districts and commanders appointed in them; and, it is urged, that this, in a military sense, constituted them the theatre of military operations; and, as in this case, Indiana had been and was again threatened with invasion by the enemy, the occasion was furnished to establish martial law. The conclusion does not follow from the premises. If armies were collected in Indiana, they were to be employed in another locality, where the laws were obstructed and the national authority disputed. On *her* soil there was no hostile foot; if once invaded, that invasion was at an end, and with it all pretext for martial law. Martial law cannot arise from a *threatened* invasion. The necessity must be actual and present; the invasion real, such as effectually closes the courts and deposes the civil administration.

. . . There are occasions when martial rule can be properly applied. If, in foreign invasion or civil war, the courts are actually closed, and it is impossible to administer criminal justice according to law, *then,* on the theatre of active military operations, where war really prevails, there is a necessity to furnish a substitute for the civil authority, thus overthrown, to preserve the safety of the army and society; and as no power is left but the military, it is allowed to govern by martial rule until the laws can have their free course. As necessity creates the rule, so it limits its duration; for, if this government is continued *after* the courts are reinstated, it is a gross usurpation of power. Martial rule can never exist where the courts are open, and in the proper and unobstructed exercise of their jurisdiction. It is also confined to the locality of actual war. . . .

If the military trial of Milligan was contrary to law, then he was entitled, on the facts stated in his petition, to be discharged from custody by the terms of the act of Congress of March 3d, 1863. . . .

Chief Justice **Chase,** *joined by Justices* **Wayne, Swayne,** *and* **Miller,** *concurring in part, and* ***dissenting*** *in part.*

* * *

We think that Congress had power, though not exercised, to authorize the military commission which was held in Indiana. . . .

The Constitution itself provides for military government as well as for civil government. And we do not understand it to be claimed that the civil safeguards of the Constitution have application in cases within the proper sphere of the former. . . .

It is not denied that the power to make rules for the government of the army and navy is a power to provide for trial and punishment by military courts without a jury. It has been so understood and exercised from the adoption of the Constitution to the present time.

Nor, in our judgment, does the fifth, or any other amendment, abridge that power. "Cases arising in the land and naval forces, or in the militia in actual service in time of war or public danger," are expressly excepted from the fifth amendment, "that no person shall be held to answer for a capital or otherwise infamous crime, unless on a presentment or indictment of a grand jury," and it is admitted that the exception applied to the other amendments as well as to the fifth.

Congress has the power not only to raise and support and govern armies but to declare war. It has, therefore, the power to provide by law for carrying on war. This power necessarily extends to all legislation essential to the prosecution of war with vigor and success, except such as interferes with the command of the forces and the conduct of campaigns. That power and duty belong to the President as commander in chief. Both these powers are derived from the Constitution, but neither is defined by that instrument. Their extent must be determined by their nature, and by the principles of our institutions. . . .

We by no means assert that Congress can establish and apply the laws of war where no war has been declared or exists.

Where peace exists the laws of peace must prevail. What we do maintain is, that when the nation is involved in war, and some portions of the country are invaded, and all are exposed to invasion, it is within the power of Congress to determine in what states or districts such great and imminent public danger exists as justifies the authorization of military tribunals for the trial of crimes and offences against the discipline or security of the army or against the public safety. . . .

We cannot doubt that, in such a time of public danger, Congress had power, under the Constitution, to provide for the organization of a military commission, and for trial by that commission of persons engaged in this conspiracy. The fact that the Federal courts were open was regarded by Congress as a sufficient reason for not exercising the power; but that fact could not deprive Congress of the right to exercise it. Those courts might be open and undisturbed in the execution of their functions, and yet wholly incompetent to avert threatened danger, or to punish, with adequate promptitude and certainty, the guilty conspirators. . . .

We have confined ourselves to the question of power. It was for Congress to determine the question of expediency. And Congress did determine it. That body did not see fit to authorize trials by military commission in Indiana, but by the strongest implication prohibited them. With that prohibition we are satisfied, and should have remained silent if the answers to the questions certified had been put on that ground, without denial of the existence of a power which we believe to be constitutional and important to the public safety,—a denial which . . . seems to draw in question the power of Congress to protect from prosecution the members of military commissions who acted in obedience to their superior officers, and whose action, whether warranted by law or not, was approved by that upright and patriotic President under whose administration the Republic was rescued from threatened destruction.

. . . . There is no law for the government of the citizens, the armies or the navy of the United States, within American jurisdiction, which is not contained in or derived from the Constitution. And wherever our army or navy may go beyond our territorial limits, neither can go beyond the authority of the President or the legislation of Congress.

We think that the power of Congress, in such times and in such localities, to authorize trials for crimes against the security and safety of the national forces, may be derived from its constitutional authority to raise and support armies and to declare war, if not from its constitutional authority to provide for governing the national forces.

We have no apprehension that this power, under our American system of government, in which all official authority is derived from the people, and exercised under direct responsibility to the people, is more likely to be abused than the power to regulate commerce, or the power to borrow money. And we are unwilling to give our assent by silence to expressions of opinion which seem to us calculated, though not intended, to cripple the constitutional powers of the government, and to augment the public dangers in times of invasion and rebellion.

MISSISSIPPI V. JOHNSON

4 Wallace (71 U.S.) 475 (1866)

In March 1867, Congress passed the Reconstruction Acts over President Johnson's veto. These Acts were designed to insure that "peace and good order should be enforced in the rebel States until loyal and republican State governments could be legally established." Under the Acts the southern states were divided into five military districts, each governed by a military officer. The Acts were to be rescinded only upon the acceptance of each state's representatives in Congress.

Representatives of the state of Mississippi, who were concerned that the Reconstruction Acts infringed liberties protected by the Bill of Rights, brought suit to enjoin President Johnson from enforcing the Acts.

Chief Justice **Chase** delivered the opinion of the Court:

. . . . The single point which requires consideration is this: Can the President be restrained by injunction from carrying into effect an act of Congress alleged to be unconstitutional?

It is assumed by the counsel for the State of Mississippi, that the President, in the execution of the Reconstruction Acts, is required to perform a mere ministerial duty. In this assumption there is, we think, a confounding of the terms ministerial and executive, which are by no means equivalent in import.

A ministerial duty, the performance of which may, in proper cases, be required of the head of a department, by judicial process, is one in respect to which nothing is left to discretion. It is a simple, definite duty, arising under conditions admitted or proved to exist, and imposed by law. . . .

Very different is the duty of the President in the exercise of the power
to see that the laws are faithfully executed, and among these laws the acts
named in the bill. By the first of these acts he is required to assign generals
to command in the several military districts, and to detail sufficient military
force to enable such officers to discharge their duties under the law. By the
supplementary act, other duties are imposed on the several commanding
generals, and these duties must necessarily be performed under the supervision of the President as commander in chief. The duty thus imposed on the
President is in no just sense ministerial. It is purely executive and political.

An attempt on the part of the judicial department of the government to
enforce the performance of such duties by the President might be justly
characterized, in the language of Chief Justice Marshall, as "an absurd and
excessive extravagance."

It is true that in the instance before us the interposition of the court is
not sought to enforce action by the Executive under constitutional legislation, but to restrain such action under legislation alleged to be unconstitutional. But we are unable to perceive that this circumstance takes the case
out of the general principles which forbid judicial interference with the
exercise of Executive discretion.

It was admitted in the argument that the application now made to us is
without a precedent; and this is of much weight against it. . . .

The fact that no such application was ever before made in any case
indicates the general judgment of the profession that no such application
should be entertained.

It will hardly be contended that Congress can interpose, in any case, to
restrain the enactment of an unconstitutional law; and yet how can the right
to judicial interposition to prevent such an enactment, when the purpose is
evident and the execution of that purpose certain, be distinguished, in
principle, from the right to such interposition against the execution of such a
law by the President?

The Congress is the legislative department of the government; the President is the executive department. Neither can be restrained in its action by
the judicial department; though the acts of both, when performed, are, in
proper cases, subject to its cognizance.

The impropriety of such interference will be clearly seen upon consideration of its possible consequences.

Suppose the bill filed and the injunction prayed for allowed. If the
President refuses obedience, it is needless to observe that the court is without power to enforce its process. If, on the other hand, the President com-
plies with the order of the court and refuses to execute the acts of Congress,
is it not clear that a collision may occur between the executive and legislative departments of the government? May not the House of Representatives
impeach the President for such refusal? And in that case could this court
interfere, in behalf of the President, thus endangered by compliance with its
mandate, and restrain by injunction the Senate of the United States from
sitting as a court of impeachment? Would the strange spectacle be offered to
the public world of an attempt by this court to arrest proceedings in that
court?

These questions answer themselves.

The motion for leave to file the bill is, therefore,

Denied.

Ex Parte Quirin

317 U.S. 1 (1942)

Four German saboteurs, armed with explosive devices, were landed by submarine on Amagansett Beach, Long Island, on the night of June 13, 1942. A similar group of four were landed in Florida, June 17, 1942. All were taken into custody by agents of the FBI in New York City and Chicago. At the time of their arrest, all were wearing civilian clothing.

Following their apprehension, President Roosevelt appointed a military commission and directed it to try the petitioners according to the laws and articles of war. The president also prescribed regulations for the procedure of the trial and proclaimed that all persons acting under the instruction of enemy nations were to be denied access to the civil courts. Petitioners filed for a writ of habeas corpus, *and claimed that such trial violated their right to trial by jury under the Fifth and Sixth Amendments.*

Their petition was denied by the district court, and the Supreme Court convened in a special term, June 29, 1942, to hear an emergency appeal.

Chief Justice **Stone** delivered the opinion of the Court:

Petitioners' main contention is that the President is without any statutory or constitutional authority to order the petitioners to be tried by military tribunal for offenses with which they are charged; that in consequence they are entitled to be tried in the civil courts with the safeguards, including trial by jury, which the Fifth and Sixth Amendments guarantee to all persons charged in such courts with criminal offenses. In any case it is urged that the President's Order, in prescribing the procedure of the Commission and the method for review of its findings and sentence, and the proceedings of the Commission under the Order, conflict with Articles of War adopted by Congress ... and are illegal and void....

We are not here concerned with any question of the guilt or innocence of petitioners. Constitutional safeguards for the protection of all who are charged with offenses are not to be disregarded in order to inflict merited punishment on some who are guilty.... But the detention and trial of petitioners—ordered by the President in the declared exercise of his powers as Commander in Chief of the Army in time of war and of grave public danger—are not to be set aside by the courts without the clear conviction that they are in conflict with the Constitution or laws of Congress constitutionally enacted.

Congress and the President, like the courts, possess no power not derived from the Constitution. But one of the objects of the Constitution, as declared by its preamble, is to "provide for the common defence." As a means to that end, the Constitution gives to Congress the power to "provide for the common Defence," Art. I, [sections] 8, cl. 1; "To raise and support Armies," "To provide and maintain a Navy," Art. I, [sections] 8, cl. 12, 13;

and "To make Rules for the Government and Regulation of the land and naval Forces," Art. I, [sections]. 8, cl. 14. Congress is given authority "To declare War, grant Letters of Marque and Reprisal, and make Rules concerning Captures on Land and Water," Art. I, [sections] 8, cl. 11; and "To define and punish Piracies and Felonies committed on the high Seas, and Offences against the Law of Nations," Art. I, [sections] 8, cl. 10. And finally, the Constitution authorizes Congress "To make all Laws which shall be necessary and proper for carrying into Execution the foregoing Powers, and all other Powers vested by this Constitution in the Government of the United States, or in any Department or Officer thereof." Art. I, [sections] 8, cl. 18.

The Constitution confers on the President the "executive Power," Art. II, [sections] 1, cl. 1, and imposes on him the duty to "take Care that the Laws be faithfully executed." Art. II, [sections] 3. It makes him the Commander in Chief of the Army and Navy, Art. II, [sections] 2, cl. 1, and empowers him to appoint and commission officers of the United States. Art. II, [sections] 3, cl. 1.

The Constitution thus invests the President, as Commander in Chief, with the power to wage war which Congress has declared, and to carry into effect all laws passed by Congress for the conduct of war and for the government and regulation of the Armed Forces, and all laws defining and punishing offenses against the law of nations, including those which pertain to the conduct of war....

From the very beginning of its history this Court has recognized and applied the law of war as including that part of the law of nations which prescribes, for the conduct of war, the status, rights and duties of enemy nations as well as of enemy individuals. By the Articles of War, and especially Article 15, Congress has explicitly provided, so far as it may constitutionally do so, that military tribunals shall have jurisdiction to try offenders or offenses against the law of war in appropriate cases. Congress, in addition to making rules for the government of our Armed Forces, has thus exercised its authority to define and punish offenses against the law of nations by sanctioning, within constitutional limitations, the jurisdiction of military commissions to try persons for offenses which, according to the rules and precepts of the law of nations, and more particularly the law of war, are cognizable by such tribunals. And the President, as Commander in Chief, by his Proclamation in time of war has invoked that law. By his Order creating the present Commission he has undertaken to exercise the authority conferred upon him by Congress, and also such authority as the Constitution itself gives the Commander in Chief, to direct the performance of those functions which may constitutionally be performed by the military arm of the nation in time of war.

An important incident to the conduct of war is the adoption of measures by the military command not only to repel and defeat the enemy, but to seize and subject to disciplinary measures those enemies who in their attempt to thwart or impede our military effort have violated the law of war. It is unnecessary for present purposes to determine to what extent the President as Commander in Chief has constitutional power to create military commissions without the support of Congressional legislation. For here

Congress has authorized trial of offenses against the law of war before such commissions. We are concerned only with the question whether it is within the constitutional power of the National Government to place petitioners upon trial before a military commission for the offenses with which they are charged. We must therefore first inquire whether any of the acts charged is an offense against the law of war cognizable before a military tribunal, and if so whether the Constitution prohibits the trial. We may assume that there are acts regarded in other countries, or by some writers on international law, as offenses against the law of war which would not be triable by military tribunal here, either because they are not recognized by our courts as violations of the law of war or because they are of that class of offenses constitutionally triable only by a jury. It was upon such grounds that the Court denied the right to proceed by military tribunal in *Ex parte Milligan.* But as we shall show, these petitioners were charged with an offense against the law of war which the Constitution does not require to be tried by jury.

. . . . The law of war cannot rightly treat those agents of enemy armies who enter our territory, armed with explosives intended for the destruction of war industries and supplies, as any the less belligerent enemies than are agents similarly entering for the purpose of destroying fortified places or our Armed Forces. By passing our boundaries for such purposes without uniform or other emblem signifying their belligerent status, or by discarding that means of identification after entry, such enemies become unlawful belligerents subject to trial and punishment.

But petitioners insist that, even if the offenses with which they are charged are offenses against the law of war, their trial is subject to the requirement of the Fifth Amendment that no person shall be held to answer for a capital or otherwise infamous crime unless on a presentment or indictment of a grand jury, and that such trials by Article III, [sections] 2, and the Sixth Amendment must be by jury in a civil court. . . .

Presentment by a grand jury and trial by a jury of the vicinity where the crime was committed were at the time of the adoption of the Constitution familiar parts of the machinery for criminal trials in the civil courts. But they were procedures unknown to military tribunals, which are not courts in the sense of the Judiciary Article, *Ex parte Vallandigham* . . . and which in the natural course of events are usually called upon to function under conditions precluding resort to such procedures. As this Court has often recognized, it was not the purpose or effect of [sections] 2 of Article III, read in the light of the common law, to enlarge the then existing right to a jury trial. The object was to preserve unimpaired trial by jury in all those cases in which it had been recognized by the common law and in all cases of a like nature as they might arise in the future . . . but not to bring within the sweep of the guaranty those cases in which it was then well understood that a jury trial could not be demanded as of right. . . .

We cannot say that Congress in preparing the Fifth and Sixth Amendments intended to extend trial by jury to the cases of alien or citizen offenders against the law of war otherwise triable by military commission, while withholding it from members of our own armed forces charged with infractions of the Articles of War punishable by death. It is equally inadmissible to construe the Amendments ... as either abolishing all trials by military tribunals, save those of the personnel of our own armed forces, or, what in effect comes to the same thing, on all such tribunals the necessity of proceeding against unlawful enemy belligerents only on presentment and trial by jury. We conclude that the Fifth and Sixth Amendments did not restrict whatever authority was conferred by the Constitution to try offenses against the law of war by military commission, and that petitioners, charged with such an offense not required to be tried by jury at common law, were lawfully placed on trial by the Commission without a jury....

Accordingly, we conclude that Charge I, on which petitioners were detained for trial by the Military Commission, alleged an offense which the President is authorized to order tried by military commission; that his Order convening the Commission was a lawful order and that the Commission was lawfully constituted; that the petitioners were held in lawful custody and did not show cause for their discharge. It follows that the orders of the District Court should be affirmed, and that leave to file petitions for *habeas corpus* in this Court should be denied.

———————— KOREMATSU V. UNITED STATES ————————

323 U.S. 214 (1944)

Pursuant to legislation by Congress and an Executive Order of the president, the U.S. military commander of the Western Defense Command ordered the exclusion of all persons of Japanese ancestry from a large area of the Pacific coast. Korematsu, an American citizen of Japanese descent, remained at his home in the designated "military area" in violation of the Order and was arrested and convicted in the U.S. District Court. The court of appeals affirmed the conviction, and Korematsu appealed.

* * *

Justice **Black** delivered the opinion of the Court:

It should be noted, to begin with, that all legal restrictions which curtail the civil rights of a single racial group are immediately suspect. That is not to say that all such restrictions are unconstitutional. It is to say that courts must subject them to the most rigid scrutiny. Pressing public necessity may sometimes justify the existence of such restrictions; racial antagonism never can....

In the light of the principles we announced in the *Hirabayashi* case, we are unable to conclude that it was beyond the war power of Congress and the Executive to exclude those of Japanese ancestry from the West Coast war area at the time they did. True, exclusion from the area in which one's home is located is a far greater deprivation than constant confinement to the home from 8 p.m. to 6 a.m. Nothing short of apprehension by the proper military authorities of the gravest imminent danger to the public safety can constitutionally justify either. But exclusion from a threatened area, no less than curfew, has a definite and close relationship to the prevention of espionage and sabotage. The military authorities, charged with the primary responsibility of defending our shores, concluded that curfew provided inadequate protection and ordered exclusion. They did so, as pointed out in our *Hirabayashi* opinion, in accordance with Congressional authority to the military to say who should, and who should not, remain in the threatened areas. . . .

Here, as in the *Hirabayashi* case, ". . . we cannot reject as unfounded the judgment of the military authorities and of Congress that there were disloyal members of that population, whose number and strength could not be precisely and quickly ascertained. We cannot say that the war-making branches of the Government did not have ground for believing that in a critical hour such persons could not readily be isolated and separately dealt with, and constituted a menace to the national defense and safety, which demanded that prompt and adequate measures be taken to guard against it."

Like curfew, exclusion of those of Japanese origin was deemed necessary because of the presence of an unascertained number of disloyal members of the group, most of whom we have no doubt were loyal to this country. It was because we could not reject the finding of the military authorities that it was impossible to bring about an immediate segregation of the disloyal from the loyal that we sustained the validity of the curfew order as applying to the whole group. In the instant case, temporary exclusion of the entire group was rested by the military on the same ground. The judgment that exclusion of the whole group was for the same reason a military imperative answers the contention that the exclusion was in the nature of group punishment based on antagonism to those of Japanese origin. That there were members of the group who retained loyalties to Japan has been confirmed by investigations made subsequent to the exclusion. Approximately five thousand American citizens of Japanese ancestry refused to swear unqualified allegiance to the United States and to renounce allegiance to the Japanese Emperor, and several thousand evacuees requested repatriation to Japan.

We uphold the exclusion order as of the time it was made and when the petitioner violated it. In doing so, we are not unmindful of the hardships imposed by it upon a large group of American citizens. But hardships are part of war, and war is an aggregation of hardships. All citizens alike, both in and out of uniform, feel the impact of war in greater or lesser measure. Citizenship has its responsibilities as well as its privileges, and in time of war the burden is always heavier. Compulsory exclusion of large groups of citizens from their homes, except under circumstances of direct emergency and peril, is inconsistent with our basic governmental institutions. But when under conditions of modern warfare our shores are threatened by hostile forces, the power to protect must be commensurate with the threatened danger.

It is said that we are dealing here with the case of imprisonment of a citizen in a concentration camp solely because of his ancestry, without evidence or inquiry concerning his loyalty and good disposition towards the United States. Our task would be simple, our duty clear, were this a case involving the imprisonment of a loyal citizen in a concentration camp because of racial prejudice. Regardless of the true nature of the assembly and relocation centers . . . we are dealing specifically with nothing but an exclusion order. To cast this case into outlines of racial prejudice, without reference to the real military dangers which were presented, merely confuses the issue. Korematsu was not excluded from the Military Area because of hostility to him or his race. He *was* excluded because we are at war with the Japanese Empire, because the properly constituted military authorities feared an invasion of our West Coast and felt constrained to take proper security measures, because they decided that the military urgency of the situation demanded that all citizens of Japanese ancestry be segregated from the West Coast temporarily, and finally, because Congress, reposing its confidence in this time of war in our military leaders—as inevitably it must—determined that they should have the power to do just this. There was evidence of disloyalty on the part of some, the military authorities considered that the need for action was great, and time was short. We cannot—by availing ourselves of the calm perspective of hindsight—now say that at that time these actions were unjustified.

Affirmed

*Justice **Roberts**, dissenting.*

Justice **Murphy,** dissenting: .... The judicial test of whether the Government, on a plea of military necessity, can validly deprive an individual of any of his constitutional rights is whether the deprivation is reasonably related to a public danger that is so "immediate, imminent, and impending" as not to admit of delay and not to permit the intervention of ordinary constitutional processes to alleviate the danger.... Civilian Exclusion Order No. 34, banishing from a prescribed area of the Pacific Coast "all persons of Japanese ancestry, both alien and non-alien," clearly does not meet that test. Being an obvious racial discrimination, the order deprives all those within its scope of the equal protection of the laws as guaranteed by the Fifth Amendment. It further deprives these individuals of their constitutional rights to live and work where they will, to establish a home where they choose and to move about freely. In excommunicating them without benefit of hearings, this order also deprives them of all their constitutional rights to procedural due process. Yet no reasonable relation to an "immediate, imminent, and impending" public danger is evident to support this racial restriction which is one of the most sweeping and complete deprivations of constitutional rights in the history of this nation in the absence of martial law.

It must be conceded that the military and naval situation in the spring of 1942 was such as to generate a very real fear of invasion of the Pacific Coast, accompanied by fears of sabotage and espionage in that area. The military command was therefore justified in adopting all reasonable means necessary to combat these dangers. In adjudging the military action taken in light of the then apparent dangers, we must not erect too high or too meticulous standards; it is necessary only that the action have some reasonable relation to the removal of the dangers of invasion, sabotage and espionage. But the exclusion, either temporarily or permanently, of all persons with Japanese blood in their veins has no such reasonable relation. And that relation is lacking because the exclusion order necessarily must rely for its reasonableness upon the assumption that *all* persons of Japanese ancestry may have a dangerous tendency to commit sabotage and espionage and to aid our Japanese enemy in other ways. It is difficult to believe that reason, logic or experience could be marshalled in support of such an assumption.

The main reasons relied upon by those responsible for the forced evacuation, therefore, do not prove a reasonable relation between the group characteristics of Japanese Americans and the dangers of invasion, sabotage and espionage. The reasons appear, instead, to be largely an accumulation of much of the misinformation, half-truths and insinuations that for years have been directed against Japanese Americans by people with racial and economic prejudices—the same people who have been among the foremost advocates of the evacuation. A military judgment based upon such racial and sociological considerations is not entitled to the great weight ordinarily given the judgments based upon strictly military considerations. Especially is this so when every charge relative to race, religion, culture, geographical location, and legal and economic status has been substantially discredited by independent studies made by experts in these matters.

I dissent from this legalization of racism. Racial discrimination in any form and in any degree has no justifiable part whatever in our democratic way of life. It is unattractive in any setting but it is utterly revolting among a free people who have embraced the principles set forth in the Constitution of the United States. All residents of this nation are kin in some way by blood or culture to a foreign land. Yet they are primarily and necessarily a part of the new and distinct civilization of the United States. They must accordingly be treated at all times as the heirs of the American experiment and as entitled to all the rights and freedoms guaranteed by the Constitution.

Justice **Jackson**, *dissenting*. . . .

————————————— IN RE YAMASHITA —————————————

327 U.S. 1 (1946)

General Yamashita commanded the 14th Army Group of the Imperial Japanese Army in the Philippines from October 9, 1944 until its surrender September 3, 1945. (The reconquest of the Philippines by the United States began approximately at the time when General Yamashita assumed command.) Yamashita's forces numbered some 260,000 troops scattered throughout the Philippines, but the geography of the islands, plus increasing American pressure, made it virtually impossible for General Yamashita to retain effective control. After his surrender, he was charged as a war criminal with violating the rules of war for failing to discharge his duty to control the operations and activities of those under his command. He was tried by special military commission, convicted and sentenced to hang. On General Yamashita's behalf, his counsel filed for a writ of habeas corpus.

Chief Justice **Stone** delivered the opinion of the Court:

. . . . The petitions for *habeas corpus* . . . [contend] . . . that the [U.S.] military commission was without lawful authority or jurisdiction to place petitioner on trial. . . .

The Supreme Court of the Philippine Islands, after hearing argument, denied the petition for *habeas corpus* ... on the ground ... that its jurisdiction was limited to an inquiry as to the jurisdiction of the commission to place petitioner on trial for the offense charged, and that the commission, being validly constituted by the order of General Styer [U.S. commander in the Philippines], had jurisdiction over the person of petitioner and over the trial for the offense charged.

* * *

The authority to create the commission.... An important incident to the conduct of war is the adoption of measures by the military commander, not only to repel and defeat the enemy, but to seize and subject to disciplinary measures those enemies who, in their attempt to thwart or impede our military effort, have violated the law of war. The trial and punishment of enemy combatants who have committed violations of the law of war is thus not only a part of the conduct of war operating as a preventive measure against such violations, but is an exercise of the authority sanctioned by Congress to administer the system of military justice recognized by the law of war. That sanction is without qualification as to the exercise of this authority so long as a state of war exists—from its declaration until peace is proclaimed.... The war power, from which the commission derives its existence, is not limited to victories in the field, but carries with it the inherent power to guard against the immediate renewal of the conflict, and to remedy, at least in ways Congress has recognized, the evils which the military operations have produced....

We cannot say that there is no authority to convene a commission after hostilities have ended to try violations of the law of war committed before their cessation, at least until peace has been officially recognized by treaty or proclamation of the political branch of the Government. In fact, in most instances the practical administration of the system of military justice under the law of war would fail if such authority were thought to end with the cessation of hostilities. For only after their cessation could the greater number of offenders and the principal ones be apprehended and subjected to trial....

The extent to which the power to prosecute violations of the law of war shall be exercised before peace is declared rests, not with the courts, but with the political branch of the Government, and may itself be governed by the terms of an armistice or the treaty of peace. Here, peace has not been agreed upon or proclaimed. Japan, by her acceptance of the Potsdam Declaration and her surrender, has acquiesced in the trials of those guilty of violations of the law of war. The conduct of the trial by the military commission has been authorized by the political branch of the Government, by military command, by international law and usage, and by the terms of the surrender of the Japanese government....

We do not make the laws of war but we respect them so far as they do not conflict with the commands of Congress or the Constitution.... We do not here appraise the evidence on which petitioner was convicted. We do not consider what measures, if any, petitioner took to prevent the commission, by the troops under his command, of the plain violations of the law of war detailed in the bill of particulars, or whether such measures as he may have taken were appropriate and sufficient to discharge the duty imposed upon him. These are questions within the peculiar competence of the military officers composing the commission and were for it to decide. It is plain that the charge on which petitioner was tried charged him with a breach of his duty to control the operations of the members of his command, by permitting them to commit the specified atrocities. This was enough to require the commission to hear evidence tending to establish the culpable failure of petitioner to perform the duty imposed on him by the law of war and to pass upon its sufficiency to establish guilt.

Obviously charges of violations of the law of war triable before a military tribunal need not be stated with the precision of a common law indictment.... But we conclude that the allegations of the charge, tested by any reasonable standard, adequately allege a violation of the law of war and that the commission had authority to try and decide the issue which it raised.

The proceedings before the commission. The regulations prescribed by General MacArthur governing the procedure for the trial of petitioner by the commission directed that the commission should admit such evidence "as in its opinion would be of assistance in proving or disproving the charge, or such as in the commission's opinion would have probative value in the mind of a reasonable man," and that in particular it might admit affidavits, depositions or other statements taken by officers detailed for that purpose by military authority. The petitions in this case charged that in the course of the trial the commission received, over objection by petitioner's counsel, the deposition of a witness taken pursuant to military authority by a United States Army captain. It also, over like objection, admitted hearsay and opinion evidence tendered by the prosecution. Petitioner argues, as ground for the writ of *habeas corpus,* that Article 25 of the Articles of War prohibited the reception in evidence by the commission of depositions on behalf of the prosecution in a capital case, and that Article 38 prohibited the reception of hearsay and of opinion evidence....

We cannot say that the commission, in admitting evidence to which objection is now made, violated any act of Congress, treaty or military command defining the commission's authority. For reasons already stated we hold that the commission's rulings on evidence and on the mode of conducting these proceedings against petitioner are not reviewable by the courts, but only by the reviewing military authorities. From this viewpoint it is unnecessary to consider what, in other situations, the Fifth Amendment might require, and as to that no intimation one way or the other is to be implied....

It ... appears that the order convening the commission was a lawful order, that the commission was lawfully constituted, that petitioner was charged with violation of the law of war, and that the commission had authority to proceed with the trial, and in doing so did not violate any military, statutory or constitutional command. We have considered, but find it unnecessary to discuss, other contentions which we find to be without merit. We therefore conclude that the detention of petitioner for trial and his detention upon his conviction, subject to the prescribed review by the military authorities, were lawful, and that the petition for *certiorari,* and leave to file in this Court petitions for writs of *habeas corpus* and prohibition should be . . .

Denied.

Justice **Murphy,** *dissenting* . . . . The grave issue raised by this case is whether a military commission so established and so authorized may disregard the procedural rights of an accused person as guaranteed by the Constitution, especially by the due process clause of the Fifth Amendment.

The answer is plain. The Fifth Amendment guarantee of due process of law applies to "any person" who is accused of a crime by the Federal Government or any of its agencies. No exception is made as to those who are accused of war crimes or as to those who possess the status of an enemy belligerent. Indeed, such an exception would be contrary to the whole philosophy of human rights which makes the Constitution the great living document that it is. The immutable rights of the individual, including those secured by the due process clause of the Fifth Amendment, belong not alone to the members of those nations that excel on the battlefield or that subscribe to the democratic ideology. They belong to every person in the world, victor or vanquished, whatever may be his race, color or beliefs. They rise above any status of belligerency or outlawry. They survive any popular passion or frenzy of the moment. No court or legislature or executive, not even the mightiest army in the world, can ever destroy them. Such is the universal and indestructible nature of the rights which the due process clause of the Fifth Amendment recognizes and protects when life or liberty is threatened by virtue of the authority of the United States.

The failure of the military commission to obey the dictates of the due process requirements of the Fifth Amendment is apparent in this case.

[T]rial was ordered to be held in territory over which the United States has complete sovereignty. No military necessity or other emergency demanded the suspension of the safeguards of due process. Yet petitioner was rushed to trial under an improper charge, given insufficient time to prepare an adequate defense, deprived of the benefits of some of the most elementary rules of evidence and summarily sentenced to be hanged. In all this needless and unseemly haste there was no serious attempt to charge or to prove that he committed a recognized violation of the laws of war. He was not charged with personally participating in the acts of atrocity or with ordering or condoning their commission. Not even knowledge of these crimes was attributed to him. It was simply alleged that he unlawfully disregarded and failed to discharge his duty as commander to control the operations of the members of his command, permitting them to commit the acts of atrocity. The recorded annals of warfare and the established principles of international law afford not the slightest precedent for such a charge. This indictment in effect permitted the military commission to make the crime whatever it willed, dependent upon its biased view as to petitioner's duties and his disregard thereof. . . .

In my opinion, such a procedure is unworthy of the traditions of our people or of the immense sacrifices that they have made to advance the common ideals of mankind. The high feelings of the moment doubtless will be satisfied. But in the sober afterglow will come the realization of the boundless and dangerous implications of the procedure sanctioned to-day. . . . To subject an enemy belligerent to an unfair trial, to charge him with an unrecognized crime, or to vent on him our retributive emotions only antagonizes the enemy nation and hinders the reconciliation necessary to a peaceful world. . . .

International law makes no attempt to define the duties of a command-er of any army under constant and overwhelming assault; nor does it impose liability under such circumstances for failure to meet the ordinary responsi-bilities of command. The omission is understandable. Duties, as well as ability to control troops, vary according to the nature and intensity of the particular battle. To find an unlawful deviation from duty under battle conditions requires difficult and speculative calculations. Such calculations become highly untrustworthy when they are made by the victor in relation to the actions of a vanquished commander. Objective and realistic norms of conduct are then extremely unlikely to be used in forming a judgment as to deviations from duty . . . It is this consideration that undermines the charge against the petitioner in this case. The indictment permits, indeed compels, the military commission of a victorious nation to sit in judgment upon the military strategy and actions of the defeated enemy and to use its conclu-sions to determine the criminal liability of an enemy commander. Life and liberty are made to depend upon the biased will of victor rather than upon objective standards of conduct.

. . . . No one denies that inaction or negligence may give rise to liability, civil or criminal. But it is quite another thing to say that the inability to control troops under highly competitive and disastrous battle conditions renders one guilty of a war crime in the absence of personal culpability. Had there been some element of knowledge or direct connection with the atroci-ties the problem would be entirely different. Moreover, it must be remem-bered that we are not dealing here with an ordinary tort or criminal action; precedents in those fields are of little if any value. Rather we are concerned with a proceeding involving an international crime, the treatment of which may have untold effects upon the future peace of the world. That fact must be kept uppermost in our search for precedent.

The only conclusion I can draw is that the charge made against the petitioner is clearly without precedent in international law or in the annals of recorded military history. This is not to say that enemy commanders may escape punishment for clear and unlawful failures to prevent atrocities. But that punishment should be based upon charges fairly drawn in light of established rules of international law and recognized concepts of justice. . . .

At a time like this when emotions are understandably high it is difficult to adopt a dispassionate attitude toward a case of this nature. Yet now is precisely the time when that attitude is most essential. While peoples in other lands may not share our beliefs as to due process and the dignity of the individual, we are not free to give effect to our emotions in reckless disre-gard of the rights of others. We live under the Constitution, which is the embodiment of all the high hopes and aspirations of the new world. And it is applicable in both war and peace. We must act accordingly. Indeed, an uncurbed spirit of revenge and retribution, masked informal legal procedure for purposes of dealing with a fallen enemy commander, can do more lasting harm than all of the atrocities giving rise to that spirit. The people's faith in the fairness and objectiveness of the law can be seriously undercut by that spirit. The fires of nationalism can be further kindled. And the hearts of all mankind can be embittered and filled with hatred, leaving forlorn and impoverished the noble ideal of malice toward none and charity to all. These are the reasons that lead me to dissent in these terms.

YOUNGSTOWN SHEET & TUBE CO. v. SAWYER

343 U.S. 579 (1952)

To avert a nationwide strike of steelworkers which he believed would jeopardize national defense during the Korean conflict, President Truman issued an Executive Order directing the secretary of commerce [Sawyer] to seize and operate the steel mills. The Order was based generally upon the powers vested by the Constitution in the president as chief executive and commander in chief of the armed forces. The president promptly reported the seizure to Congress, but Congress took no further action. Congress, in fact, previously had refused to authorize government seizures of property to settle labor disputes when it passed the Taft–Hartley Act in 1947.

The steel companies sought injunctive relief to bar the secretary of commerce from seizing the plants. The district court issued a preliminary injunction, which the court of appeals stayed, and from which the steel companies appealed.

Justice **Black** delivered the opinion of the Court:

We are asked to decide whether the President was acting within his constitutional power when he issued an order directing the Secretary of Commerce to take possession of and operate most of the Nation's steel mills. The mill owners argue that the President's order amounts to lawmaking, a legislative function which the Constitution has expressly confided to the Congress and not to the President. The Government's position is that the order was made on findings of the President that his action was necessary to avert a national catastrophe which would inevitably result from a stoppage of steel production, and that in meeting this grave emergency the President was acting within the aggregate of his constitutional powers as the Nation's Chief Executive and the Commander in Chief of the Armed Forces of the United States. . . .

The President's power, if any, to issue the order must stem either from an act of Congress or from the Constitution itself. There is no statute that expressly authorizes the President to take possession of property as he did here. Nor is there any act of Congress to which our attention has been directed from which such a power can fairly be implied. Indeed, we do not understand the Government to rely on statutory authorization for this seizure. There are two statutes which do authorize the President to take both personal and real property under certain conditions. However, the Government admits that these conditions were not met and that the President's order was not rooted in either of the statutes. . . .

[T]he use of the seizure technique to solve labor disputes in order to prevent work stoppages was not only unauthorized by any congressional enactment; prior to this controversy, Congress had refused to adopt that method of settling labor disputes. When the Taft–Hartley Act was under consideration in 1947, Congress rejected an amendment which would have authorized such governmental seizures in cases of emergency. Apparently it was thought that the technique of seizure, like that of compulsory arbitration, would interfere with the process of collective bargaining. Consequently, the plan Congress adopted in that Act did not provide for seizure under any circumstances. Instead, the plan sought to bring about settlements by use of the customary devices of mediation, conciliation, investigation by boards of inquiry, and public reports. . . .

It is clear that if the President had authority to issue the order he did, it must be found in some provision of the Constitution. And it is not claimed that express constitutional language grants this power to the President. The contention is that presidential power should be implied from the aggregate of his powers under the Constitution. Particular reliance is placed on provisions in Article II which say that "The executive Power shall be vested in a President . . ."; that "he shall take Care that the Laws be faithfully executed"; and that he "shall be Commander in Chief of the Army and Navy of the United States."

The order cannot properly be sustained as an exercise of the President's military power as Commander in Chief of the Armed Forces. The Government attempts to do so by citing a number of cases upholding broad powers in military commanders engaged in day-to-day fighting in a theater of war. . . . Even though "theater of war" be an expanding concept, we cannot with faithfulness to our constitutional system hold that the Commander in Chief of the Armed Forces has the ultimate power as such to take possession of private property in order to keep labor disputes from stopping production. This is a job for the Nation's lawmakers, not for its military authorities.

Nor can the seizure order be sustained because of the several constitutional provisions that grant executive power to the President. In the framework of our Constitution, the President's power to see that the laws are faithfully executed refutes the idea that he is to be a lawmaker. The Constitution limits his functions in the lawmaking process to the recommending of laws he thinks wise and the vetoing of laws he thinks bad. And the Constitution is neither silent nor equivocal about who shall make laws which the President is to execute. The first section of the first article says that "All legislative Powers herein granted shall be vested in a Congress of the United States. . . ." Article I goes on to provide that Congress may "make all Laws which shall be necessary and proper for carrying into Execution the foregoing Powers, and all other Powers vested by this Constitution in the Government of the United States, or in any Department or Officer thereof."

The President's order does not direct that a congressional policy be executed in a manner prescribed by Congress—it directs that a presidential policy be executed in a manner prescribed by the President. . . . The power of Congress to adopt such public policies as those proclaimed by the order is beyond question. It can authorize the taking of private property for public use. It can make laws regulating the relationships between employers and employees, prescribing rules designed to settle labor disputes, and fixing wages and working conditions in certain fields of our economy. The Constitution does not subject this lawmaking power of Congress to presidential or military supervision or control.

It is said that other Presidents without congressional authority have taken possession of private business enterprises in order to settle labor disputes. But even if this be true, Congress has not thereby lost its exclusive constitutional authority to make laws necessary and proper to carry out the powers vested by the Constitution "in the Government of the United States, or any Department or Officer thereof."

The Founders of this Nation entrusted the lawmaking power to the Congress alone in both good and bad times. It would do no good to recall the historical events, the fears of power and the hopes for freedom that lay behind their choice. Such a review would but confirm our holding that this seizure order cannot stand.

The judgment of the District Court is

Affirmed.

Justice **Frankfurter,** *concurring.... ...* Apart from his vast share of responsibility for the conduct of our foreign relations, the embracing function of the President is that "he shall take Care that the Laws be faithfully executed...." Art. II, [section] 3. The nature of that authority has for me been comprehensively indicated by Mr. Justice Holmes. "The duty of the President to see that the laws be executed is a duty that does not go beyond the laws or require him to achieve more than Congress sees fit to leave within his power." The powers of the President are not as particularized as are those of Congress. But unenumerated powers do not mean undefined powers. The separation of powers built into our Constitution gives essential content to undefined provisions in the frame of our government.

To be sure, the content of the three authorities of government is not to be derived from an abstract analysis. The areas are partly interacting, not wholly disjointed. The Constitution is a framework for government. Therefore the way the framework has consistently operated fairly establishes that it has operated according to its true nature. Deeply embedded traditional ways of conducting government cannot supplant the Constitution or legislation, but they give meaning to the words of a text or supply them. It is an inadmissibly narrow conception of American constitutional law to confine it to the words of the Constitution and to disregard the gloss which life has written upon them. In short, a systematic, unbroken, executive practice, long pursued to the knowledge of the Congress and never before questioned, engaged in by Presidents who have also sworn to uphold the Constitution, making as it were such exercise of power part of the structure of our government, may be treated as a gloss on "executive Power" noted in the President by section 1 of Art. II.

Justice **Douglas,** *concurring:* There can be no doubt that the emergency which caused the President to seize these steel plants was one that bore heavily on the country. But the emergency did not create power; it merely marked an occasion when power should be exercised. And the fact that it was necessary that measures be taken to keep steel in production does not mean that the President, rather than the Congress, had the constitutional authority to act. The Congress, as well as the President, is trustee of the national welfare. The President can act more quickly than the Congress.... Legislative power, by contrast, is slower to exercise.... [But we] cannot decide this case by determining which branch of government can deal most expeditiously with the present crisis. The answer must depend on the allocation of powers under the Constitution....

If we sanctioned the present exercise of power by the President, we would be expanding Article II of the Constitution and rewriting it to suit the political conveniences of the present emergency. Article II which vests the "executive Power" in the President defines that power with particularity. Article II, Section 2 makes the Chief Executive the Commander in Chief of the Army and Navy. But our history and tradition rebel at the thought that the grant of military power carries with it authority over civilian affairs. Article II, Section 3 provides that the President shall "from time to time give to the Congress Information of the State of the Union, and recommend to their Consideration such Measures as he shall judge necessary and expedient." The power to recommend legislation, granted to the President, serves only to emphasize that it is his function to recommend and that it is the function of the Congress to legislate. Article II, Section 3 also provides that the President "shall take Care that the Laws be faithfully executed." But, as Mr. Justice Black and Mr. Justice Frankfurter point out, the power to execute the laws starts and ends with the laws Congress has enacted.

Justice **Jackson,** *concurring:* The actual art of governing under our Constitution does not and cannot conform to judicial definitions of the power of any of its branches based on isolated clauses or even single Articles torn from context. While the Constitution diffuses power the better to secure liberty, it also contemplates that practice will integrate the dispersed powers into a workable government. It enjoins upon its branches separateness but interdependence, autonomy but reciprocity. Presidential powers are not fixed but fluctuate, depending upon their disjunction or conjunction with those of Congress. We may well begin by a somewhat over-simplified grouping of practical situations in which a President may doubt, or others may challenge, his powers, and by distinguishing roughly the legal consequences of this factor of relativity.

1. When the President acts pursuant to an express or implied authorization of Congress, his authority is at its maximum, for it includes all that he possesses in his own right plus all that Congress can delegate....

2. When the President acts in absence of either a congressional grant or denial of authority, he can only rely upon his own independent powers, but there is a zone of twilight in which he and Congress may have concurrent authority, or in which its distribution is uncertain. Therefore,

congressional inertia, indifference or quiescence may sometimes, at least as a practical matter, enable, if not invite, measures on independent presidential responsibility....

3. When the President takes measures incompatible with the expressed or implied will of Congress, his power is at its lowest ebb, for then he can rely only upon his own constitutional powers minus any constitutional powers of Congress over the matter. Courts can sustain exclusive presidential control in such a case only by disabling the Congress from acting upon the subject. Presidential claim to a power at once so conclusive and proclusive must be scrutinized with caution, for what is at stake is the equilibrium established by our constitutional system....

[T]he current seizure [is] to be justified only by the severe tests under the third grouping....

The clause [of the Constitution] which the Government next relies is that "The President shall be Commander in Chief of the Army and Navy of the United States...." These cryptic words have given rise to some of the most persistent controversies in our constitutional history. Of course, they imply something more than an empty title. But just what authority goes with the name has plagued presidential advisers who would not waive or narrow it by nonassertion yet cannot say where it begins or ends. It undoubtedly puts the Nation's armed forces under presidential command. Hence, this loose appellation is sometimes advanced as support for any presidential action, internal or external, involving use of force, the idea being that it vests power to do anything, anywhere, that can be done with an army or navy.

That seems to be the logic of an argument tendered at our bar—that the President having, on his own responsibility, sent American troops abroad derives from that act "affirmative power" to seize the means of producing a supply of steel for them....

I cannot foresee all that it might entail if the Court should endorse this argument. Nothing in our Constitution is plainer than that declaration of a war is entrusted only to Congress. Of course, a state of war may in fact exist without a formal declaration. But no doctrine that the Court could promulgate would seem to me more sinister and alarming than that a President whose conduct of foreign affairs is so largely uncontrolled, and often even is unknown, can vastly enlarge his mastery over the internal affairs of the country by his own commitment of the Nation's armed forces to some foreign venture....

We should not use this occasion to circumscribe, much less to contract, the lawful role of the President as Commander in Chief. I should indulge the widest latitude of interpretation to sustain his exclusive function to command the instruments of national force, at least when turned against the outside world for the security of our society. But, when it is turned inward, not because of rebellion but because of a lawful economic struggle between industry and labor, it should have no such indulgence. His command power is not such an absolute as might be implied from that office in a militaristic system but is subject to limitations consistent with a constitutional Republic whose law and policy-making branch is a representative Congress. The purpose of lodging dual titles in one man was to insure that the civilian would control the military, not to enable the military to subordinate the presidential office. No penance would ever expiate the sin against free government of holding that a President can escape control of executive powers by law through assuming his military role. What the power of command may include I do not try to envision, but I think it is not a military prerogative, without support of law, to seize persons or property because they are important or even essential for the military and naval establishment.

*Justice **Burton** and Justice **Clark** filed separate **concurring** Opinions. Chief Justice **Vinson,** joined by Justice **Reed** and Justice **Minton,** dissented.*

———————— NEW YORK TIMES V. UNITED STATES ————————

403 U.S. 713 (1971)

The United States sought to enjoin the New York Times and Washington Post from publishing the contents of a classified Defense Department study, "History of U.S. Decision-Making Process on Viet Nam Policy"—a 7000 page, 47 volume collection of documents detailing U.S. policy through 1968, and popularly known as the "Pentagon Papers." The Court of Appeals for the District of Columbia Circuit declined to issue the injunction in the case of the Washington Post; the Court of Appeals for the Second Circuit enjoined the New York Times from publishing, and the cases were joined on certiorari.

Per Curiam: . . . . "Any system of prior restraints of expression comes to this Court bearing a heavy presumption against its constitutional validity."

. . . . The judgment of the Court of Appeals for the District of Columbia Circuit is therefore affirmed. The order of the Court of Appeals for the Second Circuit is reversed. . . .

So ordered.

Justice **Black,** with whom Justice **Douglas** joins, *concurring:*

I adhere to the view that the Government's case against the *Washington Post* should have been dismissed and that the injunction against the *New York Times* should have been vacated without oral argument when the cases were first presented to this Court. I believe that every moment's continuance of the injunctions against these newspapers amounts to a flagrant, indefensible, and continuing violation of the First Amendment. . . . . In my view it is unfortunate that some of my Brethren are apparently willing to hold that the publication of news may sometimes be enjoined. Such a holding would make a shambles of the First Amendment.

Our Government was launched in 1789 with the adoption of the Constitution. The Bill of Rights, including the First Amendment, followed in 1791. Now, for the first time in the 182 years since the founding of the Republic, the federal courts are asked to hold that the First Amendment does not mean what it says, but rather means that the Government can halt the publication of current news of vital importance to the people of this country.

In seeking injunctions against these newspapers and in its presentation to the Court, the Executive Branch seems to have forgotten the essential purpose and history of the First Amendment. When the Constitution was adopted, many people strongly opposed it because the document contained no Bill of Rights to safeguard certain basic freedoms. They especially feared that the new powers granted to a central government might be interpreted to permit the government to curtail freedom of religion, press, assembly, and speech. In response to an overwhelming public clamor, James Madison offered a series of amendments to satisfy citizens that these great liberties would remain safe and beyond the power of government to abridge. Madison proposed what later became the First Amendment in three parts, two of which are set out below, and one of which proclaimed: "The people shall not be deprived or abridge of their right to speak, to write, or to publish their sentiments; *and the freedom of the press, as one of the great bulwarks of liberty, shall be inviolable."* [Justice Black's emphasis.] The amendments were offered to *curtail* and *restrict* the general powers granted to the Executive, Legislative, and Judicial Branches two years before in the original Constitution. The Bill of Rights changed the original Constitution into a new charter under which no branch of government could abridge the people's freedoms of press, speech, religion, and assembly. Yet the Solicitor General argues and some members of the Court appear to agree that the general powers of the Government adopted in the original Constitution should be interpreted to limit and restrict the specific and emphatic guarantees of the Bill of Rights adopted later. I can imagine no greater perversion of history....

In the First Amendment the Founding Fathers gave the free press the protection it must have to fulfill its essential role in our democracy. The press was to serve the governed, not the governors. The Government's power to censor the press was abolished so that the press would remain forever free to censure the Government. The press was protected so that it could bare the secrets of government and inform the people. Only a free and unrestrained press can effectively expose deception in government. And paramount among the responsibilities of a free press is the duty to prevent any part of the government from deceiving the people and sending them off to distant lands to die of foreign fevers and foreign shot and shell. In my view, far from deserving condemnation for their courageous reporting, the *New York Times,* the *Washington Post,* and other newspapers should be commended for serving the purpose that the Founding Fathers saw so clearly. In revealing the workings of government that led to the Vietnam war, the newspapers nobly did precisely that which the Fathers hoped and trusted they would do....

The word "security" is a broad, vague generality whose contours should not be invoked to abrogate the fundamental law embodied in the First Amendment. The guarding of military and diplomatic secrets at the expense of informed representative government provides no real security for our Republic. The Framers of the First Amendment, fully aware of both the need to defend a new nation and the abuses of the English and Colonial governments, sought to give this new society strength and security by providing that freedom of speech, press, religion, and assembly should not be abridged.

Justice **Stewart,** with whom Justice **White** joins, *concurring.* In the governmental structure created by our Constitution, the Executive is endowed with enormous power in the two related areas of national defense and international relations. This power, largely unchecked by the Legislative and Judicial branches, has been pressed to the very hilt since the advent of the nuclear age. For better or worse, the simple fact is that a President of the United States possesses vastly greater constitutional independence in these two vital areas of power than does, say, a prime minister of a country with a parliamentary form of government.

In the absence of the governmental checks and balances present in other areas of our national life, the only effective restraint upon executive policy and power in the areas of national defense and international affairs may lie in an enlightened citizenry—in an informed and critical public opinion which alone can here protect the values of democratic government. For this reason, it is perhaps here that a press that is alert, aware, and free most vitally serves the basic purpose of the First Amendment. For without an informed and free press there cannot be an enlightened people.

Yet it is elementary that the successful conduct of international diplomacy and the maintenance of an effective national defense require both confidentiality and secrecy.... In the area of basic national defense the frequent need for absolute secrecy is, of course, self-evident.

I think there can be but one answer to this dilemma, if dilemma it be. The responsibility must be where the power is. If the Constitution gives the Executive a large degree of unshared power in the conduct of foreign affairs and the maintenance of our national defense, then under the Constitution the Executive must have the largely unshared duty to determine and preserve the degree of internal security necessary to exercise that power successfully.... [T]he hallmark of a truly effective internal security system would be the maximum possible disclosure, recognizing that secrecy can best be preserved only when credibility is truly maintained. But be that as it may, it is clear to me that it is the constitutional duty of the Executive—as a matter of sovereign prerogative and not as a matter of law as the courts know law—through the promulgation and enforcement of executive regulations, to protect the confidentiality necessary to carry out its responsibilities in the fields of international relations and national defense.

This is not to say that Congress and the courts have no role to play. Undoubtedly Congress has the power to enact specific and appropriate criminal laws to protect government property and preserve government secrets.... [I]f Congress should pass a specific law authorizing civil proceedings in this field, the courts would likewise have the duty to decide the constitutionality of such a law as well as its applicability to the facts proved.

But in the cases before us we are asked neither to construe specific regulations nor to apply specific laws. We are asked, instead, to perform a function that the Constitution gave to the Executive, not the Judiciary. We are asked, quite simply, to prevent the publication by two newspapers of material that the Executive Branch insists should not, in the national interest, be published. I am convinced that the Executive is correct with respect to some of the documents involved. But I cannot say that disclosure of any of them will surely result in direct, immediate, and irreparable damage to our Nation or its people. That being so, there can under the First Amendment be but one judicial resolution of the issues before us. I join the judgments of the Court.

Justice **Marshall,** *concurring.* The problem here is whether in these particular cases the Executive Branch has authority to invoke the equity jurisdiction of the courts to protect what it believes to be the national interest.... Of course, it is beyond cavil that the President has broad powers by virtue of his primary responsibility for the conduct of our foreign affairs and his position as Commander in Chief.

And in some situations it may be that under whatever inherent powers the Government may have, as well as the implicit authority derived from the President's mandate to conduct foreign affairs and to act as Commander in Chief, there is a basis for the invocation of the equity jurisdiction of this Court as an aid to prevent the publication of material damaging to "national security," however that term may be defined.

It would, however, be utterly inconsistent with the concept of separation of powers for this Court to use its power of contempt to prevent behavior that Congress has specifically declined to prohibit. There would be a similar damage to the basic concept of these coequal branches of Government if when the Executive Branch has adequate authority granted by Congress to protect "national security" it can choose instead to invoke the contempt power of a court to enjoin the threatened conduct. The Constitution provides that Congress shall make laws, the President execute laws, and courts interpret laws.... It did not provide for government by injunction in which the courts and the Executive Branch can "make law" without regard to the action of Congress.

Justice **Harlan,** with whom the **Chief Justice** and Justice **Blackmun** join, *dissenting.* Forced as I am to reach the merits of these cases, I dissent from the opinion and judgments of the Court.

It is plain to me that the scope of the judicial function in passing upon the activities of the Executive Branch of the Government in the field of foreign affairs is very narrowly restricted. This view is, I think, dictated by the concept of separation of powers upon which our constitutional system rests.

In a speech on the floor of the House of Representatives, Chief Justice John Marshall, then a member of that body, stated:

> "The President is the sole organ of the nation in its external relations, and
> its sole representative with foreign nations."

From that time, shortly after the founding of the Nation, to this, there has been no substantial challenge to this description of the scope of executive power.

From this constitutional primacy in the field of foreign affairs, it seems to me that certain conclusions necessarily follow. Some of these were stated concisely by President Washington, declining the request of the House of Representatives for the papers leading up to the negotiation of the Jay Treaty:

> The nature of foreign negotiations requires caution, and their success must often depend on secrecy; and even when brought to a conclusion a full disclosure of all the measures, demands, or eventual concessions which may have been proposed or contemplated would be extremely impolitic; for this might have a pernicious influence on future negotiations, or produce immediate inconveniences, perhaps danger and mischief, in relation to other powers.

The power to evaluate the "pernicious influence" of premature disclosure is not, however, lodged in the Executive alone. I agree that, in performance of its duty to protect the values of the First Amendment against political pressures, the judiciary must review the initial Executive determination to the point of satisfying itself that the subject matter of the dispute does lie within the proper compass of the President's foreign relations power. Constitutional considerations forbid "a complete abandonment of judicial control." . . . Moreover, the judiciary may properly insist that the determination that disclosure of the subject matter would irreparably impair the national security be made by the head of the Executive Department concerned—here the Secretary of State or the Secretary of Defense—after actual personal consideration by that officer. . . .

But in my judgment the judiciary may not properly go beyond these two inquiries and redetermine for itself the probable impact of disclosure on the national security.

LAIRD V. TATUM

408 U.S. 1 (1972)

The President enjoys Constitutional and statutory authority to use the armed forces to quell insurrection and other domestic violence. Pursuant to this authority, President Johnson ordered federal troops to assist local authorities to suppress racial disturbances in Detroit in 1967, and later during the violence that followed the assassination of Dr. Martin Luther King. These events led Army authorities to believe that more attention should be given to contingency planning to permit effective military response to such situations with a minimum of force.

The Army established a system of domestic surveillance of public activities that were thought to have some potential for civil disorder, reporting that information to Army Intelligence headquarters in Maryland where it was stored in a computer data bank. By the early 1970s Congress became concerned with the scope of these operations and hearings were held. The Army also conducted its own review and ordered a significant reduction in its domestic intelligence activities.

A class action was brought by Tatum and others against the secretary of defense claiming that the Army's data gathering system involved the "surveillance of lawful and peaceful civilian political activity", and thus had a "chilling effect" on the exercise of First Amendment rights. The district court denied Tatum's request for injunctive relief, the Court of Appeals for the District of Columbia reversed, and the government appealed.

Chief Justice **Burger** delivered the opinion of the Court:

... Stripped to its essentials, what respondents appear to be seeking is a broad-scale investigation, conducted by themselves as private parties armed with the subpoena power of a federal district court and the power of cross-examination, to probe into the Army's intelligence-gathering activities, with the district court determining at the conclusion of that investigation the extent to which those activities may or may not be appropriate to the Army's mission. . . .

Carried to its logical end, this approach would have the federal courts as virtually continuing monitors of the wisdom and soundness of Executive action; such a role is appropriate for the Congress acting through its committees and the "power of the purse"; it is not the role of the judiciary, absent actual present or immediately threatened injury resulting from unlawful governmental action.

We, of course, intimate no view with respect to the propriety or desirability, from a policy standpoint, of the challenged activities of the Department of the Army; our conclusion is a narrow one, namely, that on this record the respondents have not presented a case for resolution by the courts.

The concerns of the Executive and Legislative Branches in response to disclosure of the Army surveillance activities—and indeed the claims alleged in the complaint—reflect a traditional and strong resistance of Americans to any military intrusion into civilian affairs. That tradition has deep roots in our history and found early expression, for example, in the Third Amendment's explicit prohibition against quartering soldiers in private homes without consent and in the constitutional provisions for civilian control of the military. Those prohibitions are not directly presented by this case, but their philosophical underpinnings explain our traditional insistence on limitations on military operations in peacetime. Indeed, when presented with claims of judicial cognizable injury resulting from military intrusion into the civilian sector, federal courts are fully empowered to consider claims of those asserting such injury; there is nothing in our Nation's history or in this Court's decided cases, including our holding today, that can properly be seen as giving any indication that actual or threatened injury by reason of unlawful activities of the military would go unnoticed or unremedied.

Reversed.

*Justice **Douglas**, with whom Justice **Marshall** concurs, **dissenting**.*

I

If Congress had passed a law authorizing the armed services to establish surveillance over the civilian population, a most serious constitutional problem would be presented. There is, however, no law authorizing surveillance over civilians, which in this case the Pentagon concededly had undertaken. The question is whether such authority may be implied. One can search the Constitution in vain for any such authority. . . .

The present controversy is not a remote, imaginary conflict. Respondents were targets of the Army's surveillance. First, the surveillance was not casual but massive and comprehensive. Second, the intelligence reports were regularly and widely circulated and were exchanged with reports of the FBI, state and municipal police departments, and the CIA. Third, the Army's surveillance was not collecting material in public records but staking out teams of agents, infiltrating undercover agents, creating command posts inside meetings, posing as press photographers and newsmen, posing as TV newsmen, posing as students, and shadowing public figures.

Finally, we know from the hearings conducted by Senator Ervin that the Army has misused or abused its reporting functions. Thus, Senator Ervin concluded that reports of the Army have been "taken from the Intelligence Command's highly inaccurate civil disturbance teletype and filed in Army dossiers on persons who have held, or were being considered for, security clearances, thus contaminating what are supposed to be investigative reports with unverified gossip and rumor. This practice directly jeopardized the employment and employment opportunities of persons seeking sensitive positions with the federal government or defense industry." [15]

Surveillance of civilians is none of the Army's constitutional business and Congress has not undertaken to entrust it with any such function. The fact that since this litigation started the Army's surveillance may have been cut back is not an end of the matter. Whether there has been an actual cutback or whether the announcements are merely a ruse can be determined only after a hearing in the District Court. . . .

The case involves a cancer in our body politic. It is a measure of the disease which afflicts us. Army surveillance, like Army regimentation, is at war with the principles of the First Amendment. Those who already walk submissively will say there is no cause for alarm. But submissiveness is not our heritage. The Constitution was designed to keep government off the backs of the people. The Bill of Rights was added to keep the precincts of belief and expression, of the press, of political and social activities free from surveillance. The Bill of Rights was designed to keep agents of government and official eavesdroppers away from assemblies of people. The aim was to allow men to be free and independent and to assert their rights against government. There can be no influence more paralyzing of that objective than Army surveillance. When an intelligence officer looks over every non-conformist's shoulder in the library, or walks invisibly by his side in a picket line, or infiltrates his club, the America once extolled as the voice of liberty heard around the world no longer is cast in the image which Jefferson and Madison designed, but more in the Russian image. . . .

*Justice **Brennan** joined by Justice **Stewart** and Justice **Marshall**, dissenting.*

––––––––––– UNITED STATES V. UNITED STATES –––––––––––
DISTRICT COURT

407 U.S. 297 (1972)

The United States brought conspiracy charges against three defendants for the dynamite bombings of an office of the CIA in Ann Arbor, Michigan. During pretrial hearings, the defendants moved to compel the government to disclose certain electronic surveillance informa-

tion it had obtained by wiretaps. The government filed an affidavit from the attorney general that he had approved the wiretaps "to gather intelligence information deemed necessary to protect the nation from attempts of domestic organizations to attack and subvert the existing structure of the Government." The district court held that the surveillance violated the Fourth Amendment, and ordered the government to make full disclosure and the government appealed.

Justice **Powell** delivered the opinion of the Court:

The issue before us is an important one for the people of our country and their Government. It involves the delicate question of the President's power, acting through the Attorney General, to authorize electronic surveillance in internal security matters without prior judicial approval. Successive Presidents for more than one-quarter of a century have authorized such surveillance in varying degrees, without guidance from the Congress or a definitive decision of this Court. This case brings the issue here for the first time. Its resolution is a matter of national concern, requiring sensitivity both to the Government's right to protect itself from unlawful subversion and attack and to the citizen's right to be secure in his privacy against unreasonable Government intrusion. . . .

We begin the inquiry by noting that the President of the United States has the fundamental duty, under Art. II. [section] 1, of the Constitution, to "preserve, protect and defend the Constitution of the United States." Implicit in that duty is the power to protect our Government against those who would subvert or overthrow it by unlawful means. In the discharge of this duty, the President—through the Attorney General—may find it necessary to employ electronic surveillance to obtain intelligence information on the plans of those who plot unlawful acts against the Government. . . .

Though the Government and respondents debate their seriousness and magnitude, threats and acts of sabotage against the Government exist in sufficient number to justify investigative powers with respect to them. The covertness and complexity of potential unlawful conduct against the Government and the necessary dependency of many conspirators upon the telephone make electronic surveillance an effective investigatory instrument in certain circumstances. The marked acceleration in technological developments and sophistication in their use have resulted in new techniques for the planning, commission, and concealment of criminal activities. It would be contrary to the public interest for Government to deny to itself the prudent and lawful employment of those very techniques which are employed against the Government and its law-abiding citizens.

It has been said that "[t]he most basic function of any government is to provide for the security of the individual and of his property." And unless Government safeguards its own capacity to function and to preserve the security of its people, society itself could become so disordered that all rights and liberties would be endangered. As Chief Justice Hughes reminded us in *Cox v. New Hampshire:*

> "Civil liberties, as guaranteed by the Constitution, imply the existence of
> an organized society maintaining public order without which liberty itself
> would be lost in the excesses of unrestrained abuses."

But a recognition of these elementary truths does not make the employment by Government of electronic surveillance a welcome development—even when employed with restraint and under judicial supervision. There is, understandably, a deep-seated uneasiness and apprehension that this capability will be used to intrude upon cherished privacy of law-abiding citizens. We look to the Bill of Rights to safeguard this privacy. . . .

As the Fourth Amendment is not absolute in its terms, our task is to examine and balance the basic values at stake in this case: the duty of Government to protect the domestic security, and the potential danger posed by unreasonable surveillance to individual privacy and free expression. If the legitimate need of Government to safeguard domestic security requires the use of electronic surveillance, the question is whether the needs of citizens for privacy and free expression may not be better protected by requiring a warrant before such surveillance is undertaken. We must also ask whether a warrant requirement would unduly frustrate the efforts of Government to protect itself from acts of subversion and overthrow directed against it. . . .

The Fourth Amendment direct[s] that, where practical, a governmental search and seizure should represent both the efforts of the officer to gather evidence of wrongful acts that the judgment of the magistrate and the collected evidence is sufficient to justify invasion of a citizen's private premises or conversation. Inherent in the concept of a warrant is its issuance by a "neutral and detached magistrate." . . . The further requirement of "probable cause" instructs the magistrate that baseless searches shall not proceed.

These Fourth Amendment freedoms cannot properly be guaranteed if domestic security surveillances may be conducted solely within the discretion of the Executive Branch. The Fourth Amendment does not contemplate the executive officers of Government as neutral and disinterested magistrates. Their duty and responsibility are to enforce the laws, to investigate, and to prosecute. . . . But those charged with this investigative and prosecutorial duty should not be the sole judges of when to utilize constitutionally sensitive means in pursuing their tasks. The historical judgment, which the Fourth Amendment accepts, is that unreviewed executive discretion may yield too readily to pressures to obtain incriminating evidence and overlook potential invasions of privacy and protected speech. . . .

It may well be that, in the instant case, the Government's surveillance . . . was a reasonable one which readily would have gained prior judicial approval. But this Court "has never sustained a search upon the sole ground that officers reasonably expected to find evidence of a particular crime and voluntarily confined their activities to the least intrusive means consistent with that end." The Fourth Amendment contemplates a prior judicial judgment, not the risk that executive discretion may be reasonably exercised. This judicial role accords with our basic constitutional doctrine that individual freedoms will best be preserved through a separation of powers and division of functions among the different branches and levels of Government. The independent check upon executive discretion is not satisfied, as the Government argues, by "extremely limited" post-surveillance judicial review.... Prior review by a neutral and detached magistrate is the time-tested means of effectuating Fourth Amendment rights.

The Government argues that the special circumstances applicable to domestic security surveillances necessitate a further exception to the warrant requirement. It is urged that the requirement of prior judicial review would obstruct the President in the discharge of his constitutional duty to protect domestic security. We are told further that these surveillances are directed primarily to the collecting and maintaining of intelligence with respect to subversive forces, and are not an attempt to gather evidence for specific criminal prosecutions. It is said that this type of surveillance should not be subject to traditional warrant requirements which were established to govern investigation of criminal activity, not ongoing intelligence gathering....

The Government further insists that courts "as a practical matter would have neither the knowledge nor the techniques necessary to determine whether there was probable cause to believe that surveillance was necessary to protect national security." These security problems, the Government contends, involve "a large number of complex and subtle factors" beyond the competence of courts to evaluate.

As a final reason for exemption from a warrant requirement, the Government believes that disclosure to a magistrate of all or even a significant portion of the information involved in domestic security surveillances "would create serious potential dangers to the national security and to the lives of informants and agents.... Secrecy is the essential ingredient in intelligence gathering; requiring prior judicial authorization would create a greater 'danger of leaks ..., because in addition to the judge, you have the clerk, the stenographer and some other officer like a law assistant or bailiff who may be apprised of the nature' of the surveillance."

These contentions in behalf of a complete exemption from the warrant requirement, when urged on behalf of the President and the national security in its domestic implications, merit the most careful consideration. We certainly do not reject them lightly, especially at a time of worldwide ferment and when civil disorders in this country are more prevalent than in the less turbulent periods of our history. There is, no doubt, pragmatic force to the Government's position.

But we do not think a case has been made for the requested departure from Fourth Amendment standards. The circumstances described do not justify complete exemption of domestic security surveillance from prior judicial scrutiny. Official surveillance, whether its purpose be criminal investigation or ongoing intelligence gathering, risks infringement of constitutionally protected privacy of speech. Security surveillances are especially sensitive because of the inherent vagueness of the domestic security concept, the necessarily broad and continuing nature of intelligence gathering, and the temptation to utilize such surveillances to oversee political dissent. We recognize ... the constitutional basis of the President's domestic security role, but we think it must be exercised in a manner compatible with the Fourth Amendment. In this case we hold that this requires an appropriate prior warrant procedure.

We cannot accept the Government's argument that internal security matters are too subtle and complex for judicial evaluation. Courts regularly deal with the most difficult issues of our society. There is no reason to believe that federal judges will be insensitive to or uncomprehending of the issues involved in domestic security cases. Certainly courts can recognize that domestic security surveillance involves different considerations from the surveillance of "ordinary crime." If the threat is too subtle or complex for our senior law enforcement officers to convey its significance to a court, one may question whether there is probable cause for surveillance.

Nor do we believe prior judicial approval will fracture the secrecy essential to official intelligence gathering. The investigation of criminal activity has long involved imparting sensitive information to judicial officers who have respected the confidentialities involved. . . .

[W]e conclude that the Government's concerns do not justify departure in this case from the customary Fourth Amendment requirement of judicial approval prior to initiation of a search or surveillance. Although some added burden will be imposed upon the Attorney General, this inconvenience is justified in a free society to protect constitutional values. Nor do we think the Government's domestic surveillance powers will be impaired to any significant degree. A prior warrant establishes presumptive validity of the surveillance and will minimize the burden of justification in post-surveillance judicial review. By no means of least importance will be the reassurance of the public generally that indiscriminate wiretapping and bugging of law-abiding citizens cannot occur.

> *The judgment of the Court of Appeals is hereby*
>
> *Affirmed.*

--------------------- UNITED STATES V. NIXON ---------------------

418 U.S. 683 (1974)

After several members of the White House staff were indicted for violation of federal statutes following the break-in at the Democratic National Headquarters at Watergate, the special prosecution filed for a subpoena duces tecum asking for production before trial of certain tapes and records of conversations between the president and others. President Nixon, claiming executive privilege, filed to quash the subpoena. The district court rejected the president's contentions (a) that the dispute between him and the special prosecuter was nonjusticiable as an "intra-executive" conflict, and (b) that the judiciary lacked authority to review the president's assertion of executive privilege. The district court thereafter issued an order for an in camera examination of the subpoenaed material, but stayed its order pending appeal, and the Supreme Court granted immediate certiorari because of the public importance of the issues presented and the need for prompt resolution.

Chief Justice **Burger** delivered the opinion of the Court:

JUSTICIABILITY

. . . . demands of and the resistance to the subpoena present an obvious controversy in the ordinary sense, but that alone is not sufficient to meet constitutional standards. In the constitutional sense, controversy means more than disagreement and conflict; rather it means the kind of controversy courts traditionally resolve. Here at issue is the production or nonproduction of specified evidence deemed by the Special Prosecutor to be relevant and admissible in a pending criminal case. It is sought by one official of the Executive Branch within the scope of his express authority; it is resisted by the Chief Executive on the ground of his duty to preserve the confidentiality of the communications of the President. Whatever the correct answer on the merits, these issues are "of a type which are traditionally justiciable." The independent Special Prosecutor with his asserted need for the subpoenaed material in the underlying criminal prosecution is opposed by the President with his steadfast assertion of privilege against disclosure of the material....

THE CLAIM OF PRIVILEGE

.... [W]e turn to the claim that the subpoena should be quashed because it demands "confidential conversations between a President and his close advisors that it would be inconsistent with the public interest to produce." The first contention is a broad claim that the separation of powers doctrine precludes judicial review of a President's claim of privilege. The second contention is that if he does not prevail on the claim of absolute privilege, the court should hold as a matter of constitutional law that the privilege prevails over the subpoena *duces tecum.*

In the performance of assigned constitutional duties each branch of the Government must initially interpret the Constitution, and the interpretation of its powers by any branch is due great respect from the others. The President's counsel, as we have noted, reads the Constitution as providing an absolute privilege of confidentiality for all Presidential communications. Many decisions of this Court, however, have unequivocally reaffirmed the holding of *Marbury v. Madison* that "[i]t is emphatically the province and duty of the judicial department to say what the law is." ...

In support of his claim of absolute privilege, the President's counsel urges two grounds, one of which is common to all governments and one of which is peculiar to our system of separation of powers. The first ground is the valid need for protection of communications between high Government officials and those who advise and assist them in the performance of their manifold duties; the importance of this confidentiality is too plain to require further discussion. Human experience teaches that those who expect public dissemination of their remarks may well temper candor with a concern for appearances and for their own interests to the detriment of the decision making process. Whatever the nature of the privilege of confidentiality of Presidential communications in the exercise of Art. II powers, the privilege can be said to derive from the supremacy of each branch within its own assigned area of constitutional duties. Certain powers and privileges flow from the nature of enumerated powers; the protection of the confidentiality of Presidential communications has similar constitutional underpinnings.

The second ground asserted by the President's counsel in support of the claim of absolute privilege rests on the doctrine of separation of powers.

Here it is argued that the independence of the Executive Branch within its own sphere . . . insulates a President from a judicial subpoena in an ongoing criminal prosecution, and thereby protects confidential Presidential communications.

However, neither the doctrine of separation of powers, nor the need for confidentiality of high-level communications, without more, can sustain an absolute, unqualified Presidential privilege of immunity from judicial process under all circumstances. The President's need for complete candor and objectivity from advisers calls for great deference from the courts. However, when the privilege depends solely on the broad, undifferentiated claim of public interest in the confidentiality of such conversations, a confrontation with other values arises. Absent a claim of need to protect military, diplomatic, or sensitive national security secrets, we find it difficult to accept the argument that even the very important interest in confidentiality of Presidential communications is significantly diminished by production of such material for *in camera* inspection with all the protection that a district court will be obliged to provide.

The impediment that an absolute, unqualified privilege would place in the way of the primary constitutional duty of the Judicial Branch to do justice in criminal prosecutions would plainly conflict with the function of the courts under Art. III. In designing the structure of our Government and dividing and allocating the sovereign power among three coequal branches, the Framers of the Constitution sought to provide a comprehensive system, but the separate powers were not intended to operate with absolute independence. . . . To read the Art. II powers of the President as providing an absolute privilege as against a subpoena essential to enforcement of criminal statutes on no more than a generalized claim of the public interest in confidentiality of nonmilitary and nondiplomatic discussions would upset the constitutional balance of "a workable government" and gravely impair the role of the courts under Art. III.

Since we conclude that the legitimate needs of the judicial process may outweigh Presidential privilege, it is necessary to resolve those competing interests in a manner that preserves the essential functions of each branch. The right and indeed the duty to resolve that question does not free the Judiciary from according high respect to the representations made on behalf of the President.

The expectation of a President to the confidentiality of his conversations and correspondence, like the claim of confidentiality of judicial deliberations, for example, has all the values to which we accord deference for the privacy of all citizens and, added to those values, is the necessity for protection of the public interest in candid, objective, and even blunt or harsh opinions in Presidential decision-making. A President and those who assist him must be free to explore alternatives in the process of shaping policies and making decisions and to do so in a way many would be unwilling to express except privately. These are the considerations justifying a presumptive privilege for Presidential communications. The privilege is fundamental to the operation of Government and inextricably rooted in the separation of powers under the Constitution. . . .

But this presumptive privilege must be considered in light of our historic commitment to the rule of law. . . . We have elected to employ an adversary system of criminal justice in which the parties contest all issues before a court of law. The need to develop all relevant facts in the adversary system is both fundamental and comprehensive. The ends of criminal justice would be defeated if judgments were to be founded on a partial or speculative presentation of the facts. The very integrity of the judicial system and public confidence in the system depend on full disclosure of all the facts, within the framework of the rules of evidence. To ensure that justice is done, it is imperative to the function of courts that compulsory process be available for the production of evidence needed either by the prosecution or by the defense. . . .

In this case the President challenges a subpoena served on him as a third party requiring the production of materials for use in a criminal prosecution; he does so on the claim that he has a privilege against disclosure of confidential communications. He does not place his claim of privilege on the ground they are military or diplomatic secrets. As to these areas of Art. II duties the courts have traditionally shown the utmost deference to Presidential responsibilities. In *C. & S. Air Lines v. Waterman S.S. Corp.*, dealing with Presidential authority involving foreign policy considerations, the Court said:

> "The President, both as Commander in Chief and as the Nation's organ for foreign affairs, has available intelligence services whose reports are not and ought not to be published to the world. It would be intolerable that courts, without the relevant information, should review and perhaps nullify actions of the Executive taken on information properly held secret."

In *United States v. Reynolds,* the Court also remarked:

> "It may be possible to satisfy the court, from all the circumstances of the case, that there is a reasonable danger that compulsion of the evidence will expose military matters which, in the interest of national security, should not be divulged. When this is the case, the occasion for the privilege is appropriate, and the court should not jeopardize the security which the privilege is meant to protect by insisting upon an examination of the evidence, even by the judge alone, in chambers."

No case of the Court, however, has extended this high degree of deference to a President's generalized interest in confidentiality. *Nowhere in the Constitution* . . . is there any explicit reference to a privilege of confidentiality, yet to the extent this interest relates to the effective discharge of a President's powers, it is constitutionally based.

The right to the production of all evidence at a criminal trial similarly has constitutional dimensions. The Sixth Amendment explicitly confers upon every defendant in a criminal trial the right "to be confronted with the witnesses against him" and "to have compulsory process for obtaining witnesses in his favor." Moreover, the Fifth Amendment also guarantees that no person shall be deprived of liberty without due process of law. It is the manifest duty of the courts to vindicate those guarantees, and to accomplish that it is essential that all relevant and admissible evidence be produced.

In this case we must weigh the importance of the general privilege of confidentiality of Presidential communications in performance of the President's responsibilities against the inroads of such a privilege on the fair administration of criminal justice. The interest in preserving confidentiality is weighty indeed and entitled to great respect. However, we cannot conclude that advisers will be moved to temper the candor of their remarks by the infrequent occasions of disclosure because of the possibility that such conversations will be called for in the context of a criminal prosecution ...

We conclude that when the ground for asserting privilege as to subpoenaed materials sought for use in a criminal trial is based only on the generalized interest in confidentiality, it cannot prevail over the fundamental demands of due process of law in the fair administration of criminal justice. The generalized assertion of privilege must yield to the demonstrated, specific need for evidence in a pending criminal trial....

Affirmed.

——————— DAMES & MOORE V. REGAN ———————

453 U.S. 654 (1981)

On November 14, 1979, President Carter declared a national emergency in response to the seizure of American Embassy personnel as hostages in Tehran. Pursuant to the International Emergency Economic Powers Act [IEEPA], he blocked the removal or transfer of all assets of the Iranian government that were subject to the jurisdiction of the United States.

On December 19, 1979, Dames & Moore, a U.S. engineering firm, filed suit in U.S. District Court against the government of Iran alleging that the company was owed a large sum of money for services rendered under a contract with the Iranian Atomic Energy Corporation. The district court issued an attachment order against Iranian property in the United States to secure any judgment that might be entered.

Subsequently, the American hostages were set free under terms of an agreement with Iran under which the United States agreed to terminate all executive legal proceedings in U.S. courts involving American claims against Iran, and that all attachments and judgments would be nullified. According to that agreement, all claims were to be settled through binding arbitration in a special Iran–United States Claims Tribunal, soon to be created.

Dames & Moore filed action against the secretary of the treasury seeking to prevent enforcement of the agreement.

Justice **Rehnquist** delivered the opinion of the Court:

[B]efore turning to the facts and law which we believe determine the result in this case, we stress that the expeditious treatment of the issues involved by all of the courts which have considered the President's actions makes us acutely aware of the necessity to rest decision on the narrowest possible ground capable of deciding the case.... This does not mean that reasoned analysis may give way to judicial fiat. It does mean that the statement of Justice Jackson—that we decide difficult cases presented to us by virtue of our commissions, not our competence—is especially true here. We attempt to lay down no general "guidelines" covering other situations not involved here, and attempt to confine the opinion only to the very questions necessary to decision of the case.

Perhaps it is because it is so difficult to reconcile the . . . definition of Art. III judicial power with the broad range of vitally important day-to-day questions regularly decided by Congress or the Executive, without either challenge or interference by the Judiciary, that the decisions of the Court in this area have been rare, episodic, and afford little precedential value for subsequent cases. . . . [W]e are obviously deciding only one more episode in the never-ending tension between the President exercising the executive authority in a world that presents each day some new challenge with which he must deal and the Constitution under which we all live and which no one disputes embodies some sort of system of checks and balances. . . .

Because the President's action in nullifying the attachments and ordering the transfer of the assets was taken pursuant to specific congressional authorization, it is "supported by the strongest of presumptions and the widest latitude of judicial interpretation, and the burden of persuasion would rest heavily upon any who might attack it." Under the circumstances of this case, we cannot say that petitioner has sustained that heavy burden. A contrary ruling would mean that the Federal Government as a whole lacked the power exercised by the President, and that we are not prepared to say.

Although we have concluded that the IEEPA constitutes specific congressional authorization to the President to nullify the attachments and order the transfer of Iranian assets, there remains the question of the President's authority to suspend claims pending in American courts. Such claims have, of course, an existence apart from the attachments which accompanied them. In terminating these claims through Executive Order, the President purported to act under authority of both the IEEPA and the so-called "Hostage Act." . . .

We conclude that although the IEEPA authorized the nullification of the attachments, it cannot be read to authorize the suspension of the claims. The claims of American citizens against Iran are not in themselves transactions involving Iranian property or efforts to exercise any rights with respect to such property. An *in personam* lawsuit, although it might eventually be reduced in judgment and that judgment might be executed upon, is an effort to establish liability and fix damages and does not focus on any particular property within the jurisdiction. The terms of the IEEPA therefore do not authorize the President to suspend claims in American courts. This is the view of all the courts which have considered the question. . . .

Concluding that neither the IEEPA nor the Hostage Act constitutes specific authorization of the President's action suspending claims, however, is not to say that these statutory provisions are entirely irrelevant to the question of the validity of the President's action. We think both statutes highly relevant in the looser sense of indicating congressional acceptance of a broad scope for executive action in circumstances such as those presented in this case. . . . [T]he IEEPA delegates broad authority to the President to act in times of national emergency with respect to property of a foreign country. The Hostage Act similarly indicates congressional willingness that the President have broad discretion when responding to the hostile acts of foreign sovereigns. . . .

Although we have declined to conclude that the IEEPA or the Hostage Act directly authorizes the President's suspension of claims for the reasons noted, we cannot ignore the general tenor of Congress' legislation in this area in trying to determine whether the President is acting alone or at least with the acceptance of Congress. As we have noted, Congress cannot anticipate and legislate with regard to every possible action the President may find it necessary to take or every possible situation in which he might act. Such failure of Congress specifically to delegate authority does not, "especially . . . in the areas of foreign policy and national security," imply "congressional disapproval" of action taken by the Executive. On the contrary, the enactment of legislation closely related to the question of the President's authority in a particular case which evinces legislative intent to accord the President broad discretion may be considered to "invite" "measures on independent presidential responsibility." At least this is so where there is no contrary indication of legislative intent and when, as here, there is a history of congressional acquiescence in conduct of the sort engaged in by the President.

Not infrequently in affairs between nations, outstanding claims by nationals of one country against the government of another country are "sources of friction" between the two sovereigns. To resolve these difficulties, nations have often entered into agreements settling the claims of their respective nationals. . . . the United States has repeatedly exercised its sovereign authority to settle the claims of its nationals against foreign countries. Though those settlements have sometimes been made by treaty, there has also been a longstanding practice of settling such claims by executive agreement without the advice and consent of the Senate. Under such agreements, the President has agreed to renounce or extinguish claims of United States nationals against foreign governments in return for lump-sum payments or the establishment of arbitration procedures. To be sure, many of these settlements were encouraged by the United States claimants themselves, since a claimant's only hope of obtaining any payment at all might lie in having his Government negotiate a diplomatic settlement on his behalf. But it is also undisputed that the "United States has sometimes disposed of the claims of its citizens without their consent, or even without consultation with them, usually without exclusive regard for their interests, as distinguished from those of the nation as a whole." . . .

[W]e conclude that the President was authorized to suspend pending claims pursuant to Executive Order. As Justice Frankfurter pointed out in *Youngstown,* "a systematic, unbroken, executive practice, long pursued to the knowledge of the Congress and never before questioned . . . may be treated as a gloss on 'Executive Power' vested in the President by [section] 1 of Art. II." Past practice does not, by itself, create power, but "long-continued practice, known to and acquiesced in by Congress, would raise a presumption that the [action] had been [taken] in pursuance of its consent. . . ." Such practice is present here and such a presumption is also appropriate. In light of the fact that Congress may be considered to have consented to the President's action in suspending claims, we cannot say that action exceeded the President's powers. . . . It is important to remember that we have already held that the President has the *statutory* authority to nullify attachments and to transfer the assets out of the country. The President's power to do so does not depend on his provision of a forum whereby claimants can recover on those claims. The fact that the President has provided such a forum here means that the claimants are receiving something in return for the suspension of their claims, namely, access to an international tribunal before which they may well recover something on their claims. Because there does appear to be a real "settlement" here, this case is more easily analogized to the more traditional claim settlement cases of the past.

Just as importantly, Congress has not disapproved of the action taken here. Though Congress has held hearings on the Iranian Agreement itself, Congress has not enacted legislation, or even passed a resolution, indicating its displeasure with the Agreement. Quite the contrary, the relevant Senate Committee has stated that the establishment of the Tribunal is "of vital importance to the United States." We are thus clearly not confronted with a situation in which Congress has in some way resisted the exercise of Presidential authority.

Finally, we reemphasize the narrowness of our decision. We do not decide that the President possesses plenary power to settle claims, even as against foreign governmental entities. As the Court of Appeals for the First Circuit stressed, "[t]he sheer magnitude of such a power, considered against the background of the diversity and complexity of modern international trade, cautions against any broader construction of authority than is necessary." But where, as here, the settlement of claims has been determined to be a necessary incident to the resolution of a major foreign policy dispute between our country and another, and where, as here, we can conclude that Congress acquiesced in the President's action, we are not prepared to say that the President lacks the power to settle such claims.

NIXON V. FITZGERALD

457 U.S. 731 (1982)

Ernest Fitzgerald was a management analyst with the Department of the Air Force. In 1968 he testified before a congressional subcommittee about cost-overruns in the development of the C5–A airplane that could run to $2 billion. In January 1970, Fitzgerald was dismissed from his job in a department reorganization. He complained to the Civil Service Commission that his separation represented unlawful retaliation for his congressional testimony. The Commission rejected his claim, but found that Fitzgerald's dismissal violated applicable regulations and ordered him reinstated. Fitzgerald filed suit for damages in U.S. District Court against various defense department officials and White House aides allegedly responsible for his dismissal. President Nixon was subsequently added as a defendant. The president's claim for absolute immunity was rejected by both the district court and the court of appeals, and the president appealed.

Justice **Powell** delivered the opinion of the Court.

The plaintiff in this lawsuit seeks relief in civil damages from a former President of the United States. The claim rests on actions allegedly taken in the former President's official capacity during his tenure in office. The issue before us is the scope of the immunity possessed by the President of the United States....

This Court consistently has recognized that government officials are entitled to some form of immunity from suits for civil damages.... Drawing upon principles of immunity developed in English cases at common law, the Court concluded that "[t]he interests of the people" required a grant of absolute immunity to public officers. In the absence of immunity, the Court reasoned, executive officials would hesitate to exercise their discretion in a way "injuriously affect[ing] the claims of particular individuals," even when the public interest required bold and unhesitating action. Considerations of "public policy and convenience" therefore compelled a judicial recognition of immunity from suits arising from official acts....

This case now presents the claim that the President of the United States is shielded by absolute immunity from civil damages liability. In the case of the President the inquiries into history and policy, though mandated independently by our cases, tend to converge. Because the Presidency did not exist through most of the development of common law, any historical analysis must draw its evidence primarily from our constitutional heritage and structure.... This inquiry involves policies and principles that may be considered implicit in the nature of the President's office in a system structured to achieve effective government under a constitutionally mandated separation of powers.

Here a former President asserts his immunity from civil damages claims of two kinds. He stands named as a defendant in a direct action under the Constitution and in two statutory actions under federal laws of general applicability. In neither case has Congress taken express legislative action to subject the President to civil liability for his official acts.

Applying the principles of our cases to claims of this kind, we hold that the petitioner, as a former President of the United States, is entitled to absolute immunity from damages liability predicated on his official acts. We consider this immunity a functionally mandated incident of the President's unique office, rooted in the constitutional tradition of the separation of powers and supported by our history. Justice Story's analysis remains persuasive:

> "There are ... incidental powers, belonging to the executive department, which are necessarily implied from the nature of the functions, which are confided to it. Among these, must necessarily be included the power to perform them.... The president cannot, therefore, be liable to arrest, imprisonment, or detention, while he is in the discharge of the duties of his office; and for this purpose his person must be deemed, in civil cases at least, to possess an official inviolability." [16]

The President occupies a unique position in the constitutional scheme. Article II, [section] 1, of the Constitution provides that "[t]he executive

Power shall be vested in a President of the United States. . . ." This grant of authority establishes the President as the chief constitutional officer of the Executive Branch, entrusted with supervisory and policy responsibilities of utmost discretion and sensitivity. These include the enforcement of federal law—it is the President who is charged constitutionally to "take Care that the Laws be faithfully executed"; the conduct of foreign affairs—a realm in which the Court has recognized that "[i]t would be intolerable that courts, without the relevant information, should review and perhaps nullify actions of the Executive taken on information properly held secret"; and management of the Executive Branch—a task for which "imperative reasons requir[e] an unrestricted power [in the President] to remove the most important of his subordinates in their most important duties."

In arguing that the President is entitled only to qualified immunity, the respondent relies on cases in which we have recognized immunity of this scope for governors and cabinet officers. We find these cases to be inapposite. The President's unique status under the Constitution distinguishes him from other executive officials. Because of the singular importance of the President's duties, diversion of his energies by concern with private lawsuits would raise unique risks to the effective functioning of government. As is the case with prosecutors and judges—for whom absolute immunity now is established—a President must concern himself with matters likely to "arouse the most intense feelings." Yet, as our decisions have recognized, it is in precisely such cases that there exists the greatest public interest in providing an official "the maximum ability to deal fearlessly and impartially with" the duties of his office. This concern is compelling where the officeholder must make the most sensitive and far-reaching decisions entrusted to any official under our constitutional system. Nor can the sheer prominence of the President's office be ignored. In view of the visibility of his office and the effect of his actions on countless people, the President would be an easily identifiable target for suits for civil damages. Cognizance of this personal vulnerability frequently could distract a President from his public duties, to the detriment of not only the President and his office but also the Nation that the Presidency was designed to serve.

Courts traditionally have recognized the President's constitutional responsibilities and status as factors counseling judicial deference and restraint. . . . We have recognized that the Presidential privilege is "rooted in the separation of powers under the Constitution." It is settled law that the separation-of-powers doctrine does not bar every exercise of jurisdiction over the President of the United States. See, *e.g., United States v. Nixon; United States v. Burr; cf. Youngstown Sheet & Tube Co. v. Sawyer.* But our cases also have established that a court, before exercising jurisdiction, must balance the constitutional weight of the interest to be served against the dangers of intrusion on the authority and functions of the Executive Branch. When judicial action is needed to serve broad public interests—as when the Court acts, not in derogation of the separation of powers, but to maintain their proper balance, or to vindicate the public interest in an ongoing criminal prosecution, the exercise of jurisdiction has been held warranted. In the case of this merely private suit for damages based on a President's official acts, we hold it is not....

A rule of absolute immunity for the President will not leave the Nation without sufficient protection against misconduct on the part of the Chief Executive. There remains the constitutional remedy of impeachment. In addition, there are formal and informal checks on Presidential action that do not apply with equal force to other executive officials. The President is subjected to constant scrutiny by the press. Vigilant oversight by Congress also may serve to deter Presidential abuses of office, as well as to make credible the threat of impeachment. Other incentives to avoid misconduct may include a desire to earn reelection, the need to maintain prestige as an element of Presidential influence, and a President's traditional concern for his historical stature.

The existence of alternative remedies and deterrents establishes that absolute immunity will not place the President "above the law." For the President, as for judges and prosecutors, absolute immunity merely precludes a particular private remedy for alleged misconduct in order to advance compelling public ends.

For the reasons stated in this opinion, the decision of the Court of Appeals is reversed, and the case is remanded for action consistent with this opinion.

So ordered.

Chief Justice **Burger,** *concurring.* ...

Justice **White,** joined by Justices **Brennan, Marshall** and **Blackmun,** *dissenting:* ...

Attaching absolute immunity to the Office of the President, rather than to particular activities that the President might perform, places the President above the law. It is a reversion to the old notion that the King can do no wrong. Until now, this concept had survived in this country only in the form of sovereign immunity. That doctrine forecloses suit against the Government itself and against Government officials, but only when the suit against the latter actually seeks relief against the sovereign. Suit against an officer, however, may be maintained where it seeks specific relief against him for conduct contrary to his statutory authority or to the Constitution. Now, however, the Court clothes the Office of the President with sovereign immunity, placing it beyond the law.

In *Marbury v. Madison,* The Chief Justice, speaking for the Court, observed: "The Government of the United States has been emphatically termed a government of laws, and not of men. It will certainly cease to deserve this high appellation, if the laws furnish no remedy for the violation of a vested legal right." Until now, the Court has consistently adhered to this proposition....

Unfortunately, the Court now abandons basic principles that have been powerful guides to decision. It is particularly unfortunate since the judgment in this case has few, if any, *indicia* of a judicial decision; it is almost wholly a policy choice, a choice that is without substantial support and that in all events is ambiguous in its reach and import. . . .

The majority may be correct in its conclusion that "[a] rule of absolute immunity . . . will not leave the Nation without sufficient protection against misconduct on the part of the Chief Executive." Such a rule will, however, leave Mr. Fitzgerald without an adequate remedy for the harms that he may have suffered. More importantly, it will leave future plaintiffs without a remedy, regardless of the substantiality of their claims. The remedies in which the Court finds comfort were never designed to afford relief for individual harms. Rather, they were designed as political safety valves. Politics and history, however, are not the domain of the courts; the courts exist to assure each individual that he, as an individual, has enforceable rights that he may pursue to achieve a peaceful redress of his legitimate grievances.

I find it ironic, as well as tragic, that the Court would so casually discard its own role of assuring "the right of every individual to claim the protection of the laws," *Marbury v. Madison,* in the name of protecting the principle of separation of powers. Accordingly, I dissent.

─────────────── C.I.A. v. Sims ───────────────

471 U.S. 159 (1985)

Between 1953 and 1966 the Central Intelligence Agency funded various research projects to counter Soviet and Chinese advances in brainwashing and interrogation techniques. In 1977, John Sims and others filed a request with the CIA under the Freedom of Information Act seeking the names of the institutions and individuals who had performed research under that program. The CIA declined, citing section 102(d)(3) of the National Security Act, which states that "the Director of Central Intelligence shall be responsible for protecting intelligence sources and methods from unauthorized disclosure." The district court held that the identities of the individuals and institutions did not have to be released, the court of appeals reversed insofar as the names of individual researchers were concerned, and the C.I.A. appealed.

Chief Justice **Burger** delivered the opinion of the Court:

* * *

Congress has made the Director of Central Intelligence "responsible for protecting intelligence sources and methods from unauthorized disclosure." As part of its postwar reorganization of the national defense system, Congress chartered the Agency with the responsibility of coordinating intelligence activities relating to national security. In order to carry out its mission, the Agency was expressly entrusted with protecting the heart of all intelligence operations—"sources and methods." . . . .

Plainly the broad sweep of this statutory language comports with the nature of the Agency's unique responsibilities. To keep informed of other nations' activities bearing on our national security the Agency must rely on a host of sources. At the same time, the Director must have the authority to shield those Agency activities and sources from any disclosures that would unnecessarily compromise the Agency's efforts. . . .

Congress knew quite well that the Agency would gather intelligence from almost an infinite variety of diverse sources. Indeed, one of the primary reasons for creating the Agency was Congress' recognition that our Government would have to shepherd and analyze a "mass of information" in order to safeguard national security in the postwar world....

Congress expressly made the Director of Central Intelligence responsible for "protecting intelligence sources and methods from unauthorized disclosure." This language stemmed from President Truman's Directive of January 22, 1946, in which he established the National Intelligence Agency and the Central Intelligence Group, the Agency's predecessors. These institutions were charged with "assur[ing] the most effective accomplishment of the intelligence mission related to the national security," and accordingly made "responsible for fully protecting intelligence sources and methods." The fact that the mandate of [the current Act] derives from this Presidential Directive reinforces our reading of the legislative history that Congress gave the Agency broad power to control the disclosure of intelligence sources.

[T]he Director, in exercising his authority under [the statute], has power to withhold superficially innocuous information on the ground that it might enable an observer to discover the identity of an intelligence source....

Here the Director concluded that disclosure of the institutional affiliations of the MKULTRA (code name for the project) researchers could lead to identifying the researchers themselves and thus the disclosure posed an unacceptable risk of revealing protected "intelligence sources." The decisions of the Director, who must of course be familiar with "the whole picture," as judges are not, are worthy of great deference given the magnitude of the national security interests and potential risks at stake. It is conceivable that the mere explanation of why information must be withheld can convey valuable information to a foreign intelligence agency....

The national interest sometimes makes it advisable, or even imperative, not to disclose information that may lead to the identity of intelligence sources. And it is the responsibility of the Director of Central Intelligence, not that of the judiciary, to weigh the variety of complex and subtle factors in determining whether disclosure of information may lead to an unacceptable risk of compromising the Agency's intelligence-gathering process....

We hold that the Director of Central Intelligence properly invoked [section] 102(d)(3) of the National Security Act of 1947 to withhold disclosure of the identities of the individual MKULTRA researchers as protected "intelligence sources." We also hold that the [Freedom of Information Act] does not require the Director to disclose the institutional affiliations of the exempt researchers in light of the record which supports the Agency's determination that such disclosure would lead to an unacceptable risk of disclosing the sources' identities.

Justice **Marshall**, *joined by Justice* **Brennan**, *concurring.*

Suggested Reading

No one should undertake a review of the presidency without Professor EDWARD S. CORWIN'S THE PRESIDENT: OFFICE AND POWERS (1957). CLINTON ROSSITER, THE SUPREME COURT AND THE COMMANDER–IN–CHIEF (1951), and ROBERT SCIGLIANO, THE SUPREME COURT AND THE PRESIDENCY also provide useful starting points. More recent studies include LOUIS FISHER, CONSTITUTIONAL CONFLICTS BETWEEN CONGRESS AND THE PRESIDENT (1985); ABRAHAM D. SOFAER, WAR, FOREIGN AFFAIRS AND CONSTITUTIONAL POWER (1976); and James Q. Wilson, *Does the Separation of Powers Still Work?,* 86 THE PUBLIC INTEREST 36 (1987).

The TOWER COMMISSION REPORT (1987) provides an essential case study of the nature of the president's authority in foreign affairs. Parts I and II of the *Report* crisply restate the origin and nature of the presidential power. Other more specialized studies include Raoul Berger, *War–Making by the President,* 121 UNIVERSITY OF PENNSYLVANIA LAW REVIEW 29 (1972); FRANCIS WORMUTH, THE VIETNAM WAR: THE PRESIDENT VS. THE CONSTITUTION (1974); Barton J. Bernstein, *The Road to Watergate and Beyond: The Growth and Abuse of Executive Power Since 1940,* 40 LAW AND CONTEMPORARY PROBLEMS (1976); W.T. Reveley, III, *Presidential War–Making: Constitutional Prerogative or Usurpation,* 55 VIRGINIA LAW REVIEW 1243 (1969); as well as the collection of essays in ERNEST R. MAY (ed.), THE ULTIMATE DECISION: THE PRESIDENT AS COMMANDER IN CHIEF (1961). Other useful studies include, Jordan J. Paust, *Is the President Bound by the Supreme Law of the Land: Foreign Affairs and National Security Re-examined,* 18 HASTINGS CONSTITUTIONAL LAW QUARTERLY 719 (1982); Kent A. Jordan, *The Extent of Independent Presidential Authority to Conduct Foreign Affairs Activities,* 42 GEORGETOWN LAW JOURNAL 1855 (1984); and Arthur S. Miller, *Reasons of State and The Emergent Constitution of Control,* 55 MINNESOTA LAW REVIEW 585 (1980).

On the Logan Act, see Detlev F. Vagts, *The Logan Act: Paper Tiger or Sleeping Giant,* 60 AMERICAN JOURNAL OF INTERNATIONAL LAW 268 (1966), as well as the earlier study by Charles Warren, *History of Laws Prohibiting Correspondence With a Foreign Government,* SENATE DOC. No. 696, 64th Cong., 2d Sess. (1917).

For reaction to the Steel Seizure Case, see Corwin, *The Steel Seizure Case: Judicial Bricks Without Straw,* 53 COLUMBIA LAW REVIEW 53 (1953); MAEVA MARCUS, TRUMAN AND THE STEEL SEIZURE CASE: THE LIMITS OF PRESIDENTIAL POWER (1977); as well as RICHARD F. HAYNES, THE AWESOME POWER: HARRY S. TRUMAN AS COMMANDER IN CHIEF (1973).

The Court's decision in the Iranian Hostage Case is treated effectively in ARTHUR S. MILLER, DAMES & MOORE V. REGAN: *A Political Decision by a Political Court,* 29 UCLA LAW REVIEW 1104 (1982). On the question of electronic surveillance, see ATHAN THEOHARIS, SPYING ON AMERICANS: POLITICAL SURVEILLANCE FROM HOOVER TO THE HUSTON PLAN (1978), and Richard W. Steele, *Franklin D. Roosevelt and His Foreign Policy Critics,* 94 Political Science Quarterly (1979).

Notes

1. "Opinion on the Question Whether the Senate Has the Right to Negative the Grade of Persons Appointed by the Executive to All Foreign Missions", April 24, 1790. 5 T. JEFFERSON, WRITINGS 161, 162 (Ford ed. 1895).

Three years later on July 10, 1793, Jefferson recorded the following conversation with Citizen Gênet: "He asked if they [Congress] were not the sovereign. I told him no. . . . 'But,' he said, 'at least Congress are bound to see that treaties are observed.' I told him no; . . . that the President is to see that treaties are observed. 'If he decides against a treaty, to whom is a nation to appeal?' I told him the Constitution had made the President the last appeal. He made a bow, and . . . expressed the utmost astonishment . . . and seemed never before to have had such an idea." 4 J. MOORE, INTERNATIONAL LAW DIGEST 680–681 (1906).

2. 10 ANNALS OF CONGRESS 613 (1800).

3. C. Warren, *History of Laws Prohibiting Correspondence With a Foreign Government,* SENATE DOC. No. 696, 64th Cong.2d Sess. (1917) p. 17.

4. 3 J. MOORE, INTERNATIONAL LAW DIGEST 243–244 (1906).

5. 135 U.S. 1 (1890).

6. *In re Debs,* 158 U.S. 564 (1895).

7. Also see *Hirabayashi v. United States,* 320 U.S. 81 (1943), in which the Court, speaking through Chief Justice Stone, upheld an earlier Presidential order imposing a curfew on Japanese living on the West Coast. In 1986, a U.S. District Court in California reversed Dr. Hirabayashi's conviction on the grounds that the government had suppressed evidence at the trial, and the court of appeals affirmed.

8. *Duncan v. Kahanamoku,* 327 U.S. 304 (1946).

9. 272 U.S. 52 (1926).

10. National Security Act of 1947. The statutory members of the National Security Council are the president, vice president, secretary of state, and secretary of defense.

11. For an excellent analysis of the passage of the National Security Act of 1947, see DEMITRIOS CARALEY, THE POLITICS OF MILITARY UNIFICATION (New York: Columbia University Press, 1966), especially pp. 313–314.

12. Former Senator John Tower, former Senator and Secretary of State Edmund Muskie, and former National Security Adviser, Maj. Gen. Brent Scowcroft.

13. THE TOWER COMMISSION REPORT 6 (New York: Bantam Books, 1987).

14. [For the current version of the *Logan Act,* see 18 U.S.C. [section] 5; 72 Stat. 126 (1932).]

15. *Hearings on Federal Data Banks, Computers and the Bill of Rights* before the Subcommittee on Constitutional Rights of the Senate Committee on the Judiciary, 92d Congress, 1st Session (1971).

16. 3 J. STORY, COMMENTARIES ON THE CONSTITUTION OF THE UNITED STATES [section] 1563, pp. 418–419 (1st ed. 1833).

6

THE WAR POWERS OF CONGRESS

THE WAR POWERS of the United States reside wholly in the national government. Article I, section 10 of the Constitution explicitly prohibits each state from keeping "Troops or Ships of War in time of Peace," or to "engage in War, unless actually invaded, or in such imminent Danger as will not admit of delay." The clauses of the Constitution which give Congress authority "to declare war, to raise and support armies, to provide and maintain a navy," and so forth, were not inserted to give the national government those powers, but to designate which branch of the government should exercise them.

Beginning with the Declaration of Independence in 1776, the war powers rested exclusively with the Continental Congress, and the Articles of Confederation confirmed that decision. In formulating the Constitution, the Framers were challenged with the task of dividing legislative from executive responsibility over the military, and the formula that resulted has been fraught with tension.

Writing in *Federalist* 23, Hamilton maintained that the war power was an aggregate of the particular powers granted to Congress in Article I, section 8 of the Constitution:

The Congress shall have power ...

To declare War, grant Letters of Marque and Reprisal, and make Rules concerning Captures on Land and Water.

To raise and support Armies, but no Appropriation of Money to that Use shall be for a longer Term than two Years.

To provide and maintain a Navy.

To make Rules for the Government and Regulation of the land and naval Forces.

In the early case of *Penhallow v. Doane* (1795), the Court spoke extensively of the war powers concentrated in Congress. Six years later in *Talbot v.*

Seeman, Chief Justice Marshall stated "The whole powers of war [were] by the Constitution . . . vested in Congress." Marshall also held the view that Congress' power to declare war implied the power to wage war. In the leading case of *McCulloch v. Maryland,* Marshall listed the power "to declare *and conduct* a war" as one of the enumerated powers from which he developed the doctrine of implied powers.[1] Chief Justice Chase, speaking for four Justices in *Ex Parte Milligan,* spoke of Congress' power to declare war as "necessarily" extending "to all legislation essential to the prosecution of war with vigor and success, except such as interferes with the command of the forces and the conduct of campaigns." Subsequently, Chief Justice White referred to the war power of Congress as "complete and undivided," [2] while Chief Justice Hughes in *Home Building and Loan Association v. Blaisdell* [3] described it as the "power to wage war successfully, [which] thus permits the harnessing of the entire energies of the people in a supreme cooperative effort to preserve the nation."

In the more recent case of *Lichter v. United States,* the Supreme Court spoke explicitly of the "war powers of Congress" in upholding the 1942 Renegotiation Act that was designed to recover excess profits from defense contractors. According to the Court:

> The Renegotiation Act was developed as a major wartime policy of Congress comparable to that of the Selective Service Act. The authority of Congress to exercise each of them sprang from its war powers. Each was part of a national policy adopted in time of crisis in the conduct of total global warfare by a nation dedicated to the preservation, practice and development of the maximum measure of individual freedom consistent with the unity of effort essential to success.

The war power of Congress emerged naturally from the powers vested in the Continental Congress. It also reflected the idea that the executive should be limited strictly to the command of the armed forces, whereas the responsibility for raising and equipping these forces, as well as the fundamental decisions of war and peace, should be in other hands. As Justice Story expressed in his *Commentaries:*

> In England, the King possessed the power of raising armies in time of peace according to his own good pleasure. And this prerogative was justly esteemed dangerous to the public liberties. Upon the revolution of 1688, Parliament wisely insisted upon a bill of rights, which should furnish an adequate security for the future. But how was this done? Not by prohibiting standing armies altogether . . . but by prohibiting them *without the consent of Parliament.* This is the very proposition contained in the Constitution: for Congress can alone raise armies; and may put them down, whenever they choose.

Ironically, since Story wrote in 1833 the power of Parliament over the Crown has steadily increased, while the power of Congress *vis-à-vis* the president has just as inexorably receded.

The authority to "declare war" gives Congress the sole authority to initiate an offensive war. However the president, as Commander in Chief, enjoys the power to respond to instant attacks or threats of attack on the

United States. This distinction reflects the deliberate intent of the Framers, but occasionally it has led to competition and friction between the two branches, as the passage of the 1973 War Powers Resolution indicates.

The Committee of Detail's first draft at the Federal Convention gave Congress the power "to make war." James Madison and Elbridge Gerry succeeded in amending the draft to read "declare war" to make clear that the military responsibility for the conduct of the war rested with the president, and the ensuing debate both in Philadelphia and in the state ratification conventions leaves no doubt as to the Framer's intent.

The Supreme Court quickly recognized that military action might occur without a formal declaration of war. In *Bas v. Tingy,* a case arising out of American difficulties with revolutionary France, the Court distinguished between officially declared wars which placed the entire nation in a state of belligerency and partial, limited wars that were fought without a solemn declaration. As to these latter wars, the Court stated:

> [H]ostilities may subsist between two nations, more confined in nature and extent; being limited as to places, persons and things; and this is more properly termed imperfect war: . . . Still, however, it is public war, because it is an external contention by force, between some of the members of the two nations, authorized by the legitimate powers.

After the Bey of Tripoli declared war on the United States in 1801, President Jefferson dispatched a squadron of frigates to the Mediterranean to protect American commerce. When one of the frigates was attacked by a Tripolitainian cruiser, the frigate returned fire and in the ensuing battle defeated and captured the cruiser. After disarming the vessel and its crew, the American frigate released them because, as Jefferson told Congress, the president was unauthorized "to go beyond the line of defense" without congressional approval. Hamilton promptly disputed Jefferson's view of Congress' power. Said Hamilton:

> It is the peculiar and exclusive province of Congress, *when the nation is at peace* to change that state into a state of war; . . . in other words, it belongs to Congress only *to go to war.* But when a foreign nation declares or openly and avowedly makes war upon the United States, they are then . . . *already at war,* and any declaration on the part of Congress is nugatory; it is at least unnecessary. [Hamilton's emphasis.]

Congress apparently shared Hamilton's view that a declaration of war was unnecessary. It authorized the president to instruct the Navy to "seize and make prize of all vessels, goods and effects, belonging to the Bey of Tripoli," and to take whatever additional acts *"the state of war* will justify." (Emphasis added.)

Over the years, Hamilton's view rather than Jefferson's has prevailed. But with the tide of isolationism running high in the 1930s, a constitutional amendment requiring a nationwide referendum before the United States could go to war was considered by Congress. Introduced in 1937 by Representative Louis L. Ludlow of Indiana, the House of Representatives narrowly defeated the amendment following the personal intervention of President Franklin Roosevelt and Speaker of the House William Bankhead.

MILITARY CONSCRIPTION

During the Revolutionary War, at least nine states provided for compulsory military service. In the War of 1812, James Monroe, who was then secretary of war, proposed a limited form of national conscription, but the war ended before legislation could be adopted. Lincoln resorted to the draft during the Civil War, and at his request Congress passed compulsory military service legislation, but it was never tested in the courts. After the Civil War, adoption of the Thirteenth Amendment prohibiting involuntary servitude was considered by some to place a future military draft in jeopardy. But in *Butler v. Perry* [4] in 1916, the Court (while dealing with a different issue) observed that the Amendment "introduced no novel doctrine with respect to services always treated as exceptional, and certainly was not intended to interdict enforcement of those duties which individuals owe to the State, such as services in the army, militia, ... etc. The great purpose in view [of the Thirteenth Amendment] was liberty under the protection of effective government, not the destruction of the latter by depriving it of essential services." Subsequently, in the *Selective Draft Law Cases* during World War I, the Supreme Court abruptly dismissed the notion that the Thirteenth Amendment would affect military conscription. Said Chief Justice White speaking for a unanimous Court:

> It may not be doubted that the very conception of a just government and its duty to the citizen includes the reciprocal obligation of the citizen to render military service in case of need and the right to compel it.

Thirteen years later in *United States v. Macintosh,* the Supreme Court confronted the question of conscientious objectors to military service. Justice Sutherland, speaking for the majority, rejected the premise that the Constitution provided protection for conscientious objectors, holding that protection was merely a matter of legislative discretion. In the course of the decision, Sutherland spoke at length about "the well-nigh limitless extent of the war powers." "[W]e are a Nation with a duty to survive," said Sutherland. Accordingly,

> From its very nature, the war power, when necessity calls for its exercise, tolerates no qualifications or limitations, unless found in the Constitution or in applicable principles of international law.

Although Chief Justice Hughes, joined by Justices Brandeis, Holmes and Stone dissented, *United States v. Macintosh,* like Sutherland's opinions in *Curtiss–Wright* and *United States v. Belmont,* continues to define the parameters of the war powers. During the Vietnam war, for example, the Supreme Court consistently refused to grant *certiorari* to cases arising from conscientious objectors challenging the government's authority to impose noncombatant military service upon them.[5]

Similarly in *United States v. O'Brien* in 1968, an all but unanimous Court, speaking through Chief Justice Warren, held that the First Amendment's protection of free speech did not extend to burning draft cards as a symbol of protest. In the 1985 case of *Wayte v. United States,* the Court rejected the

argument that selective prosecution of public protesters for refusal to register for the draft constituted an infringement of First Amendment freedoms.
Said Justice Powell, "Few interests can be more compelling than a nation's
need to ensure its own security.... Unless a society has the capability and
will to defend itself against the oppressions of others, constitutional protections of any sort have little meaning."

The broad discretion afforded Congress in military matters is reflected
in the Court's decision in *Rostker v. Goldberg*, upholding Congress' authority to
require men, but not women, to register for the draft. In rejecting claims of
sex-based discrimination, the Court observed: "The case arises in the context of Congress' authority over national defense and military affairs, and
perhaps in no other area has the Court afforded Congress greater deference...." According to Justice Rehnquist, Congress is not "free to disregard
the Constitution when it acts in the area of military affairs."

> In that area, as any other, Congress remains subject to the limitations of
> the Due Process Clause.... but the tests and limitations to be applied
> may differ because of the military context. We of course do not abdicate
> our ultimate responsibility to decide the constitutional question, but sim-
> ply recognize that the Constitution itself requires such deference to con-
> gressional choice.

But that deference does not extend to trying civilian dependents of
servicemen in military courts martial (*Reid v. Covert*), nor in subjecting former
service personnel to military trials once they have been separated from the
armed forces. In the words of Justice Black, "Free countries of the world
have tried to restrict military tribunals to the narrowest jurisdiction deemed
absolutely essential to maintaining discipline among troops in active service."

THE WAR POWERS IN DOMESTIC CONTEXT

Although the constitutional provisions designed to protect individual rights
are operative in war as well as in peace, the government enjoys far greater
discretion in wartime to take whatever action is necessary to preserve national security. The power of Congress to punish seditious speech and censor the press is limited by the First Amendment, but the Court nevertheless
sustained a series of convictions for seditious utterances during World War I
under the Espionage Act of 1917.[6] As Justice Holmes said in his famous
opinion in *Schenck v. United States*, "When a nation is at war many things that
might be said in time of peace are such a hindrance to its effort that their
utterance will not be endured so long as men fight and that no Court could
regard them as protected by any constitutional right."

The war power of Congress is not limited to the period of actual
hostilities. As the Supreme Court observed after the Civil War, "The power
is not limited to victories in the field and the dispersion of the [enemy]
forces. It carries with it inherently the power to guard against the immediate
renewal of the conflict, and to remedy the evils which have arisen from its

rise and progress." [7] This principle was given much broader application after World War I in *Hamilton v. Kentucky Distilleries Co.* where the War–Time Prohibition Act, which was actually passed by Congress after the signing of the armistice, was upheld as an appropriate measure for increasing war efficiency. As Justice Brandeis said for the Court:

> To Congress in the exercise of its powers, not least the war power upon which the very life of the nation depends, a wide latitude of discretion must be accorded; and it would require a clear case to justify a court in declaring that such an act, passed for such a purpose, had ceased to have force because the power of Congress no longer continued.

The following year in *Ruppert v. Caffey,* a sharply divided Court, again speaking through Brandeis, upheld the Volsted Act of 1919 which extended the ban on intoxicating liquors to beer and wine. This, too, was considered by the majority to be a legitimate exercise of the war power although Justices McReynolds, Day, Van Devanter, and Clarke dissented vigorously.[8] And in *Yakus v. United States* in 1943, the Court upheld the authority of Congress to fix prices and rents during wartime.

After World War II, in *Woods v. Miller,* the Court applied the same reasoning to uphold a rent control act passed by Congress in 1947 under the war power. As Justice Douglas pointed out: "We recognize the force of the argument that the effects of war under modern conditions may be felt in the economy for years and years, and that if the war power can be used in days of peace to treat all the wounds which war inflicts on society, it may not only swallow up all other powers of Congress but largely obliterate the Ninth and the Tenth Amendments as well." Somewhat disingenuously Douglas added, "There are no such implications in today's decision." The following year in *Ludecke v. Watkins* a divided Court upheld the power of Congress to authorize the deportation of enemy aliens long after the war had ended.

The power to wage war obviously includes the power to prepare for war. The potential extent of that authority may not be obvious. The Tennessee Valley Authority, the Atomic Energy Act of 1946, the interstate highway program, and the extensive federal aid to post-secondary education under the Defense Education Act are peacetime examples of the war power of Congress. Justice Story commented on the possibilities as early as 1833. Writing in his *Commentaries,* Story noted:

> It is important also to consider, that the surest means of avoiding war is to be prepared for it in peace.... How could a readiness for war in time of peace be safely prohibited, unless we could in like manner prohibit the preparations and establishments of every hostile nation?

In *Ashwander v. T.V.A.*, the Supreme Court, speaking through Chief Justice Hughes, provided authoritative endorsement for Story's views. The issue involved the commercial sale of electric power from the government's dam at Muscle Shoals, Alabama which had been constructed pursuant to the National Defense Act of 1916. The Court sustained both the construction of the dam as well as the sale of the electricity generated. Said Hughes, "We may take judicial notice of the international situation at the time the Act of

1916 was passed, and it cannot be successfully disputed that the Wilson Dam and its auxiliary plants, including the hydro-electric power plant, are, and were intended to be, adapted to the purposes of national defense." [9] But the establishment of the Atomic Energy Commission in 1946, with total control over the licensing and development of nuclear power for medical, industrial and military purposes, represents the broadest application of the war power when no "shooting war" was in progress.

CALLING THE WAR POWER TO ACCOUNT

As a general rule, the accountability of the president as Commander in Chief and of Congress under the war power is essentially a political matter. The control emanates from the ballot box and the constitutional system of checks and balances rather than through judicial review. Individuals who have been personally injured may, of course, enter the courts to seek redress, but the rules of standing and justiciability are exceedingly rigorous.

In 1940 President Roosevelt transferred fifty recently refitted and recommissioned destroyers to Great Britain in return for certain base rights in the Western Atlantic.[10] There was an immediate outcry that the president's actions not only contravened the Neutrality Act but violated Article IV, section 3 of the Constitution [11] as well. But the federal courts refused to hear any case that sought to contest to the president's authority. In the view of the court, those who brought legal actions lacked standing to sue; they could not show personal injury.

During the Vietnam war, the Court consistently refused to grant *certiorari* to suits that contested the war's constitutionality.[12] In *Massachusetts v. Laird,* the Supreme Court denied without comment the right of the Commonwealth of Massachusetts to file a bill of complaint against the secretary of defense. Subsequently, in the companion cases of *United States v. Richardson* and *Schlesinger v. Reservists to Stop the War* (1974), the Court discussed at length the nature of legal standing when it rejected taxpayers' suits challenging secret CIA expenditures or the right of Congress members to serve in the reserves of the armed forces. In *Richardson* the issue involved a taxpayer's attempt to obtain information concerning CIA expenditures pursuant to Article I, section 9 of the Constitution which provides that "a regular Statement of Account of the Receipts and Expenditures of all public Money shall be published from time to time." In delivering the opinion of the Court, Chief Justice Burger held that allowing the suit to proceed would make the federal courts the ultimate overseer of the government. "While we can hardly dispute that this respondent has a genuine interest in the use of funds," said Burger, "and that his interest may be prompted by his status as a taxpayer, he has not alleged that as a taxpayer, he is in danger of suffering any particular concrete injury...." In Burger's view, "The Constitution created a *representative* Government," and the remedy was in the elective process, not the Courts.

> Slow, cumbersome, unresponsive though the traditional electoral process
> may be thought at times, our system provides for changing members of

the political branches when dissatisfied citizens convince a sufficient number of their fellow electors that elected officials are delinquent in performing duties committed to them.

Again speaking through the Chief Justice in *Schlesinger*, the Supreme Court rejected taxpayers' arguments based on Article I, section 6 of the Constitution that senators and representatives serving in the Reserves were in violation of the provision prohibiting members of Congress from "holding any office under the United States." The petitioners, said Burger, had merely a generalized interest in the issue and lacked a personal stake in the outcome. "To permit a complainant who has no concrete injury to require a court to rule on important constitutional issues in the abstract would create the potential for abuse of the judicial process...."

AUTHORIZATION TO USE FORCE

The division of the war powers between the president and Congress can lead to constitutional as well as practical problems. While Congress enjoys the exclusive authority to initiate an offensive war, the president, as Commander in Chief, may not deem it appropriate to fight the war. One such example involved the jingoist agitation in the late nineteenth century to free Cuba from Spanish control. A delegation from Congress called on President Cleveland and told him "We have about decided to declare war against Spain over the Cuban question." Cleveland quickly intervened: "There will be no war with Spain over Cuba while I am President." When a member of Congress reminded Cleveland that the Constitution gave Congress the right to declare war, the president responded that he was commander in chief. "I will not mobilize the army," he said. "It would be an outrage to declare war." [13]

Despite Congress' vast constitutional authority over the military, the executive usually makes the decision to deploy the armed forces. Presidents from Jefferson to Reagan have used the military in combat when, in their judgment, the national interest required military action. President Lincoln's decision to save the Union, President Truman's decision to respond to Communist aggression in Korea, and the successive decisions of American presidents from Kennedy to Nixon to defend South Vietnam unquestionably represent the most extensive use of presidential discretion over the deployment of the military.

Each of these decisions raised important constitutional issues. Although the president's decision ultimately was supported, there were considerable repercussions and misgivings. Such misgivings against the war in Korea, for example, undoubtedly helped to bring General Eisenhower to the White House in 1953. And Eisenhower, who viewed Congress' role with great respect, declined throughout his presidency to employ U.S. military forces abroad without explicit congressional sanction.

In 1955 when China threatened military action against Chiang Kai Shek's forces in the Pescadores and Formosa, Eisenhower asked Congress for authority to use American forces in their defense. The Formosa Resolution

of 1955, which Congress passed immediately thereafter, explicitly "authorized" the president "to employ the Armed Forces of the United States as he
deems necessary" to protect Formosa. Two years later when Lebanon threatened to erupt in civil war, Eisenhower again asked Congress for permission
to intervene. The 1957 Joint Resolution to Promote Peace and Stability in
the Middle East again explicitly "authorized" the president's use of the
armed forces.

Neither President Kennedy nor President Johnson subscribed to Eisenhower's view of Congress' role. When JFK interdicted Soviet missiles in
Cuba, he did so on his own authority as commander in chief without
seeking official Congressional approval. Likewise, the initial deployment of
U.S. military forces in Vietnam under Kennedy and Johnson was accom-
plished by the president's actions alone. In 1964, when massive intervention
appeared necessary, President Johnson asked Congress for a resolution of
support. But the Tonkin Gulf Resolution of 1964 differed fundamentally
from the Formosa and Middle East Resolutions of the 1950s. Congress was
no longer asked to *authorize* presidential action but to approve and support
"the determination of the president . . . to take all necessary measures to
repel any armed attack against the forces of the United States and to prevent
further aggression." The change in wording reflected more than presidential
predilections; it involved a fundamental shift in the role of Congress from
one of ultimate authority to one of subordinate support.

It was dissatisfaction with this supporting role and the disaster in Vietnam that led to the repeal of the Tonkin Gulf Resolution in 1971 and then to
passage over President Nixon's veto of the War Powers Resolution of 1973.
The stated purpose of the Resolution was to "insure that the collective
judgment of both the Congress and the President will apply to the introduction of United States Armed Forces into hostilities, or into situations where
imminent involvement in hostilities is clearly indicated by the circumstances. . . ." The War Powers Resolution established an elaborate system of
consultation between the president and Congress before the armed forces
could be deployed and required the president to submit periodic reports to
Congress as the military situation evolved. It also required the president to
terminate U.S. military involvement after sixty days unless Congress declares war, approves an extension, or is unable to meet. The constitutionality
of this "legislative veto" is doubtful following the Supreme Court's decision
in *INS v. Chadha* in 1983.[14] More importantly, while some presidents have
occasionally consulted informally with Congress before using military forces
abroad, all have adhered to the position that the decision remains their
responsibility as commander in chief.

Since passage of the Resolution, history supports this view. President
Ford used the military to evacuate American citizens and Vietnamese civilians from Danang in 1975, to evacuate Saigon and Phnom Penh that same
year, and to liberate the *Mayaguez* from its Cambodian captors—all without
congressional approval as required by the War Powers Resolution. President
Carter sent the Air Force to evacuate diplomatic personnel and American
civilians in combat situations in Zaire and Cyprus and initiated the ill-fated
hostage rescue mission in Iran without prior Congressional authorization.

President Reagan's 1982 deployment of Marines in Lebanon was taken pursuant to his "constitutional authority with respect to the conduct of foreign relations and as Commander in Chief of the United States Armed Forces," [15] as was the intervention in Grenada, and the dispatch of military advisers to El Salvador. When Congress passed the 1983 Lebanon Resolution authorizing the president to keep U.S. forces in Lebanon for eighteen months, President Reagan made it clear when he signed the measure that he might continue military operations beyond the eighteen months without congressional reauthorization.[16]

Nevertheless, the passage of the 1973 War Powers Resolution, regardless of its constitutionality, reflects the basic tension between the war power of Congress and the commander in chief authority of the president. While this tension may be unavoidable in the system of checks and balances, it occasionally makes the smooth functioning of national power difficult. Congress' ultimate military check on the president lies in the appropriations process. Whether it was the bombing of Cambodia in 1973 or military support for the Contras under President Reagan, Congress' authority to provide or withdraw funds is final. This has led to efforts in the 100th Congress to tie the War Powers Resolution more closely to the appropriations process.

PENHALLOW V. DOANE

3 Dallas (3 U.S.) 54 (1795)

This is an important early case because of its analysis of the war power of Congress. During the Revolutionary War, the Continental Congress commissioned various sea captains to capture and make prize of enemy vessels and cargo. In October 1777, the American ship McClary, *duly commissioned by Congress, captured the brig* Susanna. *John Penhallow and other owners of the* McClary *brought condemnation proceedings in the maritime court of New Hampshire against the* Susanna *and its cargo—which were also claimed by Elisha Doane of Massachusetts. The maritime court ruled in favor of Penhallow and that decision was affirmed by the Superior Court of New Hampshire.*

Doane appealed to Congress, which referred the case to a newly created federal court of appeals. The commissioners of the court of appeals reversed the New Hampshire decision, and Penhallow appealed, questioning the authority of Congress to institute such tribunals. (The opinions of the Justices were delivered seriatim.*)*

Justice **Paterson:** . . . .

I. The question first in order, is, whether the Commissioners of Appeals had jurisdiction, or, in other words, whether Congress, before the ratification of the articles of confederation, had authority to institute such a tribunal, with appellate jurisdiction in cases of prize?

. . . . The powers of Congress were revolutionary in their nature, arising out of events, adequate to every national emergency, and coextensive with the object to be attained. Congress was the general, supreme, and controlling council of the nation, the centre of union, the centre of force, and the sun of the political system. To determine what their powers were, we must enquire what powers they exercised. Congress raised armies, fitted out a navy, and prescribed rules for their government: Congress conducted all military operations both by land and sea: Congress emitted bills of credit, received and sent ambassadors, and made treaties: Congress commissioned privateers to cruise against the enemy, directed what vessels should be liable to capture, and prescribed rules for the distribution of prizes. These high acts of sovereignty were submitted to, acquiesced in, and approved of, by the people of *America*. In Congress were vested, because by Congress were exercised with the approbation of the people, the rights and powers of war and peace. In every government, whether it consists of many states, or of a few, or whether it be of a federal or consolidated nature, there must be a supreme power or will; the rights of war and peace are component parts of this supremacy, and incidental thereto is the question of prize. The question of prize grows out of the nature of the thing. If it be asked, in whom, during our revolution war, was lodged, and by whom was exercised this supreme authority? No one will hesitate for an answer. It was lodged in, and exercised by, Congress; it was there, or no where; the states individually did not, and, with safety, could not exercise it. Disastrous would have been the issue of the contest, if the States, separately, had exercised the powers of war. For, in such case, there would have been as many supreme wills as there were states, and as many wars as there were wills. . . . As to war and peace, and their necessary incidents, Congress, by the unanimous voice of the people, exercised exclusive jurisdiction, and stood, like Jove, amidst the deities of old, paramount, and supreme. The truth is, that the States, individually, were not known nor recognized as sovereign, by foreign nations, nor are they now; the States collectively, under Congress, as the connecting point, or head, were acknowledged by foreign powers as sovereign, particularly in that acceptation of the term, which is applicable to all great national concerns, and in the exercise of which other sovereigns would be more immediately interested; such, for instance, as the rights of war and peace, of making treaties, and sending and receiving ambassadors. . . .

. . . . Before the articles of confederation were ratified, or even formed, a league of some kind subsisted among the states; and, whether that league originated in compact, or a sort of tacit consent, resulting from their situation, the exigencies of the times, and the nature of the warfare, or from all combined, is utterly immaterial. The States, when in Congress, stood on the floor of equality; and, until otherwise stipulated, the majority of them must control. In such a confederacy, for a state to bind others, and not, in similar cases, be bound herself, is a solecism. . . .

Justice **Iredell:** . . . . The powers of Congress at first were indeed little more than advisory; but, in proportion as the danger increased, their powers were gradually enlarged, either by express grant, or by implication arising from a kind of indefinite authority, suited to the unknown exigencies that might arise. That an undefined authority is dangerous, and ought to be entrusted as cautiously as possible, every man must admit, and none could take more pains, than Congress for a long time did, to get their authority regularly defined by a ratification of the articles of confederation. But that previously thereto they did exercise, with the acquiescence of the States, high powers of what I may, perhaps, with propriety for distinction, call *external sovereignty,* is unquestionable.... Whether among these powers comprehended within their general authority, was that of instituting courts for the trial of all prize causes, was a great and awful question; a question that demanded deep consideration, and not perhaps susceptible of an easy decision. That in point of prudence and propriety it was a power most fit for Congress to exercise, I have no doubt.

BAS V. TINGY

4 Dallas (4 U.S.) 37 (1800)

In 1793, as relations between the United States and republican France deteriorated, President Washington issued a Declaration of American Neutrality to avoid U.S. involvement in the growing war between Great Britain and France. France reacted strongly, believing Washington's proclamation violated U.S. treaty commitments to France. The United States and France commenced sporadic naval action against one another's shipping, although no formal declaration of war was made.

The controversy in this case involved two subsequent acts of Congress. An act of June 28, 1798, declared that when an American vessel captured by the French was recaptured by another American ship, one-eighth of the value of the vessel and its cargo was to be awarded to the rescuers. A subsequent act (March 2, 1799) provided that if ninety-six or more hours had elapsed before recapture of a vessel taken by the "enemy," then the rescuers were entitled to one-half the original value.

The Eliza, *a U.S. merchant vessel, was taken on the high seas by a French privateer, March 31, 1799. It was retaken by Captain Tingy, April 21, and pursuant to the second act of Congress, the district court awarded Tingy one-half of the value of* Eliza, *and the circuit court affirmed.*

Washington, Justice.

The decision of this question must depend upon ... is, whether, at the time of passing the act of congress of the 2d of March 1799, there subsisted a state of war between the two nations? It may, I believe, be safely laid down, that every contention by force, between two nations, in external matters, under the authority of their respective governments, is not only war, but public war. If it be declared in form, it is called solemn, and is of the perfect kind; because one whole nation is at war with another whole nation; and all the members of the nation declaring war are authorized to commit hostilities against all the members of the other, in every place and under every circumstance. In such a war, all the members act under a general authority, and all the rights and consequences of war attach to their condition.

But hostilities may subsist between two nations, more confined in its nature and extent; being limited as to places, persons and things; and this is more properly termed imperfect war; because not solemn, and because those who are authorized to commit hostilities act under special authority, and can go no further than to the extent of their commission. Still, however, it is public war, because it is an external contention by force, between some of the members of the two nations, though all the members are not authorized to commit hostilities, such as in a solemn war, where the government restrains the general power.

Now, if this be the true definition of war, let us see, what was the situation of the United States in relation to France. In March 1799, congress had raised an army; stopped all intercourse with France; dissolved our treaty; built and equipped ships of war; and commissioned private armed ship; enjoining the former, and authorizing the latter, to defend themselves against the armed ships of France, to attack them on the high seas, to subdue and take them as prize, and to recapture armed vessels found in their possession. Here, then, let me ask, what were the technical characters of an American and French armed vessel, combating on the high seas, with a view, the one to subdue the other, and to make prize of his property? They certainly were not friends, because there was a contention by force; nor were they private enemies, because the contention was external, and authorized by the legitimate authority of the two governments. If they were not our enemies, I know not what constitutes an enemy.

But secondly, it is said, that a war of the imperfect kind, is more properly called acts of hostility or reprisal, and that congress did not mean to consider the hostility subsisting between France and the United States, as constituting a state of war. In support of this position, it has been observed, that in no law, prior to March 1799, is France styled our enemy, nor are we said to be at war. This is true; but neither of these things were necessary to be done: because, as to France, she was sufficiently described by the title of the French republic; and as to America, the degree of hostility meant to be carried on, was sufficiently described, without declaring war, or declaring that we were at war. Such a declaration by congress, might have constituted a perfect state of war, which was not intended by the government....

.... The two laws, upon the whole, cannot be rendered consistent, unless the court could wink so hard as not to see and know, that in fact, in the view of congress, and to every intent and purpose, the possession by a French armed vessel of an American vessel, was the possession of an enemy: and therefore, in my opinion, the decree of the circuit court ought to be affirmed.

Justice Chase and Justice Patterson, concurring.

By the Court—Let the decree of the circuit court be affirmed.

——————————— SELECTIVE DRAFT LAW CASES ———————————

245 U.S. 366 (1918)

Following the United States' declaration of war against Germany in 1917, Congress passed the Selective Draft Law Act which provided for military conscription. These cases, which were joined for trial, involved certain draftees who refused to register for the draft and were prosecuted under the Act. The defendants argued that the Draft Act was unconstitutional, but their arguments had been dismissed by the trial courts.

Chief Justice **White** delivered the opinion of the Court:

.... The possession of authority to enact the statute must be found in the clauses of the Constitution giving Congress power "to declare war; ... to raise and support armies, but no appropriation of money to that use shall be for a longer term than two years; ... to make rules for the government and regulation of the land and naval forces." Article I, [section] 8. And of course the powers conferred by these provisions like all other powers given carry with them as provided by the Constitution the authority "to make all laws which shall be necessary and proper for carrying into execution the forego- ing powers." Article I, [section] 8.

As the mind cannot conceive an army without the men to compose it, on the face of the Constitution the objection that it does not give power to provide for such men would seem to be too frivolous for further notice. It is said, however, that since under the Constitution as originally framed state citizenship was primary and United States citizenship but derivative and dependent thereon, therefore the power conferred upon Congress to raise armies was only coterminous with United States citizenship and could not be exerted so as to cause that citizenship to lose its dependent character and dominate state citizenship. But the proposition simply denies to Congress the power to raise armies which the Constitution gives. That power by the very terms of the Constitution, being delegated, is supreme. Article VI. In truth the contention simply assails the wisdom of the framers of the Consti- tution in conferring authority on Congress and in not retaining it as it was under the Confederation in the several States. Further it is said, the right to provide is not denied by calling for volunteer enlistments, but it does not and cannot include the power to exact enforced military duty by the citizen. This however but challenges the existence of all power, for a governmental power which has no sanction to it and which therefore can only be exercised provided the citizen consents to its exertion is in no substantial sense a power. It is argued, however, that although this is abstractly true, it is not concretely so because as compelled military service is repugnant to a free government and in conflict with all the great guarantees of the Constitution as to individual liberty, it must be assumed that the authority to raise armies was intended to be limited to the right to call an army into existence counting alone upon the willingness of the citizen to do his duty in time of public need, that is, in time of war. But the premise of this proposition is so devoid of foundation that it leaves not even a shadow of ground upon which to base the conclusion.... It may not be doubted that the very conception of a just government and its duty to the citizen includes the reciprocal obligation of the citizen to render military service in case of need and the right to compel it. To do more than state the proposition is absolute- ly unnecessary in view of the practical illustration afforded by the almost universal legislation to that effect now in force....

When the Constitution came to be formed it may not be disputed that one of the recognized necessities for its adoption was the want of power in Congress to raise an army and the dependence upon the States for their quotas. In supplying the power it was manifestly intended to give it all and leave none to the States, since besides the delegation to Congress of authori- ty to raise armies the Constitution prohibited the States, without the consent of Congress, from keeping troops in time of peace or engaging in war. Article I, [section] 10. . . .

Thus sanctioned as is the act before us by the text of the Constitution, and by its significance as read in the light of the fundamental principles with which the subject is concerned, by the power recognized and carried into effect in many civilized countries, by the authority and practice of the colonies before the Revolution, of the States under the Confederation and of the Government since the formation of the Constitution, the want of merit in the contentions that the act in the particulars which we have been previously called upon to consider was beyond the constitutional power of Congress, is manifest. . . . In reviewing the subject, we have hitherto considered it, as it has been argued, from the point of view of the Constitution as it stood prior to the adoption of the Fourteenth Amendment. But to avoid all misapprehension we briefly direct attention to that Amendment for the purpose of pointing out, as has been frequently done in the past, how completely it broadened the national scope of the Government under the Constitution by causing citizenship of the United States to be paramount and dominant instead of being subordinate and derivative, and therefore, operating as it does upon all the powers conferred by the Constitution, leaves no possible support for the contentions made, if their want of merit was otherwise not so clearly made manifest. . . .

Finally, as we are unable to conceive upon what theory the exaction by government from the citizen of the performance of his supreme and noble duty of contributing to the defense of the rights and honor of the nation, as the result of a war declared by the great representative body of the people, can be said to be the imposition of involuntary servitude in violation of the prohibitions of the Thirteenth Amendment, we are constrained to the conclusion that the contention to that effect is refuted by its mere statement.

Affirmed.

HAMILTON V. KENTUCKY DISTILLERIES CO.

251 U.S. 146 (1919)

Ten days after the armistice with Germany was signed, Congress passed and the president signed the War-Time Prohibition Act. That Act provided that until the war and demobilization were complete ["the state of which shall be determined and proclaimed by the President"] it would be illegal "to sell for beverage purposes any distilled spirits." Kentucky Distilleries sought an injunction against the collector of internal revenue (Hamilton) to prevent enforcement of the Act. The U.S. District Court granted the injunction, and the government appealed.

Justice **Brandeis** delivered the opinion of the Court: . . . .

The present contention may be stated thus: That notwithstanding the Act was a proper exercise of the war power of Congress at the date of its approval and contains its own period of limitation—"until the conclusion of the present war and thereafter until the termination of demobilization,"—

the progress of events since that time had produced so great a change of conditions and there now is so clearly a want of necessity for conserving the manpower of the nation, for increased efficiency in the production of arms, munitions and supplies, that the prohibition of the sale of distilled spirits for beverage purposes can no longer be enforced, because it would be beyond the constitutional authority of Congress in the exercise of the war power to impose such a prohibition under present circumstances. Assuming that the implied power to enact such a prohibition must depend not upon the existence of a technical state of war, terminable only with the ratification of a treaty of peace or a proclamation of peace ... but upon some actual emergency or necessity arising out of the war or incident to it, still, as was said in *Stewart v. Kahn,* 11 Wall. 493, 507, "The power is not limited to victories in the field and the dispersion of the [resurgent] forces. It carries with it inherently the power to guard against the immediate renewal of the conflict, and to remedy the evils which have arisen from its rise and progress."

No principle of our constitutional law is more firmly established than that this court may not, in passing upon the validity of a statute, enquire into the motives of Congress.... Nor may the court enquire into the wisdom of the legislation.... Nor may it pass upon the necessity for the exercise of a power possessed, since the possible abuse of a power is not an argument against its existence.... Conceding, then, for the purposes of the present case, that the question of the continued validity of the War–Time Prohibition Act under the changed circumstances depends upon whether it appears that there is no longer any necessity for the prohibition of the sale of distilled spirits for beverage purposes, it remains to be said that on obvious grounds every reasonable intendment must be made in favor of its continuing validity, the prescribed period of limitation not having arrived; that to Congress in the exercise of its powers, not least the war power upon which the very life of the nation depends, a wide latitude of discretion must be accorded; and that it would require a clear case to justify a court in declaring that such an act, passed for such a purpose, had ceased to have force because the power of Congress no longer continued. In view of facts of public knowledge ... that the treaty of peace has not yet been concluded, that the railways are still under national control by virtue of the war powers, that other war activities have not been brought to a close, and that it can not even be said that the manpower of the nation has been restored to a peace footing, we are unable to conclude that the act has ceased to be valid....

The War–Time Prohibition Act being thus valid and still in force, the decree is reversed and the case is remanded to the District Court with directions to dismiss the bill....

UNITED STATES V. MACINTOSH

283 U.S. 605 (1931)

A Canadian by birth, Macintosh came to the United States as a graudate student at the University of Chicago and in 1907 was ordained a Baptist minister. In 1909 he began to teach at Yale and at the time of litigation was Chaplain of the Yale Graduate School and

Dwight Professor of Theology. (In World War I, Macintosh had served as a chaplain with the Canadian army at the front in France.) In 1925, Macintosh applied for naturalization as a United States citizen. The U.S. District Court denied the application because Macintosh would not promise to bear arms for the United States as the Naturalization Act required, unless he believed the war to be morally justified. The circuit court of appeals reversed, and the government appealed.

Justice **Sutherland** delivered the opinion of the Court:

. . . . There are few finer or more exalted sentiments than that which finds expression in opposition to war. Peace is a sweet and holy thing, and war is a hateful and an abominable thing to be avoided by any sacrifice or concession that a free people can make. But thus far mankind has been unable to devise any method of indefinitely prolonging the one or of entirely abolishing the other; and, unfortunately, there is nothing which seems to afford positive ground for thinking that the near future will witness the beginning of the reign of perpetual peace for which good men and women everywhere never cease to pray. The Constitution, therefore, wisely contemplating the ever-present possibility of war, declares that one of its purposes is to "provide for the common defense." In express terms Congress is empowered "to declare war," which necessarily connotes the plenary power to wage war with all the force necessary to make it effective; and "to raise . . . armies," which necessarily connotes the like power to say who shall serve in them and in what way.

From its very nature, the war power, when necessity calls for its exercise, tolerates no qualifications or limitations, unless found in the Constitution or in applicable principles of international law. In the words of John Quincy Adams—"This power is tremendous; it is strictly constitutional; but it breaks down every barrier so anxiously erected for the protection of liberty, property and of life." To the end that war may not result in defeat, freedom of speech may, by act of Congress, be curtailed or denied so that the morale of the people and the spirit of the army may not be broken by seditious utterances; freedom of the press curtailed to preserve our military plans and movements from the knowledge of the enemy; deserters and spies put to death without indictment or trial by jury; ships and supplies requisitioned; property of alien enemies, theretofore under the protection of the Constitution, seized without process and converted to the public use without compensation and without due process of law in the ordinary sense of that term; prices of food and other necessities of life fixed or regulated; railways taken over and operated by the government; and other drastic powers, wholly inadmissable in time of peace, exercised to meet the emergencies of war.

These are but illustrations of the breadth of the power; and it necessarily results from their consideration that whether any citizen shall be exempt from serving in the armed forces of the Nation in time of war is dependent upon the will of Congress and not upon the scruples of the individual, except as Congress provides. That body, thus far, has seen fit, by express enactment, to relieve from the obligation of armed service those persons who belong to the class known as conscientious objectors; and this policy is of such long standing that it is thought by some to be beyond the possibility of alteration. Indeed, it seems to be assumed in this case that the privilege is one that Congress itself is powerless to take away.... ... Of course, there is no such principle of the Constitution, fixed or otherwise. The conscientious objector is relieved from the obligation to bear arms in obedience to no constitutional provision, express or implied; but because, and only because, it has accorded with the policy of Congress thus to relieve him. The alien, when he becomes a naturalized citizen, acquires, with one exception, every right possessed under the Constitution by those citizens who are native born but he acquires no more. The privilege of the native-born conscientious objector to avoid bearing arms comes not from the Constitution, but from the acts of Congress. That body may grant or withhold the exemption as in its wisdom it sees fit; and if it be withheld, the native-born conscientious objector cannot successfully assert the privilege. No other conclusion is compatible with the well-nigh limitless extent of the war powers as above illustrated, which include, by necessary implication, the power, in the last extremity, to compel the armed service of any citizen in the land, without regard to his objections or his views in respect of the justice or morality of the particular war or of war in general....

The applicant for naturalization here is unwilling to become a citizen with this understanding. He is unwilling to leave the question of his future military service to the wisdom of Congress where it belongs, and where every native born or admitted citizen is obliged to leave it. In effect, he offers to take the oath of allegiance only with the qualification that the question whether the war is necessary or morally justified must, so far as his support is concerned, be conclusively determined by reference to his opinion.

When he speaks of putting his allegiance to the will of God above his allegiance to the government, it is evident, in the light of his entire statement, that he means to make *his own interpretation* of the will of God the decisive test which shall conclude the government and stay its hand. We are a Christian people according to one another the equal right of religious freedom, and acknowledging with reverence the duty of obedience to the will of God. But, also, we are a Nation with the duty to survive; a Nation whose Constitution contemplates war as well as peace; whose government must go forward upon the assumption, and safely can proceed upon no other, that unqualified allegiance to the Nation and submission and obedience to the laws of the land, as well those made for war as those made for peace, are not inconsistent with the will of God....

It is not within the province of the courts to make bargains with those who seek naturalization. They must accept the grant and take the oath in accordance with the terms fixed by the law, or forego the privilege of citizenship. There is no middle choice....

The decree of the court of appeals is reversed and that of the district court is affirmed.

Chief Justice **Hughes**, *joined by Justices* **Holmes**, **Brandeis**, *and* **Stone**,
dissenting.

———————————— THE LUDLOW AMENDMENT ————————————

75th Congress, 1st Session
House Joint Resolution 199

Proposing an amendment to the Constitution of the United States to provide for a referendum on war.

Resolved by the Senate and House of Representatives of the United States of America in Congress assembled (two-thirds of each House concurring therein). That the following article is proposed as an amendment to the Constitution of the United States, which shall be valid to all intents and purposes as a part of the Constitution when ratified by the legislatures of three-fourths of the several States.

"SECTION 1. Except in the event of an invasion of the United States or its Territorial possessions and attack upon its citizens residing therein, the authority of Congress to declare war shall not become effective until confirmed by a majority of all votes cast thereon in a Nationwide referendum. Congress, when it deems a national crisis to exist, may by concurrent resolution refer the question of war or peace to the citizens of the States, the question to be voted on being, Shall the United States declare war on _____? Congress may otherwise by law provide for the enforcement of this section."

[The Ludlow Amendment, sponsored by Representative Louis Ludlow of Indiana, was never acted upon by the House of Representatives. Introduced February 5, 1937, it had remained in the Judiciary Committee until January 10, 1938, when Representative Ludlow sought to bring it to the Floor by a special discharge resolution. President Roosevelt, Speaker Bankhead and Majority Leader Sam Rayburn urged that the motion to consider be defeated, and after spirited debate, the motion failed 209–188, ending the possibility of consideration for that session.]

———————————— YAKUS V. UNITED STATES ————————————

321 U.S. 414 (1944)

In an effort to stabilize commodity prices and prevent wartime inflation during World War II, Congress passed the Emergency Price Control Act of 1942. The Act was a temporary wartime measure which authorized the fixing of maximum prices for commodities and rents. Yakus was convicted of selling wholesale cuts of beef at prices above the maximum prescribed. He appealed, claiming the Act violated his rights under the Due Process Clause of the Fifth Amendment. The court of appeals affirmed the conviction, and the Supreme Court granted certiorari.

Chief Justice **Stone** delivered the opinion of the Court:

. . . . Congress enacted the Emergency Price Control Act in pursuance of a defined policy and required that the prices fixed by the Administrator should further that policy and conform to standards prescribed by the Act. . . . The purposes of the Act specified in [section] 1 denote the objective to be sought by the Administrator in fixing prices—the prevention of inflation and its enumerated consequences. The standards set out in [section] 2 define the boundaries within which prices having that purpose must be fixed. It is enough to satisfy the statutory requirements that the Administrator finds that the prices fixed will tend to achieve that objective and will conform to those standards, and that the courts in an appropriate proceeding can see that substantial basis for those findings is not wanting. . . .

The essentials of the legislative function are the determination of the legislative policy and its formulation and promulgation as a defined and binding rule of conduct—here the rule, with penal sanctions, that prices shall not be greater than those fixed by maximum price regulations which conform to standards and will tend to further the policy which Congress has established. These essentials are preserved when Congress has specified the basic conditions of fact upon whose existence or occurrence, ascertained from relevant data by a designated administrative agency, it directs that its statutory command shall be effective. It is no objection that the determination of facts and the inferences to be drawn from them in the light of the statutory standards and declaration of policy call for the exercise of judgment, and for the formulation of subsidiary administrative policy within the prescribed statutory framework.

Nor does the doctrine of separation of powers deny to Congress power to direct that an administrative officer properly designated for that purpose have ample latitude within which he is to ascertain the conditions which Congress has made prerequisite to the operation of its legislative command. Acting within its constitutional power to fix prices it is for Congress to say whether the data on the basis of which prices are to be fixed are to be confined within a narrow or a broad range. In either case the only concern of courts is to ascertain whether the will of Congress has been obeyed. This depends not upon the breadth of the definition of the facts or conditions which the administrative officer is to find but upon the determination whether the definition sufficiently marks the field within which the Administrator is to act so that it may be known whether he has kept within it in compliance with the legislative will. . . .

Our decisions leave no doubt that when justified by compelling public interest the legislature may authorize summary action subject to later judicial review of its validity. It may insist on the immediate collection of taxes. It may take possession of property presumptively abandoned by its owner, prior to determination of its actual abandonment. For the protection of public health it may order the summary destruction of property without prior notice or hearing. It may summarily requisition property immediately needed for the prosecution of the war. As a measure of public protection the property of alien enemies may be seized, and property believed to be owned by enemies taken without prior determination of its true ownership. Similarly public necessity in time of war may justify allowing tenants to remain in possession against the will of the landlord. Even the personal liberty of the citizen may be temporarily restrained as a measure of public safety. Measured by these standards we find no denial of due process under the circumstances in which this Act was adopted and must be applied, in its denial of any judicial stay pending determination of a regulation's validity. . . .

Affirmed.

Justice **Roberts** and Justice **Rutledge, dissenting.**

───────────────── WOODS V. MILLER ─────────────────

333 U.S. 138 (1948)

On December 31, 1946, President Truman proclaimed the termination of hostilities arising from World War II. The following year, Congress enacted the Housing and Rent Act of 1947 which limited rents for housing in "defense rental areas." Woods, the U.S. housing expediter, sought an injunction to prevent landlord Miller from increasing rents in the "Cleveland Defense–Rental area," and the U.S. District Court refused, holding the Act to be unconstitutional.

Justice **Douglas** delivered the opinion of the Court:

. . . . We conclude, in the first place, that the war power sustains this legislation. . . . . [T]he war power includes the power "to remedy the evils which have arisen from its rise and progress" and continues for the duration of that emergency. Whatever may be the consequences when war is officially terminated, the war power does not necessarily end with the cessation of hostilities. We [have] held that it is adequate to support the preservation of rights created by wartime legislation. . . . But it has a broader sweep. In *Hamilton v. Kentucky Distilleries Co.,* and *Ruppert v. Caffey,* prohibition laws which were enacted after the Armistice in World War I were sustained as exercises of the war power because they conserved manpower and increased efficiency of production in the critical days during the period of demobilization, and helped to husband the supply of grains and cereals depleted by the war effort. Those cases followed the reasoning of *Stewart v. Kahn,* which held that Congress had the power to toll the statute of limitations of the States during the period when the process of their courts was not available to litigants due to the conditions obtaining in the Civil War.

The constitutional validity of the present legislation follows *a fortiori* from those cases. The legislative history of the present Act makes abundantly clear that there has not yet been eliminated the deficit in housing which in considerable measure was caused by the heavy demobilization of veterans and by the cessation or reduction in residential construction during the period of hostilities due to the allocation of building materials to military projects. Since the war effort contributed heavily to that deficit, Congress has the power even after the cessation of hostilities to act to control the forces that a short supply of the needed article created. If that were not true, the Necessary and Proper Clause, Art. I, [section] 8, cl. 18, would be drastically limited in its application to the several war powers. The Court has declined to follow that course in the past. . . . We decline to take it today. The result would be paralyzing. It would render Congress powerless to remedy conditions the creation of which necessarily followed from the mobilization of men and materials for successful prosecution of the war. So to read the Constitution would be to make it self-defeating.

We recognize the force of the argument that the effects of war under modern conditions may be felt in the economy for years and years, and that if the war power can be used in days of peace to treat all the wounds which war inflicts on our society, it may not only swallow up all other powers of Congress but largely obliterate the Ninth and the Tenth Amendment as well. There are no such implications in today's decision. We deal here with the consequences of a housing deficit greatly intensified during the period of hostilities by the war effort. Any power, of course, can be abused. But we cannot assume that Congress is not alert to its constitutional responsibilities. And the question whether the war power has been properly employed in cases such as this is open to judicial inquiry.

Justice **Jackson,** concurring. I agree with the result in this case, but the arguments that have been addressed to us lead me to utter more explicit misgivings about war powers than the Court has done. The Government asserts no constitutional basis for this legislation other than this vague, undefined and undefinable "war power."

No one will question that this power is the most dangerous one to free government in the whole catalogue of powers. It usually is invoked in haste and excitement when calm legislative consideration of constitutional limitation is difficult. It is executed in a time of patriotic fervor that makes moderation unpopular. And, worst of all, it is interpreted by judges under the influence of the same passions and pressures. Always, as in this case, the Government urges hasty decision to forestall some emergency or serve some purpose and pleads that paralysis will result if its claims to power are denied or their confirmation delayed.

Particularly when the war power is invoked to do things to the liberties of people, or to their property or economy that only indirectly affect conduct of the war and do not relate to the management of the war itself, the constitutional basis should be scrutinized with care.

I think we can hardly deny that the war power is as valid a ground for federal rent control now as it has been at any time. We still are technically in a state of war. I would not be willing to hold that war powers may be indefinitely prolonged merely by keeping legally alive a state of war that had in fact ended. I cannot accept the argument that war powers last as long as the effects and consequences of war, for if so they are permanent—as permanent as the war debts. But I find no reason to conclude that we could find fairly that the present state of war is merely technical. We have armies abroad exercising our war power and have made no peace terms with our allies, not to mention our principle enemies. I think the conclusion that the war power has been applicable during the lifetime of this legislation is unavoidable.

—————————————— LICHTER V. UNITED STATES ——————————————

334 U.S. 742 (1948)

During World War II, Congress enacted the so called "Renegotiation Act of 1942" to recapture excess profits from defense contractors. Pursuant to the Act, the under secretary of war determined that $70,000 of the profits realized by Lichter's construction firm under defense contracts in 1942 were excessive profits and undertook to recapture them. Although Lichter challenged the constitutionality of the Renegotiation Act, both the district court and the circuit court of appeals upheld its validity.

Justice **Burton** delivered the opinion of the Court: . . . .

The Renegotiation Act was developed as a major war-time policy of Congress comparable to that of the Selective Service Act. The authority of Congress to authorize each of them sprang from its war powers. Each was a part of a national policy adopted in time of crisis in the conduct of total global warfare by a nation dedicated to the preservation, practice and development of the maximum measure of individual freedom consistent with the unity of effort essential to success.

With the advent of such warfare, mobilized property in the form of equipment and supplies became as essential as mobilized manpower. Mobilization of effort extended not only to the uniformed armed services but to the entire population. Both Acts were a form of mobilization. The language of the Constitution authorizing such measures is broad rather than restrictive. It says "The Congress shall have Power . . . To raise and support Armies, but no appropriation of Money to that Use shall be for a longer Term than two Years; . . . ." Art. 1, [section] 8, cl. 12. This places emphasis upon the supporting as well as upon the raising of armies. The power of Congress as to both is inescapably express, not merely implied. The conscription of manpower is a more vital interference with the life, liberty and property of the individual than is the conscription of his property or his profits or any substitute for such conscription of them. For his hazardous, full-time service in the armed forces a soldier is paid whatever the Government deems to be a fair but modest compensation. Comparatively speaking, the manufacturer of war goods undergoes no such hazard to his personal safety as does a front-line soldier and yet the Renegotiation Act gives him far better assurance of a reasonable return for his wartime services than the Selective Service Act and all its related legislation give to the men in the armed forces. The constitutionality of the conscription of manpower for military service is beyond question. The constitutional power of Congress to support the armed forces with equipment and supplies is no less clear and sweeping. It is valid, *a fortiori.*

In view of this power "To raise and support Armies, . . ." and the power granted in the same Article of the Constitution "To make all Laws which shall be necessary and proper for carrying into Execution the foregoing Powers, . . ." the only question remaining is whether the Renegotiation Act was a law "necessary and proper for carrying into Execution" the war powers of Congress and especially its power to support armies. The results [of World War II] amply demonstrated the infinite value of [war] production in winning the war. It proved to be a *sine qua non* condition of the survival of the nation. Not only was it "necessary and proper" for Congress to provide for such production in the successful conduct of the war, but it was well within the outer limits of the constitutional discretion of Congress and the President to do so under the terms of the Renegotiation Act. Accordingly, the question before us as to the constitutionality of the Renegotiation Act is not that of the power of the government to renegotiate and recapture war profits. The only questions are whether the particular method of renegotiation and the administrative procedure prescribed conformed to the constitutional limitations under which Congress was permitted to exercise its basic powers.

Our first question relates to the method of adjusting net compensation for war services through the compulsory "renegotiation" of profits under existing contracts between private parties, including recourse to unilateral orders for payments into the Treasury of the United States of such portions of those profits as were determined by the administrative officials of that Government to be "excessive profits." . . .

One approach to the question of the constitutional power of Congress over the profits on these contracts is to recognize that Congress, in time of war, unquestionably has the fundamental power . . . to conscript men and to requisition the properties necessary and proper to enable it to raise and support its Armies. Congress futhermore has a primary obligation to bring about whatever production of war equipment and supplies shall be necessary to win a war. Given this mission, Congress then had to choose between possible alternatives for its performance. In the light of the compelling necessity for the immediate production of vast quantities of war goods, the first alternative, all too clearly evident to the world, was that which Congress did not choose, namely, that of mobilizing the productive capacity of the nation into a governmental unit on the totalitarian model. This would have meant the conscription of property and of workmen. It would have meant the raising of supplies for the Armies in much the same manner as that in which Congress raised the manpower for such Armies. Already the nation had some units of production of military supplies in the form of arsenals, navy yards, and in the increasing number of governmentally owned, if not operated, war material plants. The production of the atomic bombs was one example of a war industry owned and operated exclusively by the Government. Faced with this ironical alternative of converting the nation in effect into a totalitarian state in order to preserve itself from totalitarian domination, that alternative was steadfastly rejected. The plan for Renegotiation of Profits which was chosen in its place by Congress appears in its true light as the very symbol of a free people united in reaching unequalled productive capacity and yet retaining the maximum of individual freedom consistent with a general mobilization of effort. . . .

[I]t is of the highest importance that the fundamental purposes of the Constitution be kept in mind and given effect in order that, through the Constitution, the people of the United States may in time of war as in peace bring to the support of those purposes the full force of their united action. In time of crisis nothing could be more tragic and less expressive of the intent of the people than so to construe their Constitution that by its own terms it would substantially hinder rather than help them in defending their national safety.

In an address by Honorable Charles E. Hughes, of New York, on "War Powers Under The Constitution," September 5, 1917, he said:

> "The power to wage war is the power to wage war successfully. The framers of the Constitution were under no illusions as to war. They had emerged from a long struggle which had taught them the weakness of a mere confederation, and they had no hope that they could hold what they had won save as they established a Union which could fight with the strength of one people under one government entrusted with the common defense. In equipping the National Government with the needed authority in war, they tolerated no limitations inconsistent with that object, as they realized that the very existence of the Nation might be at stake and that every resource of the people must be at command. . . .

> *   *   *

> "The extraordinary circumstances of war may bring particular busi-ness[es] and enterprises clearly into the category of those which are affect-ed with a public interest and which demand immediate and thoroughgo-ing public regulation. The production and distribution of foodstuffs, articles of prime necessity, those which have direct relation to military efficiency, those which are absolutely required for the support of the people during the stress of conflict, are plainly of this sort. Reasonable regulations to safeguard the resources upon which we depend for military success must be regarded as being within the powers confided to enable it to prosecute a successful war. . . .

> "Similarly, it may be said that the power has been expressly given to Congress to prosecute war, and to pass all laws which shall be necessary and proper for carrying that power into execution. That power explicitly conferred and absolutely essential to the safety of the Nation is not destroyed or impaired by any later provision of the constitution or by any one of the amendments. These may all be construed so as to avoid making the constitution self-destructive, so as to preserve the rights of the citizen from unwarrantable attack, while assuring beyond all hazard the common defense and the perpetuity of our liberties. These rest upon the preserva-tion of the nation.

> "It has been said that the constitution marches. That is, there are con-stantly new applications of unchanged powers, and it is ascertained that in novel and complex situations, the old grants contain, in their general words and true significance, needed and adequate authority. So, also, we have a *fighting constitution. We cannot at this time fail to appreciate the wisdom of the fathers, as under this charter, one hundred and thirty years old—the constitution of Washington—the people of the United States fight with the power of unity,—as we fight for the freedom of our children and that hereafter the sword of autocrats may never threaten the world."*

The war powers of Congress and the president are only those which are to be derived from the Constitution but, in the light of the language just quoted, the primary implication of a war power is that it shall be an effective power to wage the war successfully. Thus, while the constitutional structure and controls of our Government are our guides equally in war and in peace, they must be read with the realistic purposes of the entire instrument fully in mind. . . .

The recovery by the Government of excessive profits received or receivable upon war contracts is in the nature of the regulation of maximum prices under war contracts or the collection of excess profits taxes, rather than the requisitioning or condemnation of private property for public use. One of the primary purposes of the renegotiation plan for redetermining the allowable profit on contracts for the production of war goods by private persons was the avoidance of requisitioning or condemnation proceedings leading to governmental ownership and operation of the plants producing war materials. . . . The collection of renegotiated excessive profits on a war subcontract also is not in the nature of a penalty and is not a deprivation of a subcontractor of his property without due process of law in violation of the Fifth Amendment. . . .

Affirmed.

*Justice **Jackson** and Justice **Douglas**, concurring in part and **dissenting** in part.*

FORMOSA RESOLUTION OF 1955

84th Congress, 1st Session
[H.J.Res. 159]

Joint Resolution authorizing the President to employ the Armed Forces of the United States for protecting the security of Formosa, the Pescadores and related positions and territories of that area.

Whereas the primary purpose of the United States, in its relations with all other nations, is to develop and sustain a just and enduring peace for all; and Whereas certain territories in the West Pacific under the jurisdiction of the Republic of China are now under armed attack, and threats and declarations have been and are being by the Chinese Communists that such armed attack is in aid of and in preparation for armed attack on Formosa and the Pescadores,

Whereas such armed attack if continued would gravely endanger the peace and security of the West Pacific Area and particularly of Formosa and the Pescadores; and

Whereas the secure possession by friendly governments of the Western Pacific Island chain, of which Formosa is a part, is essential to the vital interests of the United States and all friendly nations in or bordering upon the Pacific Ocean; and

Whereas the President of the United States on January 6, 1955, submitted to the Senate for its advice and consent to ratification a Mutual Defense Treaty between the United States of America and the Republic of China, which recognizes that an armed attack in the West Pacific area directed against territories, therein described, in the region of Formosa and the Pescadores, would be dangerous to the peace and safety of the parties to the treaty: Therefore be it

Resolved by the Senate and House of Representatives of the United States of America in Congress assembled, That:

The President of the United States be and he hereby is authorized to employ the Armed Forces of the United States as he deems necessary for the specific purpose of securing and protecting Formosa and the Pescadores against armed attack, this authority to include the securing and protection of such related positions and territories of that area now in friendly hands and the taking of such other measures as he judges to be required or appropriate in assuring the defense of Formosa and the Pescadores.

This resolution shall expire when the President shall determine that the peace and security of the area is reasonably assured by international conditions created by action of the United Nations or otherwise, and shall so report to the Congress.

Approved January 29, 1955.

JOINT RESOLUTION TO PROMOTE PEACE AND STABILITY IN THE MIDDLE EAST

85th Congress, 1st Session, March 9, 1957
[H.J.Res. 117]

Resolved by the Senate and the House of Representatives of the United States of America in Congress assembled, That:

The President be and hereby is authorized to cooperate with and assist any nation or group of nations in the general area of the Middle East desiring such assistance in the development of economic strength dedicated to the maintenance of national independence.

* * *

Sec. 2. The President is authorized to undertake, in the general area of the Middle East, military assistance programs with any nation or group of nations of that area desiring such assistance. Furthermore, the United States regards as vital to the national interest and world peace the preservation of the independence and integrity of the nations of the Middle East. To this end, if the President determines the necessity thereof, the United States is prepared to use armed forces to assist any such nation or group of such nations requesting assistance against armed aggression from any country controlled by international communism: *Provided,* That such employment shall be consonant with the treaty obligations of the United States and with the Constitution of the United States.

* * *

Sec. 5. The President shall within the months of January and July of each year report to the Congress his action hereunder.

Sec. 6. This joint resolution shall expire when the President shall determine that the peace and security of the nations in the general area of the Middle East are reasonably assured by international conditions created by action of the United Nations or otherwise except that it may be terminated earlier by a concurrent resolution of the two Houses of Congress.

───────── Tonkin Gulf Resolution ─────────

August 10, 1964
Public Law 88–408; 78 Stat. 384

JOINT RESOLUTION

To promote the maintenance of international peace and security in southeast Asia.

Whereas naval units of the Communist regime in Vietnam, in violation of the principles of the Charter of the United Nations and of international law, have deliberately and repeatedly attacked United States naval vessels lawfully present in international waters, and have thereby created a serious threat to international peace; and

Whereas these attacks are part of a deliberate and systematic campaign of aggression that the Communist regime in North Vietnam has been waging against its neighbors and the nations joined with them in the collective defense of their freedom; and

Whereas the United States is assisting the peoples of southeast Asia to protect their freedom and has no territorial, military or political ambitions in that area, but desires only that these peoples should be left in peace to work out their own destinies in their own way: Now, therefore, be it

Resolved by the Senate and House of Representatives of the United States of America in Congress assembled, That the Congress approves and supports the determination of the President, as Commander in Chief, to take all necessary measures to repel any armed attack against the forces of the United States and to prevent further aggression.

Sec. 2. The United States regards as vital to its national interest and to world peace the maintenance of international peace and security in southeast Asia. Consonant with the Constitution of the United States and the Charter of the United Nations and in accordance with its obligations under the Southeast Asia Collective Defense Treaty, the United States is, therefore, prepared, as the President determines, to take all necessary steps, including the use of armed force, to assist any member or protocol state of the Southeast Asia Collective Defense Treaty requesting assistance in defense of its freedom.

Sec. 3. This resolution shall expire when the President shall determine that the peace and security of the area is reasonably assured by international conditions created by action of the United Nations or otherwise, except that it may be terminated earlier by concurrent resolution of the Congress.

Approved August 10, 1964.

[*Congress repealed the Tonkin Gulf Resolution, January 2, 1971.*]

──────────── UNITED STATES V. O'BRIEN ────────────

391 U.S. 367 (1968)

On the morning of March 31, 1966, David O'Brien and three companions burned their draft registration cards on the steps of the South Boston Courthouse. O'Brien was indicted, tried and convicted of violating the Universal Military Training Act, which provided that any person who "knowingly destroys" or "knowingly mutilates" a draft certificate is guilty of a felony. O'Brien contended that that portion of the Act was an unconstitutional abridgement of free speech and served no useful purpose. The district court rejected O'Brien's contention, the court of appeals reversed, and the government appealed.

Chief Justice **Warren** delivered the opinion of the Court: . . .

We cannot accept the view that an apparently limitless variety of conduct can be labeled "speech" whenever the person engaging in the conduct intends thereby to express an idea. However, even on the assumption that the alleged communicative element in O'Brien's conduct is sufficient to bring into play the First Amendment, it does not necessarily follow that the destruction of a registration certificate is constitutionally protected activity. This Court has held that when "speech" and "nonspeech" elements are combined in the same course of conduct, a sufficiently important governmental interest in regulating the nonspeech element can justify incidental limitations on First Amendment freedoms. To characterize the quality of the governmental interest which must appear, the Court has employed a variety of descriptive terms: compelling; substantial; subordinating; paramount; cogent; strong. Whatever imprecision inheres in these terms, we think it clear that a government regulation is sufficiently justified if it is within the constitutional power of the Government; if it furthers an important or substantial government interest; if the governmental interest is unrelated to the suppression of free expression; and if the incidental restriction on alleged First Amendment freedoms is no greater than is essential to the furtherance of that interest. We find that the Act meets all of these requirements, and consequently that O'Brien can be constitutionally convicted for violating it.

The constitutional power of Congress to raise and support armies and to make all laws necessary and proper to that end is broad and sweeping. . . . The power of Congress to classify and conscript manpower for military service is "beyond question." Pursuant to this power, Congress may establish a system of registration for individuals liable for training and service, and may require such individuals within reason to cooperate in the registration system. The issuance of certificates indicating the registration and eligibility classification of individuals is a legitimate and substantial administrative aid in the functioning of this system. And legislation to insure the continuing availability of issued certificates serves a legitimate and substantial purpose in the system's administration. . . .

We think it apparent that the continuing availability to each registrant of his Selective Service certificates substantially furthers the smooth and proper functioning of the system that Congress has established to raise armies. We think it also apparent that the Nation has a vital interest in having a system for raising armies that functions with maximum efficiency and is capable of easily and quickly responding to continually changing circumstances. For these reasons, the Government has a substantial interest in assuring the continuing availability of issued Selective Service certificates. . . .

In conclusion, we find that because of the Government's substantial interest in assuring the continuing availability of issued Selective Service certificates, because [the Act] is an appropriately narrow means of protecting this interest and condemns only the independent noncommunicative impact of conduct within its reach, and because the noncommunicative impact of O'Brien's act of burning his registration certificate frustrated the Government's interest, a sufficient governmental interest has been shown to justify O'Brien's conviction. . . .

Since the 1965 Amendment to ss 12(b)(3) of the Universal Military Training and Service Act is constitutional as enacted and as applied, the Court of Appeals should have affirmed the judgment of conviction entered by the District Court. Accordingly, we vacate the judgment of the Court of Appeals, and reinstate the judgment and sentence of the District Court.

It is so ordered.

Justice **Harlan,** *concurring* . . . .

Justice **Douglas,** *dissenting* . . . .

MASSACHUSETTS V. LAIRD

400 U.S. 886 (1970)

The Supreme Court denied without comment the right of the Commonwealth of Massachusetts to file an original bill of complaint against the secretary of defense, contesting the constitutionality of the war in Vietnam.

Justice **Harlan** and Justice **Stewart** *dissent.* They would set the motion for argument on questions of standing and justiciability.

Justice **Douglas,** *dissenting.*

This motion was filed by the Commonwealth of Massachusetts against the Secretary of Defense, a citizen of another State. It is brought pursuant to a mandate contained in an act of the Massachusetts Legislature. Massachusetts seeks to obtain an adjudication of the constitutionality of the United States' participation in the Indochina war. It requests that the United States' participation be declared "unconstitutional in that it was not initially authorized or subsequently ratified by Congressional declaration"; it asks that the Secretary of Defense be enjoined "from carrying out, issuing or causing to be issued any further orders which would increase the present level of United States troops in Indochina"; and it asks that, if appropriate congressional action is not forthcoming within 90 days of this Court's decree, the Secretary of Defense be enjoined "from carrying out, issuing, or causing to be issued any further orders directing any inhabitant of the Commonwealth of Massachusetts to Indochina for the purpose of participating in combat or supporting combat troops in the Vietnam war." Today this Court denies leave to file the complaint. I dissent.

The threshold issues for granting leave to file a complaint in this case are standing and justiciability. I believe that Massachusetts has standing and the controversy is justiciable. At the very least, however, it is apparent that the issues are not so clearly foreclosed as to justify a summary denial of leave to file. . . .

STANDING

In *Massachusetts v. Mellon,* the Court held that a State lacked standing to challenge, as *parens patriae,* a federal grant-in-aid program under which the Federal Government was allegedly usurping powers reserved to the States. The Solicitor General argues that *Mellon* stands as a bar to this suit.

Yet the ruling of the Court in that case is not dispositive of this one. The opinion states: "We need not go so far as to say that a State may never intervene by suit to protect its citizens against any form of enforcement of unconstitutional acts of Congress; but we are clear that the right to do so does not arise here." Thus the case did not announce a *per se* rule to bar all suits against the Federal Government as *parens patriae.*

It has been settled, at least since 1901, that "if the health and comfort of the inhabitants of a State are threatened, the State is the proper party to represent and defend them," *Missouri v. Illinois,* in an original action in this Court. . . . Massachusetts would clearly seem to have standing as *parens patriae* to represent, as alleged in its complaint, its male citizens being drafted for overseas combat in Indochina.

JUSTICIABILITY

A question that is "political" is opposed to one that is "justiciable." [We reviewed] the dimensions of the "political" question. . . . in *Baker v. Carr.*

─────── WAR POWERS RESOLUTION ───────

Public Law 93–148; 87 Stat. 555; November 7, 1973

JOINT RESOLUTION

Concerning the war powers of Congress and the President.

Resolved by the Senate and House of Representatives of the United States of America in Congress assembled,

Short Title

Sec. 1. This joint resolution may be cited as the "War Powers Resolution."

Purpose and Policy

Sec. 2. (a) It is the purpose of this joint resolution to fulfill the intent of the framers of the Constitution of the United States and insure that the collective judgment of both the Congress and the President will apply to the introduction of United States Armed Forces into hostilities, or into situations where imminent involvement in hostilities is clearly indicated by the circumstances, and to the continued use of such forces in hostilities or in such situations.

(b) Under article I, section 8, of the Constitution, it is specifically provided that the Congress shall have the power to make all laws necessary and proper for carrying into execution, not only its own powers but also all other powers vested by the Constitution in the Government of the United States, or in any department or officer thereof.

(c) The constitutional powers of the President as Commander in Chief to introduce United States Armed Forces into hostilities or into situations where imminent involvement in hostilities is clearly indicated by the circumstances, are exercised only pursuant to (1) a declaration of war, (2) specific statutory authorization, or (3) a national emergency created by attack upon the United States, its territories or possessions, or its armed forces.

Consultation

Sec. 3. The President in every possible instance shall consult with Congress before introducing United States Armed Forces into hostilities or into situations where imminent involvement in hostilities is clearly indicated by the circumstances, and after every such introduction shall meet regularly with the Congress until United States Armed Forces are no longer engaged in hostilities or have been removed from such situations.

Reporting

Sec. 4. (a) In the absence of a declaration of war, in any case in which United States Armed Forces are introduced—

1. into hostilities or into situations where imminent involvement in hostilities is clearly indicated by the circumstances;

2. into the territory, airspace or waters of a foreign nation, while equipped for combat, except for deployments which relate solely to supply, replacement, repair, or training of such forces; or

3. in numbers which substantially enlarge United States Armed Forces equipped for combat already located in a foreign nation;

the President shall submit within 48 hours to the Speaker of the House of Representatives and to the President *pro tempore* of the Senate a report, in writing, setting forth—

    (A) the circumstances necessitating the introduction of United States Armed Forces;

(B) the constitutional and legislative authority under which such introduction took place; and

(C) the estimated scope and duration of the hostilities or involvement.

(b) The President shall provide such other information as the Congress may request in the fulfillment of its constitutional responsibilities with respect to committing the Nation to war and to the use of United States Armed Forces abroad.

(c) Whenever United States Armed Forces are introduced into hostilities or into any situation described in subsection (a) of this section, the President shall, so long as such armed forces continue to be engaged in such hostilities or situation, report to the Congress periodically on the status of such hostilities or situation as well as on the scope and duration of such hostilities or situation, but in no event shall he report to the Congress less often than once every six months.

Congressional Action

* * *

Sec. 5. (b) Within sixty calendar days after a report is submitted or is required to be submitted pursuant to section 4(a)(1), whichever is earlier, the President shall terminate any use of United States Armed Forces with respect to which such report was submitted (or required to be submitted), unless the Congress (1) has declared war or has enacted a specific authorization for such use of United States Armed Forces, (2) has extended by law such sixty-day period, or (3) is physically unable to meet as a result of an armed attack upon the United States. Such sixty-day period shall be extended for not more than an additional thirty days if the President determines and certifies to the Congress in writing that unavoidable military necessity respecting the safety of United States Armed Forces requires the continued use of such armed forces in the course of bringing about a prompt removal of such forces.

(c) Notwithstanding subsection (b), at any time that United States Armed Forces are engaged in hostilities outside the territory of the United States, its possessions and territories without a declaration of war or specific statutory authorization, such forces shall be removed by the President if the Congress so directs by concurrent resolution.

* * *

Interpretation of Joint Resolution

Sec. 8. (a) Authority to introduce United States Armed Forces into hostilities or into situations wherein involvement in hostilities is clearly indicated by the circumstances shall not be inferred—

1. from any provision of law (whether or not in effect before the date of the enactment of this joint resolution), including any provision con-

tained in any appropriation Act, unless such provision specifically authorizes the introduction of United States Armed Forces into hostilities or into such situations and states that it is intended to constitute specific statutory authorization within the meaning of this joint resolution; or

2. from any treaty heretofore or hereafter ratified unless such treaty is implemented by legislation specifically authorizing the introduction of United States Armed Forces into hostilities or into such situations and stating that it is intended to constitute specific statutory authorization within the meaning of this joint resolution.

(b) Nothing in this joint resolution shall be construed to require any further specific statutory authorization to permit members of United States Armed Forces to participate jointly with members of the armed forces of one or more foreign countries in the headquarters operations of high-level military commands which were established prior to the date of enactment of this joint resolution and pursuant to the United Nations Charter or any treaty ratified by the United States prior to such date.

(c) For purposes of this joint resolution, the term "introduction of United States Armed Forces" includes the assignment of members of such armed forces to command, coordinate, participate in the movement of, or accompany the regular or irregular military forces of any foreign country or government when such military forces are engaged, or there exists an imminent threat that such forces will become engaged, in hostilities.

(d) Nothing in this joint resolution—

1. is intended to alter the constitutional authority of the Congress or of the President, or the provisions of existing treaties; or

2. shall be construed as granting any authority to the President with respect to the introduction of United States Armed Forces into hostilities or into situations wherein involvement in hostilities is clearly indicated by the circumstances which authority he would not have had in the absence of this resolution.

Separability Clause

* * *

[Passed over Presidential veto, November 7, 1973.]

──────────── UNITED STATES V. RICHARDSON ────────────

418 U.S. 166 (1974)

Richardson sought unsuccessfully to obtain from the government detailed information concerning CIA expenditures. He then brought suit, as a federal taxpayer, to test the constitutionality of the Central Intelligence Agency Act which permits the Agency to account for its funds "solely on the certificate of the Director." The district court held that Richardson lacked standing to bring the suit, the court of appeals reversed, and the United States appealed.

Chief Justice **Burger** delivered the opinion of the Court:

We granted *certiorari* in this case to determine whether the respondent has standing to bring an action as a federal taxpayer alleging that certain provisions concerning public reporting of expenditures under the Central Intelligence Agency Act of 1949 violate Art. I, [section] 9, cl. 7, of the Constitution which provides:

> No Money shall be drawn from the Treasury, but in Consequence of Appropriations made by law; and a regular Statement and Account of the Receipts and Expenditures of all public Money shall be published from time to time.

* * *

I

As far back as *Marbury v. Madison* this Court held that judicial power may be exercised only in a case properly before it—a "case or controversy" not suffering any of the limitations of the political-question doctrine, not then moot or calling for an advisory opinion. In *Baker v. Carr* this limitation was described in terms that a federal court cannot

> 'pronounce any statute, either of a State or of the United States, void, because irreconcilable with the Constitution, except as it is called upon to adjudge the legal rights of litigants in actual controversies.'

III

The respondent's claim is that without detailed information on CIA expenditures—and hence its activities—he cannot intelligently follow the actions of Congress or the Executive, nor can he properly fulfill his obligations as a member of the electorate in voting for candidates seeking national office.

This is surely the kind of a generalized grievance described in both *Frothingham* and *Flast* since the impact on him is plainly undifferentiated and "common to all members of the public." While we can hardly dispute that this respondent has a genuine interest in the use of funds and that his interest may be prompted by his status as a taxpayer, he has not alleged that, as a taxpayer, he is in danger of suffering any particular concrete injury as a result of the operation of this statute. As the Court noted in *Sierra Club v. Morton:*

> [A] mere 'interest in a problem,' no matter how longstanding the interest and no matter how qualified the organization is in evaluating the problem, is not sufficient by itself to render the organization 'adversely affected' or 'aggrieved' within the meaning of the APA.

It can be argued that if respondent is not permitted to litigate this issue, no one can do so. In a very real sense, the absence of any particular individual or class to litigate these claims gives support to the argument that the subject matter is committed to the surveillance of Congress, and ultimately to the political process. Any other conclusion would mean that the Founding Fathers intended to set up something in the nature of an Athenian democracy or a New England town meeting to oversee the conduct of the National

Government by means of lawsuits in federal courts. The Constitution created a *representative* Government with the representatives directly responsible to their constituents at stated periods of two, four, and six years; that the Constitution does not afford a judicial remedy does not, of course, completely disable the citizen who is not satisfied with the "ground rules" established by the Congress for reporting expenditures of the Executive Branch. Lack of standing within the narrow confines of Art. III jurisdiction does not impair the right to assert his views in the political forum or at the polls. Slow, cumbersome, and unresponsive though the traditional electoral process may be thought at times, our system provides for changing members of the political branches when dissatisfied citizens convince a sufficient number of their fellow electors that elected representatives are delinquent in performing duties committed to them.

As our society has become more complex, our numbers more vast, our lives more varied, and our resources more strained, citizens increasingly request the intervention of the courts on a greater variety of issues than at any period of our national development. The acceptance of new categories of judicially cognizable injury has not eliminated the basic principle that to invoke judicial power the claimant must have a "personal stake in the outcome," *Baker v. Carr,* or a "particular, concrete injury," *Sierra Club,* or "a direct injury," *Ex parte Lévitt; in short, something more than "generalized grievances." Respondent has failed to meet these fundamental tests; accordingly, the judgment of the Court of Appeals is*

Reversed.

Justices **Douglas, Brennan, Stewart** and **Marshall, dissenting.**

SCHLESINGER V. RESERVISTS TO STOP THE WAR

418 U.S. 208 (1974)

The Reservists Committee to Stop the War brought a class action on behalf of all American citizens and taxpayers against the secretary of defense challenging the holding of reserve commissions by members of Congress as a violation of the Incompatibility Clause of the Constitution which provides that: "no Person holding any Office under the United States, shall be a member of either House during his Continuance in Office." (Art. I, sec. 6, cl. 2) The district court held that the Reservists had standing to sue as citizens but not as taxpayers, and the court of appeals affirmed.

Chief Justice **Burger** delivered the opinion of the Court:

* * *

CITIZEN STANDING

To have standing to sue as a class representative it is essential that a plaintiff must be a part of that class, that is, he must possess the same interest and suffer the same injury shared by all members of the class he represents. In granting respondents standing to sue as representatives of the class of all United States citizens, the District Court therefore necessarily—and correctly—characterized respondents' interest as "undifferentiated" from that of all other citizens.

The only interest all citizens share in the claim advanced by respondents is one which presents injury in the abstract. Respondents seek to have the Judicial Branch compel the Executive Branch to act in conformity with the Incompatibility Clause, an interest shared by all citizens. The very language of respondents' complaint reveals that it is nothing more than a matter of speculation whether the claimed nonobservance of that Clause deprives citizens of the faithful discharge of the legislative duties of reservist Members of Congress. And that claimed nonobservance, standing alone, would adversely affect only the generalized interest of all citizens in constitutional governance, and that is an abstract injury. The Court has previously declined to treat "generalized grievances" about the conduct of Government as a basis for taxpayer standing. We consider now whether a citizen has standing to sue under such a generalized complaint.

. . . . [S]tanding to sue may not be predicated upon an interest of the kind alleged here which is held in common by all members of the public, because of the necessarily abstract nature of the injury all citizens share. Concrete injury, whether actual or threatened, is that indispensable element of a dispute which serves in part to cast it in a form traditionally capable of judicial resolution. It adds the essential dimension of specificity to the dispute by requiring that the complaining party have suffered a particular injury caused by the action challenged as unlawful. This personal stake is what the Court has consistently held enables a complainant authoritatively to present to a court a complete perspective upon the adverse consequences flowing from the specific set of facts undergirding his grievance. Such authoritative presentations are an integral part of the judicial process, for a court must rely on the parties' treatment of the facts and claims before it to develop its rules of law. Only concrete injury presents the factual context within which a court, aided by parties who argue within the context, is capable of making decisions.

Moreover, when a court is asked to undertake constitutional adjudication, the most important and delicate of its responsibilities, the requirement of concrete injury further serves the function of insuring that such adjudication does not take place unnecessarily. This principle is particularly applicable here, where respondents seek an interpretation of a constitutional provision which has never before been construed by the federal courts. First, concrete injury removes from the realm of speculation whether there is a real need to exercise the power of judicial review in order to protect the interests of the complaining party. . . . Second, the discrete factual context within which the concrete injury occurred or is threatened insures the framing of relief no broader than required by the precise facts to which the court's ruling would be applied. This is especially important when the relief sought produces a confrontation with one of the coordinate branches of the Government; here the relief sought would, in practical effect, bring about conflict with two coordinate branches.

To permit a complainant who has no concrete injury to require a court to rule on important constitutional issues in the abstract would create the potential for abuse of the judicial process, distort the role of the Judiciary in its relationship to the Executive and the Legislature and open the Judiciary to an arguable charge of providing "government by injunction." . . .

Accordingly, the judgment of the Court of Appeals is reversed, and the case is remanded to the District Court for further proceedings consistent with this opinion.

It is so ordered.

Justices **Douglas, Brennan** and **Marshall,** dissenting.

--------------- ROSTKER, DIRECTOR OF SELECTIVE ---------------
SERVICE, v. GOLDBERG

453 U.S. 57 (1981)

In 1980, at President Carter's request, Congress passed legislation requiring young men to register for the draft. The Congress declined to follow Carter's recommendation that women also be required to register. Mr. Goldberg and others thereupon reinstituted an earlier suit on behalf of "all male persons . . . subject to registration," contesting the constitutionality of the Act based on sex discrimination in violation of the Due Process Clause of the Fifth Amendment. The district court held in favor of the plaintiffs, and permanently enjoined the government from enforcing the Act. The government appealed directly to the Supreme Court.

Justice **Rehnquist** delivered the opinion of the Court: . . . .

II

Whenever called upon to judge the constitutionality of an Act of Congress—"the gravest and most delicate duty that this Court is called upon to perform,"—the Court accords "great weight to the decisions of Congress." The Congress is a coequal branch of government whose Members take the same oath we do to uphold the Constitution of the United States. As Justice Frankfurter noted in *Joint Anti–Fascist Refugee Committee v. McGrath,* (concurring opinion), we must have "due regard to the fact that this Court is not exercising a primary judgment but is sitting in judgment upon those who also have taken the oath to observe the Constitution and who have the responsibility for carrying on government." The customary deference accorded the judgments of Congress is certainly appropriate when, as here, Congress specifically considered the question of the Act's constitutionality.

This is not, however, merely a case involving the customary deference accorded congressional decisions. The case arises in the context of Congress' authority over national defense and military affairs, and perhaps in no other area has the Court accorded Congress greater deference. . . .

The operation of a healthy deference to legislative and executive judgments in the area of military affairs is evident in several recent decisions of this Court. In *Parker v. Levy,* 417 U.S. 733, 756, 758 (1974), the Court rejected both vagueness and overbreadth challenges to provisions of the Uniform

Code of Military Justice, noting that "Congress is permitted to legislate both with greater breadth and with greater flexibility when the statute governs military society, and that "[w]hile the members of the military are not excluded from the protection granted by the First Amendment, the different character of the military community and of the military mission requires a different application of those protections." In *Middendorf v. Henry,* 425 U.S. 25 (1976), the Court noted that in considering due process claims in the context of a summary court-martial it "must give particular deference to the determination of Congress, made under its authority to regulate the land and naval forces, U.S. Const., Art. I, [section] 8," concerning what rights were available. Deference to the judgment of other branches in the area of military affairs also played a major role in *Greer v. Spock,* 424 U.S. 828, 837, 838 (1976), where the Court upheld a ban on political speeches by civilians on a military base, and in *Brown v. Glines,* 444 U.S. 348 (1980), where the Court upheld regulations imposing a prior restraint on the right to petition military personnel. See also *Burns v. Wilson,* 346 U.S. 137 (1953); *United States v. MacIntosh,* 283 U.S. 605, 622 (1931). . . .

None of this is to say that Congress is free to disregard the Constitution when it acts in the area of military affairs. In that area, as any other, Congress remains subject to the limitations of the Due Process Clause. . . ., but the tests and limitations to be applied may differ because of the military context. We of course do not abdicate our ultimate responsibility to decide the constitutional question, but simply recognize that the Constitution itself requires such deference to congressional choice. In deciding the question before us we must be particularly careful not to substitute our judgment of what is desirable for that of Congress, or our own evaluation of evidence for a reasonable evaluation by the Legislative Branch. . . .

We find [the District Court's] efforts to divorce registration from the military and national defense context, with all the deference called for in that context, singularly unpersuasive. *United States v. O'Brien,* 391 U.S. 367 (1968), recognized the broad deference due Congress in the selective service area before us in this case. Registration is not an end in itself in the civilian world but rather the first step in the induction process into the military one, and Congress specifically linked its consideration of registration to induction. Congressional judgments concerning registration and the draft are based on judgments concerning military operations and needs, ("the starting point for any discussion of the appropriateness of registering women for the draft is the question of the proper role of women in combat"), and the deference unquestionably due the latter judgments is necessarily required in assessing the former as well. Although the District Court stressed that it was not intruding on military questions, its opinion was based on assessments of military need and flexibility in a time of mobilization. It would be blinking reality to say that our precedents requiring deference to Congress in military affairs are not implicated by the present case. . . .

. . . . In this case the courts are called upon to decide whether Congress, acting under an explicit constitutional grant of authority, has by that action transgressed an explicit guarantee of individual rights which limits the authority so conferred. Simply labeling the legislative decision "military" on the one hand or "gender-based" on the other does not automatically guide a court to the correct constitutional result.

No one could deny that under the test of *Craig v. Boren,* the Government's interest in raising and supporting armies is an "important governmental interest." Congress and its Committees carefully considered and debated two alternative means of furthering that interest: the first was to register only males for potential conscription, and the other was to register both sexes. Congress chose the former alternative. When that decision is challenged on equal protection grounds, the question a court must decide is not which alternative it would have chosen, had it been the primary decisionmaker, but whether that chosen by Congress denies equal protection of the laws. . . .

III

This case is quite different from several of the gender-based discrimination cases we have considered in that, despite appellees' assertions, Congress did not act "unthinkingly" or "reflexively and not for any considered reason." The question of registering women for the draft not only received considerable national attention and was the subject of wide-ranging public debate, but also was extensively considered by Congress in hearings, floor debate, and in committee.

Congress determined that any future draft, which would be facilitated by the registration scheme, would be characterized by a need for combat troops. . . . Congress' determination that the need would be for combat troops if a draft took place was sufficiently supported by testimony adduced at the hearings so that the courts are not free to make their own judgment on the question. The purpose of registration, therefore, was to prepare for a draft *of combat troops.*

Women as a group, however, unlike men as a group, are not eligible for combat. The restrictions on the participation of women in combat in the Navy and Air Force are statutory. Under 10 U.S.C. [section] 6015 "women may not be assigned to duty on vessels or in aircraft that are engaged in combat missions," and under 10 U.S.C. [section] 8549 female members of the Air Force "may not be assigned to duty in aircraft engaged in combat missions." The Army and Marine Corps preclude the use of women in combat as a matter of established policy. Congress specifically recognized and endorsed the exclusion of women from combat in exempting women from registration. In the words of the Senate Report:

> "The principle that women should not intentionally and routinely engage in combat is fundamental, and enjoys wide support among our people. It is universally supported by military leaders who have testified before the Committee. . . . Current law and policy exclude women from being assigned to combat in our military forces, and the Committee reaffirms this policy."

. . . . The existence of the combat restrictions clearly indicates the basis for Congress' decision to exempt women from registration. The purpose of registration was to prepare for a draft of combat troops. Since women are excluded from combat, Congress concluded that they would not be needed in the event of a draft, and therefore decided not to register them. . . .

The District Court stressed that the military need for women was irrelevant to the issue of their registration. As that court put it: "Congress could not constitutionally require registration under the MSSA of only black citizens or only white citizens, or single out any political or religious group simply because those groups contain sufficient persons to fill the needs of the Selective Service System." This reasoning is beside the point. The reasons women are exempt from registration is not because military needs can be met by drafting men. This is not a case of Congress arbitrarily choosing to burden one of two similarly situated groups, such as would be the case with an all-black or all-white, or an all-Catholic or all-Lutheran, or an all-Republican or all-Democratic registration. Men and women, because of the combat restrictions on women, are simply not similarly situated for purposes of a draft or registration for a draft.

Congress' decision to authorize the registration of only men, therefore, does not violate the Due Process Clause. The exemption of women from registration is not only sufficiently but also closely related to Congress' purpose in authorizing registration. The fact that Congress and the Executive have decided that women should not serve in combat fully justifies Congress in not authorizing their registration, since the purpose of registration is to develop a pool of potential combat troops. As was the case in *Schlesinger v. Ballard,* "the gender classification is not individious, but rather realistically reflects the fact that the sexes are not similarly situated" in this case. The Constitution requires that Congress treat similarly situated persons similarly, not that it engage in gestures of superficial equality. . . .

. . . . The District Court was quite wrong in undertaking an independent evaluation of this evidence, rather than adopting an appropriately deferential examination of *Congress'* evaluation of that evidence.

In light of the foregoing, we conclude that Congress acted well within its constitutional authority when it authorized the registration of men, and not women, under the Military Selective Service Act. The decision of the District Court holding otherwise is accordingly,

Reversed.

Justices **White, Brennan** *and* **Marshall, dissenting.**

──────────── **WAYTE V. UNITED STATES** ────────────

470 U.S. 598 (1985)

David Wayte declined to register for the draft as required by law, and instead wrote to the president and other government officials stating that he had not registered and refused to do so. Subsequently, the Selective Service adopted a policy of "passive enforcement" under which it would investigate and prosecute only those non-registrants called to its attention. Wayte came within that category. He was thereafter twice notified that his refusal to register could lead to prosecution, and he failed to respond. When he was indicted for failure to register, the district court dismissed the indictment based on the government's "selective prosecution." The court of appeals reversed.

Justice **Powell** delivered the opinion of the Court:

The question presented is whether a passive enforcement policy under which the Government prosecutes only those who report themselves as having violated the law, or who are reported by others, violates the First and Fifth Amendments. . . .

In our criminal justice system, the Government retains "broad discretion" as to whom to prosecute. "[S]o long as the prosecutor has probable cause to believe that the accused committed an offense defined by statute, the decision whether or not to prosecute, and what charge to file or bring before a grand jury, generally rests entirely in his discretion." This broad discretion rests largely on the recognition that the decision to prosecute is particularly ill-suited to judicial review. Such factors as the strength of the case, the prosecution's general deterrence value, the Government's enforcement priorities, and the case's relationship to the Government's overall enforcement plan are not readily susceptible to the kind of analysis the courts are competent to undertake. Judicial supervision in this area, moreover, entails systemic costs of particular concern. Examining the basis of a prosecution delays the criminal proceeding, threatens to chill law enforcement by subjecting the prosecutor's motives and decisionmaking to outside inquiry, and may undermine prosecutorial effectiveness by revealing the Government's enforcement policy. All these are substantial concerns that make the courts properly hesitant to examine the decision whether to prosecute. . . .

It is appropriate to judge selective prosecution claims according to ordinary equal protection standards. Under our prior cases, these standards require petitioner to show both that the passive enforcement system had a discriminatory effect and that it was motivated by a discriminatory purpose. All petitioner has shown here is that those eventually prosecuted, along with many not prosecuted, reported themselves as having violated the law. He has not shown that the enforcement policy selected nonregistrants for prosecution on the basis of their speech. Indeed, he could not have done so given the way the "beg" policy was carried out. The Government did not prosecute those who reported themselves but later registered. Nor did it prosecute those who protested registration but did not report themselves or were not reported by others. In fact, the Government did not even investigate those who wrote letters to Selective Service criticizing registration unless their letters stated affirmatively that they had refused to comply with the law. The Government, on the other hand, did prosecute people who reported themselves or were reported by others but who did not publicly protest. These facts demonstrate that the Government treated all reported nonregistrants similarly. It did not subject vocal nonregistrants to any special burden. Indeed, those prosecuted in effect selected themselves for prosecution by refusing to register after being reported and warned by the Government.

Even if the passive policy had a discriminatory effect, petitioner has not shown that the Government intended such a result. The evidence he presented demonstrated only that the Government was aware that the passive enforcement policy would result in prosecution of vocal objectors and that they would probably make selective prosecution claims. As we have noted, however, " '[d]iscriminatory purpose' ... implies more than ... intent as awareness of consequences. It implies that the decisionmaker ... selected or reaffirmed a particular course of action at least in part 'because of,' not merely 'in spite of,' its adverse effects upon an identifiable group." In the present case, petitioner has not shown that the Government prosecuted him *because of* his protest activities. Absent such a showing, his claim of selective prosecution fails.

IV

Petitioner also challenges the passive enforcement policy directly on First Amendment grounds. In particular, he claims that "[e]ven though the [Government's passive] enforcement policy did not overtly punish protected speech as such, it inevitably created a content-based regulatory system with a concomitantly disparate, content-based impact on nonregistrants. This Court has held that when, as here, " 'speech' and 'nonspeech' elements are combined in the same course of conduct, a sufficiently important governmental interest in regulating the nonspeech element can justify incidental limitations on First Amendment freedoms." ...

Few interests can be more compelling than a nation's need to ensure its own security. It is well to remember that freedom as we know it has been suppressed in many countries. Unless a society has the capability and will to defend itself from the aggression of others, constitutional protections of any sort have little meaning. Recognizing this fact, the Framers listed "provid[ing] for the common defence," U.S. Const., Preamble, as a motivating purpose for the Constitution and granted Congress the power to "provide for the common Defence and general Welfare of the United States," Art. I, [section] 8, cl. 1. This Court, moreover, has long held that the power "to raise and support armies ... is broad and sweeping," and that the "power ... to classify and conscript manpower for military service is 'beyond question,'....

We think it important to note as a final matter how far the implications of petitioner's First Amendment argument would extend. Strictly speaking, his argument does not concern passive enforcement but self-reporting. The concerns he identifies would apply to all nonregistrants who report themselves even if the Selective Service engaged only in active enforcement. For example, a nonregistrant who wrote a letter informing Selective Service of his failure to register could, when prosecuted under an active system, claim that the Selective Service was prosecuting him only because of his "protest." Just as in this case, he could have some justification for believing that his letter had focused inquiry upon him. Prosecution in either context would equally "burden" his exercise of First Amendment rights. Under the petitioner's view, then, the Government could not constitutionally prosecute a self-reporter—even in an active enforcement system—unless perhaps it could prove that it would have prosecuted him without his letter. On principle, such a view would allow any criminal to obtain immunity from prosecution simply by reporting himself and claiming that he did so in order to "protest" the law. The First Amendment confers no such immunity from prosecution.

V

We conclude that the Government's passive enforcement system together with its "beg" policy violated neither the First nor Fifth Amendments. Accordingly, we affirm the judgment of the Court of Appeals.

It is so ordered.

Justice **Marshall** *and Justice* **Brennan, dissenting.**

Suggested Reading

Two useful surveys of Congress' role in foreign affairs are the recent works by LOUIS FISHER, THE CONSTITUTION BETWEEN FRIENDS: CONGRESS, THE PRESIDENT AND THE LAW (1978), and CONSTITUTIONAL CONFLICTS BETWEEN THE PRESIDENT AND CONGRESS (1985). Also see CECIL V. CRABB, JR. and PAT M. HOLT, INVITATION TO STRUGGLE (1984).

For a spirited defense of presidential authority, see Senator John Tower's *Congress versus President: The Formulation and Implementation of American Foreign Policy*, 56 FOREIGN AFFAIRS 226 (1978), as well as Warren Christopher, *Ceasefire Between the Branches*, 60 FOREIGN AFFAIRS 889 (1982). The case for Congress is made by Newell L. Highsmith in *Policing Executive Adventurism: Congressional Oversight of Military and Paramilitary Operations*, 12 HARVARD JOURNAL OF LITIGATION 328 (1982), and Douglas J. Bennet, *Congress in Foreign Policy: Who Needs It?*, 56 FOREIGN AFFAIRS 40 (1978). Also see JOHN SPANIER and JOSEPH NOGEE, eds., CONGRESS, THE PRESIDENT, AND AMERICAN FOREIGN POLICY (1981); THOMAS FRANCK and EDWARD WEISBAND, FOREIGN POLICY BY CONGRESS (1979), and FRANCIS O. WILCOX, CONGRESS, THE EXECUTIVE AND FOREIGN POLICY (1971).

Earlier works include ROBERT DAHL, CONGRESS AND FOREIGN POLICY (1950); *Congress and Foreign Relations* published in the ANNALS OF THE AMERICAN ACADEMY OF POLITICAL AND SOCIAL SCIENCE (1953); JAMES ROBINSON, CONGRESS AND FOREIGN–POLICY MAKING (rev. ed. 1967); and H. CARROLL, THE HOUSE OF REPRESENTATIVES AND FOREIGN AFFAIRS (1958).

For a discussion of Congress' war power, see Thomas M. Franck, *After the Fall: The New Procedural Framework for Congressional Control Over the War Power*, 71 AMERICAN JOURNAL OF INTERNATIONAL LAW 605 (1977); JACOB JAVITS, WHO MAKES WAR: THE PRESIDENT VERSUS CONGRESS (1973); W. TAYLOR REVELEY, WAR POWERS OF THE PRESIDENT AND CONGRESS (1981); and W.B. Spong, Jr., *Can Balance be Restored in the Constitutional War Powers of the President and Congress?*, 6 UNIVERSITY OF RICHMOND LAW REVIEW 11 (1971); as well as the Note at 81 HARVARD LAW REVIEW 1771 (1968), *Congress, the President and the Power to Commit Forces to Combat.*

On the War Powers Resolution itself, see ROBERT F. TURNER, THE WAR POWERS RESOLUTION: ITS IMPLEMENTATION IN THEORY AND PRACTICE (1983); Michael J. Glennon, *The War Powers Resolution Ten Years Later: More Politics Than Law*, 78 AMERICAN JOURNAL OF INTERNATIONAL LAW 571 (1984); Representative Clement Zablocki, *War Powers Resolu-*

tion: Its Past Record and Future Promise, 17 LOYOLA OF LOS ANGELES LAW REVIEW 579 (1984); and Eugene V. Rostow, *Great Cases Make Bad Law: The War Powers Act,* 50 TEXAS LAW REVIEW 833 (1972).

More specialized articles include Paul Ehrlich, *The Legal Process in Foreign Affairs: Military Intervention—A Testing Case,* 27 STANFORD LAW REVIEW 637 (1975); and, with reference to *United States v. Richardson,* see Note, *The CIA's Secret Funding and the Constitution,* 84 YALE LAW JOURNAL 608 (1975). The issue of sex discrimination in *Rostker v. Goldberg* is treated in James Graney, *Gender Based Equal Protection versus the War Power,* 15 JOHN MARSHALL LAW REVIEW 725 (1984).

Notes

1. 4 Wheat. (17 U.S.) 316, 407 (1819). Emphasis added.

2. *Northern Pacific Railway v. North Dakota,* 250 U.S. 135, 149 (1919).

3. 290 U.S. 398 (1934).

4. 240 U.S. 328, 333 (1916).

5. See *United States v. Holmes,* 387 F.2d 781, cert. denied, 391 U.S. 936 (1967). Compare the concurring opinion of Justice Cardozo in *Hamilton v. Regents of the University of California,* 293 U.S. 245, 265.

6. *Schenck v. United States,* 249 U.S. 47 (1919); *Debs v. United States,* 249 U.S. 211 (1919); *Sugarman v. United States,* 249 U.S. 182 (1919); *Frohwerk v. United States,* 249 U.S. 204 (1919); *Abrams v. United States,* 250 U.S. 616 (1919).

7. *Stewart v. Kahn,* 11 Wall. (78 U.S.) 493, 507 (1871).

8. 251 U.S. 264 (1920).

9. 297 U.S. 288 (1936).

10. Hull–Lothian Agreement, September 2, 1940.

11. "The Congress shall have Power to dispose of . . . property belonging to the United States. . . ."

12. See, for example, *McArthur v. Clifford,* 393 U.S. 1002 (1968); *Da Costa v. Laird,* 405 U.S. 979 (1972); *Velvel v. Nixon,* 396 U.S. 1042 (1970); *Mora v. McNamara,* 389 U.S. 934 (1967).

13. ROBERT McELROY, 2 GROVER CLEVELAND 249–250 (1923).

14. 462 U.S. 919 (1983).

15. 18 WEEKLY COMPILATION OF PRESIDENTIAL DOCUMENTS 1232 (September 29, 1982).

16. 19 *Id.,* at 1422–23 (October 12, 1983).

7

CITIZENSHIP, THE RIGHT TO TRAVEL, AND THE DIPLOMATIC PROTECTION OF CITIZENS ABROAD

THE CONSTITUTION as drafted and ratified did not define citizenship. It provided that "the Citizens of each State shall be entitled to all Privileges and Immunities of Citizens of the several States" (Article IV), and it gave to Congress the authority to establish uniform rules of naturalization (Article I). But nowhere did the Constitution discuss the qualifications of citizenship or what citizenship entailed.

Initially the United States accepted the ancient British doctrine that citizenship was perpetual and unchangeable; [1] that it involved indelible allegiance to the country of one's birth and could not be renounced without that country's permission. For a nation of immigrants, the British rule soon proved unworkable. In 1868, Congress enacted legislation expressly recognizing the right of everyone to expatriate himself (that is, to renounce his original allegiance) and choose another country. These new citizens, as Chief Justice Marshall had stated earlier, each "become a member of the society, possessing all the rights of a native citizen, and standing, in the view of the Constitution, on the footing of a native." [2] But the United States continued to view citizenship as exclusive: one could owe allegiance to one country only, and naturalization in the U.S. involved explicit renunciation of all previous citizenship.

But the precise meaning of citizenship remained unclear. In the famous *Dred Scott* case of 1857,[3] Chief Justice Taney held for a bitterly divided Court that national citizenship was derivative from state citizenship and Negroes were ineligible. In 1868 the issue was finally resolved by adoption of the Fourteenth Amendment which defined citizenship in the following terms:

> All persons born or naturalized in the United States, and subject to the jurisdiction thereof, are citizens of the United States and of the State wherein they reside.

273

The leading case to discuss citizenship in the context of the Fourteenth Amendment is *United States v. Wong Kim Ark,* decided in 1898. The issue involved the nationality of a child born in the United States to Chinese alien laborers who were ineligible for U.S. citizenship themselves. The Supreme Court, speaking through Justice Gray, held the child to be a U.S. citizen by birth, regardless of the status of his parents. Said Gray:

> Whatever considerations ... might influence the legislative or the executive branch of the Government to decline to admit persons of the Chinese race to the status of citizens of the United States, there are none that can constrain or permit the judiciary to refuse to give full effect to the peremptory and explicit language of the Fourteenth Amendment....

There are certain exceptions. Children born in the United States to parents of foreign diplomats do not become citizens because they are not "subject to the jurisdiction" of the United States. Similarly, persons born on foreign airplanes or ships in the U.S. are not considered to have been born within the jurisdiction of the United States. Children born abroad of American parents become U.S. citizens by descent based on congressional legislation not by constitutional guarantee of the Fourteenth Amendment. And as the Court held in *Harisiades v. Shaughnessy,* an alien in the United States may be deported at any time. His or her status is not a matter of right, "but is a matter of permission and tolerance." More recently, in *Kleindienst v. Mandel* in 1972, the Supreme Court, speaking through Justice Blackmun, upheld the broad right of Congress to exclude aliens from entry into the United States, even if freedom of speech may be involved. "The Court without exception has sustained Congress' 'plenary power to make rules for the admission of aliens and to exclude those who possess those characteristics which Congress has forbidden.' " "We are not inclined to reconsider this line of cases," said Blackmun.

EXPATRIATION

It was not until 1907 that the United States enacted legislation making citizenship revocable.[4] The most common reasons for which an American could be involuntarily expatriated traced to the concept that U.S. citizenship was exclusive. Accordingly, acts that suggested divided loyalty or a lack of complete allegiance, such as becoming a citizen of another country, serving in the armed forces of a foreign country, desertion from the military in wartime, or voting in foreign elections were considered sufficient to terminate American citizenship. For a female U.S. citizen, marrying a foreign national at one time worked a forfeiture of U.S. citizenship.[5]

In *Perez v. Brownell* in 1958 the Supreme Court confronted the case of a native-born American citizen of Mexican heritage who had once voted in a Mexican election and was ordered deported from the United States as a result. A divided Court sustained the authority of Congress to provide for the loss of citizenship in such circumstances, based on Congress' "power to deal with foreign affairs". But in two companion cases, *Trop v. Dulles*[6] and

Nishikawa v. Dulles [7], the Court struck down legislation that would have deprived a soldier of his citizenship for desertion in wartime or for being conscripted into the Japanese army in 1941. "Citizenship is not a license that expires upon misbehavior," said Chief Justice Warren in the *Trop* case.

Five years later in two more companion cases, *Kennedy v. Mendoza–Martinez* and *Rusk v. Cort,* the Court ruled that Congress had no power to withdraw citizenship from native-born Americans who sought to evade the draft by fleeing to a foreign country (*Mendoza–Martinez*) or remaining in a foreign country (*Cort*). And in *Schneider v. Rusk* in 1964, speaking through Justice Douglas, the Court overturned the requirement that naturalized American citizens residing in the country of their birth must return periodically to the United States to retain their citizenship. As Justice Douglas remarked, "Living abroad . . . is no badge of lack of allegiance." Finally, in the leading case of *Afroyim v. Rusk* in 1967, the Supreme Court overruled *Perez,* holding that Americans could not be deprived of their citizenship unless they voluntarily renounced it.

The *Afroyim* Court reverted to the Federalist ideas of Marshall and Story that citizens formed the Union, and as a consequence citizenship antedated both the Constitution and the government.

> Citizenship in the Nation is a cooperative affair. Its citizenry is the country and the country its citizenry. The very nature of our free government makes it completely incongruous to have a rule of law under which a group of citizens temporarily in office can deprive another group of citizens of their citizenship. We hold that the Fourteenth Amendment was designed to, and does, protect every citizen of the nation against a congressional forcible destruction of his citizenship. . . . unless he voluntarily relinquishes that citizenship.

Although the *Afroyim* holding was distinguished for persons who had acquired their citizenship by descent (not born or naturalized in the United States) in *Rogers v. Bellei,* its basic premise that citizens could not be stripped of their citizenship appears to command unanimous Court support.[8]

RIGHT TO TRAVEL

The right to travel abroad was recognized by the Supreme Court in *Kent v. Dulles* as "an important aspect of a citizen's liberty." According to Justice Douglas who spoke for the Court, "Freedom of movement across frontiers in either direction, and inside frontiers as well, was a part of our heritage. Travel abroad, like travel within the country . . . may well be as close to the heart of the individual as the choice of what he eats, or wears, or reads. Freedom of movement is basic to our scheme of values."

Six years later in *Aptheker v. Secretary of State,* the Court overturned portions of the Subversive Activities Control Act that denied passports to members of Communist organizations. "The restrictive effect of the legislation cannot be gainsaid by emphasizing, as the government seems to do, that a member of a [Communist] organization could recapture his freedom to travel by simply . . . abandoning his membership in the organization."

Both *Kent* and *Aptheker* dealt with travel restrictions aimed at particular groups of individuals. In *Zemel v. Rusk* the Court confronted restrictions placed on travel to Cuba for reasons of national security. Speaking through Chief Justice Warren, the Court differentiated between "area restrictions"— which enjoyed a long history of use in American foreign policy—and travel restrictions aimed at particular individuals because of their political beliefs. According to Warren, "the fact that a liberty cannot be inhibited without due process of law does not mean that it can under no circumstances be inhibited."

> We think ... that the Secretary [of State] has justifiably concluded that travel to Cuba by American citizens might involve the Nation in dangerous international incidents, and that the Constitution does not require him to validate passports for such travel.

But two years later in *United States v. Laub,* the Court ruled in the negative when considering whether travel to Cuba with an otherwise valid passport was a criminal offense. The result produced a somewhat anomalous situation in which the government could impose area travel restrictions for reasons of national security and could deny U.S. diplomatic protection to anyone who travelled to that area. But the government could not indict that traveller for a criminal offense for ignoring the travel restriction. That anomaly was partially rectified by passage of the International Emergency Economic Powers Act in 1977 which gave the president broad discretionary powers to prohibit commercial activities with foreign countries in the interest of national security. Pursuant to the Act, the Treasury Department promulgated a series of regulations prohibiting travel-related financial transactions with Cuba as well as general tourist and business travel to the island. These economic restrictions (which effectively barred all travel to Cuba) were upheld by a sharply divided [5–4] Supreme Court in *Regan v. Wald* in 1984. Said Justice Rehnquist for the majority, "we think there is adequate basis under the Due Process Clause of the Fifth Amendment to sustain the President's decision to curtail the flow of hard currency to Cuba—currency that could be used in support of Cuba adventurism—by restricting travel...."

The right to travel abroad is similar to the constitutional right of interstate travel, except the Court has recognized that national security considerations may legitimately intervene to restrict foreign travel. As Justice Stewart stated in *Califano v. Aznavorian:* [9]

> The constitutional right of interstate travel is virtually unqualified. By contrast the "right" of international travel has been considered no more than an aspect of the "liberty" protected by the Due Process Clause of the Fifth Amendment.... As such, this "right" ... can be regulated within the bounds of due process.

The most restrictive holding pertaining to the right to travel abroad came in 1981 when the Court dealt with the revocation of the passport of Philip Agee, a former CIA agent living abroad.[10] Following his resignation from the CIA, Agee had undertaken a public campaign to expose U.S. intelligence operations overseas. The Supreme Court, speaking through

Chief Justice Burger, upheld the government's action because "it is 'obvious and unarguable' that no governmental interest is more compelling than the security of the nation."

At one level it would appear that *Haig v. Agee* represents a substantial backtracking from the guarantee of individual travel proclaimed in *Kent* and *Aptheker*. But unlike the petitioners in the former cases, Agee was actively involved in undermining American intelligence activities abroad by disclosing highly classified information—including the names and addresses of active agents—in public media. The link between Agee's actions and the threat to national security was real and immediate. In that context the decision might be seen as one restricted to the particular facts of the case. Indeed, as Justice Brennan said in dissent, "I suspect that this case is a prime example of the adage that 'bad facts make bad law'."

DIPLOMATIC PROTECTION ABROAD

The idea of providing diplomatic protection to citizens abroad stems from ancient feudal concepts involving "protection" and "allegiance." The protection provided by monarchs for their people was reciprocated in the citizens' allegiance to their king. The doctrine was formulated by Lord Chief Justice Sir Edward Coke in *Calvin's Case* in 1608 as *protectio trahit subjectionem, et subjectio protectionem*.[11] As Professor Hirsch Lauterpacht has pointed out, "That reciprocity of benefit and duty, of allegiance and protection, is not, of course, an artificial or obsolete formula of a past period. It is expressive of a compelling principle of political ethics and, above all, of the security of the State."[12]

As early as 1873 in the *Slaughter House Cases*[13] the Supreme Court recognized the constitutional obligation to protect American citizens abroad. Speaking for the Court, Justice Miller identified the "right to demand protection of the Federal Government on the high seas, or abroad" as one of the privileges and immunities of United States citizenship guaranteed by the Fourteenth Amendment.

The Supreme Court has seen little litigation concerning diplomatic protection abroad. Although in *In re Neagle* the Court, again speaking through Justice Miller, noted with approval the decisive action of U.S. naval authorities in Turkish waters to free an American national from Austrian imprisonment. Previously in *Durand v. Hollins*,[14] Justice Nelson, then on circuit, justified the U.S. naval bombardment of Greytown, Nicaragua after an attack by a mob on the United States consul there in 1854.

> As the Executive head of the nation, the President is made the only legitimate organ of the General Government . . . in matters concerning the interests of the country or of its citizens. It is to him [that] the citizen abroad must look for protection of person and of property, and for the faithful execution of the laws existing and intended for their protection. . . .
>
> Now, as it respects the interposition of the Executive abroad, for the protection of the lives or property of the citizen, the duty must, of necessi-

ty, rest in the discretion of the President. Acts of lawless violence, or of threatened violence to the citizen or his property, cannot be anticipated or provided for; and the protection, to be effectual or of any avail, may, not infrequently, require the most prompt and decided action.

Under our system of government, the citizen abroad is as much entitled to protection as the citizen at home. The great object and duty of government is the protection of the lives, liberty and property of the people composing it, whether abroad or at home, and any Government failing in the accomplishment of the object, or the performance of the duty, is not worth preserving.

The earliest legislation concerning protection abroad was enacted by Congress in 1868 and still remains on the statute books. It calls upon the president to seek the immediate release of any American citizen held unlawfully by a foreign government and to "use such means, not amounting to acts of war, as he may think necessary." [15]

In 1984, federal kidnapping legislation was amended to make it a crime to seize, detain or threaten to kill an American national whether in the United States or abroad and to make the offense punishable by imprisonment "for any term of years or for life." [16]

UNITED STATES V. WONG KIM ARK

169 U.S. 649 (1898)

Wong Kim Ark was born in San Francisco in 1873, the son of Chinese resident aliens. In 1890, he departed with his parents on a temporary visit to China and returned later that year. He was permitted to enter on the grounds that he was a native born American citizen. He visited China again in 1894, but upon his return to the U.S. was denied entry on the sole ground that he was not a United States citizen and was taken into custody. Ark petitioned the U.S. District Court for a writ of habeas corpus which was granted, and he was ordered released. The government appealed.

Justice **Gray** delivered the opinion of the Court:

. . . . The Fourteenth Amendment affirms the ancient and fundamental rule of citizenship by birth within the territory, in the allegiance and under the protection of the country, including all children here born of resident aliens. . . . The Amendment, in clear words and in manifest intent, includes the children born, within the territory of the United States, of all other persons, of whatever race or color, domiciled within the United States. Every citizen or subject of another country, while domiciled here, is within the allegiance and the protection, and consequently subject to the jurisdiction, of the United States. His allegiance to the United States is direct and immediate, and, although . . . but local and temporary, continuing only so long as he remains within our territory, is yet, in the words of Lord Coke, in *Calvin's Case,* "strong enough to make a natural subject, for if he hath issue here, that issue is a natural-born subject," and his child, as said by Mr. Binney in his essay before quoted [*Alienigenae of the United States,* Philadelphia, 1853], "if born in the country, is as much a citizen as the natural-born child of a citizen, and by operation of the same principle.". . . .

To hold that the Fourteenth Amendment of the Constitution excludes from citizenship the children, born in the United States, of citizens or subjects of other countries, would be to deny citizenship to thousands of persons of English, Scotch, Irish, German or other European parentage, who have always been considered and treated as citizens of the United States.

. . . . Whatever considerations, in the absence of a controlling provision of the Constitution, might influence the legislative or the executive branch of the Government to decline to admit persons of the Chinese race to the status of citizens of the United States, there are none that can constrain or permit the judiciary to refuse to give full effect to the preemptory and explicit language of the Fourteenth Amendment, which declares and ordains that "All persons born or naturalized in the United States, and subject to the jurisdiction thereof, are citizens of the United States."

The Fourteenth Amendment of the Constitution, in the declaration that "all persons born or naturalized in the United States, and subject to the jurisdiction thereof, are citizens of the United States and of the State wherein they reside," contemplates two sources of citizenship, and two only: birth and naturalization. Citizenship by naturalization can only be acquired by naturalization under the authority and in the forms of law. But citizenship by birth is established by the mere fact of birth under the circumstances defined in the Constitution. Every person born in the United States, and subject to the jurisdiction thereof, becomes at once a citizen of the United States, and needs no naturalization. A person born out of the jurisdiction of the United States can only become a citizen by being naturalized, either by treaty, as in the case of the annexation of foreign territory; or by authority of Congress. . . .

The power of naturalization, vested in Congress by the Constitution, is a power to confer citizenship, not a power to take it away. "A naturalized citizen," said Chief Justice Marshall, "becomes a member of the society, possessing all the rights of a native citizen, and standing, in the view of the Constitution, on the footing of a native. The Constitution does not authorize Congress to enlarge or abridge those rights. The simple power of the National Legislature is to prescribe a uniform rule of naturalization, and the exercise of this power exhausts it, so far as respects the individual. . . . The Fourteenth Amendment, while it leaves the power, where it was before, in Congress, to regulate naturalization, has conferred no authority upon Congress to restrict the effect of birth, declared by the Constitution to constitute a sufficient and complete right of citizenship. . . .

The fact, therefore, that acts of Congress or treaties have not permitted Chinese persons born out of this country to become citizens by naturalization, cannot exclude Chinese persons born in this country from the operation of the broad and clear words of the Constitution, "All persons born in the United States, and subject to the jurisdiction thereof, are citizens of the United States." . . .

The evident intention, and the necessary effect, of the submission of this case to the decision of the court upon the facts agreed by the parties, were to present for determination the single question, stated at the beginning of this opinion, namely, whether a child born in the United States, of parents of Chinese descent, who, at the time of his birth, are subjects of the Emperor of China, but have a permanent domicile and residence in the United States, and are there carrying on business, and are not employed in any diplomatic or official capacity under the Emperor of China, becomes at the time of his birth a citizen of the United States. For the reasons above stated, this court is of opinion that the question must be answered in the affirmative.

Order affirmed.

Chief Justice **Fuller**, *joined by Justice* **Harlan**, *dissenting.*

——————— HARISIADES V. SHAUGHNESSY, ———————
DISTRICT DIRECTOR OF IMMIGRATION AND NATURALIZATION

342 U.S. 580 (1952)

The Alien Registration Act of 1940 authorized the deportation of resident aliens because of membership in the Communist Party. In 1946 three permanent residents of the United States—citizens of Greece, Italy and Russia respectively—received deportation notices because of their affiliation with the Communist Party. All three appealed, contending that admission as permanent residents conferred "vested rights" equal to that of the citizen to remain within the country and that an alien was entitled to the Constitutional protection of the Fifth Amendment. The U.S. District Court denied this appeal and the court of appeals affirmed.

Justice **Jackson** delivered the opinion of the Court:

Under our law, the alien in several respects stands on an equal footing with citizens, but in others has never been conceded legal parity with the citizen. Most importantly, to protract this ambiguous status within the country is not his right but is a matter of permission and tolerance. The Government's power to terminate its hospitality has been asserted and sustained by this Court since the question first arose.

War, of course, is the most usual occasion for extensive resort to the power. Though the resident alien may be personally loyal to the United States, if his nation becomes our enemy his allegiance prevails over his personal preference and makes him also our enemy, liable to expulsion or internment, and his property becomes subject to seizure and perhaps confiscation. But it does not require war to bring the power of deportation into existence or to authorize its exercise. Congressional apprehension of foreign or internal dangers short of war may lead to its use. So long as the alien elects to continue the ambiguity of his allegiance his domicile here is held by a precarious tenure.

That aliens remain vulnerable to expulsion after long residence is a practice that bristles with severities. But it is a weapon of defense and reprisal confirmed by international law as a power inherent in every sovereign state. Such is a traditional power of the Nation over the alien and we leave the law on the subject as we find it. . . .

It is pertinent to observe that any policy toward aliens is vitally and intricately interwoven with contemporaneous policies in regard to the conduct of foreign relations, the war power, and the maintenance of a republican form of government. Such matters are so exclusively entrusted to the political branches of government as to be largely immune from judicial inquiry or interference.

These restraints upon the judiciary, occasioned by different events, do not control today's decision but they are pertinent. It is not necessary and probably not possible to delineate a fixed and precise line of separation in these matters between political and judicial power under the Constitution. Certainly, however, nothing in the structure of our Government or the text of our Constitution would warrant judicial review by standards which would require us to equate our political judgment with that of Congress. . . .

We think that, in the present state of the world, it would be rash and irresponsible to reinterpret our fundamental law to deny or qualify the Government's power of deportation. However desirable world-wide amelioration of the lot of aliens, we think it is peculiarly a subject for international diplomacy. It should not be initiated by judicial decision which can only deprive our own Government of a power of defense and reprisal without obtaining for American citizens abroad any reciprocal privileges or immunities. Reform in this field must be entrusted to the branches of the Government in control of our international relations and treaty-making powers.

We hold that the Act is not invalid under the Due Process Clause. These aliens are not entitled to judicial relief. . . .

Affirmed.

Justice **Frankfurter,** *concurring:* It is not for this Court to reshape a world order based on politically sovereign States. In such an international ordering of the world a national State implies a special relationship of one body of people, *i.e.,* citizens of that State, whereby the citizens of each State are aliens in relation to every other State. Ever since national States have come into being, the right of people to enjoy the hospitality of a State of which they are not citizens has been a matter of political determination by each State. (I put to one side the oddities of dual citizenship.) Though as a matter of political outlook and economic need this country has traditionally welcomed aliens to come to its shores, it has done so exclusively as a matter of political outlook and national self-interest. This policy has been a political policy, belonging to the political branch of the Government wholly outside the concern and the competence of the Judiciary. . . .

The Court's acknowledgement of the sole responsibility of Congress for these matters has been made possible by Justices whose cultural outlook, whose breadth of view and robust tolerance were not exceeded by those of Jefferson. In their personal views, libertarians like Mr. Justice Holmes and Mr. Justice Brandeis doubtless disapproved of some of these policies, departures as they were from the best traditions of this country and based as they have been in part on discredited racial theories or manipulation of figures in formulating what is known as the quota system. But whether immigration laws have been crude and cruel, whether they may have reflected xenophobia in general or anti-Semitism or anti-Catholicism, the responsibility belongs to Congress. Courts do enforce the requirements imposed by Congress upon officials in administering immigration laws, and the requirement of Due Process may entail certain procedural observances. But the underlying policies of what classes of aliens shall be allowed to enter and what classes of aliens shall be allowed to stay, are for Congress exclusively to determine even though such determination may be deemed to offend American traditions and may, as has been the case, jeopardize peace.

In recognizing this power and this responsibility of Congress, one does not in the remotest degree align oneself with fears unworthy of the American spirit or with hostility to the bracing air of the free spirit. One merely recognizes that the place to resist unwise or cruel legislation touching aliens is the Congress, not this Court.

*Justice **Douglas**, joined by Justice **Black**, dissenting.*

PEREZ V. BROWNELL

356 U.S. 44 (1958)

The Nationality Act of 1940 required the expatriation of American citizens for voting in foreign elections. Perez was born in Texas in 1909. He lived in the United States until he was eleven, then moved with his parents to Mexico where he lived without interruption until 1943. In that year Perez was granted permission to enter the United States on a temporary basis as an alien laborer. He returned to Mexico in 1944 but shortly thereafter reentered the United States, again as an alien laborer. He returned to Mexico in 1947, attempted to reenter the United States as an American citizen but was excluded for having voted in a Mexican election, thereby expatriating himself. In 1952, Perez was again granted entry as an alien but was ordered deported in 1953 for an invalid visa. Perez brought suit, seeking a declaratory judgment that he was a U.S. citizen. The district court concluded that Perez had expatriated himself, and the court of appeals affirmed the judgment. Perez appealed.

Justice **Frankfurter** delivered the opinion of the Court:

. . . . The first step in our inquiry must be to answer the question: what is the source of power on which Congress must be assumed to have drawn? Although there is in the Constitution no specific grant to Congress of power to enact legislation for the effective regulation of foreign affairs, there can be no doubt of the existence of this power in the law-making organ of the Nation. The States that joined together to form a single Nation and to create, through the Constitution, a Federal Government to conduct the affairs of that Nation must be held to have granted that Government the powers indispensable to its functioning effectively in the company of sovereign nations. The Government must be able not only to deal affirmatively with foreign nations, as it does through the maintenance of diplomatic relations with them and the protection of American citizens sojourning within their territories. It must also be able to reduce to a minimum the frictions that are unavoidable in a world of sovereigns sensitive in matters touching their dignity and interests.

The inference is fairly to be drawn from the congressional history of the Nationality Act of 1940, read in light of the historical background of expatriation in this country, that, in making voting in foreign elections (among other behavior) an act of expatriation, Congress was seeking to effectuate its power to regulate foreign affairs. The legislators, counseled by those on whom they rightly relied for advice, were concerned about actions by citizens in foreign countries that create problems of protection and are inconsistent with American allegiance. Moreover, we cannot ignore the fact that embarrassments in the conduct of foreign relations were of primary concern in the consideration of the Act of 1907, of which the loss of nationality provisions of the 1940 Act are a codification and expansion.

Broad as the power in the National Government to regulate foreign affairs must necessarily be, it is not without limitation. The restrictions confining Congress in the exercise of any of the powers expressly delegated to it in the Constitution apply with equal vigor when that body seeks to regulate our relations with other nations. Since Congress may not act arbitrarily, a rational nexus must exist between the content of a specific power in Congress and the action of Congress in carrying that power into execution. More simply stated, the means—in this case, withdrawal of citizenship—must be reasonably related to the end—here, regulation of foreign affairs. The inquiry—and, in the case before us, the sole inquiry—into which this Court must enter is whether or not Congress may have concluded not unreasonably that there is a relevant connection between this fundamental source of power and the ultimate legislative action.

Our starting point is to ascertain whether the power of Congress to deal with foreign relations may reasonably be deemed to include a power to deal generally with the active participation, by way of voting, of American citizens in foreign political elections. Experience amply attests that, in this day of extensive international travel, rapid communication and widespread use of propaganda, the activities of the citizens of one nation when in another country can easily cause serious embarrassments to the government of their own country as well as to their fellow citizens. We cannot deny to Congress the reasonable belief that these difficulties might well become acute, to the point of jeopardizing the successful conduct of international relations, when a citizen of one country chooses to participate in the political or governmental affairs of another country. The citizen may by his action unwittingly promote or encourage a course of conduct contrary to the interests of his own government; moreover, the people or government of the foreign country may regard his action to be the action of his government, or at least as a reflection if not an expression of its policy. . . .

The question must finally be faced whether, given the power to attach some sort of consequence to voting in a foreign political election, Congress, acting under the Necessary and Proper Clause, Art. I, s. 8, cl. 18, could attach loss of nationality to it. Is the means, withdrawal of citizenship, reasonably calculated to effect the end that is within the power of Congress to achieve, the avoidance of embarrassment in the conduct of our foreign relations attributable to voting by American citizens in foreign political elections? The importance and extreme delicacy of the matters here sought to be regulated demand that Congress be permitted ample scope in selecting appropriate modes for accomplishing its purpose. The critical connection between this conduct and loss of citizenship is the fact that it is the possession of American citizenship by a person committing the act that makes the act potentially embarrassing to the American Government and pregnant with the possibility of embroiling this country in disputes with other nations. The termination of citizenship terminates the problem. Moreover, the fact is not without significance that Congress has interpreted this conduct, not irrationally, as importing not only something less than complete and unswerving allegiance to the United States but also elements of an allegiance to another country in some measure, at least, inconsistent with American citizenship.

Of course, Congress can attach loss of citizenship only as a consequence of conduct engaged in voluntarily. But it would be a mockery of this Court's decisions to suggest that a person, in order to lose his citizenship, must intend or desire to do so. . . .

It cannot be said, then, that Congress acted without warrant when, pursuant to its power to regulate the relations of the United States with foreign countries, it provided that anyone who votes in a foreign election of significance politically in the life of another country shall lose his American citizenship. To deny the power of Congress to enact the legislation challenged here would be to disregard the constitutional allocation of governmental functions that it is this Court's solemn duty to guard. . . .

Judgment affirmed.

Chief Justice **Warren,** joined by Justices **Black** and **Douglas,** *dissenting:*
. . . . What is this Government, whose power is here being asserted? And what is the source of that power? The answers are the foundation of our Republic. To secure the inalienable rights of the individual, "Governments are instituted among Men, deriving their just powers from the consent of the governed." I do not believe the passage of time has lessened the truth of this proposition. It is basic to our form of government. This Government was born of its citizens, it maintains itself in a continuing relationship with them, and, in my judgment, it is without power to sever the relationship that gives rise to its existence. I cannot believe that a government conceived in the spirit of ours was established with power to take from the people their most basic right. . . .

My conclusions are as follows. The Government is without power to take citizenship away from a native-born or lawfully naturalized American. The Fourteenth Amendment recognizes that this priceless right is immune from the exercise of governmental powers. If the Government determines that certain conduct by United States citizens should be prohibited because of anticipated injurious consequences to the conduct of foreign affairs or to some other legitimate governmental interest, it may within the limits of the Constitution proscribe such activity and assess appropriate punishment. But every exercise of governmental power must find its source in the Constitution. The power to denationalize is not within the letter or the spirit of the powers with which our Government was endowed. The citizen may elect to renounce his citizenship, and under some circumstances he may be found to have abandoned his status by voluntarily performing acts that compromise his undivided allegiance to his country. The mere act of voting in a foreign election, however, without regard to the circumstances attending the participation, is not sufficient to show a voluntary abandonment of citizenship. The record in this case does not disclose any of the circumstances under which this petitioner voted. We know only the bare fact that he cast a ballot. The basic right of American citizenship has been too dearly won to be so lightly lost.

––––––––––––––––––––––– TROP V. DULLES –––––––––––––––––––––––

356 U.S. 86 (1958)

The Nationality Act of 1940 provided for the loss of citizenship upon conviction by court martial for desertion from the military in time of war. In 1944, Trop, a native-born American citizen, was a private in the U.S. Army serving in French Morocco. In May of that year he escaped from a military stockade in Casablanca, where he had been confined following a previous breach of discipline. Trop was apprehended the following day, convicted of desertion by a General Court Martial, and sentenced to three years hard labor and a dishonorable discharge. In 1952 Trop applied for a U.S. passport but was denied on the grounds that he had lost his U.S. citizenship pursuant to his conviction and discharge.

Chief Justice **Warren** delivered the opinion of the Court:

.... It is my conviction that citizenship is not subject to the general powers of the National Government and therefore cannot be divested in the exercise of those powers. The right may be voluntarily relinquished or abandoned either by express language or by language and conduct that show a renunciation of citizenship.

Under these principles, this petitioner has not lost his citizenship. Desertion in wartime, though it may merit the ultimate penalty, does not necessarily signify allegiance to a foreign state.... This soldier committed a crime for which he should be and was punished, but he did not involve himself in any way with a foreign state....

Citizenship is not a license that expires upon misbehavior. The duties of citizenship are numerous, and the discharge of many of these obligations is essential to the security and well-being of the Nation. The citizen who fails to pay his taxes or to abide by the laws safe-guarding the integrity of elections deals a dangerous blow to his country. But could a citizen be deprived of his nationality for evading these basic responsibilities of citizenship? In time of war the citizen's duties include not only the military defense of the Nation but also full participation in the manifold activities of the civilian ranks. Failure to perform any of these obligations may cause the Nation serious injury, and, in appropriate circumstances, the punishing power is available to deal with derelictions of duty. But citizenship is not lost every time a duty of citizenship is shirked. And the deprivation of citizenship is not a weapon that the Government may use to express its displeasure at a citizen's conduct, however reprehensible that conduct may be. As long as a person does not voluntarily renounce or abandon his citizenship, and this petitioner has done neither, I believe his fundamental right of citizenship is secure. On this ground alone the judgment in this case should be reversed.

II

Since a majority of the Court concluded in *Perez v. Brownell* [see p. 282] that citizenship may be divested in the exercise of some governmental power, I deem it appropriate to state additionally why the action taken in this case exceeds constitutional limits, even under the majority's decision in *Perez*. The Court concluded in *Perez* that citizenship could be divested in the exercise of the foreign affairs power. In this case, it is urged that the war power is adequate to support the divestment of citizenship. But there is a vital difference between the two statutes that purport to implement these powers by decreeing loss of citizenship. The statute in *Perez* decreed loss of citizenship—so the majority concluded—to eliminate those international problems that were thought to arise by reason of a citizen's having voted in a foreign election. The statute in this case, however, is entirely different. Section 401(g) decrees loss of citizenship for those found guilty of the crime of desertion. . . .

In form Section 401(g) appears to be a regulation of nationality. The statute deals initially with the status of nationality and then specifies the conduct that will result in loss of that status. But surely a form cannot provide the answer to this inquiry. A statute providing that "a person shall lose his liberty by committing bank robbery," though in form a regulation of liberty, would nonetheless be penal. Nor would its penal effect be altered by labeling it a regulation of banks or by arguing that there is a rational connection between safeguarding banks and imprisoning bank robbers. The inquiry must be directed to substance.

. . . . In deciding whether or not a law is penal, this Court has generally based its determination upon the purpose of the statute. If the statute imposes a disability for the purposes of punishment—that is, to reprimand the wrongdoer, to deter others, etc.—it has been considered penal. But a statute has been considered nonpenal if it imposes a disability, not to punish, but to accomplish some other legitimate governmental purpose. The Court has recognized that any statute decreeing some adversity as a consequence of certain conduct may have both a penal and a nonpenal effect. The controlling nature of such statutes normally depends on the evident purpose of the legislature. . . .

The same reasoning applies to Section 401(g). The purpose of taking away citizenship from a convicted deserter is simply to punish him. There is no other legitimate purpose that the statute could serve. Denationalization in this case is not even claimed to be a means of solving international problems, as was argued in *Perez*. Here the purpose is punishment, and therefore the statute is a penal law. . . .

Section 401(g) is a penal law, and we must face the question whether the Constitution permits the Congress to take away citizenship as a punishment for crime. If it is assumed that the power of Congress extends to divestment of citizenship, the problem still remains as to this statute whether denationalization is a cruel and unusual punishment within the meaning of the Eighth Amendment. Since wartime desertion is punishable by death, there can be no argument that the penalty of denationalization is excessive in relation to the gravity of the crime. The question is whether this penalty subjects the individual to a fate forbidden by the principle of civilized treatment guaranteed by the Eighth Amendment....

We believe, as did Chief Judge Clark in the court below, that use of denationalization as a punishment is barred by the Eighth Amendment. There may be involved no physical mistreatment, no primitive torture. There is instead the total destruction of the individual's status in organized society. It is a form of punishment more primitive than torture, for it destroys for the individual the political existence that was centuries in the development. The punishment strips the citizen of his status in the national and international political community. His very existence is at the sufferance of the country in which he happens to find himself....

In concluding as we do that the Eighth Amendment forbids Congress to punish by taking away citizenship, we are mindful of the gravity of the issue inevitably raised whenever the constitutionality of an Act of the National Legislature is challenged. No member of the Court believes that in this case the statute before us can be construed to avoid the issue of constitutionality. That issue confronts us, and the task of resolving it is inescapably ours. This task requires the exercise of judgment, not the reliance upon personal preferences. Courts must not consider the wisdom of statutes but neither can they sanction as being merely unwise that which the Constitution forbids....

The provisions of the Constitution are not time-worn adages or hollow shibboleths. They are vital, living principles that authorize and limit governmental powers in our Nation. They are the rules of government. When the constitutionality of an Act of Congress is challenged in this Court, we must apply those rules. If we do not, the words of the Constitution become little more than good advice.

When it appears that an Act of Congress conflicts with one of these provisions, we have no choice but to enforce the paramount commands of the Constitution. We are sworn to do no less. We cannot push back the limits of the Constitution merely to accommodate challenged legislation. We must apply those limits as the Constitution prescribes them, bearing in mind both the broad scope of legislative discretion and the ultimate responsibility of constitutional adjudication. We do well to approach this task cautiously, as all our predecessors have counseled. But the ordeal of judgment cannot be shirked. In some 81 instances since this Court was established it has determined that congressional action exceeded the bounds of the Constitution. It is so in this case.

The judgment of the Court of Appeals for the Second Circuit is reversed and the cause is remanded to the District Court for appropriate proceedings.

Reversed and remanded.

Justice **Frankfurter,** *joined by Justices* **Burton, Clark,** *and* **Harlan,** *dissenting.*

———— KENNEDY V. MENDOZA–MARTINEZ [17] ————

372 U.S. 144 (1963)

Mendoza–Martinez and Cort were native born citizens of the United States. Mendoza–Martinez had attempted to evade military service in 1942 by fleeing to Mexico and remaining there until 1946. When he returned to the United States he was convicted of draft evasion and thereupon served the imposed prison sentence of one year and one day. Upon his release, he resided undisturbed in the United States until 1953, when he was served with a deportation order.

Cort, a graduate of the Yale School of Medicine, went to England in 1951 to assume a position as research fellow at Cambridge University. He had properly registered for the draft before leaving, but when his draft board notified him in 1953 that he was required to report for an Army induction physical, Cort refused. He was indicted for violating the Selective Service Act, and when his residence permit expired in England, he moved with his family to Czechoslovakia. In 1959, Cort's application for a new U.S. passport was denied by the American Embassy in Prague. Mendoza–Martinez sought a declaratory judgment from the U.S. District Court that he was a U.S. citizen. After extended litigation, the district court ruled in his favor, citing the decision of the Supreme Court in Trop v. Dulles, *supra. A similar judgment was handed down in favor of Cort by a three-judge panel of the U.S. District Court for the District of Columbia, and affirmed by the court of appeals. The government appealed both cases.*

Justice **Goldberg** delivered the opinion of the Court:

We are called upon in these two cases to decide the grave and fundamental problem, common to both, of the constitutionality of Acts of Congress which divest an American of his citizenship for "[d]eparting from or remaining outside of the jurisdiction of the United States in time of war or ... national emergency for the purpose of evading or avoiding training and service" in the Nation's armed forces....

We deal with the contending constitutional arguments in the context of certain basic and sometimes conflicting principles. Citizenship is a most precious right. It is expressly guaranteed by the Fourteenth Amendment to the Constitution, which speaks in the most positive terms. The Constitution is silent about the permissibility of involuntary forfeiture of citizenship rights. While it confirms citizenship rights, plainly there are imperative obligations of citizenship, performance of which Congress in the exercise of its powers may constitutionally exact. One of the most important of these is to serve the country in time of war and national emergency. The powers of Congress to require military service for the common defense are broad and far-reaching, for while the Constitution protects against invasions of individual rights, it is not a suicide pact. Similarly, Congress has broad power under the Necessary and Proper Clause to enact legislation for the regulation of foreign affairs. Latitude in this area is necessary to ensure effectuation of this indispensable function of government....

It is fundamental that the great powers of Congress to conduct war and to regulate the Nation's foreign relations are subject to the constitutional requirements of due process. The imperative necessity for safeguarding these rights to procedural due process under the gravest of emergencies has existed throughout our constitutional history, for it is then, under the pressing exigencies of crisis, that there is the greatest temptation to dispense with fundamental constitutional guarantees which, it is feared, will inhabit governmental action. "The Constitution of the United States is a law for rulers and people, equally in war and in peace, and covers with the shield of its protection all classes of men, at all times, and under all circumstances."

We hold [sections] 401(j) [Nationality Act of 1940] and 349(a)(10) [Immigration and Nationality Act of 1952] invalid because in them Congress has plainly employed the sanction of deprivation of nationality as a punishment—for the offense of leaving or remaining outside the country to evade military service—without affording the procedural safeguards guaranteed by the Fifth and Sixth Amendments....

It is argued that our holding today will have the unfortunate result of immunizing the draft evader who has left the United States from having to suffer any sanction against his conduct, since he must return to this country before he can be apprehended and tried for his crime. The compelling answer to this is that the Bill of Rights which we guard so jealously and the procedures it guarantees are not to be abrogated merely because a guilty man may escape prosecution or for any other expedient reason. Moreover, the truth is that even without being expatriated, the evader living abroad is not in a position to assert the vast majority of his component rights as an American citizen. If he wishes to assert those rights in any real sense he must return to this country, and by doing that he will subject himself to prosecution. In fact, while he is outside the country evading prosecution, the United States may, by proper refusal to exercise its largely discretionary power to afford him diplomatic protection, decline to invoke its sovereign power on his behalf. Since the substantial benefits of American citizenship only come into play upon return to face prosecution, the draft evader who wishes to exercise his citizenship rights will inevitably come home and pay his debt, which within constitutional limits Congress has the power to define. This is what Mendoza–Martinez did, what Cort says he is willing to do, and what others have done. Thus our holding today does not frustrate the effective handling of the problem of draft evaders who leave the United States.

We conclude, for the reasons stated, that [sections] 401(j) and 349(a)(10) are punitive and as such cannot constitutionally stand, lacking as they do the procedural safeguards which the Constitution commands. We recognize that draft evasion, particularly in time of war, is a heinous offense, and should and can be properly punished. Dating back to Magna Carta, however, it has been an abiding principle governing the lives of civilized men that "no freeman shall be taken or imprisoned or diseased or outlawed or exiled ... without the judgment of his peers or by the law of the land...." What we hold is only that, in keeping with this cherished tradition, punishment cannot be imposed "without due process of law." Any lesser holding would ignore the constitutional mandate upon which our essential liberties depend. Therefore the judgments of the District Courts in these cases are

Affirmed.

Justices **Harlan, Clark, Stewart** and **White, dissenting.**

─────────── SCHNEIDER V. RUSK ───────────

377 U.S. 163 (1964)

Mrs. Schneider was born in Germany, came to the United States with her parents as a child, and acquired American citizenship derivatively through her mother's naturalization in the U.S. After graduating from Smith College, she moved to Germany, married a German citizen, and except for two visits back to the United States, remained domiciled in Germany. In 1959, her application for an American passport was denied on the grounds that she had lost her American citizenship pursuant to the Immigration and Nationality Act of 1952 which provided that a naturalized citizen would lose his or her U.S. citizenship after three years of continuous residence in a foreign state of which that person was formerly a national. Schneider appealed, claiming that the legislation provided no restrictions on the length of foreign residence for native-born citizens. The U.S. District Court for the District of Columbia denied her request for a declaratory judgment that she remained a U.S. citizen, and Schneider appealed to the Supreme Court.

Justice **Douglas** delivered the opinion of the Court:

. . . . We start from the premise that the rights of citizenship of the native born and of the naturalized person are of the same dignity and are coextensive. The only difference drawn by the Constitution is that only the "natural born" citizen is eligible to be President.

While the rights of citizenship of the native born derive from [section] 1 of the Fourteenth Amendment and the rights of the naturalized citizen derive from satisfying, free of fraud, the requirements set by Congress, the latter, apart from the exception noted, "becomes a member of the society, possessing all the rights of a native citizen, and standing, in the view of the constitution, on the footing of a native. The constitution does not authorize Congress to enlarge or abridge those rights. The simple power of the national Legislature, is to prescribe a uniform rule of naturalization, and the exercise of this power exhausts it, so far as respects the individual." . . .

This statute proceeds on the impermissible assumption that naturalized citizens as a class are less reliable and bear less allegiance to this country than do the native born. This is an assumption that is impossible for us to make. Moreover, while the Fifth Amendment contains no equal protection clause, it does forbid discrimination that is "so unjustifiable as to be violative of due process." A native born citizen is free to reside abroad indefinitely without suffering loss of citizenship. The discrimination aimed at naturalized citizens drastically limits their rights to live and work abroad in a way that other citizens may. It creates indeed a second-class citizenship. Living abroad, whether the citizen be naturalized or native born, is no badge of lack of allegiance and in no way evidences a voluntary renunciation of nationality and allegiance. It may indeed be compelled by family, business, or other legitimate reasons.

Reversed.

*Justice **Clark**, joined by Justices **Harlan** and **White**, dissenting.*

—————————— AFROYIM V. RUSK ——————————

387 U.S. 253 (1967)

Afroyim was born in Poland in 1893. He immigrated to the United States in 1912 and was naturalized in 1926. In 1950, he immigrated to Israel and voted in an Israeli election. When he attempted to renew his U.S. passport in 1960, he was refused on the grounds that he had expatriated himself by voting in a foreign election. Afroyim challenged the statutory provisions that required expatriation for voting in foreign elections. (See Perez v. Brownell, *supra.) The U.S. District Court ruled against Afroyim, citing the foreign relations power of Congress, and the court of appeals affirmed the judgment. Afroyim appealed.*

Justice **Black** delivered the opinion of the Court:

. . . . The fundamental issue before this Court here, as it was in *Perez,* is whether Congress can consistently with the Fourteenth Amendment enact a law stripping an American of his citizenship which he has never voluntarily renounced or given up. . . .

First we reject the idea expressed in *Perez* that, aside from the Fourteenth Amendment, Congress has any general power, express or implied, to take away an American citizen's citizenship without his assent. This power cannot, as *Perez* indicated, be sustained as an implied attribute of sovereignty possessed by all nations. Other nations are governed by their own constitutions, if any, and we can draw no support from theirs. In our country the people are sovereign and the Government cannot sever its relationship to the people by taking away their citizenship. Our Constitution governs us and we must never forget that our Constitution limits the Government to those powers specifically granted or those that are necessary and proper to carry out the specifically granted ones. The Constitution, of course, grants Congress no express power to strip people of their citizenship, whether in the exercise of the implied power to regulate foreign affairs or in the exercise of any specifically granted power. And even before the adoption of the Fourteenth Amendment, views were expressed in Congress and by this court that under the Constitution the Government was granted no power, even under its express power to pass a uniform rule of naturalization, to determine what conduct should and should not result in the loss of citizenship. . . .

. . . . It is in this setting that . . . in *Osborn v. Bank of the United States,* this Court, speaking through Chief Justice Marshall, declared in what appears to be a mature and well-considered dictum that Congress, once a person becomes a citizen, cannot deprive him of that status. . . .

Although these legislative and judicial statements may be regarded as inconclusive and must be considered in the historical context in which they were made, any doubt as to whether prior to the passage of the Fourteenth Amendment Congress had the power to deprive a person against his will of citizenship once obtained should have been removed by the unequivocal terms of the Amendment itself. It provides its own constitutional rule in language calculated completely to control the status of citizenship: "All persons born or naturalized in the United States . . . are citizens of the United States. . . ." There is no indication in these words of a fleeting citizenship, good at the moment it is acquired but subject to destruction by the

Government at any time. Rather the Amendment can most reasonably be read as defining a citizenship which a citizen keeps unless he voluntarily relinquishes it. Once acquired, this Fourteenth Amendment citizenship was not to be shifted, canceled, or diluted at the will of the Federal Government, the States, or any other governmental unit. . . .

To uphold Congress' power to take away a man's citizenship because he voted in a foreign election in violation of [section] 401(e) [of the Act] would be equivalent to holding that Congress has the power to "abridge," "affect," "restrict the effect of," and "take . . . away" citizenship. Because the Fourteenth Amendment prevents Congress from doing any of these things, we agree with the Chief Justice's dissent in the *Perez* case that the Government is without power to rob a citizen of his citizenship. . . .

Because the legislative history of the Fourteenth Amendment and of the expatriation proposals which preceded and followed it, like most other legislative history, contains many statements from which conflicting inferences can be drawn, our holding might be unwarranted if it rested entirely or principally upon that legislative history. But it does not. Our holding we think is the only one that can stand in view of the language and the purpose of the Fourteenth Amendment, and our construction of that Amendment, we believe, comports more nearly than *Perez* with the principles of liberty and equal justice to all that the entire Fourteenth Amendment was adopted to guarantee. Citizenship is no light trifle to be jeopardized any moment Congress decides to do so under the name of one of its general or implied grants of power. In some instances, loss of citizenship can mean that a man is left without the protection of citizenship in any country in the world—as a man without a country. Citizenship in this Nation is a part of a cooperative affair. Its citizenry is the country and the country is its citizenry. The very nature of our free government makes it completely incongruous to have a rule of law under which a group of citizens temporarily in office can deprive another group of citizens of their citizenship. We hold that the Fourteenth Amendment was designed to, and does, protect every citizen of this Nation against congressional forcible destruction of his citizenship, whatever his creed, color, or race. Our holding does no more than to give to this citizen that which is his own, a constitutional right to remain a citizen in a free country unless he voluntarily relinquishes that citizenship.

Perez v. Brownell is overruled. The judgment is

Reversed.

Justice **Harlan,** *joined by Justices* **Clark, Stewart,** *and* **White,** *dissenting.*

─────────────── ROGERS V. BELLEI ───────────────

401 U.S. 815 (1971)

Aldo Bellei was born in Italy in 1939. His father was an Italian citizen and his mother a native born U.S. citizen. Bellei thus became an Italian citizen by birth, and acquired American citizenship by descent, pursuant to U.S. legislation. U.S. statutes also required that a person who acquired U.S. citizenship by descent must reside in the United States continu-

ously for five years between the ages of 14 and 28 to retain that citizenship. Although Bellei had visited the United States on several occasions, and had been warned of the danger of losing his citizenship, he did not meet the residence requirement.

In 1964, four years after he had registered for the draft with the American Consul in Rome, Bellei was informed that he had no further obligation for American military service because he had lost his U.S. citizenship. Bellei challenged the residence requirement as a violation of the Fifth Amendment. A three-judge panel of the U.S. District Court held in favor of Bellei, and the government appealed.

Justice **Blackmun** delivered the opinion of the Court:

. . . . The central fact, in our weighing of the plaintiff's claim to continuing and therefore current United States citizenship, is that he was born abroad. He was not born in the United States. And he has not been subject to the jurisdiction of the United States. All this being so, it seems indisputable that the first sentence of the Fourteenth Amendment has no application to plaintiff Bellei. He simply is not a Fourteenth-Amendment-first-sentence citizen. His posture contrasts with that of Mr. Afroyim, who was naturalized in the United States, and with that of Mrs. Schneider, whose citizenship was derivative by her presence here and by her mother's naturalization here.

The plaintiff's claim thus must center in the statutory power of Congress and in the appropriate exercise of that power within the restrictions of any pertinent constitutional provisions other than the Fourteenth Amendment's first sentence. . . .

This takes us, then, to the issue of the constitutionality of the exercise of that congressional power when it is used to impose the condition subsequent that confronted plaintiff Bellei. We conclude that its imposition is not unreasonable, arbitrary, or unlawful, and that it withstands the present constitutional challenge.

1. The Congress has an appropriate concern with problems attendant on dual nationality. . . .

* * *

4. The solution to the dual nationality dilemma provided by the Congress by way of required residence surely is not unreasonable. It may not be the best that could be devised, but here, too, we cannot say that it is irrational or arbitrary or unfair. . . .

5. We feel that it does not make good constitutional sense, or comport with logic, to say, on the one hand, that Congress may impose a condition precedent, with no constitutional complication, and yet be powerless to impose precisely the same condition subsequent. Any such distinction, of course, must rest, if it has any basis at all, on the asserted "premise that the rights of citizenship of the native born and of the naturalized person are of the same dignity and are coextensive," and on the announcement that Congress has no "power, express or implied, to take away an American citizen's citizenship without his assent." But . . . these were utterances bottomed upon Fourteenth Amendment citizenship and that Amendment's direct reference to "persons born or naturalized in the United States." We do not accept the notion that those utterances are

now to be judicially extended to citizenship not based upon the Fourteenth Amendment and to make citizenship an absolute. That it is not an absolute is demonstrated by the fact that even Fourteenth Amendment citizenship by naturalization, when unlawfully procured, may be set aside.

6. A contrary holding would convert what is congressional generosity into something unanticipated and obviously undesired by the Congress. Our National Legislature indulged the foreign-born child with presumptive citizenship, subject to subsequent satisfaction of a reasonable residence requirement, rather than to deny him citizenship outright, as concededly it had the power to do, and relegate the child, if he desired American citizenship, to the more arduous requirements of the usual naturalization process. The plaintiff here would force the Congress to choose between unconditional conferment of United States citizenship at birth and deferment of citizenship until a condition precedent is fulfilled. We are not convinced that the Constitution requires so rigid a choice. If it does, the congressional response seems obvious.

7. Neither are we persuaded that a condition subsequent in this area impresses one with "second-class citizenship." That cliché is too handy and too easy, and, like most clichès, can be misleading. That the condition subsequent may be beneficial is apparent in the light of the conceded fact that citizenship to this plaintiff was fully deniable. The proper emphasis is on what the statute permits him to gain from the possible starting point of noncitizenship, not on what he claims to lose from the possible starting point of full citizenship to which he has no constitutional right in the first place. His citizenship, while it lasts, although conditional, is not "second-class."

8. The plaintiff is not stateless. His Italian citizenship remains. He has lived practically all his life in Italy. He has never lived in this country; although he has visited here five times, the stipulated facts contain no indication that he ever will live here. He asserts no claim of ignorance or of mistake or even of hardship. He was warned several times of the provision of the statute and of his need to take up residence in the United States prior to his 23d birthday.

We hold that ss 301(b) has no constitutional infirmity in its application to plaintiff Bellei. The judgment of the District Court is reversed.

Justices **Black, Douglas, Marshall** *and* **Brennan,** *dissenting.*

—————————— KENT V. DULLES ——————————

357 U.S. 116 (1958)

Regulations promulgated by the secretary of state prohibited the issuance of U.S. passports to persons with Communist affiliations. Rockwell Kent applied for a passport to attend a meeting of the "World Council of Peace" in Helsinki, Finland but was denied one on the grounds that he was a Communist and had demonstrated "a consistent and prolonged adherence to the Communist Party line." Kent was informed that before a passport could be issued he must submit an affidavit as to whether he was then, or ever had been, a Communist. Kent refused to submit the affidavit and filed suit for declaratory relief. The district court granted summary judgment for the secretary of state, the court of appeals affirmed by divided vote, and the Supreme Court granted certiorari.

Justice **Douglas** delivered the opinion of the Court:

.... Under the 1926 Act and its predecessor a large body of precedents grew up which repeat over and again that the issuance of passports is "a discretionary act" on the part of the Secretary of State. The scholars, the courts, the Chief Executive, and the Attorneys General, all so said. This long-continued executive construction should be enough, it is said, to warrant the inference that Congress had adopted it. But the key to that problem, as we shall see, is in the manner in which the Secretary's discretion was exercised, not in the bare fact that he had discretion.

The right to travel is a part of the "liberty" of which the citizen cannot be deprived without due process of law under the Fifth Amendment. So much is conceded by the Solicitor General. In Anglo–Saxon law that right was emerging at least as early as the Magna Carta.... Freedom of movement across frontiers in either direction, and inside frontiers as well, was a part of our heritage. Travel abroad, like travel within the country, may be necessary for a livelihood. It may be as close to the heart of the individual as the choice of what he eats, or wears, or reads. Freedom of movement is basic in our scheme of values.... We need not decide the extent to which it can be curtailed. We are first concerned with the extent, if any, to which Congress has authorized its curtailment.

The difficulty is that while the power of the Secretary of State over the issuance of passports is expressed in broad terms, it was apparently long exercised quite narrowly. So far as material here, the cases of refusal of passports generally fell into two categories. First, questions pertinent to the citizenship of the applicant and his allegiance to the United States had to be resolved by the Secretary, for the command of Congress was that "No passport shall be granted or issued to or verified for any other persons than those owing allegiance, whether citizens or not, to the United States." Second, was the question whether the applicant was participating in illegal conduct, trying to escape the toils of the law, promoting passport frauds, or otherwise engaging in conduct which would violate the laws of the United States.

The grounds for refusal asserted here do not relate to citizenship or allegiance on the one hand or to criminal or unlawful conduct on the other. Yet, so far as relevant here, those two are the only ones which it could fairly be argued were adopted by Congress in light of prior administrative practice. One can find in the records of the State Department rulings of subordinates covering a wider range of activities than the two indicated. But as respects Communists these are scattered rulings and not consistently of one pattern. We can say with assurance that whatever may have been the practice after

1926, at the time the Act of July 3, 1926, was adopted, the administrative practice, so far as relevant here, had jelled only around the two categories mentioned. We, therefore, hesitate to impute to Congress, when in 1952 it made a passport necessary for foreign travel and left its issuance to the discretion of the Secretary of State, a purpose to give him unbridled discretion to grant or withhold a passport from a citizen for any substantive reason he may choose. . . .

Since we start with an exercise by an American citizen of an activity included in constitutional protection, we will not readily infer that Congress gave the Secretary of State unbridled discretion to grant or withhold it. If we were dealing with political questions entrusted to the Chief Executive by the Constitution we would have a different case. But there is more involved here. . . . [A passport's] function today is control over exit. And, as we have seen, the right of exit is a personal right included within the word "liberty" as used in the Fifth Amendment. If that "liberty" is to be regulated, it must be pursuant to the law-making functions of the Congress. And if that power is delegated, the standards must be adequate to pass scrutiny by the accepted tests. Where activities or enjoyment, natural and often necessary to the well-being of an American citizen, such as travel, are involved, we will construe narrowly all delegated powers that curtail or dilute them. We hesitate to find in this broad generalized power an authority to trench so heavily on the rights of the citizen.

. . . . [W]e deal here with a constitutional right of the citizen, a right which we must assume Congress will be faithful to respect. We would be faced with important constitutional questions were we to hold that Congress had given the Secretary authority to withhold passports to citizens because of their beliefs or associations. Congress has made no such provision in explicit terms; and absent one, the Secretary may not employ that standard to restrict the citizens' right of free movement.

Reversed.

Justice **Clark,** *joined by Justices* **Burton, Harlan,** *and* **Whittaker,** *dissenting.*

———————————————— APTHEKER ET AL. V. ————————————————
SECRETARY OF STATE

378 U.S. 500 (1964)

In 1961, Congress enacted legislation to prohibit members of Communist organizations from applying for or using U.S. passports. Herbert Aptheker, editor of the Party's publication Political Affairs, *and Elizabeth Gurley Flynn, chairman of the Communist Party of the United States, both native born American citizens, held valid U.S. passports prior to the Act taking effect. They were subsequently notified by the State Department that their passports were revoked. After exhausting their appeals under State Department procedures, they filed suit asking that the Act be declared unconstitutional as a violation of the Due Process Clause of the Fifth Amendment. A three-judge panel of the U.S. District Court held the statute to be constitutional and Aptheker and his associates appealed.*

Justice **Goldberg** delivered the opinion of the Court:

.... The present case, is the first in which this Court has been called upon to consider the constitutionality of the [legislative] restrictions ... on the right to travel.

The substantiality of the restrictions cannot be doubted. The denial of a passport, given existing domestic and foreign laws, is a severe restriction upon, and in effect a prohibition against, world-wide foreign travel....

The restrictive effect of the legislation cannot be gainsaid by emphasizing, as the Government seems to do, that a member of a registering organization could recapture his freedom to travel by simply in good faith abandoning his membership in the organization. Since freedom of association is itself guaranteed in the First Amendment, restrictions imposed upon the right to travel cannot be dismissed by asserting that the right to travel could be fully exercised if the individual would first yield up his membership in a given association.

Although previous cases have not involved the constitutionality of statutory restrictions upon the right to travel abroad, [see *Kent v. Dulles*] there are well-established principles by which to test whether the restrictions here imposed are consistent with the liberty guaranteed by the Fifth Amendment. It is a familiar and basic principle ... that "a governmental purpose to control or prevent activities constitutionally subject to state regulation may not be achieved by means which sweep unnecessarily broadly and thereby invade the area of protected freedoms." ...

In our view the foregoing considerations compel the conclusion that [section] 6 of the Control Act is unconstitutional on its face. The section, judged by its plain import and by the substantive evil which Congress sought to control, sweeps too widely and too indiscriminately across the liberty guaranteed in the Fifth Amendment. The prohibition against travel is supported only by a tenuous relationship between the bare fact of organizational membership and the activity Congress sought to proscribe. The broad and enveloping prohibition indiscriminately excludes plainly relevant considerations such as the individual's knowledge, activity, commitment, and purposes in and places for travel. The section therefore is patently not a regulation "narrowly drawn to prevent the supposed evil," yet here, as elsewhere, precision must be the touchstone of legislation so affecting basic freedoms....

It must be remembered that "[a]lthough this Court will often strain to construe legislation so as to save it against constitutional attack, it must not and will not carry this to the point of perverting the purpose of a statute ..." or judicially rewriting it.... [S]ince freedom of travel is a constitutional liberty closely related to rights of free speech and association, we believe that appellants in this case should not be required to assume the burden of demonstrating that Congress could not have written a statute constitutionally prohibiting their travel.

Accordingly the judgment of the three-judge District Court is reversed and the cause remanded for proceedings in conformity with this opinion.

Reversed and remanded.

Justice **Clark,** *joined by Justice* **Harlan** *and* **White,** *dissenting.*

ZEMEL V. RUSK

381 U.S. 1 (1965)

In 1961, the United States broke diplomatic relations with Cuba and directed that special passport validation be required for travel to Cuba. In early 1962, Zemel applied to the State Department to have his passport validated for travel to Cuba "to satisfy [his] curiosity . . . and to make him a better informed citizen." Zemel's request was denied, and he filed suit, claiming that the travel restrictions constituted an unconstitutional interference with his right to travel. The U.S. District Court dismissed his complaint.

Chief Justice **Warren** delivered the opinion of the Court: . . . .

We think that the Passport Act of 1926, embodies a grant of authority to the Executive to refuse to validate the passports of United States citizens for travel to Cuba. That Act provides, in pertinent part:

> "The Secretary of State may grant and issue passports . . . under such rules as the President shall designate and prescribe for and on behalf of the United States. . . ."

The legislative history of the 1926 Act and its predecessors does not, it is true, affirmatively indicate an intention to authorize area restrictions. However, its language is surely broad enough to authorize area restrictions, and there is no legislative history indicating an intent to exclude such restrictions from the grant of authority. . . .

This construction of the Act is reinforced by the State Department's continued imposition of area restrictions during both times of war and periods of peace since 1926. [The Court at this point traces the history of such restrictions.]. . . . Under some circumstances, Congress' failure to repeal or revise in the face of such administrative interpretation has been held to constitute persuasive evidence that that interpretation is the one intended by Congress. In this case, however, the inference is supported by more than mere congressional inaction. For in 1952 Congress, substantially reenacting laws which had been passed during the First and Second World Wars, provided that after the issuance of a presidential proclamation of war or national emergency, it would be unlawful to leave or enter the United States without a valid passport. . . . Despite 26 years of executive interpretation of the 1926 Act as authorizing the imposition of area restrictions, Congress in 1952, though it once again enacted legislation relating to passports, left completely untouched the broad rule-making authority granted in the earlier Act.

This case is therefore not like *Kent v. Dulles,* where we were unable to find, with regard to the sort of passport refusal involved there, an administrative practice sufficiently substantial and consistent to warrant the conclusion that Congress had implicitly approved it. It must be remembered, in reading this passage, that the issue involved in *Kent* was whether a citizen could be denied a passport because of his political beliefs or associations. In finding that history did not support the position of the Secretary in that case, we summarized that history "so far as material here"—that is, so far as material to passport refusals based on the character of the particular applicant. In this case, however, the Secretary has refused to validate appellant's passport not because of any characteristic peculiar to appellant, but rather because of foreign policy considerations affecting all citizens.

Having concluded that the Secretary of State's refusal to validate appellant's passport for travel to Cuba is supported by the authority granted by Congress in the Passport Act of 1926, we must next consider whether that refusal abridges any constitutional right of appellant. . . .

The requirements of due process are a function not only of the extent of the governmental restriction imposed, but also of the extent of the necessity for the restriction. Cuba is the only area in the Western Hemisphere controlled by a Communist government. It is, moreover, the judgment of the State Department that a major goal of the Castro regime is to export its Communist revolution to the rest of Latin America. The United States and other members of the Organization of American States have determined that travel between Cuba and the other countries of the Western Hemisphere is an important element in the spreading of subversion, and many have therefore undertaken measures to discourage such travel. It also cannot be forgotten that in the early days of the Castro regime, United States citizens were arrested and imprisoned without charges. We think, particularly in view of the President's statutory obligation to "use such means, not amounting to acts of war, as he may think necessary and proper" to secure the release of an American citizen unjustly deprived of his liberty by a foreign government, that the Secretary has justifiably concluded that travel to Cuba by American citizens might involve the Nation in dangerous international incidents, and that the Constitution does not require him to validate passports for such travel.

. . . . That the restriction which is challenged in this case is supported by the weightiest considerations of national security is perhaps best pointed up by recalling that the Cuban missile crisis of October 1962 preceded the filing of appellant's complaint by less than two months.

Finally, appellant challenges the 1926 Act on the ground that it does not contain sufficiently definite standards for the formulation of travel controls by the Executive. It is important to bear in mind, in appraising this argument, that because of the changeable and explosive nature of contemporary international relations, and the fact that the Executive is immediately privy to information which cannot be swiftly presented to, evaluated by, and acted upon by the legislature, Congress—in giving the Executive authority over matters of foreign affairs—must of necessity paint with a brush broader than that it customarily wields in domestic areas. . . .

This does not mean that simply because a statute deals with foreign relations, it can grant the Executive totally unrestricted freedom of choice. However, the 1926 Act contains no such grant. We have held, and reaffirm today, that the 1926 Act must take its content from history: it authorizes only those passport refusals and restrictions "which it could fairly be argued were adopted by Congress in light of prior administrative practice." So limited, the Act does not constitute an invalid delegation.

The District Court therefore correctly dismissed the complaint, and its judgment is

Affirmed.

Justices **Black, Douglas,** *and* **Goldberg,** *dissenting.*

─────────────── UNITED STATES V. LAUB ───────────────

385 U.S. 475 (1967)

The Immigration and Nationality Act of 1952 made it unlawful for citizens to travel abroad without a valid passport during wartime or during a national emergency when the president proclaimed that such restrictions were vital to the national interest. Such proclamation was made by President Truman in 1953, and thereafter American citizens were required to carry passports when travelling abroad, except when travelling in areas exempted by the Department of State. After diplomatic relations with Cuba were severed in 1961, State Department regulations required a specially validated passport for travel to Cuba. Subsequently, Laub and others were indicted for conspiring to violate the Immigration and Nationality Act by arranging travel to Cuba for fifty-eight U.S. citizens whose passports, though otherwise valid, were not specifically endorsed for travel to Cuba. In U.S. District Court, Laub et al. moved to have the indictments dismissed, and the court agreed. The government appealed. The issue before the Supreme Court was whether area restrictions upon an otherwise valid passport were criminally enforceable under the 1952 Immigration and Nationality Act.

Justice **Fortas** delivered the opinion of the Court:

. . . . In *Zemel v. Rusk* the petitioner sought a declaratory judgment that the Secretary of State does not have statutory authorization to impose area restrictions on travel; that if the statute were construed to authorize the Secretary to do so, it would be an impermissible delegation of power; and that, in any event, the exercise of the power to restrict travel denied to petitioner his rights under the First and Fifth Amendments. This Court rejected petitioner's claims and sustained the Secretary's statutory power to refuse to validate passports for travel to Cuba. It found authority for area restrictions in the general passport authority vested in the Secretary of State by the 1926 Act, relying upon the successive "imposition of area restrictions during both times of war and periods of peace" before and after the enactment of the Act of 1926.

The Court [in *Zemel v. Rusk*] specifically declined the Solicitor General's invitation to rule also that "travel in violation of an area restriction imposed on an otherwise valid passport is unlawful under the 1952 Act."

We now confront that question. . . .

As this Court has observed, "The right to travel is a part of the 'liberty' of which the citizen cannot be deprived without due process of law. . . ."

Under [section] 215(b) and its predecessor statutes, Congress authorized the requirement that a citizen possess a passport for departure from and entry into the United States, and there is no doubt that with the adoption and promulgation of the "Excluding Cuba" regulation, a passport was required for departure from this country for Cuba and for entry into this country from Cuba. Departure for Cuba or entry from Cuba without a passport would be a violation of [section] 215(b), exposing the traveler to the criminal penalties provided in that section. But it does not follow that travel to Cuba with a passport which is not specifically validated for that country is a criminal offense. Violation of the "area restriction"—"invalidating" passports for travel in or to Cuba and requiring specific validation of passports if they are to be valid for travel to or in Cuba—is quite a different matter from violation of the requirement of [section] 215(b) and the regulations thereunder that a citizen bear a "valid passport" for departure from or entry into the United States.

The area restriction applicable to Cuba was promulgated by a "Public Notice" and a press release, neither of which referred to [section] 215(b) or to criminal sanctions. On the contrary, the only reference to the statutory base of the announcement appears in the "Public Notice," and this is a reference to the nonpenal 1926 Act and the Executive Order adopted thereunder in 1938. These merely authorize the Secretary of State to impose area restrictions incidental to his general powers with respect to passports. They do not purport to make travel to the designated area unlawful.

The press release issued by the Department of State at the time expressly explained the action as being "in view of the U.S. Government's inability ... to extend normal protective services to Americans visiting Cuba." It explained that the action was taken in conformity with the Department's "normal practice," of limiting travel to countries with which we do not have diplomatic relations. That "normal practice," as will be discussed, has not included criminal sanctions. In short, the relevant State Department promulgations are not only devoid of a suggestion that travel to Cuba without a specially validated passport is prohibited, or that such travel would be criminal conduct, but they also contain positive suggestions that the purpose and effect of the restriction were merely to make clear that the passport was not to be regarded by the traveler in Cuba as a voucher on the protective services normally afforded by the State Department.

In 1957, the Senate Foreign Relations Committee asked the Department: "What does it mean when a passport is stamped 'not valid to go to country X'?" After three months, the Department sent its official reply. It stated that this stamping of a passport "means that if the bearer enters country X he *cannot be assured of the protection* of the United States. . . . [but it] *does not necessarily mean that if the bearer travels to country X he will be violating the criminal law."* [Justice **Fortas'** italics.] Similarly, in hearings before another Senate Committee, a Department official explained that when a passport is marked "invalid" for travel to stated countries, this means that "this Government is not sponsoring the entry of the individual into those countries and does not give him permission to go in there under the protection of this Government." . . .

In view of this overwhelming evidence that [section] 215(b) does not authorize area restrictions, we agree with the District Court that the indictment herein does not allege a crime. If there is a gap in the law, the right and the duty, if any, to fill it do not devolve upon the courts. The area travel restriction, requiring special validation of passports for travel to Cuba, was a valid civil regulation under the 1926 Act. But it was not and was not intended or represented to be an exercise of authority under [section] 215(b), which provides the basis of the criminal charge in this case....

In view of our decision that appellees were charged with conspiracy to violate a nonexistent criminal prohibition, we need not consider other issues which the case presents.

Accordingly, the judgment of the District Court is

Affirmed.

-------------------------- REGAN V. WALD --------------------------

468 U.S. 222 (1984)

The International Emergency Economic Powers Act (IEEPA) gives the president broad authority to impose comprehensive embargoes on foreign countries to deal with peacetime emergencies which threaten national security. A Treasury Department regulation, first promulgated in 1963 as part of the Cuban Assets Control Regulations, prohibited any transaction involving property in which Cuba had "any interest of any nature whatsoever, direct or indirect." This 1963 regulation was based generally on the president's "national emergency authority" deriving from the Trading with the Enemy Act. When the IEEPA was enacted in 1977, Congress "grandfathered" the president's action. At the same time, a new regulation was implemented which generally permitted travel related economic transactions with Cuba. This regulation was amended in 1982 to restrict travel to Cuba, prohibiting general tourist and business travel. Ruth Wald and several other American citizens wanted to travel to Cuba, but were prevented from doing so under the revised regulation. Wald sought injunctive relief in the U.S. District Court to prevent the government from enforcing the regulation. The district court denied the motion, the court of appeals reversed, and the government appealed.

Justice **Rehnquist** delivered the opinion of the Court:

.... Respondents finally urge that if we do find that the President is authorized by Congress to enforce the regulations here in question, their enforcement violates respondents' right to travel guaranteed by the Due Process Clause of the Fifth Amendment. Respondents rely on a number of our prior decisions which recognized such a right, beginning in 1958 with *Kent v. Dulles* ....

In *Kent,* the Court held that Congress had not authorized the Secretary of State to inquire of passport applicants as to affiliation with the Communist Party. The Court noted that the right to travel "is a part of the 'liberty' of which the citizen cannot be deprived without due process of law," and stated that it would "construe narrowly all delegated powers that curtail or dilute" that right. Subsequently, in *Aptheker v. United States,* the Court held that a provision of the Subversive Control Act of 1950, forbidding the issuance of a passport to a member of the Communist Party, "sweeps too widely and too indiscriminately across the liberty guaranteed in the Fifth Amendment."

Both *Kent* and *Aptheker*, however, were qualified the following term in *Zemel v. Rusk.* In that case, the Court sustained against constitutional attack a refusal by the Secretary of State to validate the passports of United States citizens for travel to Cuba. The Secretary of State in *Zemel*, as here, made no effort selectively to deny passports on the basis of political belief or affiliation, but simply imposed a general ban on travel to Cuba following the break in diplomatic and consular relations with that country in 1961 . . .

We see no reason to differentiate between the travel restrictions imposed by the President in the present case and the passport restrictions imposed by the Secretary of State in *Zemel*. Both have the practical effect of preventing travel to Cuba by most American citizens, and both are justified by weighty concerns of foreign policy.

Respondents apparently feel that only a Cuban missile crisis in the offing will make area restrictions on international travel constitutional. They argue that there is no "emergency" at the present time and that the relations between Cuba and the United States are subject to "only the 'normal' tensions inherent in contemporary international affairs." The holding in *Zemel*, however, was not tied to the Court's independent foreign policy analysis. Matters relating "to the conduct of foreign relations . . . are so exclusively entrusted to the political branches of governments as to be largely immune from judicial inquiry or interference." Our holding in *Zemel* was merely an example of this classical deference to the political branches in matters of foreign policy. . . .

In the opinion of the State Department, Cuba, with the political, economic, and military backing of the Soviet Union, has provided widespread support for armed violence and terrorism in the Western Hemisphere. Cuba also maintains close to 40,000 troops in various countries in Africa and the Middle East in support of objectives inimical to United States foreign policy interests. Given the traditional deference to executive judgment "[i]n this vast external realm," we think there is an adequate basis under the Due Process Clause of the Fifth Amendment to sustain the President's decision to curtail the flow of hard currency to Cuba—currency that could then be used in support of Cuban adventurism—by restricting travel. . . .

The judgment of the Court of Appeals is

Reversed.

Justice **Blackmun,** *joined by Justices* **Brennan, Marshall** *and* **Powell,** *dissenting.*

————————— KLEINDIENST V. MANDEL —————————

408 U.S. 753 (1972)

In 1969, Ernst Mandel, a Belgian journalist and Marxist theoretician, applied to the American consul in Brussels for a visa to participate in a series of academic conferences in the

United States to which he had been invited. Mandel's application was refused under the Immigration and Nationality Act of 1952 which provided for the exclusion of aliens who advocate "the economic, international, and governmental doctrines of world communism." The attorney general declined to exercise his statutory authority to waive Mandel's exclusion on the ground that "previous abuses by Mandel," involving unscheduled activities on an earlier visit to the United States, "made it inappropriate to grant a waiver again." Mandel was joined by eight American university professors in an action against the attorney general alleging that the application of the statute to Mandel was arbitrary and capricious and that citizens of the United States had a First Amendment right to hear him. The U.S. District Court for the eastern district of New York granted the injunction Mandel requested and the government appealed.

Justice **Blackmun** delivered the opinion of the Court:

Until 1875 alien migration to the United States was unrestricted. The Act of March 3, 1875 barred convicts and prostitutes. Seven years later Congress passed the first general immigration statute. Other legislation followed. A general revision of the immigration laws was effected by the Act of Mar. 3, 1903. Section 2 of that Act made ineligible for admission "anarchists, or persons who believe in or advocate the overthrow by force or violence of the Government of the United States or of all government or of all forms of law." By the Act of Oct. 16, 1918, Congress expanded the provisions for the exclusion of subversive aliens. Title II of the Alien Registration Act of 1940 amended the 1918 Act to bar aliens who, at any time, had advocated or were members of or affiliated with organizations that advocated violent overthrow of the United States Government.

In the years that followed, after extensive investigation and numerous reports by congressional committees, Congress passed the Internal Security Act of 1950. This Act dispensed with the requirement of the 1940 Act of a finding in each case, with respect to members of the Communist Party, that the party did in fact advocate violent overthrow of the Government. These provisions were carried forward into the Immigration and Nationality Act of 1952.

We thus have almost continuous attention on the part of Congress since 1875 to the problems of immigration and of excludability of certain defined classes of aliens. The pattern generally has been one of increasing control with particular attention, for almost 70 years now, first to anarchists and then to those with communist affiliation or views.

III

It is clear that Mandel personally, as an unadmitted and nonresident alien, had no constitutional right of entry to this country as a nonimmigrant or otherwise. . . .

The case, therefore, comes down to the narrow issue whether the First Amendment confers upon the appellee professors, because they wish to hear, speak, and debate with Mandel in person, the ability to determine that Mandel should be permitted to enter the country or, in other words, to compel the Attorney General to allow Mandel's admission.

IV

In a variety of contexts this Court has referred to a First Amendment right to "receive information and ideas." . . .

V

Recognition that First Amendment rights are implicated, however, is not dispositive of our inquiry here. In accord with ancient principles of the international law of nation-states, the Court in *The Chinese Exclusion Case,* and in *Fong Yue Ting v. United States,* held broadly that the power to exclude aliens is "inherent in sovereignty, necessary for maintaining normal international relations and defending the country against foreign encroachments and dangers—a power to be exercised exclusively by the political branches of government. . . ." Since that time, the Court's general reaffirmations of this principle have been legion. The Court without exception has sustained Congress' "plenary power to make rules for the admission of aliens and to exclude those who possess those characteristics which Congress has forbidden." . . . Mr. Justice Frankfurter ably articulated this history in *Galvan v. Press,* a deportation case, and we can do no better. After suggesting that "much could be said for the view" that due process places some limitations on congressional power in this area "were we writing on a clean slate," he continued:

> But the slate is not clean. As to the extent of the power of Congress under review, there is not merely 'a page of history' . . . but a whole volume. Policies pertaining to the entry of aliens and their right to remain here are peculiarly concerned with the political conduct of government. In the enforcement of these policies, the Executive Branch of the Government must respect the procedural safeguards of due process. . . . But that the formulation of these policies is entrusted exclusively to Congress has become about as firmly embedded in the legislative and judicial tissues of our body politic as any aspect of our government. . . .
>
> We are not prepared to deem ourselves wiser or more sensitive to human rights than our predecessors, especially those who have been most zealous in protecting civil liberties under the Constitution, and must therefore under our constitutional system recognize congressional power in dealing with aliens. . . .

We are not inclined in the present context to reconsider this line of cases. Indeed, the appellees do not ask that we do so. . . . They argue that the Executive's implementation of this congressional mandate through decision whether to grant a waiver in each individual case must be limited by the First Amendment rights of persons like appellees. . . .

. . . . Were we to endorse the proposition that governmental power to withhold a waiver must yield whenever a bona fide claim is made that American citizens wish to meet and talk with an alien excludable under [section] 212(a)(28), one of two unsatisfactory results would necessarily ensue. Either every claim would prevail, in which case the plenary discretionary authority Congress granted the Executive becomes a nullity, or courts in each case would be required to weigh the strength of the audience's interest against that of the Government in refusing a waiver to the particular alien applicant, according to some as yet undetermined standard. The dangers and the undesirability of making that determination on the basis of factors such as the size of the audience or the probity of the speaker's ideas are obvious. Indeed, it is for precisely this reason that the waiver decision has, properly, been placed in the hands of the Executive. . . .

Reversed.

Justice **Douglas**, *and Justice* **Marshall** *joined by Justice* **Brennan**, *dissenting.*

HAIG V. AGEE

453 U.S. 280 (1981)

From 1957 to 1968 Philip Agee, an American citizen, was employed by the Central Intelligence Agency and held positions in that section of the Agency responsible for covert intelligence gathering in foreign countries. In 1974, six years after leaving the CIA, Agee held a press conference in London to announce his campaign "to expose CIA officers and agents and to take the measures necessary to drive them out of the countries where they are operating." He then engaged in activities abroad which resulted in the identifications of alleged undercover CIA agents and intelligence sources in foreign countries. In 1979, the secretary of state revoked Agee's U.S. passport pursuant to regulations authorizing revocation where the secretary determines that an American citizen's activities abroad "are causing or are likely to cause serious damage to the national security or the foreign policy of the United States." Agee filed suit alleging that the regulation under which his passport was revoked was not authorized by Congress and was impermissibly vague that revocation violated his privilege to travel and his First Amendment right to criticize government policies, and that the failure to accord him a prerevocation hearing violated his Fifth Amendment right to procedural due process. The U.S. District Court ruled in favor of Agee, and instructed the State Department to restore his passport. The court of appeals affirmed the decision and the government appealed.

Chief Justice **Burger** delivered the opinion of the Court:

The question presented is whether the President, acting through the Secretary of State, has authority to revoke a passport on the ground that the holder's activities in foreign countries are causing or are likely to cause serious damage to the national security or foreign policy of the United States. . . .

The Passport Act does not in so many words confer upon the Secretary a power to revoke a passport. Nor, for that matter, does it expressly authorize denials of passport applications. Neither, however, does any statute expressly limit those powers. It is beyond dispute that the Secretary has the power to deny a passport for reasons not specified in the statutes. . . . Matters intimately related to foreign policy and national security are rarely proper subjects for judicial intervention. In *Harisiades v. Shaughnessy* [see above] the Court observed that matters relating "to the conduct of foreign relations . . . are so exclusively entrusted to the political branches of government as to be largely immune from judicial inquiry or interference." . . .

The history of passport controls since the earliest days of the Republic shows congressional recognition of Executive authority to withhold passports on the basis of substantial reasons of national security and foreign policy. Prior to 1856, when there was no statute on the subject, the common perception was that the issuance of a passport was committed to the sole discretion of the Executive and that the Executive would exercise this power in the interests of the national security and foreign policy of the United States. This derived from the generally accepted view that foreign policy was the province and responsibility of the Executive. From the outset, Congress endorsed not only the underlying premise of Executive authority in the areas of foreign policy and national security, but also its specific application to the subject of passports. Early Congresses enacted statutes expressly recognizing the Executive authority with respect to passports....

Agee argues that the only way the Executive can establish implicit congressional approval is by proof of longstanding and consistent *enforcement* of the claimed power: that is, by showing that many passports were revoked on national security and foreign policy grounds....

The Secretary has construed and applied his regulations consistently, and it would be anomalous to fault the Government because there were so few occasions to exercise the announced policy and practice. Although a pattern of actual enforcement is one indicator of Executive policy, it suffices that the Executive has "openly asserted" the power at issue....

The protection accorded beliefs standing alone is very different from the protection accorded conduct.

Beliefs and speech are only part of Agee's "campaign to fight the United States CIA." In that sense, this case contrasts markedly with the facts in *Kent* and *Aptheker*. No presumptions, rebuttable or otherwise, are involved, for Agee's conduct in foreign countries presents a serious danger to American officials abroad and serious danger to the national security.

We hold that the policy announced in the challenged regulations is "sufficiently substantial and consistent" to compel the conclusion that Congress has approved it....

Revocation of a passport undeniably curtails travel, but the freedom to travel abroad with a "letter of introduction" in the form of a passport issued by the sovereign is subordinate to national security and foreign policy considerations; as such, it is subject to reasonable governmental regulation. The Court has made it plain that the *freedom* to travel outside the United States must be distinguished from the *right* to travel within the United States....

It is "obvious and unarguable" that no governmental interest is more compelling than the security of the Nation. Protection of the foreign policy of the United States is a governmental interest of great importance, since foreign policy and national security considerations cannot neatly be compartmentalized.

Measures to protect the secrecy of our Government's foreign intelligence operations plainly serve these interests....

Not only has Agee jeopardized the security of the United States, but he has also endangered the interests of countries other than the United States— thereby creating serious problems for American foreign relations and foreign policy. Restricting Agee's foreign travel, although perhaps not certain to prevent all of Agee's harmful activities, is the only avenue open to the Government to limit these activities....

To the extent the revocation of his passport operates to inhibit Agee, "it is an inhibition of *action*," rather than of speech. Agee is as free to criticize the United States Government as he was when he held a passport—always subject, of course, to express limits on certain rights by virtue of his contract with the Government.

We reverse the judgment of the Court of Appeals and remand for further proceedings consistent with this opinion.

Reversed and remanded.

Justice **Brennan,** with whom Justice **Marshall** joins, *dissenting:* ... I suspect that this case is a prime example of the adage that "bad facts make bad law." Philip Agee is hardly a model representative of our Nation. And the Executive Branch has attempted to use one of the only means at its disposal, revocation of a passport, to stop respondent's damaging statements. But just as the Constitution protects both popular and unpopular speech, it likewise protects both popular and unpopular travelers. And it is important to remember that this decision applies not only to Philip Agee, whose activities could be perceived as harming the national security, but also to other citizens who may merely disagree with Government foreign policy and express their views.

The Constitution allocates the lawmaking function to Congress, and I fear that today's decision has handed over too much of that function to the Executive. In permitting the Secretary to stop this unpopular traveler and critic of the CIA, the Court professes to rely on, but in fact departs from, the two precedents in the passport regulation area, *Zemel* and *Kent.* Of course it is always easier to fit oneself within the safe haven of *stare decisis* than boldly to overrule precedents of several decades' standing. Because I find myself unable to reconcile those cases with the decision in this case, however, and because I disagree with the Court's *sub silentio* overruling of those cases, I dissent.

Suggested Reading

The first major study of citizenship undertaken by the government is contained in the REPORT OF THE CITIZENSHIP BOARD OF THE U.S. DEPARTMENT OF STATE, *Citizenship of the United States, Expatriation, and Protection Abroad,* published in 1907 (H.R.DOC. No. 326, 59th Cong., 2d Sess.).

For a useful survey of the question of expatriation, see Duvall, *Expatriation Under United States Law. Perez to Afroyim: The Search for an American Philosophy of Citizenship,* 56 VIRGINIA LAW REVIEW 408 (1970), as well as John Roche, *The Expatriation Cases,* 1963 SUPREME COURT REVIEW 325. Also see P. SCHUCK and R. SMITH, CITIZENSHIP WITHOUT CONSENT: ILLEGAL ALIENS IN THE AMERICAN POLITY (1985).

For recent articles on the right to travel, see Note, *Constitutional Protection of Foreign Travel,* 81 COLUMBIA LAW REVIEW 902 (1981), and Note, *Due Process, Equal Protection and the Right to Travel,* 49 JOURNAL OF AIR LAW AND COMMERCE 907 (1984). The classic study of protection abroad is PROFESSOR BORCHARD'S DIPLOMATIC PROTECTION OF CITIZENS ABROAD (1915). Numerous examples in which protection was either provided or not provided can be found in JOHN BASSETT MOORE, DIGEST OF INTERNATIONAL LAW, volume 3 (1908). Also see GREEN HACHWORTH, DIGEST OF INTERNATIONAL LAW, volume 3 (1951); and CHARLES CHANEY HYDE, INTERNATIONAL LAW CHIEFLY AS INTERPRETED BY THE UNITED STATES (2nd ed. 1945). On the evolution of allegiance and protection, see Kettner, *The Development of American Citizenship in the Revolutionary Era: The Idea of Volitional Allegiance,* 18 AMERICAN JOURNAL OF LEGAL HISTORY 208 (1974), as well as the work of W.W. Willoughby, *Citizenship and Allegiance in Constitutional and International Law,* 1 AMERICAN JOURNAL OF INTERNATIONAL LAW 914 (1908).

Notes

1. *Shanks v. Dupont,* 3 Peters (28 U.S.) 242, 246 (1830).
2. *Osborn v. United States Bank,* 9 Wheat. (22 U.S.) 738, 827 (1824). Also see *Knauer v. United States,* 328 U.S. 654 (1946).
3. *Scott v. Sandford,* 19 How. (60 U.S.) 393 (1856).
4. Act of March 2, 1907, 34 Stat. 1228.
5. *Mackenzie v. Hare,* 239 U.S. 299, 309–312 (1915). In this case, a now obsolete statute (34 Stat. 1228) which divested the citizenship of a woman marrying an alien was upheld.
6. 356 U.S. 86 (1958).
7. 356 U.S. 129 (1958).
8. *Vance v. Terranzas,* 444 U.S. 252 (1980).
9. 439 U.S. 170 (1978).
10. *Haig v. Agee,* 453 U.S. 280 (1981).
11. "Protection draws with it subjection, and subjection protection," 7 Coke's Reports 1, 5a (1608).
12. H. Lauterpacht, "Allegiance, Diplomatic Protection and Criminal Jurisdiction over Aliens," 9 Camb.Law J. 330, 334–335 (1947).
13. 16 Wall. (83 U.S.) 36 (1872).
14. Fed.Cas. 111 (No. 4186) (C.C.S.D.N.Y.1860).
15. Hostages Act of 1868, 15 Stat. 224; 22 U.S.C. 1732.
16. 98 Stat. 2186; 18 U.S.C. 1203.
17. Along with companion case, *Rusk v. Cort,* 372 U.S. 144 (1963).

GLOSSARY OF KEY TERMS

Abdicate To voluntarily renounce.

Ab intestato From someone who dies without a will.

Adjudicate To deprive one of something as a result of a judgment.

Abstain To hold back.

Acquit To release someone from an obligation. To declare that the accused is innocent of the crime.

Ad hoc For this special thing or purpose (e.g. ad hoc committee).

Ad subjiciendum A writ directed to a person detaining another to release the prisoner.

Advisory opinion A formal opinion expressed by a judge on a legal question, but not as part of a lawsuit. Judges provide advisory opinions when, for example, public officials request judges to give their opinion on a question of law. In the United States, Supreme Court precedent bars advisory opinions.

A fortiori With stronger reason.

Amicus curiae Friend of the court.

Amnis ratihabitio retrotrahitur et mandato equiparatur The retroactive forgiveness for past actions at the express command of the sovereign power.

Autarkic The characteristic of being independent and nationally self-sufficient.

Casus foederis A treaty obligation.

Class action A lawsuit initiated by representative members of a larger group on behalf of all of the members of the group.

Comity   A doctrine of courtesy and respect. Courts may use comity to defer to the jurisdictional authority of another court.

Compendium   A comprehensive summary.

Continuance   The adjournment or postponement of a session, hearing, trial, or other proceeding to a later day or time.

Declaratory judgment   A judicial determination on a legal question or the rights of parties short of awarding damages or ordering any actions to be taken. Parties may seek declaratory judgments if a genuine, not a theoretical, legal problem exists.

De facto   In fact.

Defendant   The person defending or denying; the person against whom relief or recovery is sought.

De jure   Legitimate, lawful or sanctioned.

De jure belli ac pacis   The law of war and peace.

De jure naturae et gentium   The law of nature and humankind.

Demurrer   An admission, for the sake of argument, of the allegations of fact made by the other party in order to show that even if they are true, they are insufficient to entitle this party to relief, e.g., the facts do not state a cause of action.

Desideratum (pl. desiderata)   Something desired as essential.

Dictum (pl. dicta)   An observation made by a judge in an opinion that is not essential to the determination of the case; comments that go beyond the facts before the court.

Differ   To contradict, deny, counter; to prove the contrary.

Dissent   A disagreement or difference of opinion. To disagree or withhold approval.

Escheat statute   A reversion of property to the state when no individual is available who qualifies to inherit it.

Ex majore cautela   Acting out of extreme caution.

Ex parte   Where only one side is present or represented.

Ex post facto   An action after the fact; a law which provides punishment for an act which, when committed, was not punishable.

Flagrante bello   During an actual state of war.

Immunity   Exception or freedom from duty, penalty or liability. Special treatment or privilege.

In camera   In private; in chambers.

Indicia   Circumstances that point to the existence of a given fact as probable but not certain.

Indict   To accuse formally of a crime through an indictment.

Indictment A sworn accusation of crime against one or more persons, made by grand jury; a true bill.

In personam A suit against a particular person.

In re In the matter of. Attached to a case dealing with a thing (e.g. a business) and not a dispute involving named persons.

Inter arma silent leges In time of war the laws are silent.

Ipso jure By mere operation of the law.

Jure belli According to the laws of war.

Leges posteriores contrarias abrogant Later laws abrogate prior laws that are contrary to them.

Modus vivendi A way of living.

Parens patriae As a sovereign.

Per curiam Literally means by the court; An unsigned decision rendered by the court. A per curiam decision is one supported by all judges, yet normally appears without a judge's name attached to it.

Plenary Full or complete.

Protectio trahit subjectionem, et subjectio protectionem Protection draws with it subjection, and subjection protection.

Quorum The number of members who must be present in a deliberative body before business may be transacted.

Remand To send back for further action. To return to custody.

Res judicata A thing or controversy which is finally decided and can't be reheard.

Scire facias, habeas corpus Common law writs to revive a judgment and to release a prisoner.

Sedition A communication or agreement that has as its objective the stirring up of treason or certain lesser commotions; advocating the overthrow or reformation of the government by violence; defamation of the government.

Sequestration The process by which property or funds are attached pending the outcome of the litigation.

Seriatim One by one, one following after another; successive.

Sine qua non An indispensable condition, practice, or thing.

Sovereignty The Supreme and absolute power by which an independent state is governed; supreme political authority; the power of self-government; the international independence of a state.

Stare decisis To abide by past decisions.

Statute A law passed by a legislative body.

Subpoena A judicial order requiring a person to appear in court to provide evidence or give testimony.

Subpoena duces tecum   Where, under subpoena, a person is required to appear before court with specific documents.

Sub silento   Under silence; without notice being taken.

Sustain   To affirm. To support, corroborate. To keep alive or nourish. To endure, undergo, tolerate.

Tour de force   A feat of skill or strength.

Treaty   A compact made between two or more nations.

Ultima ratio regum   Last resort of sovereigns.

Writ   An order issued by a judicial body which compels something to be done or authorizes something to be done.

Writ of certiorari   A writ by a higher court to a lower court to send up its proceedings on a case for review.

Writ of error   A writ that asks a court to reform its own judgment due to an error or mistake of fact that did not appear on the face of the record because of fraud, duress, or excusable neglect. If the facts had been known, the same judgment allegedly would not have been rendered.

Writ of habeas corpus   A writ that demands that government officials, almost always police officers, justify before a judge why a person is being held.

Writ of scire facias   A judicial writ founded on a matter of record, requiring the person against whom it is brought to show why the party bringing the writ should not have advantage of the record or why the record should not be annulled and vacated.

THE CONSTITUTION OF THE UNITED STATES OF AMERICA

PREAMBLE

We the People of the United States, in Order to form a more perfect Union, establish Justice, insure domestic Tranquility, provide for the common defence, promote the general Welfare, and secure the Blessings of Liberty to ourselves and our Posterity, do ordain and establish this Constitution for the United States of America.

ARTICLE I

Section 1. All legislative Powers herein granted shall be vested in a Congress of the United States, which shall consist of a Senate and House of Representatives.

Section 2. The House of Representatives shall be composed of Members chosen every second Year by the People of the several States, and the Electors, in each State shall have the Qualifications requisite for Electors of the most numerous Branch of the State Legislature.

No Person shall be a Representative who shall not have attained to the Age of twenty five Years, and been seven Years a Citizen of the United States, and who shall not, when elected, be an Inhabitant of that State in which he shall be chosen.

Representatives and direct Taxes shall be apportioned among the several States which may be included within this Union, according to their respective Numbers, which shall be determined by adding to the whole Number of free Persons, including those bound to Service for a Term of Years, and excluding Indians not taxed, three fifths of all other Persons. The actual Enumeration shall be made within three Years after the first Meeting of the Congress of the United States, and within every subsequent Term of ten Years, in such Manner as they shall by Law direct. The Number of Representatives shall not exceed one for every thirty Thousand, but each State shall have at Least one Representative; and until such enumeration shall be made, the State of New Hampshire shall be entitled to chuse three, Massachusetts eight, Rhode Island and Providence Plantations one, Connecticut five, New York six, New Jersey four, Pennsylvania eight, Delaware one, Maryland six, Virginia ten, North Carolina five, South Carolina five, and Georgia three.

When vacancies happen in the Representation from any State, the Executive Authority thereof shall issue Writs of Election to fill such Vacancies.

The House of Representatives shall chuse their Speaker and other Officers; and shall have the sole Power of Impeachment.

Section 3. The Senate of the United States shall be composed of two Senators from each State, chosen by the Legislature thereof, for six Years; and each Senator shall have one Vote.

Immediately after they shall be assembled in Consequence of the first Election, they shall be divided as equally as may be into three Classes. The Seats of the Senators of the first Class shall be vacated at the Expiration of the second Year, of the second Class at the Expiration of the fourth Year, and of the third Class at the Expiration of the sixth Year, so that one third may be chosen every second Year; and if Vacancies happen by Resignation, or otherwise, during the Recess of the Legislature of any State, the Executive thereof may make temporary Appointments until the next Meeting of the Legislature, which shall then fill such Vacancies.

No Person shall be a Senator who shall not have attained to the Age of thirty Years, and been nine Years a Citizen of the United States, and who shall not, when elected, be an Inhabitant of that State for which he shall be chosen.

The Vice President of the United States shall be President of the Senate, but shall have no Vote, unless they be equally divided.

The Senate shall chuse their other Officers, and also a President pro tempore, in the Absence of the Vice President, or when he shall exercise the Office of President of the United States.

The Senate shall have the sole Power to try all Impeachments. When sitting for that Purpose, they shall be on Oath or Affirmation. When the President of the United States is tried, the Chief Justice shall preside: And no Person shall be convicted without the Concurrence of two thirds of the Members present.

Judgment in Cases of Impeachment shall not extend further than to removal from Office, and disqualification to hold and enjoy any Office of honor, Trust, or Profit under the United States: but the Party convicted shall nevertheless be liable and subject to Indictment, Trial, Judgment, and Punishment, according to Law.

Section 4. The Times, Places and Manner of holding Elections for Senators and Representatives, shall be prescribed in each State by the Legislature thereof; but the Congress may at any time by Law make or alter such Regulations, except as to the Places of chusing Senators.

The Congress shall assemble at least once in every Year, and such Meeting shall be on the first Monday in December, unless they shall by Law appoint a different Day.

Section 5. Each House shall be the Judge of the Elections, Returns, and Qualifications of its own Members, and a Majority of each shall constitute a Quorum to do Business; but a smaller Number may adjourn from day to day, and may be authorized to compel the Attendance of absent Members, in such Manner, and under such Penalties as each House may provide.

Each House may determine the Rules of its Proceedings, punish its Members for disorderly Behavior, and, with the Concurrence of two thirds, expel a Member.

Each House shall keep a Journal of its Proceedings, and from time to time publish the same, excepting such Parts as may in their Judgment require Secrecy; and the Yeas and Nays of the Members of either House on any question shall, at the Desire of one fifth of those Present, be entered on the Journal.

Neither House, during the Session of Congress, shall, without the Consent of the other, adjourn for more than three days, nor to any other Place than that in which the two Houses shall be sitting.

Section 6. The Senators and Representatives shall receive a Compensation for their Services, to be ascertained by Law, and paid out of the Treasury of the United States. They shall in all Cases, except Treason, Felony and Breach of the Peace, be privileged from Arrest during their Attendance at the Session of their respective Houses, and in going to and returning from the same; and for any Speech or Debate in either House, they shall not be questioned in any other Place.

No Senator or Representative shall, during the Time for which he was elected, be appointed to any civil Office under the Authority of the United States, which shall have been created, or the Emoluments whereof shall have been increased during such time and no Person holding any Office under the United States, shall be a Member of either House during his Continuance in Office.

Section 7. All Bills for raising Revenue shall originate in the House of Representatives; but the Senate may propose or concur with Amendments as on other Bills.

Every Bill which shall have passed the House of Representatives and the Senate, shall, before it become a Law, be presented to the President of the United States; If he approve he shall sign it, but if not he shall return it, with his Objections to the House in which it shall have originated, who shall enter the Objections at large on their Journal, and proceed to reconsider it. If after such Reconsideration two thirds of that House shall agree to pass the Bill, it shall be sent together with the Objections, to the other House, by which it shall likewise be reconsidered, and if approved by two thirds of that House, it shall become a law. But in all such Cases the Votes of both Houses shall be determined by Yeas and Nays, and the Names of the

Persons voting for and against the Bill shall be entered on the Journal of each House respectively. If any Bill shall not be returned by the President within ten Days (Sundays excepted) after it shall have been presented to him, the Same shall be a Law, in like Manner as if he had signed it, unless the Congress by their Adjournment prevent its Return in which Case it shall not be a Law.

Every Order, Resolution, or Vote, to Which the Concurrence of the Senate and House of Representatives may be necessary (except on a question of Adjournment) shall be presented to the President of the United States; and before the Same shall take Effect, shall be approved by him, or being disapproved by him, shall be repassed by two thirds of the Senate and House of Representatives, according to the Rules and Limitations prescribed in the Case of a Bill.

Section 8. The Congress shall have Power To lay and collect Taxes, Duties, Imposts and Excises, to pay the Debts and provide for the common Defence and general Welfare of the United States; but all Duties, Imposts and Excises shall be uniform throughout the United States;

To borrow money on the credit of the United States;

To regulate Commerce with foreign Nations, and among the several States, and with the Indian Tribes;

To establish an uniform Rule of Naturalization, and uniform Laws on the subject of Bankruptcies throughout the United States;

To coin Money, regulate the Value thereof, and of foreign Coin, and fix the Standard of Weights and Measures;

To provide for the Punishment of counterfeiting the Securities and current Coin of the United States;

To Establish Post Offices and Post Roads;

To promote the Progress of Science and useful Arts, by securing for limited Times to Authors and Inventors the exclusive Right to their respective Writings and Discoveries;

To constitute Tribunals inferior to the supreme Court;

To define and punish Piracies and Felonies committed on the high Seas, and Offenses against the Law of Nations;

To declare War, grant Letters of Marque and Reprisal, and make Rules concerning Captures on Land and Water;

To raise and support Armies, but no Appropriation of Money to that Use shall be for a longer Term than two Years;

To provide and maintain a Navy;

To make Rules for the Government and Regulation of the land and naval Forces;

To provide for calling forth the Militia to execute the Laws of the Union, suppress Insurrections and repel Invasions;

To provide for organizing, arming, and disciplining, the Militia, and for governing such Part of them as may be employed in the Service of the United States, reserving to the States respectively, the Appointment of the Officers, and the Authority of training the Militia according to the discipline prescribed by Congress.

To exercise exclusive Legislation in all Cases whatsoever, over such District (not exceeding ten Miles square) as may, by Cession of particular States, and the Acceptance of Congress, become the Seat of the Government of the United States, ánd to exercise like Authority over all Places purchased by the Consent of the Legislature of the State in which the Same shall be, for the Erection of Forts, Magazines, Arsenals, dock-Yards, and other needful Buildings;—And

To make all Laws which shall be necessary and proper for carrying into Execution the foregoing Powers, and all other Powers vested by this Constitution in the Government of the United States, or in any Department or Officer thereof.

Section 9. The Migration or Importation of Such Persons as any of the States now existing shall think proper to admit, shall not be prohibited by the Congress prior to the Year one thousand eight hundred and eight, but a Tax or duty may be imposed on such Importation, not exceeding ten dollars for each Person.

The privilege of the Writ of Habeas Corpus shall not be suspended, unless when in Cases of Rebellion or Invasion the public Safety may require it.

No Bill of Attainder or ex post facto Law shall be passed.

No Capitation, or other direct, Tax shall be laid, unless in Proportion to the Census or Enumeration herein before directed to be taken.

No Tax or Duty shall be laid on Articles exported from any State.

No Preference shall be given by any Regulation of Commerce or Revenue to the Ports of one State over those of another: nor shall Vessels bound to, or from, one State be obliged to enter, clear, or pay Duties in another.

No money shall be drawn from the Treasury, but in Consequence of Appropriations made by Law; and a regular Statement and Account of the Receipts and Expenditures of all public Money shall be published from time to time.

No Title of Nobility shall be granted by the United States: And no Person holding any Office of Profit or Trust under them, shall, without the Consent of the Congress, accept of any present, Emolument, Office, or Title, of any kind whatever, from any King, Prince, or foreign State.

Section 10. No State shall enter into any Treaty, Alliance, or Confederation; grant Letters of Marque and Reprisal; coin Money; emit Bills of Credit; make any Thing but gold and silver Coin a Tender in Payment of Debts; pass any Bill of Attainder, ex post facto Law, or Law impairing the Obligation of Contracts, or grant any Title of Nobility.

No State shall, without the Consent of the Congress, lay any Imposts or Duties on Imports or Exports, except what may be absolutely necessary for executing its inspection Laws: and the net Produce of all Duties and Imposts, laid by any State on Imports or Exports, shall be for the Use of the Treasury of the United States; and all such Laws shall be subject to the Revision and Controul of the Congress.

No State shall, without the Consent of Congress, lay any Duty of Tonnage, keep Troops, or Ships of War in time of Peace, enter into any Agreement or Compact with another State, or with a foreign Power, or engage in War, unless actually invaded, or in such imminent Danger as will not admit of delay.

ARTICLE II

Section 1. The executive Power shall be vested in a President of the United States of America. He shall hold his Office during the Term of four Years, and, together with the Vice President, chosen for the same term, be elected, as follows:

Each State shall appoint, in such Manner as the Legislature thereof may direct, a Number of Electors, equal to the whole Number of Senators and Representatives to which the State may be entitled in the Congress; but no Senator or Representative, or Person holding an Office of Trust or Profit under the United States, shall be appointed an Elector.

The Electors shall meet in their respective States, and vote by Ballot for two Persons, of whom one at least shall not be an Inhabitant of the same State with themselves. And they shall make a List of all the Persons voted for, and of the Number of Votes for each; which List they shall sign and certify, and transmit sealed to the Seat of the Government of the United States, directed to the President of the Senate. The President of the Senate shall, in the Presence of the Senate and House of Representatives, open all the Certificates, and the Votes shall then be counted. The Person having the greatest Number of Votes shall be the President, if such Number be a Majority of the whole Number of Electors appointed; and if there be more than one who have such Majority, and have an equal Number of Votes, then the House of Representatives shall immediately chuse by Ballot one of them for President; and if no Person have a Majority, then from the five highest on the List the said House shall in like Manner chuse the President. But in chusing the President, the Votes shall be taken by States the Representation from each State having one Vote; A quorum for this Purpose shall consist of a Member or Members from two thirds of the States, and a Majority of all the States shall be necessary to a Choice. In every Case, after the Choice of the President, the Person having the greater Number of Votes of the Electors shall be the Vice President. But if there should remain two or more who have equal Votes, the Senate shall chuse from them by Ballot the Vice President.

The Congress may determine the Time of chusing the Electors, and the Day on which they shall give their Votes; which Day shall be the same throughout the United States.

No person except a natural born Citizen, or a Citizen of the United States, at the time of the Adoption of this Constitution, shall be eligible to the Office of President; neither shall any Person be eligible to that Office who shall not have attained to the Age of thirty five Years, and been fourteen Years a Resident within the United States.

In case of the removal of the President from Office, or of his Death, Resignation or Inability to discharge the Powers and Duties of the said Office, the Same shall devolve on the Vice President, and the Congress may by Law provide for the Case of Removal, Death, Resignation or Inability, both of the President and Vice President, declaring what Officer shall then act as President, and such Officer shall act accordingly, until the Disability be removed, or a President shall be elected.

The President shall, at stated Times, receive for his Services, a Compensation, which shall neither be increased nor diminished during the Period for which he shall have been elected, and he shall not receive within that Period any other Emolument from the United States, or any of them.

Before he enter on the Execution of his Office, he shall take the following Oath or Affirmation: "I do solemnly swear (or affirm) that I will faithfully execute the Office of President of the United States, and will to the best of my Ability, preserve, protect and defend the Constitution of the United States."

Section 2. The President shall be Commander in Chief of the Army and Navy of the United States, and of the militia of the several States, when called into the actual Service of the United States; he may require the Opinion, in writing, of the principal Officer in each of the Executive Departments, upon any Subject relating to the Duties of their respective Offices, and he shall have Power to grant Reprieves and Pardons for Offenses against the United States, except in Cases of Impeachment.

He shall have Power, by and with the Advice and Consent of the Senate to make Treaties, provided two thirds of the Senators present concur; and he shall nominate, and by and with the Advice and Consent of the Senate, shall appoint Ambassadors, other public Ministers and Consuls, Judges of the supreme Court, and all other Officers of the United States, whose Appointments are not herein otherwise provided for, and which shall be established by Law; but the Congress may by Law vest the Appointment of such inferior Officers, as they think proper, in the President alone, in the Courts of Law, or in the Heads of Departments.

The President shall have Power to fill up all Vacancies that may happen during the Recess of the Senate, by granting Commissions which shall expire at the End of their next Session.

Section 3. He shall from time to time give to the Congress Information of the State of the Union, and recommend to their Consideration such Measures as he shall judge necessary and expedient; he may, on extraordinary Occasions, convene both Houses, or either of them, and in Case of Disagreement between them, with Respect to the Time of Adjournment, he may adjourn them to such Time as he shall think proper; he shall receive Ambassadors and other public Ministers; he shall take Care that the Laws be faithfully executed, and shall Commission all the Officers of the United States.

Section 4. The President, Vice President and all civil Officers of the United States, shall be removed from Office on Impeachment for, and Conviction of, Treason, Bribery, or other high Crimes and Misdemeanors.

ARTICLE III

Section 1. The judicial Power of the United States, shall be vested in one supreme Court, and in such inferior Courts as the Congress may from time to time ordain and establish. The Judges, both of the supreme and inferior Courts, shall hold their Offices during good Behaviour, and shall, at stated Times, receive for their Services a Compensation, which shall not be diminished during their Continuance in Office.

Section 2. The judicial Power shall extend to all Cases, in Law and Equity, arising under this Constitution, the Laws of the United States, and Treaties made, or which shall be made, under their Authority;—to all Cases affecting Ambassadors, other public Ministers and Consuls;—to all Cases of admiralty and maritime jurisdiction;—to Controversies to which the United States shall be a Party;—to Controversies between two or more States;—between a State and Citizens of another State;—between Citizens of different States;—between Citizens of the same State claiming Lands under the Grants of different States, and between a State, or the Citizens thereof, and foreign States, Citizens or Subjects.

In all Cases affecting Ambassadors, other public Ministers and Consuls, and those in which a State shall be a Party, the supreme Court shall have original Jurisdiction. In all the other Cases before mentioned, the supreme Court shall have appellate Jurisdiction, both as to Law and Fact, with such Exceptions, and under such Regulations as the Congress shall make.

The trial of all Crimes, except in Cases of Impeachment, shall be by Jury; and such Trial shall be held in the State where the said Crimes shall have been committed; but when not committed within any State, the Trial shall be at such Place or Places as the Congress may by Law have directed.

Section 3. Treason against the United States, shall consist only in levying War against them, or, in adhering to their Enemies, giving them Aid and Comfort. No Person shall be convicted of Treason unless on the Testimony of two Witnesses to the same overt Act, or on Confession in open Court.

The Congress shall have Power to declare the Punishment of Treason, but no Attainder of Treason shall work Corruption of Blood, or Forfeiture except during the Life of the Person attainted.

ARTICLE IV

Section 1. Full Faith and Credit shall be given in each State to the public Acts, Records, and judicial Proceedings of every other State. And the Congress may by general Laws prescribe the Manner in which such Acts, Records and Proceedings shall be proved, and the Effect thereof.

Section 2. The Citizens of each State shall be entitled to all Privileges and Immunities of Citizens in the several States.

A Person charged in any State with Treason, Felony, or other Crime, who shall flee from Justice and be found in another State, shall on demand of the executive Authority of the State from which he fled, be delivered up, to be removed to the State having Jurisdiction of the Crime.

No Person held to Service or Labour in one State, under the Laws thereof, escaping into another, shall, in Consequence of any Law or Regulation therein, be discharged from such Service or Labour, but shall be delivered up on Claim of the Party to whom such Service or Labour may be due.

Section 3. New States may be admitted by the Congress into this Union; but no new State shall be formed or erected within the Jurisdiction of any other State; nor any State be formed by the Junction of two or more States, or Parts of States, without the Consent of the Legislatures of the States concerned as well as of the Congress.

The Congress shall have Power to dispose of and make all needful Rules and Regulations respecting the Territory or other Property belonging to the United States; and nothing in this Constitution shall be so construed as to Prejudice any Claims of the United States, or of any particular State.

Section 4. The United States shall guarantee to every State in this Union a Republican Form of Government, and shall protect each of them against Invasion; and on Application of the Legislature, or of the Executive (when the Legislature cannot be convened) against domestic Violence.

ARTICLE V

The Congress, whenever two thirds of both Houses shall deem it necessary, shall propose Amendments to this Constitution, or, on the Application of the Legislatures of two thirds of the several States, shall call a Convention for proposing Amendments, which, in either Case, shall be valid to all Intents and Purposes, as part of this Constitution, when ratified by the Legislatures of three fourths of the several States, or by Conventions in three fourths thereof, as the one or the other Mode of Ratification may be proposed by the Congress; Provided that no Amendment which may be made prior to the Year One thousand eight hundred and eight shall in any Manner affect the first and fourth Clauses in the Ninth Section of the first Article; and that no State, without its Consent, shall be deprived of its equal Suffrage in the Senate.

ARTICLE VI

All Debts contracted and Engagements entered into, before the Adoption of this Constitution shall be as valid against the United States under this Constitution, as under the Confederation.

This Constitution, and the Laws of the United States which shall be made in Pursuance thereof; and all Treaties made, or which shall be made, under the Authority of the United States, shall be the supreme Law of the Land; and the Judges in every State shall be bound thereby, any Thing in the Constitution or Laws of any State to the Contrary notwithstanding.

The Senators and Representatives before mentioned, and the Members of the several State Legislatures, and all executive and judicial Officers, both of the United States and of the several States, shall be bound by Oath or Affirmation, to support this Constitution; but no religious Test shall ever be required as a Qualification to any Office or public Trust under the United States.

ARTICLE VII

The Ratification of the Conventions of nine States shall be sufficient for the Establishment of this Constitution between the States so ratifying the Same.

ARTICLES IN ADDITION TO, AND AMENDMENT OF, THE CONSTITUTION OF THE UNITED STATES OF AMERICA, PROPOSED BY CONGRESS, AND RATIFIED BY THE LEGISLATURES OF THE SEVERAL STATES PURSUANT TO THE FIFTH ARTICLE OF THE ORIGINAL CONSTITUTION.

AMENDMENT I [1791]

Congress shall make no law respecting an establishment of religion, or prohibiting the free exercise thereof; or abridging the freedom of speech, or of the press; or the right of the people peaceably to assemble, and to petition the Government for a redress of grievances.

AMENDMENT II [1791]

A well regulated Militia, being necessary to the security of a free State, the right of the people to keep and bear Arms, shall not be infringed.

AMENDMENT III [1791]

No Soldier shall, in time of peace be quartered in any house, without the consent of the Owner, nor in time of war, but in a manner to be prescribed by law.

AMENDMENT IV [1791]

The right of the people to be secure in their persons, houses, papers, and effects, against unreasonable searches and seizures, shall not be violated, and no Warrants shall issue, but upon probable cause, supported by Oath or affirmation, and particularly describing the place to be searched, and the persons or things to be seized.

AMENDMENT V [1791]

No person shall be held to answer for a capital, or otherwise infamous crime, unless on a presentment or indictment of a Grand Jury, except in cases arising in the land or naval forces, or in the Militia, when in actual service in time of War or public danger; nor shall any person be subject for the same offence to be twice put in jeopardy of life or limb; nor shall be compelled in any criminal case to be a witness against himself, nor be deprived of life, liberty, or property, without due process of law; nor shall private property be taken for public use, without just compensation.

AMENDMENT VI [1791]

In all criminal prosecutions, the accused shall enjoy the right to a speedy and public trial, by an impartial jury of the State and district wherein the crime shall have been committed, which district shall have been previously ascertained by law, and to be informed of the nature and cause of the accusation; to be confronted with the witnesses against him; to have compulsory process for obtaining witnesses in his favor, and to have the Assistance of Counsel for his defence.

AMENDMENT VII [1791]

In Suits at common law, where the value in controversy shall exceed twenty dollars, the right of trial by jury shall be preserved, and no fact tried to jury, shall be otherwise re-examined in any Court of the United States, than according to the rules of the common law.

AMENDMENT VIII [1791]

Excessive bail shall not be required, nor excessive fines imposed, nor cruel and unusual punishments inflicted.

AMENDMENT IX [1791]

The enumeration in the Constitution, of certain rights, shall not be construed to deny or disparage others retained by the people.

AMENDMENT X [1791]

The powers not delegated to the United States by the Constitution, nor prohibited by it to the States, are reserved to the States respectively, or to the people.

AMENDMENT XI [1798]

The Judicial power of the United States shall not be construed to extend to any suit in law or equity, commenced or prosecuted against one of the United States by Citizens of another State, or by Citizens or Subjects of any Foreign State.

AMENDMENT XII [1804]

The Electors shall meet in their respective states and vote by ballot for President and Vice-President, one of whom, at least, shall not be an inhabitant of the same state with themselves; they shall name in their ballots the person voted for as President, and in distinct ballots the person voted for as Vice-President, and they shall make distinct lists of all persons voted for as President, and of all persons voted for as Vice-President, and of the number of votes for each, which lists they shall sign and certify, and transmit sealed to the seat of the government of the United States, directed to the President of the Senate;—The President of the Senate shall, in the presence of the Senate and House of Representatives, open all the certificates and the votes shall then be counted;—The person having the greatest number of votes for President, shall be the President, if such number be a majority of the whole number of Electors appointed; and if no person have such majority, then from the persons having the highest numbers not exceeding three on the list of those voted for as President, the House of Representatives shall choose immediately, by ballot, the President. But in choosing the President, the votes shall be taken by states, the representation from each state having one vote; a quorum for this purpose shall consist of a member or members from two-thirds of the states, and a majority of all the states shall be necessary to a choice. And if the House of Representatives shall not choose a President whenever the right of choice shall devolve upon them before the fourth day of March next following, then the Vice-President shall act as President, as in the case of the death or other constitutional disability of the President.—The person having the greatest number of votes as Vice-President, shall be the Vice-President, if such number be a majority of the whole number of Electors appointed, and if no person have a majority, then from the two highest numbers on the list, the Senate shall choose the Vice-President; a quorum for the purpose shall consist of two-thirds of the whole number of Senators, and a majority of the whole number shall be necessary to a choice. But no person constitutionally ineligible to the office of President shall be eligible to that of Vice-President of the United States.

AMENDMENT XIII [1865]

Section 1. Neither slavery nor involuntary servitude, except as a punishment for crime whereof the party shall have been duly convicted, shall exist within the United States, or any place subject to their jurisdiction.

Section 2. Congress shall have power to enforce this article by appropriate legislation.

AMENDMENT XIV [1868]

Section 1. All persons born or naturalized in the United States, and subject to the jurisdiction thereof, are citizens of the United States and of the State wherein they reside. No State shall make or enforce any law which shall abridge the privileges or immunities of citizens of the United States; nor shall any State deprive any person of life, liberty, or property, without due process of law; nor deny to any person within its jurisdiction the equal protection of the laws.

Section 2. Representatives shall be apportioned among the several States according to their respective numbers, counting the whole number of persons in each State excluding Indians not taxed. But when the right to vote at any election for the choice of electors for President and Vice President of the United States, Representatives in Congress, the Executive and Judicial officers of a State, or the members of the Legislature thereof, is denied to any of the male inhabitants of such State, being twenty-one years of age, and citizens of the United States, or in any way abridged, except for participation in rebellion, or other crime, the basis of representation therein shall be reduced in the proportion which the number of such male citizens shall bear to the whole number of male citizens twenty-one years of age in such State.

Section 3. No person shall be a Senator or Representative in Congress, or elector of President and Vice President, or hold any office, civil or military, under the United States or under any State, who having previously taken an oath, as a member of Congress, or as an officer of the United States, or as a member of any State legislature, or as an executive or judicial officer of any State, to support the Constitution of the United States, shall have engaged in insurrection or rebellion against the same, or given aid or comfort to the enemies thereof. But Congress may by a vote of two-thirds of each House, remove such disability.

Section 4. The validity of the public debt of the United States, authorized by law, including debts incurred for payment of pensions and bounties for services in suppressing insurrection or rebellion, shall not be questioned. But neither the United States nor any State shall assume or pay any debt or obligation incurred in aid of insurrection or rebellion against the United States, or any claim for the loss or emancipation of any slave; but all such debts, obligations and claims shall be held illegal and void.

Section 5. The Congress shall have power to enforce, by appropriate legislation, the provisions of this article.

AMENDMENT XV [1870]

Section 1. The right of citizens of the United States to vote shall not be denied or abridged by the United States or by any State on account of race, color, or previous condition of servitude.

Section 2. The Congress shall have power to enforce this article by appropriate legislation.

AMENDMENT XVI [1913]

The Congress shall have power to lay and collect taxes on incomes, from whatever source derived, without apportionment among the several States, and without regard to any census or enumeration.

AMENDMENT XVII [1913]

The Senate of the United States shall be composed of two Senators from each State, elected by the people thereof, for six years; and each Senator shall have one vote. The electors in each State shall have the qualifications requisite for electors of the most numerous branch of the State legislatures.

When vacancies happen in the representation of any State in the Senate, the executive authority of such State shall issue writs of election to fill such vacancies: *Provided,* That the legislature of any State may empower the executive thereof to make temporary appointments until the people fill the vacancies by election as the legislature may direct.

This amendment shall not be so construed as to affect the election or term of any Senator chosen before it becomes valid as part of the Constitution.

AMENDMENT XVIII [1919]

Section 1. After one year from the ratification of this article the manufacture, sale, or transportation of intoxicating liquors within, the importation thereof into, or the exportation thereof from the United States and all territory subject to the jurisdiction thereof for beverage purposes is hereby prohibited.

Section 2. The Congress and the several States shall have concurrent power to enforce this article by appropriate legislation.

Section 3. This article shall be inoperative unless it shall have been ratified as an amendment to the Constitution by the legislatures of the several States, as provided in the Constitution, within seven years from the date of the submission hereof to the States by the Congress.

AMENDMENT XIX [1920]

The right of citizens of the United States to vote shall not be denied or abridged by the United States or by any State on account of sex.

Congress shall have power to enforce this article by appropriate legislation.

AMENDMENT XX [1933]

Section 1. The terms of the President and Vice President shall end at noon on the 20th day of January, and the terms of Senators and Representatives at noon on the 3d day of January, of the years in which such terms would have ended if this article had not been ratified; and the terms of their successors shall then begin.

Section 2. The Congress shall assemble at least once in every year, and such meeting shall begin at noon on the 3d day of January, unless they shall by law appoint a different day.

Section 3. If, at the time fixed for the beginning of the term of the President, the President elect shall have died, the Vice President elect shall become President. If the President shall not have been chosen before the time fixed for the beginning of his term, or if the President elect shall have failed to qualify, then the Vice-President elect shall act as President until a President shall have qualified; and the Congress may by law provide for the case wherein neither a President elect nor a Vice President elect shall have qualified, declaring who shall then act as President, or the manner in which one who is to act shall be selected, and such person shall act accordingly until a President or Vice President shall have qualified.

Section 4. The Congress may by law provide for the case of the death of any of the persons from whom the House of Representatives may choose a President whenever the right of choice shall have devolved upon them, and for the case of the death of any of the persons from whom the Senate may choose a Vice President whenever the right of choice shall have devolved upon them.

Section 5. Sections 1 and 2 shall take effect on the 15th day of October following the ratification of this article.

Section 6. This article shall be inoperative unless it shall have been ratified as an amendment to the Constitution by the legislatures of three-fourths of the several States within seven years from the date of its submission.

AMENDMENT XXI [1933]

Section 1. The eighteenth article of amendment to the Constitution of the United States is hereby repealed.

Section 2. The transportation or importation into any State, Territory, or possession of the United States for delivery or use therein of intoxicating liquors, in violation of the laws thereof, is hereby prohibited.

Section 3. This article shall be inoperative unless it shall have been ratified as an amendment to the Constitution by conventions in the several States, as provided in the Constitution, within seven years from the date of the submission hereof to the States by the Congress.

AMENDMENT XXII [1951]

Section 1. No person shall be elected to the office of the President more than twice, and no person who has held the office of President, or acted as President, for more than two years of a term to which some other person was elected President shall be elected to the office of President more than once. But this Article shall not apply to any person holding the office of President when this Article was proposed by the Congress, and shall not prevent any person who may be holding the office of President, or acting as President, during the term within which this Article becomes operative from holding the office of President or acting as President during the remainder of such term.

Section 2. This article shall be inoperative unless it shall have been ratified as an amendment to the Constitution by the legislatures of three-fourths of the several States within seven years from the date of its submission to the States by the Congress.

AMENDMENT XXIII [1961]

Section 1. The District constituting the seat of Government of the United States shall appoint in such manner as the Congress may direct:

A number of electors of President and Vice President equal to the whole number of Senators and Representatives in Congress to which the District would be entitled if it were a State, but in no event more than the least populous state; they shall be in addition to those appointed by the states, but they shall be considered, for the purposes of the election of President and Vice President, to be electors appointed by a state; and they shall meet in the District and perform such duties as provided by the twelfth article of amendment.

Section 2. The Congress shall have power to enforce this article by appropriate legislation.

AMENDMENT XXIV [1964]

Section 1. The right of citizens of the United States to vote in any primary or other election for President or Vice President, for electors for President or

Vice President, or for Senator or Representative in Congress, shall not be denied or abridged by the United States, or any State by reason of failure to pay any poll tax or other tax.

Section 2. The Congress shall have power to enforce this article by appropriate legislation.

AMENDMENT XXV [1967]

Section 1. In case of the removal of the President from office or of his death or resignation, the Vice President shall become President.

Section 2. Whenever there is a vacancy in the office of the Vice President, the President shall nominate a Vice President who shall take office upon confirmation by a majority vote of both Houses of Congress.

Section 3. Whenever the President transmits to the President pro tempore of the Senate and the Speaker of the House of Representatives his written declaration that he is unable to discharge the powers and duties of his office, and until he transmits to them a written declaration to the contrary, such powers and duties shall be discharged by the Vice President as Acting President.

Section 4. Whenever the Vice President and a majority of either the principal officers of the executive departments or of such other body as Congress may by law provide, transmit to the President pro tempore of the Senate and the Speaker of the House of Representatives their written declaration that the President is unable to discharge the powers and duties of his office, the Vice President shall immediately assume the powers and duties of the office as Acting President.

Thereafter, when the President transmits to the President pro tempore of the Senate and the Speaker of the House of Representatives his written declaration that no inability exists, he shall resume the powers and duties of his office unless the Vice President and a majority of either the principal officers of the executive department or of such other body as Congress may by law provide, transmit within four days to the President pro tempore of the Senate and the Speaker of the House of Representatives their written declaration and the President is unable to discharge the powers and duties of his office. Thereupon Congress shall decide the issue, assembling within forty-eight hours for that purpose if not in session. If the Congress, within twenty-one days after receipt of the latter written declaration, or, if Congress is not in session, within twenty-one days after Congress is required to assemble, determines by two-thirds vote of both Houses that the President is unable to discharge the power and duties of his office, the Vice President shall continue to discharge the same as Acting President; otherwise, the President shall resume the powers and duties of his office.

AMENDMENT XXVI [1971]

Section 1. The right of citizens of the United States, who are eighteen years of age or older, to vote shall not be denied or abridged by the United States or by any State on account of age.

Section 2. The Congress shall have power to enforce this article by appropriate legislation.

INDEX